AMC'S BEST DAY HIKES IN
THE WHITE MOUNTAINS

Four-Season Guide to 60 of the Best Trails in the White Mountains

THIRD EDITION

D0823891

ROBERT N. BUCHSBAUM

Appalachian Mountain Club Books
Boston, Massachusetts

AMC is a nonprofit organization, and sales of AMC Books fund our mission of protecting the Northeast outdoors. If you appreciate our efforts and would like to become a member or make a donation to AMC, visit outdoors.org, call 800-372-1758, or contact us at Appalachian Mountain Club, 5 Joy Street, Boston, MA 02108.

outdoors.org/publications/books

Distributed by National Book Network.

Front cover and back cover photographs © Dennis Welsh
Interior photographs © Robert N. Buchsbaum, unless otherwise noted
Maps by Ken Dumas © Appalachian Mountain Club
Ilustrations by Nancy Childs
Book design by Abigail Coyle

Library of Congress Cataloging-in-Publication Data
Names: Buchsbaum, Robert N.
Title: AMC's best day hikes in the White Mountains : four-season guide to 60
   of the best trails in the White Mountains / Robert N. Buchsbaum.
Description: 3rd Edition. | Boston, Massachusetts : Appalachian Mountain Club
   Books, [2016] | "Distributed by National Book Network"--T.p. verso. |
   Includes bibliographical references and index.
Identifiers: LCCN 2015041499 (print) | LCCN 2015047162 (ebook) | ISBN 9781628420289
(paperback) | ISBN 9781628420296 (ePub) | ISBN 9781628420302 (Mobi)
Subjects: LCSH: Hiking--White Mountain National Forest (N.H. and Me.)--Guidebooks. |
White Mountain National Forest (N.H. and Me.)--Guidebooks.
Classification: LCC GV199.42.W47 B83 2016 (print) | LCC GV199.42.W47
(ebook) | DDC 917.42/20444--dc23
LC record available at http://lccn.loc.gov/2015041499

The paper used in this publication meets the minimum requirements of the American National Standard for Information Sciences-Permanence of Paper for Printed Library Materials, ANSIZ39.48-1984. ∞

Interior pages contain 30% post-consumer recycled fiber.
Cover contains 10% post-consumer recycled fiber.
Printed in the United States of America,
using vegetable-based inks.

21 20 19 18 17 16   1 2 3 4 5

MIX
Paper from
responsible sources
FSC
www.fsc.org
FSC® C005010

This book is dedicated to all the volunteers who maintain the trails, allowing us to enjoy the wonderful vistas, waterfalls, flowers, and creatures of the mountains.

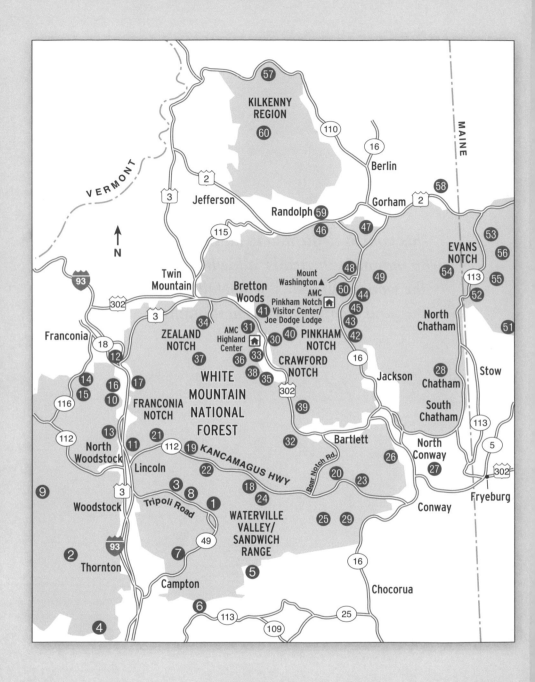

CONTENTS

AT-A-GLANCE TRIP PLANNER

TRIP NUMBER	TRIP NAME	LOCATION	DIFFICULTY	DISTANCE	ELEVATION GAIN
THE SOUTHWESTERN WHITE MOUNTAINS AND WATERVILLE VALLEY					
1	Cascade Path, Waterville Valley	Waterville Valley, NH	Easy	3.4 mi	700 ft
2	Three Ponds Loop	Ellsworth, NH	Easy	5.7 mi	749 ft
3	East Pond and Little East Pond	Livermore, NH	Moderate	5.0 mi	1,000 ft
4	Stinson Mountain Trail	Rumney, NH	Moderate	3.6 mi	1,400 ft
5	Mount Israel	Sandwich, NH	Moderate	4.2 mi	1,700 ft
6	Percival-Morgan Loop	Holderness/Campton, NH	Moderate	5.2 mi	1,550 ft
7	Welch-Dickey Loop	Thornton, NH	Moderate-Strenuous	4.4 mi	1,800 ft
8	Mount Osceola	Livermore, NH	Strenuous	6.4 mi	2,050 ft
9	Mount Moosilauke	Woodstock/Benton, NH	Strenuous	7.9 mi	2,700 ft
FRANCONIA NOTCH					
10	The Basin and Basin-Cascade Trail	Lincoln, NH	Easy	1.6 mi	400 ft
11	Flume Gorge	Lincoln, NH	Easy	2.0 mi	270 ft
12	Bald Mountain and Artist's Bluff	Franconia, NH	Moderate	1.5 mi	550 ft
13	Mount Pemigewasset Trail	Lincoln, NH	Moderate	3.6 mi	1,300 ft
14	Coppermine Trail to Bridal Veil Falls	Franconia, NH	Moderate	5.0 mi	1,100 ft
15	Bald Peak via Mount Kinsman Trail	Easton, NH	Moderate	4.6 mi	1,450 ft
16	Lonesome Lake and Hut	Lincoln, NH	Moderate	3.2 mi	1,000 ft
17	Cloudland Falls and Franconia Ridge via Falling Waters, Greenleaf, and Old Bridle Path Trails	Lincoln, NH, to Franconia, NH	Moderate-Strenuous	2.6/9.0 mi	800/3,850 ft
OFF THE KANCAMAGUS HIGHWAY					
18	Sabbaday Falls	Waterville Valley, NH	Easy	0.6 mi	100 ft
19	Forest Discovery Trail	Lincoln, NH	Easy	1.4 mi	150 ft
20	Rocky Gorge and Lovequist Loop around Falls Pond	Albany, NH	Easy	1.0 mi	150 ft

TIME	TRIP HIGHLIGHTS	PUBLIC TRANSPORT	FEE	GOOD FOR KIDS	DOG-FRIENDLY	X-C SKIING	SNOWSHOEING
2.0 hrs	Pleasant, easy walk to beautiful series of small waterfalls			🚶	🐕	⛷	❄
4.0 hrs	Level walk to scenic ponds with wildlife; waterfall a bonus			🚶	🐕	⛷	❄
4.0–5.0 hrs	Mountain ponds with wildflowers, ferns, mushrooms			🚶	🐕		❄
3.0 hrs	Sweeping view from the summit, interesting geology			🚶	🐕		❄
3.5 hrs	Great views of Sandwich Range and lakes			🚶	🐕		❄
4.5 hrs	Fun climb with extensive views of Squam Lake			🚶	🐕		
3.5–5.0 hrs	Excellent views, popular family hike		$	🚶	🐕		
5.0–6.0 hrs	Spectacular mountain vista at summit		$		🐕		
6.0 hrs	Follows rushing mountain stream to alpine summit with extensive views				🐕		❄
45 min–1.5 hrs	Beautiful waterfalls, rapids, and glacially carved potholes			🚶	🐕		❄
2.0 hrs	Waterfalls, stunning gorge, covered bridges		$	🚶			❄
1.0–2.0 hrs	Ideal family outing with views and nearby picturesque swimming beach			🚶	🐕		
4.0 hrs	Good for kids, excellent views, wildflowers, and mushrooms			🚶	🐕		❄
3.0–4.0 hrs	One of the most beautiful waterfalls in the White Mountains			🚶	🐕		❄
4.0 hrs	Pass attractive cascades to 360-degree vista			🚶	🐕		❄
4.0 hrs	Beautiful swimming lake, great views, overnight accommodation	🚌		🚶			❄
2.0–7.0 hrs	Shorter waterfall option. Longer option is one of the White Mountains' most spectacular alpine hikes	🚌			🐕		
0.5–1.0 hr	Gorge with interesting geology, ideal for very young children		$	🚶	🐕		
1.0–2.0 hrs	Interpretive trail with view of nearby forests and mountains, benches along trail			🚶	🐕		❄
0.5–1.0 hr	Good for families; small gorge, pond, fishing, picnics		$	🚶	🐕	⛷	❄

TRIP NUMBER	TRIP NAME	LOCATION	DIFFICULTY	DISTANCE	ELEVATION GAIN
21	Lincoln Woods Trail to Black Pond and/or Franconia Falls	Lincoln, NH	Moderate	6.6–8.0 mi	500 ft
22	Greeley Ponds	Lincoln/Livermore, NH	Moderate	3.2–4.6 mi	450 ft
23	Boulder Loop Trail	Albany, NH	Moderate	3.1 mi	950 ft
24	UNH Trail to Hedgehog Mountain	Albany, NH	Moderate	4.8 mi	1,450 ft
25	Mount Chocorua via Champney Falls	Albany, NH	Moderate to falls, strenuous to Mount Chocorua	3.5 mi to falls, 7.8 miles to summit	600 ft to falls, 2,250 ft to summit

CONWAY-NORTH CONWAY REGION

TRIP NUMBER	TRIP NAME	LOCATION	DIFFICULTY	DISTANCE	ELEVATION GAIN
26	Diana's Baths	Conway, NH	Easy	1.2 mi	minimal
27	Black Cap	Conway, NH	Moderate	2.2 mi	650 ft
28	Mountain Pond Loop Trail	Chatham, NH	Moderate	2.7 mi	minimal
29	White Ledge Loop	Albany, NH	Moderate	4.4 mi	1,450 ft

CRAWFORD NOTCH AND ZEALAND NOTCH

TRIP NUMBER	TRIP NAME	LOCATION	DIFFICULTY	DISTANCE	ELEVATION GAIN
30	Saco Lake and Elephant Head	Carroll, NH	Easy	1.2 mi	100 ft
31	Ammonoosuc Lake via Around the Lake Trail	Carroll, NH	Easy	1.0–2.0 mi	150 ft
32	Sawyer Pond	Livermore, NH	Moderate	3.0 mi	350 ft
33	Mount Willard	Carroll, NH, to Hart's Location, NH	Moderate	3.2 mi	900 ft
34	Sugarloaf Trail	Bethlehem, NH	Moderate	3.4 mi	700/900 ft
35	Arethusa Falls and Frankenstein Cliffs	Hart's Location, NH	Moderate	3.0/4.9 mi	1,300 ft
36	Mount Avalon	Carroll/Bethlehem, NH	Moderate	3.7 mi	1,550 ft
37	Zealand Trail to Zealand Falls Hut and Zealand Pond	Bethlehem, NH	Moderate	5.4 mi	650 ft
38	Ethan Pond and Ripley Falls	Hart's Location, NH, to Bethlehem, NH	Moderate	6.0 mi	1,600 ft
39	Mount Crawford	Hart's Location, NH, to Hadley's Purchase, NH	Strenuous	5.0 mi	2,100 ft
40	Mizpah Spring Hut and Mount Pierce	Carroll, NH, to Hart's Location, NH	Strenuous	6.6 mi	2,450 ft
41	Mount Eisenhower via Edmands Path	Crawford's Purchase, NH	Strenuous	6.6 mi	2,750 ft

TIME	TRIP HIGHLIGHTS	PUBLIC TRANSPORT	FEE	GOOD FOR KIDS	DOG-FRIENDLY	X-C SKIING	SNOWSHOEING
3.0–5.0 hrs	Old logging railroad along river to pond and waterfall, wading		$	●	●	●	●
2.0–4.0 hrs	Classic mountain ponds, rugged slopes, split-log bridges		$	●	●	●	●
2.0–4.0 hrs	Rocky ledges, fine views, covered bridge nearby		$	●	●		●
3.5–5.0 hrs	Great vistas, three overlooks, interesting wildflowers		$		●		●
2.5–6.0 hrs	Great for families up to the waterfalls; spectacular mountain scenery from Mount Chocorua		$	● to falls	● to falls		● to falls
0.5–1.0 hr	Popular family destination, wading, handicapped-accessible		$	●	●		●
1.0–2.0 hrs	Popular family hike, fine vista			●	●		●
1.5–3.0 hrs	Pond with beaver houses, spruce-fir forest, boulder piles			●	●		●
3.0–4.0 hrs	Excellent family outing; hemlock forest, esker, pasture, views		$	●	●		
1.0 hr	Easy hike to pond and vista, especially good for small children	●		●	●		●
1.0–2.0 hrs	Quiet pond with moose, beavers, wood ducks, wildflowers	●		●	●		●
1.5–2.0 hrs	Swimming, picnicking, camping, fishing, birding			●	●	●	●
3.0–4.0 hrs	One of the most beautiful views in the White Mountains	●		●	●		●
3.0–4.0 hrs	Great views, glacial boulders, abandoned quarry		$	●	●		●
2.0/4.5 hrs	Tallest waterfall in NH, great views of Crawford Notch			●	●		●
3.0–4.0 hrs	Pass attractive cascades to excellent vista	●			●		●
3.0–4.0 hrs	Premier location for beavers, birds, and other wildlife, spectacular notch view	●	$	●	●	●	●
5.0 hrs	Remote mountain pond favored by the legendary Ethan Allen Crawford	●		●	●		●
5.0 hrs	Stunning vistas, mountain birds				●		●
5.0–6.0 hrs	Great birds, old-growth red spruce forest, wildflowers, alpine vista		$		●		●
6.0 hrs	Well-graded trail to alpine zone with spectacular vistas and rare alpine plants				●		

	TRIP NUMBER / TRIP NAME	LOCATION	DIFFICULTY	DISTANCE	ELEVATION GAIN
PINKHAM NOTCH					
42	Glen Ellis Falls	Pinkham's Grant, NH	Easy	0.6 mi	short descent
43	Lost Pond	Pinkham's Grant, NH	Easy	1.0–1.8 mi	minimal
44	Thompson Falls Trail	Pinkham's Grant, NH	Easy	1.4 mi	200 ft
45	Square Ledge	Pinkham's Grant, NH	Moderate	1.0 mi	500 ft
46	Waterfall and Vista Loop in the Northern Presidentials	Randolph, NH	Easy-Strenuous	1.5–4.0 mi	400–1,450 ft
47	Pine Mountain from Pinkham B (Dolly Copp) Road	Gorham, NH	Moderate	3.5 mi	1,450 ft
48	Low's Bald Spot via Old Jackson Road	Pinkham's Grant, NH, to Sargent's Purchase, NH	Moderate	4.4 mi	950 ft
49	Nineteen Mile Brook Trail to Carter Notch Hut	Bean's Purchase, NH	Moderate	7.6 mi	1,900 ft
50	Tuckerman Ravine and Mount Washington	Pinkham's Grant, NH, to Sargent's Purchase, NH	Strenuous	8.4 mi	4,250 ft
EVANS NOTCH AND EASTERN WHITE MOUNTAINS					
51	Lord Hill	Stoneham, ME	Easy	2.8 mi	650 ft
52	Deer Hill and Deer Hill Spring	Chatham, NH, to Stow, ME	Easy-Moderate	1.6–4.0 mi	minimal–1,000 ft
53	The Roost	Batchelder's Grant, ME	Moderate	2.1 mi	650 ft
54	Basin Trail to Basin Rim	Bean's Purchase, NH	Moderate	4.6 mi	800 ft
55	Blueberry Mountain via Stone House Trail	Stow, ME, to Stoneham, ME	Moderate	4.5 mi	1,150 ft
56	Caribou Mountain	Batchelder's Grant, ME	Strenuous	6.9 mi	1,900 ft
NORTH COUNTRY					
57	Devil's Hopyard	Stark, NH	Easy	2.6 mi	250 ft
58	Mount Crag	Shelburne, NH	Moderate	2.4 mi	700 ft
59	Lookout Ledge	Randolph, NH	Moderate	2.6 mi	1,000 ft
60	Unknown Pond from Mill Brook Road	Stark, NH, to Kilkenny, NH	Moderate	4.4 mi	1,400 ft

TIME	TRIP HIGHLIGHTS	PUBLIC TRANSPORT	FEE	GOOD FOR KIDS	DOG-FRIENDLY	X-C SKIING	SNOWSHOEING
30-40 min	Impressive falls reached by very short walk, great for all ages		$	Kids	Dog		
1.0 hr	Beaver wetland, wildflowers, views of Mount Washington	Bus		Kids	Dog	Ski	Snowshoe
1.0-2.0 hrs	Short, easy walk, lots of wildflowers, waterfall, and cascades			Kids	Dog		Snowshoe
1.0-2.0 hrs	Great first experience for children on a steep trail to vista	Bus		Kids	Dog		
1.0-4.0 hrs	First part has great waterfalls and picnic spot; second offers great views, challenge			Kids (first part)	Dog		
2.0-3.5 hrs	Fascinating geology and excellent views for moderate effort			Kids	Dog		Snowshoe
3.0-4.0 hrs	Great view, interesting mushrooms, wildflowers				Dog	Ski	Snowshoe
7.0 hrs	Hike along brook to stunning mountain scenery, two pristine lakes	Bus	$		Dog	Ski	Snowshoe
8.0 hrs	Tallest mountain in New England, incomparable views, alpine community, very challenging	Bus					
2.0-4.0 hrs	Rock collecting, vista of pond			Kids	Dog		Snowshoe
1.0-4.0 hrs	Maple, beech, birch, hemlock, blueberries, great views			Kids	Dog		Snowshoe
1.0-1.5 hrs	Terrific views of Wild River and Evans Brook valleys			Kids	Dog		
4.0-6.0 hrs	Impressive glacial cirque and cliffs		$	Kids	Dog		Snowshoe
3.0-5.0 hrs	Blueberries, great views, a gorge and a deep pool			Kids	Dog		Snowshoe
6.0 hrs	Beautiful cascades and views, alpine plants			Kids	Dog		Snowshoe
1.0-2.0 hrs	Narrow, picturesque gorge, handicapped-accessible		$	Kids			Snowshoe
2.0 hrs.	Well-graded trail leading to great view of the Androscoggin Valley			Kids	Dog		Snowshoe
2.0-3.0 hrs	Wonderful view of Northern Presidentials			Kids	Dog		Snowshoe
3.5 hrs	Remote, boreal mountain pond			Kids	Dog		Snowshoe

ACKNOWLEDGMENTS

I thank the Appalachian Mountain Club for giving me the opportunity to write this book. I have had the pleasure of working with gifted editors and other staff at AMC Books. Gordon Hardy guided me through the first edition of *Nature Hikes in the White Mountains,* and I am forever grateful for his faith, encouragement, advice, and good humor. Mark Russell oversaw the second edition. Sarah Jane Shangraw oversaw the evolution of *Nature Hikes* into *Best Day Hikes in the White Mountains,* Dan Eisner and Kimberly Duncan-Mooney managed the second edition of that work, and Victoria Sandbrook Flynn and Shannon Smith managed this third edition. Walter Graff and Nancy Ritger at Pinkham Notch provided helpful recommendations on trails appropriate for children and contributed some basic ideas on how to approach this topic. Much of what I have learned about the White Mountains comes from my past association with the wonderful group of AMC volunteer naturalists.

Many people provided advice and support through my years of writing about day hikes and nature in the White Mountains. Steve Smith, co-author of the AMC *White Mountain Guide* (29th edition), reviewed all the trail descriptions in addition to providing wise counsel on the general perspective of the book and suggesting a number of hikes. Thanks to Lesley Rowse and Gary Inman for their advice on trails, particularly in Evans Notch; for sharing their knowledge of the White Mountains; and for letting my family invade their home on numerous occasions. Ed Quinlan, Leslie Nelkin, and their children, Suzanna and Michael, also shared their house with us, accompanied us on many hikes, and provided feedback. Sarah Allen and her children, Sam and Jack Van Etten, joined us on a number of hikes. David Ross, AMC New Hampshire Chapter Excursions chair, and New Hampshire AMC members Jane Gibbons and Wanda Rice gave valuable feedback and suggestions on the choice of hikes. David Govatski provided historical information on Low's Bald Spot. Russ Cohen suggested the Stinson Mountain Trail. Much of the information on the origins of place names in the White Mountains was taken from John Mudge's *The White Mountains: Names, Places, and Legends* (The Durand Press, 1995).

J. Dykstra Eusden reviewed the geology section of the natural history information in the appendix. Of course, the author takes all responsibility for any errors.

Arriving at Low's Bald Spot after
a fine hike from Pinkham Notch.
Photo by Dennis Welsh.

Very special thanks are due to my wife, Nancy Schalch, and our children, Alison and Gabriel. Nancy was my chief hiking companion, cheerfully doing more than her share of the child care on our trips so I could concentrate on taking notes and photographs. She provided continual encouragement and logistical support, reading and making useful comments on the entire manuscript. It simply would not have been possible to complete this book without her. Alison went on her first hike when she was 2 months old and, fortunately for us (and for this book project), instantly took a liking to being out on the trails. Gabriel was not here when the first version of this book came out but has more than made up for it with his running commentary and enthusiasm for the natural world whenever we have walked these trails together since then. It has been great to see the pendulum swing over the years, from Nancy and I cheerfully encouraging the children to keep up on the trails, to them now wondering what could possibly be taking their parents so long to get up the mountain.

INTRODUCTION

The White Mountains comprise a region of bare mountain summits; extensive views; deep, glacially-scoured ravines; fascinating plants and animals; enchanted evergreen forests; and cold mountain streams tumbling over boulders in fantastic patterns. The area provides some of the very best hiking opportunities in the United States. It has the largest alpine (above treeline) area in the East, where on a clear day the panoramic views can seem endless. There are also many wonderful hikes to lower mountains where the vistas are almost as extensive, and to the more-intimate trails along rivers and streams leading to waterfalls and ponds. Whether you are looking for a full day of hiking or a short walk with young children, the White Mountains have something suitable for you.

For this book, I have selected a variety of trails with different levels of difficulty, so families with young children who are beginning hikers as well as people looking for a long day hike up a steep slope should be able to find something appropriate for their interests and skill levels. The trails all have some natural highlight, whether it is a scenic vista, an interesting geologic feature, or a particularly rich area for birds or other wildlife. Most of the hikes are within the White Mountain National Forest, the largest national forest in the northeastern United States and part of the U.S. Forest Service. Other hikes are in New Hampshire state parks or on private conservation land. I have tried to select trails that are well maintained by trail crews of the national forest, AMC, and other hiking clubs.

HOW TO USE THIS BOOK

With 60 hikes to choose from, you may wonder how to decide where to go. The locator map at the front of this book will help you narrow down the trips by location, and the At-a-Glance Trip Planner that follows the table of contents will provide more information to guide you toward a decision.

Once you settle on a destination and turn to a trip in this guide, you will find a series of icons that indicate whether the hike is a good place for kids, if dogs are permitted, if you can go snowshoeing or cross-country skiing there, and if at least some part of the trail provides access to those using wheelchairs. Note that winter activities may be appropriate for only part of the trail, so be sure to read the descriptions.

Information on the basics follows: location, difficulty rating, distance, elevation gain, estimated time, and available maps. The difficulty ratings are based on the author's perception and are estimates of what the average hiker will experience. You may find the hikes to be easier or more difficult than stated. The estimated time is also based on the author's perception. Consider your own pace when planning.

The elevation gain is the sum of all the uphill climbing that is required to complete the hike. It takes into account the various ups and downs of the terrain. Information is included about the location of the hike in the *AMC White Mountain National Forest Map & Guide,* the maps of AMC's *White Mountain Guide* (29th edition), the relevant U.S. Geological Survey (USGS) topographic map, and the town(s) in which the hike is located.

The Directions explain how to reach the trailhead by car. Some trips have a public transportation icon, which means the trailhead is near a stop on the AMC Hiker Shuttle. Global positioning system (GPS) coordinates for parking lots are also included. When you enter the coordinates into your GPS device, it will provide driving directions. Whether or not you own a GPS device, it is wise to consult an atlas before leaving your home.

In the Trail Description sections, you will find instructions on following the trail or trails. It will describe where to turn at any trail junction, where there are particular challenges such as a stream crossing that could be difficult after a rainstorm, and whether there are places where you need to be particularly careful to avoid losing the trail. You will also learn about the natural and human history along your hike, along with information about flora, fauna, and any landmarks and objects you will encounter.

The trail maps that accompany each trip will help guide you along your hike. An additional resource is the *AMC White Mountain National Forest Map & Guide*. This provides a wonderful overview of the region and contains brief descriptions of almost all of the hikes described here.

Following the trail description, there is a section on Other Activities, which describes nearby swimming and fishing opportunities, places of natural or historical interest, other nearby hikes and winter activities, and so on. Each trip ends with a More Information section that provides details about the locations of bathrooms and other amenities, the land ownership of the trail, and any fees. If you are interested in nearby campgrounds, stores, restaurants, etc., refer to the background information on the region at the beginning of each regional section.

The trail descriptions are grouped by geographic region within the White Mountains. At the beginning of each regional section is a summary of local resources. The hikes are ordered by level of difficulty, with those rated easy first, those rated moderate next, and those that are more challenging last.

Also included in this book is an appendix full of advice on hiking in the Whites with children. The appendix on natural history emphasizes flora, fauna, and geologic features that are visible on many trails.

Before starting out, read the trail description to decide if the hike is right for you. Remember that the difficulty rating naturally involves some subjectivity. "Easy" means the terrain is relatively level and the hike is less than 3 miles long or that the hike is somewhat steep but very short. "Moderate" means the terrain may be rocky or that there is a steeper grade. The hike may be 2 to 5 miles long. "Strenuous" means the terrain can be difficult and generally inappropriate for young children, the elevation gain is greater than 2,000 feet, and the hike may be 5 to 10 miles long. The estimated times are for hiking and factor in some additional time for any stops to enjoy a vista or have lunch.

I hope you enjoy this book and that it is a useful companion on many great hikes in the White Mountains.

TRIP PLANNING AND SAFETY

The White Mountains are the most popular hiking destination in New England, and serious accidents are uncommon. However, there are a couple of things to keep in mind in order to ensure a safe, positive experience. The trails in the White Mountains, though generally well marked, are not manicured. Your trail will sometimes cross directly over streams without any bridges; have exposed tree roots and rocks; take you to windy, exposed locations; or require scrambling up and over boulders. Another safety consideration is the weather, notoriously fickle in the White Mountains, particularly at higher elevations. You may be several hours from "civilization," out of range of cell phone reception and other amenities, when a thunderstorm or even a summer snowstorm hits, so it is wise to be prepared. You will be more likely to have an enjoyable, safe hike if you take proper precautions. Before heading out for your hike, consider the following:

- Select a hike that everyone in your group is comfortable taking. Match the hike to the abilities of the least capable person in the group. If anyone is uncomfortable with the weather or is tired, turn around and complete the hike another day.
- Check the weather. In the White Mountains, the weather can change rapidly. Bright, sunny days can turn into cold, soaking rains, so hikers need to be prepared with rain gear and extra clothes. At low elevations, bad weather could merely be uncomfortable, but above treeline, the consequences can be deadly. Lives have been lost due to hypothermia and lightning strikes, almost always involving people who ignored weather warnings, did not carry a map and compass, and did not have the proper gear. You must be willing to turn back if the weather begins to sour. If you are planning a ridge or summit hike, especially in summer, start early so you will be off the exposed area before the afternoon hours when thunderstorms most often strike. Before heading out, particularly if planning a hike above treeline, you should get a weather forecast at AMC facilities at Pinkham and Crawford notches or at White Mountain National Forest ranger stations. In winter it is particularly critical to check on weather and snow conditions.
- Plan to be back at the trailhead before dark. Before beginning your hike, determine a turnaround time. Don't diverge from it, even if you have not reached your intended destination.
- Check current trail conditions at AMC's website, outdoors.org.

- Bring a pack with the following items:
  - ✓ Water: Two quarts per person is usually adequate, depending on the weather and the length of the trip.
  - ✓ Food: Even if you are planning just a 1-hour hike, bring high-energy snacks such as nuts, dried fruit, or granola bars. Pack a lunch for longer trips.
  - ✓ Map and compass: Be sure you know how to use them. A handheld GPS device may also be helpful, but is not always reliable, particularly under a thick canopy of spruce and fir trees.
  - ✓ Headlamp or flashlight, with spare batteries
  - ✓ Extra clothing: rain gear, wool sweater or fleece, hat, and mittens
  - ✓ Sunscreen
  - ✓ First-aid kit, including adhesive bandages, gauze, nonprescription pain-killer, and moleskin
  - ✓ Pocketknife or multitool
  - ✓ Waterproof matches and a lighter
  - ✓ Trash bag
  - ✓ Toilet paper
  - ✓ Whistle
  - ✓ Insect repellent
  - ✓ Sunglasses
  - ✓ Cell phone: Be aware that cell phone service is unreliable in the backcountry. If you are receiving a signal, use the phone only for emergencies to avoid disturbing the backcountry experience for other hikers.
  - ✓ Binoculars (optional)
  - ✓ Camera (optional)
- Wear appropriate footwear and clothing. Wool or synthetic hiking socks will keep your feet dry and help prevent blisters. Comfortable, waterproof hiking boots that are broken in before your hike will provide ankle support and good traction. Avoid wearing cotton clothing, which absorbs sweat and rain and contributes to an unpleasant hiking experience. Polypropylene, fleece, silk, and wool all wick moisture away from your body and keep you warm in wet or cold conditions. It is always wise to bring a windbreaker and extra clothes when hiking to summit ledges, even at low elevations. The weather on ledges could be cool and windy compared to that in the forest. You'll enjoy your lunch breaks at the summits much more if you have additional layers to wear.
- To limit bug bites, wear pants and a long-sleeve shirt or use insect repellents. Blackfly season in the White Mountains runs through much of May

and June, and mosquitoes can be a problem in low, swampy areas from late spring through much of summer.

- When you are ahead of the rest of your hiking group, wait at all trail junctions until the others catch up. This avoids confusion and keeps people from getting separated or lost.
- If you see downed wood that appears to be purposely covering a trail, it probably means the trail is closed due to overuse or hazardous conditions.
- If a trail is muddy, walk through the mud or on rocks, never on tree roots or plants. Waterproof boots will keep your feet comfortable. Staying in the center of the trail will keep it from eroding into a wide hiking highway.
- Leave your itinerary and the time you expect to return with someone you trust. If you see a logbook at a trailhead, be sure to sign in when you arrive, and sign out when you finish your hike.
- After you complete your hike, check for deer ticks, which carry the dangerous Lyme disease.
- If your hike takes you out into the sun, remember to wear a sun hat and sunscreen.
- Poison ivy is uncommon in the White Mountains but it does grow along some lowland trails. To identify the plant, look for clusters of three leaves that shine in the sun but are dull in the shade. If you do come into contact with poison ivy, wash the affected area with soap as soon as possible.
- Wear blaze-orange items in hunting season. In New Hampshire, deer hunting season typically runs from early November through early December.
- Rainstorms and spring snowmelt can make stream crossings difficult or even hazardous. Rocks that are fun to scramble up in dry weather can become slippery when wet or icy. I have noted these in the hike descriptions, so you can choose your hike wisely under these less-than-ideal conditions.
- Annoying insects are likely to be the only wildlife "threat" you will encounter. Bears are extremely rare and will almost always take pains to stay away from humans. To avoid surprising a mother with cubs, it is a good idea to make some noise while hiking.
- You may need more than 2 quarts of water per person for some of the longer hikes in this book, particularly if the weather is warm. Water in mountain lakes and streams is considered unsafe to drink, so fill your water bottle before beginning your hike. Read the hike description to determine if you will be passing a reliable and safe source of water along the trail (e.g., an AMC hut).
- Getting lost is an unpleasant experience. At higher elevations of the White Mountains and in bad weather, it can be dangerous. The trails in this guide are generally well marked with signs and blazes (painted spots on tree trunks or rocks); however, intersections with logging roads or unmarked trails, and

occasional faded blazes, might lead to some confusion. On open ledges and summits, trails are often marked by cairns, a Scottish Gaelic word meaning piles of rocks. Read the trail description before you depart so that you are prepared for any quirks. If you think you are off the trail, the best thing to do is to backtrack until you find the last blaze. Keep track of the blazes as you hike, which is a job you might share with children so they feel responsible for the successful navigation of the trip. Remember to stay on the trail, not only for safety, but also to protect plants and wildlife.

WHAT TO BRING ESPECIALLY FOR KIDS

First of all, you should bring along all the items necessary for hikes without children. A child who is cold or hungry is not going to be a good hiking companion. Remember that children are more likely to get chilled if you end up carrying them, so bring extra clothing, especially for backpack-sized babies.

One important safety item for children is a whistle. Train children beforehand to stay within sight, and then you won't need the whistle. However, all children should have one. If they are separated from the group, they should stay put and blow the whistle at regular intervals. Remind them that the whistle is not for play but should be used only when they sense they are lost.

Food is another critical ingredient of a successful hike with kids. Lunch is a great motivator and reward. Occasional snacks such as granola bars, fruit, or cookies can nip any crankiness before it goes too far.

Have kids carry a pack of their own when they are old enough. In addition to extra clothes and perhaps a small water bottle, make sure each child's pack has something essential for one of the group's activities (e.g., a special snack, bags for blueberries, or a lunch treat). If the kids insist they won't need jackets, suggest that they can sit on them during lunch.

Consider bringing along a child carrier, especially for longer hikes. It is a lot easier than carrying a tired child on your shoulders—and safer too.

Other small items good to have: a hand lens or magnifying glass to aid in examining small things; binoculars

It's never too early to get your kids outside.

if your destination is a view; a tea or soup strainer to make searching for aquatic life along ponds and streams more fun; and a bug box to enable children to examine insects closely. Finally, younger children can bring a favorite toy or stuffed animal in their own day packs.

See Appendix A for more advice on hiking with children.

HIKESAFE

The U.S. Forest Service and New Hampshire Fish and Game Department have developed "hikeSafe," a program to encourage hiker responsibility in the White Mountain National Forest. The hikeSafe "Hiker Responsibility Code" states that you are responsible for yourself, so be prepared:

- With knowledge and gear. Become self-reliant by learning about the terrain, conditions, local weather, and your equipment before you start.
- To leave your plans. Tell someone where you are going, the trails you are hiking, when you'll return, and your emergency plans.
- To stay together. When you start as a group, you should hike as a group, and end as a group. Pace your hike to the slowest person.
- To turn back. Weather changes quickly in the mountains. Fatigue and unexpected conditions can also affect your hike. Know your limitations and when to postpone your hike. The mountains will be there another day.
- For emergencies, even if you are headed out for just an hour. An injury, severe weather, or a wrong turn could become life threatening. Don't assume you will be rescued; know how to rescue yourself.
- To share the hiker code with others.

New Hampshire Fish and Game (NHFG) sells an annual voluntary "hikeSafe card" to raise money for the department's search and rescue fund. Cardholders will not be held responsible for search and rescue costs if rescued due to negligence; they will still be charged if their actions are deemed reckless or intentional. The cost of the card, good from time of purchase through the end of the calendar year, is $25 for individuals and $35 for families. Cards may be purchased online at wildnh.com/safe.

PARKING AND ENTRANCE FEES

The White Mountain National Forest Recreational Fee Program has existed since 1997. Your vehicle must display a sticker for you to park at certain marked trailheads within the national forest. These are generally those trailheads that have bathrooms, picnic tables, and other amenities. In 2015, the cost of the sticker was $3 for a one-day pass, $5 for seven days, and $20 for one year ($25 for two cars in the same family). Day passes are available at self-service pay stations at the trailhead. Day, weekly, and yearly passes are available at ranger stations, information centers, and at a number of businesses throughout the region. Ninety-five percent of the fee directly supports the White Mountain National Forest.

Holders of Interagency, Golden Age, or Golden Access passes do not have to pay the fee, but the card must be displayed on the dashboard of your car. You can obtain these passes at White Mountain National Forest ranger stations and information centers.

Certain sites operated by concessionaires within the national forest charge a day-use fee. These include Russell Pond (off Tripoli Road) and South Pond (North Country).

Changes to the fee program, including an increase in the amount and elimination of some of the sites that require fees, have been proposed. You can obtain the latest information at www.fs.usda.gov/detail/whitemountain/passes-permits/recreation/.

Franconia and Crawford Notch state parks do not generally charge an entrance fee for day use by hikers. If you park at the beach at Echo Lake in Franconia Notch State Park, there is a $4/$2 charge per adult/child. There is also an entrance fee for walking the trails of Flume Gorge (Trip 11), also in Franconia Notch State Park.

AMC LODGES AND HUTS

Hikers staying overnight in the White Mountains can opt for backcountry stays at AMC's huts or frontcountry comfort at AMC's Joe Dodge Lodge in Pinkham Notch and Highland Center in Crawford Notch. Two shuttle routes operate daily from June through September and on weekends until mid-October, connecting the lodge-and-hut system to major trail heads across the White Mountain National Forest. For more information about AMC's lodges and huts, visit outdoors.org/lodging; a shuttle schedule is available at outdoors.org/lodging/lodging-shuttle.cfm. For reservations, call 603-466-2727.

DOGS ON THE TRAILS

Dogs can be great hiking companions. They are permitted on trails in the White Mountain National Forest, but they must be under verbal or physical control at all times. Hikers with dogs should recognize that while dogs will likely bring smiles to the faces of many hikers on the trail, some people may find dogs intimidating, especially when those hikers are surprised on a trail. When in campgrounds, dogs must be leashed. The rules for New Hampshire state parks vary by park. Franconia Notch and Crawford Notch state parks both allow dogs in designated areas, so check when you arrive at those parks. Be aware that dogs, like people, will have more stamina for hiking if they have been getting regular exercise before you attempt to scale a mountain with them.

LEAVE NO TRACE

The Appalachian Mountain Club is a national educational partner of Leave No Trace, a nonprofit organization dedicated to promoting and inspiring responsible outdoor recreation through education, research, and partnerships.
The Leave No Trace program seeks to develop wildland ethics—ways in which people think and act in the outdoors to minimize their impact on the areas they visit and to protect our natural resources for future enjoyment. Leave No Trace unites four federal land management agencies—the U.S. Forest Service, National Park Service, Bureau of Land Management, and U.S. Fish and Wildlife Service—with manufacturers, outdoor retailers, user groups, educators, organizations such as AMC, and individuals.

The Leave No Trace ethic is guided by these seven principles:

1. **Plan Ahead and Prepare.** Know the terrain and any regulations applicable to the area you're planning to visit, and be prepared for extreme weather or other emergencies. This will enhance your enjoyment and ensure that you've chosen an appropriate destination. Small groups have less impact on resources and on the experiences of other backcountry visitors.

2. **Travel and Camp on Durable Surfaces.** Travel and camp on established trails and campsites, rock, gravel, dry grasses, or snow. Good campsites are found, not made. Camp at least 200 feet from lakes and streams, and focus activities on areas where vegetation is absent. In pristine areas, disperse use to prevent the creation of campsites and trails.

3. **Dispose of Waste Properly.** Pack it in, pack it out. Inspect your camp for trash or food scraps. Deposit solid human waste in cat holes dug 6 to 8 inches deep, at least 200 feet from water, camps, and trails. Pack out toilet paper and hygiene products. To wash yourself or your dishes, carry water 200 feet from streams or lakes and use small amounts of biodegradable soap. Scatter strained dishwater.

4. **Leave What You Find.** Cultural or historical artifacts, as well as natural objects such as plants and rocks, should be left as found.

5. **Minimize Campfire Impacts.** Cook on a stove. Use established fire rings, fire pans, or mound fires. If you build a campfire, keep it small and use dead sticks found on the ground.

6. **Respect Wildlife.** Observe wildlife from a distance. Feeding animals alters their natural behavior. Protect wildlife from your food by storing rations and trash securely.

7. **Be Considerate of Other Visitors.** Be courteous, respect the quality of other visitors' backcountry experience, and let nature's sounds prevail.

AMC is a national provider of the Leave No Trace Master Educator course. AMC offers this five-day course, designed especially for outdoor professionals and land managers, as well as the shorter two-day Leave No Trace Trainer course at locations throughout the Northeast.

For Leave No Trace information and materials, contact the Leave No Trace Center for Outdoor Ethics, P.O. Box 997, Boulder, CO 80306. Phone: 800-332-4100 or 302-442-8222; fax: 303-442-8217; web: lnt.org. For information on the AMC Leave No Trace Master Educator training course schedule, see outdoors.org/education/lnt.

THE SOUTHWESTERN WHITE MOUNTAINS AND WATERVILLE VALLEY

The southwestern corner of the White Mountains provides a variety of hiking opportunities, from short walks along beautiful cascading streams to 4,800-foot Mount Moosilauke. The region includes the towns of Plymouth, Rumney, Campton, Thornton, and Waterville Valley. From I-93, it is a relatively short drive from the big metropolitan areas of the East Coast compared with other parts of the White Mountains. The region loses its snow cover earlier in spring and cools down later in fall than more northerly sections of the White Mountain National Forest, making for a more extended hiking season.

Waterville Valley, a beautiful valley tucked in among 4,000-foot peaks, is a centerpiece of this region. This valley still feels secluded and quiet despite the presence of a major ski resort and conference center. If you are coming from the south, reach Waterville Valley from I-93 by traveling about 11 miles northeast on NH 49 (Campton, Exit 28). This is a well-paved, scenic road that parallels the Mad River. If approaching from the north, travel about 10 miles east through Thornton Gap on Tripoli Road (Exit 31 off I-93), an unpaved road for much of its length. Note that Tripoli Road is not plowed in winter.

The valley's loop hike to Welch and Dickey mountains is one of the most popular family hikes in the White Mountains (see Trip 7). There is also an extensive network of easy trails along streams.

Facing page: Many small cascades are characteristic of Waterville Valley and nearby areas of the White Mountains.

The Squam Range in the southern part of this region provides vistas of Squam, Winnipesaukee, and other lakes. Percival-Morgan Loop (Trip 6) overlooks Squam Lake south of Waterville Valley.

SUPPLIES AND LOGISTICS

Plymouth is one of the larger towns in the White Mountain region, with restaurants, gas stations, malls, and Plymouth State University, a campus of the University System of New Hampshire. The resort community of Waterville Valley has downhill ski slopes, a convention center, and condominiums. The town caters to outdoor activities, so you'll have no trouble buying last-minute supplies. If you are coming from the north, you may find it convenient to get your supplies at the Lincoln/North Woodstock exit, where there are a number of stores along NH 112.

NEARBY CAMPING

There are numerous national forest campgrounds in the region. NH 49 in the Waterville Valley area provides access to three. These are Campton Campground (close to I-93; 58 sites open in summer and a group camping area open year-round), Waterville Campground (8 miles from I-93; 27 sites; open year-round), and Osceola Vista Campground (near the junction of NH 49 and Tripoli Road just beyond the village of Waterville Valley; 11 sites). Russell Pond, a terrific spot for swimming and paddling, can be reached from Tripoli Road a few miles from I-93. It has 86 sites. The campgrounds in Franconia Notch and the western part of the Kancamagus Highway are about 30 to 45 minutes from the trails in this region.

1

CASCADE PATH, WATERVILLE VALLEY

This is a pleasant, easy walk to a beautiful series of small waterfalls in Waterville Valley near the resort community. A number of connecting trails provide a potential longer hike if you do not mind wading across a stream.

DIRECTIONS

Waterville Valley is at the end of NH 49, about 11 miles northeast of the Campton exit off I-93, or about 10 miles east of I-93 through Thornton Gap on Tripoli Road. To find the trailhead, continue on NH 49 (Valley Road) past the town square and turn right onto Boulder Path Road, following the signs to Snow's Mountain and WVAIA hiking trails. Park in the large lot just past the tennis courts and chair lift about 0.1 mile north of West Branch Road. Follow the sign to Cascade Path. New development may affect the location of the trailhead so follow the sign. *GPS coordinates: 43° 57.61′ N, 71° 30.52′ W.*

TRAIL DESCRIPTION

Cascade Path begins by climbing alongside the winding Cascade Ridge Road. At 0.2 mile, the trail, now ascending an old ski slope, passes the junction with Boulder Path. It passes through a small patch of woods, crosses the road once more, and enters the woods on the left (north) side of the old slope after about 0.3 mile. Do not turn off too soon on the cross-country ski trail.

The hiking trail, marked with yellow blazes, intersects a cross-country ski trail a short way in and then passes Elephant Rock Trail (0.5 mile). Just beyond, look for hemlocks with their short, flat needles. One hemlock root hugging a rock near the trail may particularly catch your eye.

The trail continues over a series of small wooden bridges and reaches Cascade Brook (1.2 miles) where a logging

LOCATION
Waterville Valley, NH

RATING
Easy

DISTANCE
3.4 miles round-trip

ELEVATION GAIN
700 feet

ESTIMATED TIME
2.0 hours

MAPS
AMC *White Mountain National Forest Map & Guide*, J6

AMC *White Mountain Guide*, 29th ed. Map 3 Crawford Notch–Sandwich Range, J6

USGS Topo: Waterville Valley

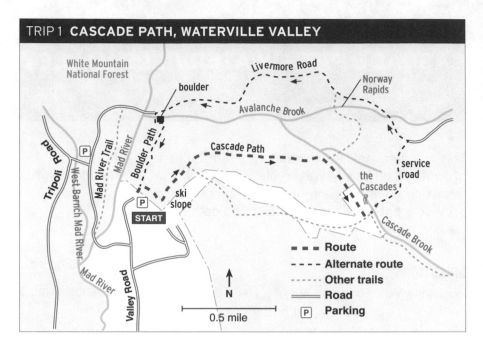

road comes in from the left. There is a nice patch of wildflowers in the middle of the trail just before the brook. Look for clintonia (bluebead lily), bunchberries, rosy twisted stalk, and asters. You could turn around here, although the cascades are not much farther and are really worth seeing. Norway Rapids Trail heads left across the brook, but continue straight on Cascade Path.

Along the brook you will pass by a marvelous example of a tree that grows on top of a rock. The woods here are dominated by northern hardwoods—beech, sugar maple, and yellow birch. Red and painted trillium, clintonia, Canada mayflower, goldthread, and mountain wood sorrel put on particularly showy displays in spring. In late summer, most of the flowers are gone, but the rich woods are a great habitat for mushrooms. Amanitas, most of which are deadly poisonous, are particularly abundant. One of the most common and attractive is fly agaric, which is your classic toadstool with a broad red cap (occasionally yellowish) covered with flecks of whitish scales. A pure white amanita is called destroying angel, which certainly brings home the message that picking any mushroom should be best left to the experts—and even they occasionally make mistakes. There are also boletes, which have tiny pores instead of gills on their undersides. After the first cascade, the trail then becomes a little rougher. It crosses the brook at the bottom of the first cascade, which can be tricky in high water, but you can go up either side of the brook. The cascades go on for a good distance, shooting through small gorges and tumbling into deep pools. Just when you think you've reached the last waterfall, you walk up a little farther and discover yet another. Although pools below several of the cascades may look inviting, you should use care, common sense, and a conservation ethic. Some are difficult to reach because of the steep sides of the bank. Others show signs of erosion where too many people have scurried down the sides to get to them, inadvertently destroying the vegetation.

Much of the streambed around the cascades consists of flat slabs of granite. A flat slab just below the bridge at the top of the trail is an excellent lunch rock. Note there and elsewhere how the granite fractured along smooth joints when eroded by streams.

You reach an unpaved maintenance road at 1.7 miles. Retrace your steps to return to the trailhead.

DID YOU KNOW?

Waterville was a quiet summer resort area until 1966, when the ski area at Mount Tecumseh was developed.

OTHER ACTIVITIES

There are many connecting trails that could make for a longer loop hike. When you reach the maintenance road at the end of Cascade Path you can turn left onto the maintenance road, follow it for 0.6 mile, and then turn left onto Livermore Road (another unpaved road—no motorized vehicles). After 1.5 more miles, turn left onto Boulder Path. The boulder, a huge glacial erratic in Avalanche Brook, is reached just a short distance from the turn. The path crosses

Waterfall along Cascade Brook. Photo by Steve Smith.

the brook, which will require wading. (If the crossing looks too challenging, then complete the loop on Livermore Road instead.) After the crossing, the trail follows the brook for about 100 yards with nice wildflowers (e.g., pink lady's slippers, Canada mayflower, oak ferns). It then ascends away from the brook and reaches an old woodland road. Turn right and follow the road back to a cul de sac. Walk alongside the cul de sac back to Cascade Path to complete the loop (4.9 miles for the complete loop).

If you turn right onto the maintenance road at the top of Cascade Path, you reach the top of Snow's Mountain Ski Area in 0.8 miles and get some views. You can then descend Elephant Rock Trail back to Cascade Path.

Norway Rapids Trail also links Cascade Path to Livermore Road in 0.5 mile, passing by impressive rapids. It too requires wading across Avalanche Brook, which should not be attempted in high water.

Livermore Road is appropriate for skiing and snowshoeing. In addition, Waterville Valley offers a host of other skiing and snowshoeing opportunities.

The resort village of Waterville Valley, famous for skiing in winter, has restaurants, a grocery store, golf, fishing, and other amenities.

MORE INFORMATION

Most of this hike is within the White Mountain National Forest; www.fs.usda.gov/whitemountain; 603-536-6100. There is no parking fee.

AQUATIC INSECTS IN THE WHITE MOUNTAINS

A number of aquatic insects are common inhabitants of the White Mountains. Most are easy to find in streams, ditches, and temporary woodland pools, and some, like mosquitoes and blackflies, actually come looking for you.

Mosquitoes begin life in small, temporary pools, such as those that form in depressions on a path after a heavy rain, or in holes in trees. The wormlike larvae (called wrigglers because of their corkscrew-like movements) survive best in these isolated pools because they are easy prey for fish, salamanders, and just about everything else that lives in more permanent bodies of water. Wrigglers typically hang down from the water surface, with their posterior end taking in air while they feed on detritus underwater. They abandon this posture and scatter toward the bottom when your shadow or any other "threat" appears over their little pool. The larvae go through several stages before forming a pupa (which also swims in the pool). The adult mosquito emerges after the pupal stage and leaves the pool to mate and search for nectar (males) or a blood meal (females).

The crane fly is a graceful fly with very long legs. It is likely to be seen hovering above the water, occasionally landing on people and causing instant panic because it looks like the world's largest mosquito. But don't worry, crane flies are harmless. Their larvae feed on detritus in streams and are important in nutrient recycling.

Blackflies spend their larval stages attached to rocks along flowing waters. They passively feed on organic matter that passes by. Unfortunately, they abandon that lifestyle as adults. While males feed solely on nectar or plant sap, females require a blood meal for optimum egg development.

Predaceous diving beetles spend most of their lives in water. You might find them in any deep pool in a stream or even in ditches along the sides of trails. They are blackish and oval and swim strongly underwater, feeding on invertebrates and even larval fish. Don't try to pick one up with your hands because they can give a surprisingly nasty bite (their larvae are named "water tigers"). Adults can fly, which is how they reach some of those out-of-the-way pools in the woods.

Water striders walk on the water's surface, supported by surface tension—  the same force that keeps cocoa powder on the surface of hot water until it is stirred. Tiny hairs on the bottoms of their legs repel water and prevent them from breaking through. If for some reason their legs do penetrate the surface, the insect "falls" underwater and must crawl up on some vegetation to dry off before it can walk on water again. If the light is just right, water striders appear to have foot pads under their legs. These are actually indentations of the water surface itself under the weight of the insect.

Humans are much too big and heavy for surface tension to hold us up, but for many small creatures, the water surface can be an impenetrable barrier. Water striders feed on small invertebrates that fall onto the surface film and get stuck. They lay eggs underwater, and the newly hatched young must swim to the surface and break through to survive.

Whirligig beetles spin around in dizzying patterns on the surface of the water, particularly when they are disturbed by your presence. They actually have two pairs of eyes, one that can look up at the sky to detect predators and another that looks into the water. They hold their antenna on the water surface and are very sensitive to vibrations that might indicate potential prey struggling there.

2

THREE PONDS LOOP

This relatively level loop hike features an attractive series of nature-rich ponds nestled among mountains, great wildlife viewing potential, and walking along rushing mountain streams. It makes use of sections of Three Ponds, Donkey Hill Cutoff, and Mount Kineo trails.

DIRECTIONS

The Three Ponds trailhead is located in the southwestern part of the White Mountain National Forest. From Exit 26 (milepost 82) off I-93, follow NH 25 west. In 4.0 miles you will go around a traffic circle, and in another 1.0 mile pass Polar Caves. At 8.5 miles from I-93, turn right onto Main Street toward Rumney Center, which you reach in 0.7 mile. Continue straight through the main intersection onto Stinson Lake Road. The trailhead parking area is 6.2 miles north of Rumney Center (6.9 miles north of NH 25). If you are coming from the Lincoln/Woodstock area, take I-93 south to Exit 29 (Thornton). Take US 3 south for 1.4 miles. Make a slight right onto Dan Webb Road and then an immediate right onto Ellsworth Hill Road. Follow Ellsworth Hill Road for 5.9 miles. It becomes Stinson Lake Road and you follow it for another 2.0 miles. Trailhead parking will be on the right. *GPS coordinates: 43° 51.13′ N, 71° 47.77′ W.*

TRAIL DESCRIPTION

This loop hike starts on Three Ponds Trail, which begins as a wide logging road. There is a short, steep ascent of about 200 feet, which is the steepest part of the hike. Mount Kineo Trail enters to the right at 0.1 mile and Carr Mountain Trail on the left at 0.5 mile. Look for typical northern hardwood trees (sugar maple, yellow birch, American beech) and an understory dominated by hobblebush along the trail. During spring and summer, birds that are likely to serenade you include black-throated green warbler

RATING
Easy

DISTANCE
5.7 miles

ELEVATION GAIN
749 feet

ESTIMATED TIME
4.0 hours including time for a picnic lunch

MAPS
AMC *White Mountain National Forest Map & Guide,* K3

AMC *White Mountain Guide,* 29th ed. Map 4 Moosilauke-Kinsman, K3

USGS Topo: Mount Kineo, NH

Middle Pond, a great lunch spot on the Three Ponds Trail.

(wheezy, slurred song) and ovenbird (a staccato *Teacher, teacher!*). There are some muddy sections. After about a half hour of hiking through forest, you get to a wetland along a stream where there is a logjam (piles of logs and leaves that are causing water to back up, creating that wetland). At 1.0 mile, the trail crosses a bridge over Sucker Brook, turns right, and then follows the brook for much of the rest of the way to the pond. The trail departs to the right from the logging road for a short distance (follow blazes), rejoins the logging road, and crosses a tributary on a snowmobile bridge. A final crossing on stones could be difficult in high water. The trail then departs from the snowmobile trail and ascends gradually through a forest with an increasing number of spruce and fir trees. The southernmost pond, Lower Pond, is to your right but there is no trail to it. Three Ponds Trail reaches Middle Pond at 2.0 miles (1.25 hours).

After you've hiked in the forest for an hour, the open views across the pond to Carr Mountain and other nearby peaks are a welcome sight. The pond is shallow and edged by marshes where birds such as swamp sparrows and common yellowthroats reside. Following along the eastern shoreline, a spur trail to Three Pond Shelter goes off to the right at 2.2 miles. There are no views from the shelter but there is a privy there if you need it. Reach it by walking past the shelter and following an unmarked trail uphill.

Back along Three Ponds Trail, the best sitting rocks for your lunch or a snack along the pond are a short distance beyond the spur trail to the shelter. On a sunny summer day, several species of dragonflies, including green darners and white and chalk-fronted corporals, are likely to be patrolling the shoreline. Green frogs and damselflies hang out along the edge of the pond, and newts are visible in the shallow water. If you look carefully in the water, you might see a leech (not the best incentive to go for a swim) or a stonefly larva (which builds a case of small twig fragments that it carries around). Moose are a possibility, as are ducks and great blue herons. The beautiful songs of hermit thrushes and white-throated sparrows emanate from the surrounding woodlands.

Continuing along Three Ponds Trail, reach the junction with Donkey Hill Cutoff at 2.5 miles. To get a look at Upper Pond, follow Three Ponds Trail for another 0.2 mile. It does require crossing over a wetland on a beaver dam, so do this only if your shoes are waterproof or if you don't mind hiking with wet feet the rest of the way. Assuming you make it across, you pass through a dense area of hobblebush. Where Three Ponds Trail continues to the left, you

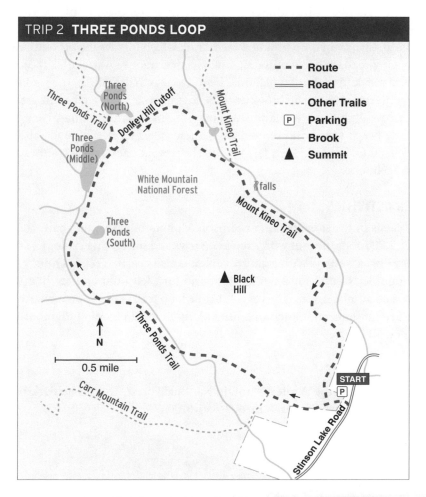

reach the edge of the pond by a grassy area off a short spur trail. The orange, dandelion-like flowers (illustrated here) are orange hawkweed, also called devil's paintbrush, a nonnative species but attractive nonetheless.

Upper Pond is smaller than Middle Pond and surrounded by shrubby wetlands. The dominant shrubs are sheep laurel, leatherleaf, sweet gale, and Labrador tea. Moose and other aquatic animals are possible here too.

Retracing your steps back across the beaver dam, return to the junction and take Donkey Hill Cutoff. This trail follows the edge of open, beaver-created wetlands (the first section follows the outlet to the north pond) and provides nice viewing opportunities of the open wetlands, Mount Kineo, and other peaks along the way. There is little overall elevation gain along this trail, though it is a bit rough in sections. Despite the proximity of the beaver wetlands, the trail manages to avoid serious mud, at least in summer. The trail runs for 1.1 miles and takes about 30 minutes. It ends at Mount Kineo Trail by Brown Brook (4.0 miles; 2.5 hours, including stop for lunch). Here, there is a large wooden bridge that seems oversized for the site, but do not cross it.

Instead, turn right onto Mount Kineo Trail, which follows the brook along an old logging road. In a few minutes, look for an attractive waterfall, a nice place to take a break. At 4.7 miles (0.7 mile from Donkey Hill Cutoff), the trail turns away to the right from the brook and the logging road. On a pleasant grade, it passes through a rich woodland with lots of ferns (e.g., Christmas, New York, and long beech ferns) and crosses over a few small rivulets. It ends at Three Ponds Trail (5.6 miles). Turn left for the short walk back to the trailhead (5.7 miles; 3.5 hours).

OTHER ACTIVITIES

This hike is in the same region as Stinson Mountain, a 3.6-mile, half-day hike up to a 2,900-foot summit with excellent views and interesting geology (Trip 4). Quincy Bog, a wetland with a nature center, is also nearby. Follow Quincy Road from Rumney Center for 2.1 miles east and turn left onto Quincy Bog Road. There is no admission fee. The easy, 1.0-mile loop trail is partly on a boardwalk.

Find restaurants and other amenities along Route 25 in West Plymouth and Rumney, NH.

MORE INFORMATION

This trail is within the White Mountain National Forest. There is no parking fee; www.fs.usda.gov/whitemountain; 603-536-6100.

3

EAST POND AND LITTLE EAST POND

East Pond and Little East Pond are two aquatic gems nestled behind Mount Osceola and Scar Ridge at 2,600 feet. They are connected by a loop trail that passes through rich woodlands carpeted with wildflowers, ferns, and mushrooms and crosses over a number of streams.

LOCATION
Livermore, NH

RATING
Moderate

DISTANCE
5.0 miles round-trip

ELEVATION GAIN
1,000 feet

ESTIMATED TIME
4.0–5.0 hours

MAPS
AMC White Mountain National Forest Map & Guide, J5

AMC *White Mountain Guide*, 29th ed. Map 4 Moosilauke–Kinsman, J5

USGS Topo: Waterville Valley and Mount Osceola

DIRECTIONS

The trailhead for East Pond Trail is off Tripoli Road, about 5.4 miles from its junction with I-93. If you are coming from Waterville Valley, the trailhead is about 6.0 miles west of the junction of Tripoli Road and NH 49. Stay to the right when the road to the ski area splits off to the left. Turn north off Tripoli Road onto a gravel side road for about 100 yards to reach the parking area. *GPS coordinates: 43° 59.63′ N, 71° 35.00′ W.*

TRAIL DESCRIPTION

This loop hike uses East Pond Trail, East Pond Loop Trail, and Little East Pond Trail. The entire loop may be long for younger children, so you can shorten the hike by walking only to East Pond and back, a moderately uphill, 1.4-mile walk in each direction.

East Pond Trail starts out on an old, wide logging road. After a few minutes, the logging road swings off to the right and East Pond Trail continues straight, still on a wide path. Look for the yellow blazes that mark the trail.

After 0.4 mile, you reach the junction with Little East Pond Trail, near where a mill once stood. This is a good spot for a number of wildflowers and ferns, notably wild sarsaparilla, red trillium, golden alexanders, clintonia, and long beech fern. Striped maple and hobblebush are the

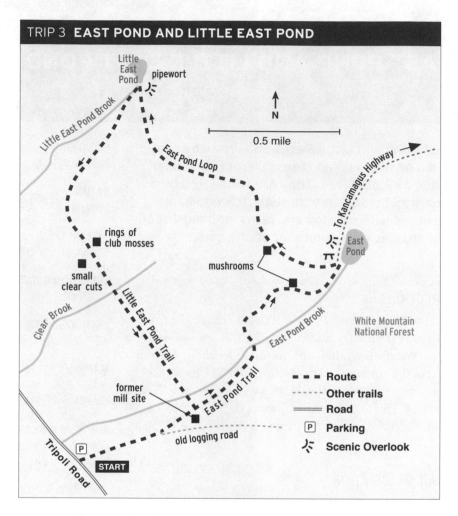

Little East Pond

pipewort

Little East Pond Brook

East Pond Loop

N

0.5 mile

To Kancamagus Highway

rings of club mosses

mushrooms

East Pond

small clear cuts

Clear Brook

Little East Pond Trail

White Mountain National Forest

East Pond Brook

former mill site

East Pond Trail

- - - Route
.... Other trails
===== Road
P Parking
⅄ᶜ Scenic Overlook

old logging road

Tripoli Road

P

START

common understory shrubs. The ruins of the mill (foundation and bricks) can be seen a couple hundred feet in the woods to the right.

Continue straight along the old logging road on a gradual uphill. The trail remains wide and, for the most part, offers easy walking. Cross East Pond Brook at 0.7 mile on a snowmobile bridge. At 1.4 miles, just below East Pond, East Pond Loop Trail diverges left toward Little East Pond. Continue straight on East Pond Trail, then take a side path to the right to reach the shore of East Pond at an open area. This is the best spot to view the pond, swim, and picnic.

East Pond is about 6.5 acres. A saddle in Scar Ridge forms the backdrop of the pond as you look out from the southern end. The pond is shallow by the gravelly "beach" area but then grades off to a depth of 27 feet.

There's much for everyone to enjoy right at the edge of the pond. If you swim, you'll be joining the abundant resident red-spotted newts. These aquatic sala-manders have green bodies with red spots and flattened tails they use to propel themselves through the water. In an unusual twist for an amphibian, immature

Southern ground cedar, a nonflowering plant also called fan club moss. Photo by Jerry Monkman.

newts—just recently graduated from being tadpoles—typically leave the water and live on the forest floor for several years in a juvenile life stage called red efts. You may have seen these brightly colored critters (orange-red bodies with green spots—the reverse of the adult color pattern) on the forest floor of the White Mountains, often a considerable distance from water. They then return to the water and transform into newts that spend their adult lives swimming about places like East Pond.

Newts have a number of companions in East Pond. The tadpoles of frogs are quite abundant at times. Leeches also inhabit the pond. A beaver lodge is visible near a big rock on the opposite shore. Dragonflies patrol the shores of the pond hunting for unwary insects, and water striders skim across the pools in the small outlet creek near the informal camping area.

For some additional perspectives of the pond, follow East Pond Trail along the west side of the pond for a couple hundred yards. (It eventually swings away and meets the Kancamagus Highway in 3.7 miles.) Explore some short spur paths to informal camping areas near the pond shore. Keep a watchful eye skyward for birds that may fly over the pond. Ravens and hawks are possibilities.

To hike the entire loop, return to the trail junction and head west on East Pond Loop Trail. It is about 1.5 miles (1.0 hour) from East Pond to Little East Pond via East Pond Loop Trail. The trail has a few minor ups and downs but almost no overall change in elevation.

East Pond Loop Trail passes through a forest of red spruce and balsam fir with occasional paper birches. Twenty years ago, the birch dominated this section of the forest, but the spruce and fir have clearly taken over now—actually returning to their former prominence. This area was originally spruce-fir forest, but after it was logged in the early twentieth century, the paper birch came in. Many of the birches were recently knocked over by windstorms.

Many small, sunny gaps in the forest are created where trees have been knocked down by the wind. These provide partial views of Mount Osceola, Scar Ridge, and the Sandwich Range. Hay-scented fern, a large, lacy fern that smells like fresh-cut grass when it dries out in fall, often colonizes forest gaps. Hay-scented fern grows as a dense colony because new individuals are produced from old ones by underground runners. So the patch you see is really a clone, technically one individual because the ferns are all connected underneath.

East Pond Loop Trail between the two ponds is a particularly good place for witch's butter. This bright yellow or yellow-orange fungus grows on dead logs. It is also called jelly fungus because it looks like a blob of jelly on a log and is somewhat sticky. Like most fungi, witch's butter gets its nutrition by breaking down dead organic matter, such as the log upon which it rests.

Listen for birds that are characteristic of spruce-fir forest in this stretch of the trail. Arguably the most beautiful is the ascending flutelike song of the Swainson's thrush. You may also here the staccato two-note *che-bunk* of the yellow-bellied flycatcher, or its more musical slurred, whistle-like call. Magnolia warblers are also common here.

About 0.5 mile from East Pond, cross a streambed that is likely to be dry in mid- to late summer. In another 1.0 mile, the trail reaches the junction of Little East Pond Trail. A short spur trail to the right leads you to the south end of Little East Pond.

Little East Pond (3.5 acres) is shallow and dotted with waterlilies and pipeworts. Pipeworts look like hatpins, with small, white, rounded balls on top of thin stalks. The "pinheads" are flower clusters. The shoreline is boggy, with abundant sphagnum, leatherleaf, mountain holly, and marsh Saint-John's-wort. Right by the trail sign, look for a patch of snowberries and bunchberries growing under small balsam fir and red spruce.

From Little East Pond, continue the loop via Little East Pond Trail. The trail descends gradually through spruce and fir for the first 0.7 mile, initially along the outlet to Little East Pond. It then makes a sharp left turn, levels out, and follows the grade of an old logging railroad through a rich northern hardwood forest. Along with the typical hobblebush and striped maples, notice the many young sugar maples coming up. Unlike many species of trees, which will die if they are kept in the shade too long, sugar maple saplings are able to survive under the forest canopy, biding their time and waiting for their moment in the sun when one of the giants around them falls. Then, finally bathed in full sunlight, the little trees grow fast toward the forest canopy.

Striking "fairy rings" of shining club moss are along Little East Pond Trail. These are almost round patches of dark-green, low plants with small, dense, needlelike leaves on upright stems. Like the hay-scented fern described earlier, this growth habit is the result of one individual spore germinating and then sending out runners that create new upright plants.

The trail crosses Clear Brook, East Pond Brook, and other smaller brooks and eventually reaches the trail junction with East Pond Trail (1.7 miles from Little East Pond). Turn right to get back to the parking area (0.4 mile from the junction) on Tripoli Road.

DID YOU KNOW?

Tripoli (or tripolite), the source of the name of the road, is a rock, also called diatomaceous earth, which can be made into a fine powder where it has a variety of uses. These include: a polish in toothpaste, an abrasive in cleaners, in water filters, and in controlling insects and other pests. Tripoli is composed of the silica derived from the skeletons of diatoms, which are microscopic marine algae. The rock was mined from the bottom of East Pond in the early part of the twentieth century and hauled down to the mill for processing.

OTHER ACTIVITIES

You can swim with the newts in East Pond. Bring water shoes because the pond bottom has gravelly and muddy spots (and unfortunately you also need to keep your eye out for broken glass). If you see leeches, keep moving—leeches are reportedly less likely to latch on to a moving target.

MORE INFORMATION

This hike is within the White Mountain National Forest; www.fs.usda.gov/whitemountain; 603-536-6100.

Restaurants and hiking supplies are available in Waterville Valley.

4

STINSON MOUNTAIN TRAIL

Stinson Mountain is a long ridge that dominates the landscape just north of Plymouth, NH, and west of I-93. There is a sweeping view from the summit south over the Lakes Region and toward Mount Cardigan.

DIRECTIONS

Stinson Mountain is in the extreme southwestern part of the White Mountain National Forest, not far from Plymouth, NH. From Exit 26 (milepost 82) off I-93, follow NH 25 west. In 4.0 miles you will go around a traffic circle, and in another 1.0 mile pass Polar Caves. At 8.5 miles from I-93, turn right onto Main Street toward Rumney Center, which you reach in 0.7 mile. Continue straight through the main intersection onto Stinson Lake Road and go 4.5 miles. Just before you reach Stinson Lake itself, make a right onto Cross Street and take it for 0.8 mile (it becomes a dirt road) until it reaches a T junction with Doetown Road. Turn right toward the parking area, 0.3 mile down the road. Space is available for about four vehicles and there is some room farther down along the side of the road for more cars to pull off. *GPS coordinates:* 43° 50.94′ N, 71° 48.10′ W.

TRAIL DESCRIPTION

The Stinson Mountain Trail is a great half-day hike, suitable for younger children but still enough of a climb to engage adults. The ascent is pleasant and relatively easy, nowhere particularly steep.

From the parking area, the trail enters the woods and climbs gradually uphill through northern hardwoods. Many large sugar maples are along this part of the trail, but also look for white ash, a tree whose bark has an attractive lattice pattern. Another distinctive feature of white ash is its compound leaves (consisting of multiple leaflets all originating from one bud) that are attached to the branches in

LOCATION
Rumney, NH

RATING
Moderate

DISTANCE
3.6 miles round-trip

ELEVATION GAIN
1,400 feet

ESTIMATED TIME
3.0 hours

MAPS
AMC White Mountain National Forest Map & Guide, K3

AMC *White Mountain Guide*, 29th ed. Map 4 Moosilauke-Kinsman, K3

USGS Topo: Rumney, NH

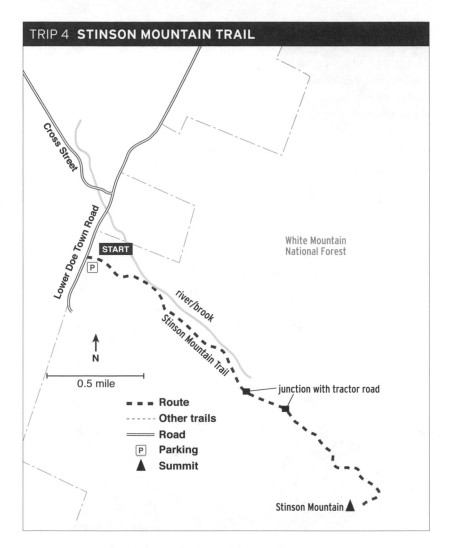

pairs (opposite each other on the branches). Birds singing in spring and summer include hermit thrushes, red-eyed vireos, black-throated blue warblers, and black-throated green warblers. Look for American toads and garter snakes scooting across the trail as you ascend. There are only occasional yellow blazes, but the trail is easy to follow as long as you don't get sidetracked on one of the logging roads that it intersects.

After about 25 minutes (0.9 mile), turn left onto an old tractor road (now used by snowmobiles) and follow the road for 0.2 mile. In late summer and early fall, the white flowers of whorled wood-aster put on a nice display along this section of the trail.

At 1.1 miles at a trail sign, Stinson Mountain Trail branches off to the right from the snowmobile road just before a wooden bridge and climbs more steeply. Hobblebush will be evident along this section of the trail. Note the gradual change from northern hardwoods to a spruce-fir forest. You'll find colonies of hay-scented fern in every small clearing where sunlight reaches the forest floor. Birds on this higher section of the trail could be Swainson's thrushes, magnolia and yellow-rumped warblers, white-throated sparrows, and dark-eyed juncos. A short distance from the summit, the trail intersects the upper part of the same snowmobile road. Continue straight to the open summit. A right turn will also get you there via a short loop.

At the open summit, the old concrete footings from the fire tower are a nice perch from which to enjoy the view to the south and east. Squam Lake to the southeast is the largest body of water visible. To the southwest, the summit of Mount Cardigan (3,150 feet) is prominent. New wind turbines on Tenny and Fletcher mountains are to the west. A view of Stinson Lake and Mount Moosilauke can be obtained by a short spur trail to the north. This spur can be a little difficult to distinguish from some dead-end trails in the northwest direction, but keep trying. Restricted views of Franconia Ridge and the 4,000-footers along the Kancamagus Highway are to the east and northeast.

Aside from the view, the layering and folds in the rocks at the summit are bound to catch your eye. The bedrocks of Stinson Mountain are metamorphic

The view north from Stinson Mountain includes Stinson Lake and Mounts Kineo and Moosilauke.

rocks that were deposited as layers of sand and mud under a prehistoric ocean about 400 million years ago. These sediments first became layers of sandstone and shale. They were later folded and re-formed as metamorphic schists and gneisses when these rocks were under intense heat and pressure and actually became flexible as they were compressed between two moving continents.

The short trees at the summit include balsam fir, red spruce, and heart-leaved birch. Lowbush blueberry and raspberries are there but neither is common enough to satisfy more than the first few hikers who get there. Wildflowers and grasses include rough-stemmed goldenrod and poverty grass, fescues, and sedges in a damp area.

On your descent, the sign indicating "Turn Right" when you reach this upper junction is intended for snowmobiles that use the tractor road. For a different perspective, you can descend via the snowmobile road to its lower junction with the hiking trail (a few damp spots). Just be careful not to miss the right turn from the road back onto the hiking trail.

OTHER ACTIVITIES

Quincy Bog, an interesting wetland with a nature center, is nearby. Follow Quincy Road from Rumney Center for 2.1 miles east and turn left onto Quincy Bog Road. There is no admission fee. The easy 1.0-mile loop trail is partly on a boardwalk.

Rumney Rocks is a popular rock-climbing area about 1.0 mile west of Rumney Village off Buffalo Road (WMNF parking fee of $3). Another 1.5 miles farther down Buffalo Road, Rattlesnake Mountain Trail provides a short, steep ascent to a loop trail on a ridge. The ridge provides an extensive view south over the Baker River Valley and east to Stinson Mountain and other nearby peaks. There is no fee for parking.

MORE INFORMATION

This trail is within the White Mountain National Forest; www.fs.usda.gov/whitemountain; 603-536-6100. There is no parking fee.

If you are hiking with your dog in summer, you should bring extra water because the streams along the trail are likely to be dry.

You will find an assortment of restaurants and other amenities along Route 25 in West Plymouth and Rumney, NH.

5

MOUNT ISRAEL

Mount Israel commands great views of the Sandwich Range, other peaks south of the Kancamangus Highway, and the Lakes Region. The ascent via the Wentworth Trail is a moderate but steady climb.

LOCATION
Sandwich, NH

RATING
Moderate

DISTANCE
4.2 miles round-trip

DIRECTIONS

From Exit 24 on I-93, follow US 3/NH 25 for 4.0 miles through Ashland to Holderness. Make a left onto NH 113 and follow it for 11.6 miles to Center Sandwich. Along the way you will pass the Squam Lake Natural Science Center and the trailheads for Mounts Morgan and Percival (Trip 6). Make a sharp left onto Grove Street and take it for 0.4 mile, then continue onto Diamond Ledge Road for 1.9 miles. Turn left onto Sandwich Notch Road for 0.2 mile and take a side road to the right (Diamond Ledge Road again) for 0.4 mile to Mead Conservation Center (formerly known as Mead Base). This is a camp that houses trail crews and is run by the Friends of Mead Base. Park in the field below the building. *GPS coordinates: 43° 49.71′ N, 71° 29.06′ W.*

ELEVATION GAIN
1,700 feet

ESTIMATED TIME
3.5 hours

MAPS
AMC *White Mountain National Forest Map & Guide*, L7

AMC *White Mountain Guide*, 29th ed. Map 3 Crawford Notch–Sandwich Range, L7

USGS Topo: Center Sandwich, NH

TRAIL DESCRIPTION

Wentworth Trail is a well-graded path marked with yellow blazes. It starts to the left of the building and enters a deciduous woodland that has the feel of a southern New Hampshire forest due to the omnipresent oak trees. Look for hop hornbeam, a tree with shaggy, vertically peeling strands of bark. This tree is noted for its very hard wood, hence its alternative name—ironwood. As a tree more common south of the White Mountains, the presence of hop hornbeam reflects the more southern exposure of this trail. Ferns are abundant along the trail, including long beech, Christmas, New York, and bracken ferns. Understory herbs include wild sarsaparilla and asters.

Wintry scene on the summit of Mount Israel. Photo by Jerry Monkman.

After about 0.3 mile (10 minutes), the trail passes through a stone wall on an old cart path, climbs up some steps above the wall, and crosses a stream on a bridge at 0.8 mile. The trail then turns right to follow the stream for about 15 minutes, making for a very pleasant walk. Note the presence of some large red pines (their long needles in bunches of two) in this area. After leaving the stream, the trail starts to climb at a slightly steeper grade. As you ascend, you will notice balsam fir trees starting to make their appearance, eventually becoming dominant.

The trail ascends on switchbacks and at 1.5 miles (about 1.5 hour) reaches a vista over Squam Lake and a partial view of Lake Winnipesaukee. An attractive grass that grows in clumps in this ledgy area is crinkled hairgrass. It has dark-maroon flowers and seed heads in summer.

Shortly after the vista, the trail levels off at the top of the ridge and is a pleasant boreal forest walk. You cross more ledges that provide a preview of the final view, go back into the forest, and then reach the true summit at 2.1 miles (2.0 hours). Here Wentworth Trail intersects Mead Trail.

Sandwich Mountain, also called Sandwich Dome, is the closest large mountain to the north. Looking farther to the northeast, you can see the slides and three summits of Mount Tripyramid. The vegetation is a mix of red spruce and balsam fir, with a few paper birches mixed in. The pale green of reindeer lichen underlain by rocks may remind you of a rock garden. Snowberry, black huckleberry, lowbush blueberries, and sheep laurel make up the understory.

Head northeast from the summit cairn to find a slightly beaten trail that leads in about 100 yards to another great vista with views to the northeast (Mounts Tripyramid and Chocorua) and south (Squam Lake). Look for a wet area containing a lush growth of haircap moss (illustrated here). The brown capsules of this species contain a mechanism for shooting its spores some distance from the parent plant, thus ensuring some measure of dispersal.

After enjoying the views and the moss, retrace your steps to the trailhead at Mead Base. A popular short extension from Mead Base is to walk north on Bearcamp River Trail to Beede Falls in Sandwich Town Park. This trail follows the river through a dark, hemlock forest and passes Cow Cave, where legend has it that a cow survived the winter. It reaches the falls 0.4 mile (10 minutes) from Mead Base. The pool created by the falls is a popular swimming/wading area (water is thigh deep), so an ideal place to end your hike. A short distance beyond the falls, Bearcamp River Trail comes out on Sandwich Notch Road.

OTHER ACTIVITIES

A fine loop can be made by using Wentworth, Mead, and Guinea Pond trails. This requires either spotting a second car at the Guinea Pond trailhead or being willing to hike 2.2 miles along Sandwich Notch Road to Sandwich Town Park, then 0.6 miles along Bearcamp River Trail to get back to the Mead Conservation Center. If you opt to spot a second car at the Guinea Pond trailhead, be aware that Sandwich Notch Road can be heavily rutted in sections, so is best traveled by a vehicle with a high clearance (our subcompact scraped bottom numerous times).

After climbing Mount Israel on Wentworth Trail, descend via Mead Trail, a gradual descent of 1.7 miles that ends in Guinea Pond Trail. A notable feature of this trail is a small ravine and stream crossing at 0.8 mile from the summit. Turn left onto Guinea Pond Trail, which is a level walk along an old forest road that leads to Sandwich Notch Road in 1.6 miles. Guinea Pond Trail passes through numerous beaver-created wetlands that are framed by nearby mountains, so the scenery is interesting and the bird life more abundant than in other parts of the loop trail. Flooding by beavers may require some sections of the trail to be relocated through an adjacent power-line right of way. Look for abundant wildflowers, such as fireweed and meadowsweet, in the right of way because it gets much more sun than the forest floor. When you reach Sandwich Notch Road, turn left for the hike back to the Mead Conservation Center (assuming you did not spot a car at the Guinea Pond trailhead). After 2.5 miles along this road, turn left at Sandwich Town Park and follow Bearcamp River Trail for 0.6 mile past Beede Falls and back to the Mead Conservation Center.

MORE INFORMATION

This trail is within the White Mountain National Forest; www.fs.usda.gov/whitemountain; 603-536-6100. There is no fee for parking at the Mead Conservation Center, although donations are accepted.

Three campsites are available to the public at the Mead Conservation Center. One is a group camping site that can accommodate up to 30 people. See https://sites.google.com/site/friendsofmead/home for information on reserving a campsite. A picnic area and bathrooms are located there as well. The main building and a number of the outbuildings are reserved for the use of the trail crew, interns, and an artist in residence.

Holderness and Ashland have restaurants, gas stations, and motels. Sandwich, a classic, small New England village, has a number of restaurants, inns, and bed-and-breakfasts.

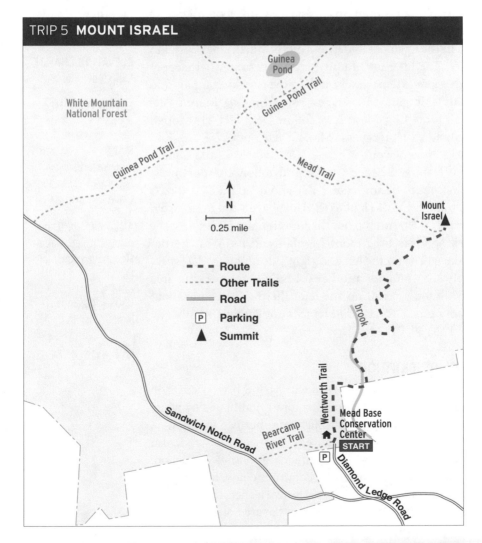

TRIP 5 **MOUNT ISRAEL**

Guinea Pond

White Mountain National Forest

Guinea Pond Trail

Guinea Pond Trail

Mead Trail

Mount Israel ▲

N

0.25 mile

- - - Route
..... Other Trails
=== Road
P Parking
▲ Summit

brook

Wentworth Trail

Sandwich Notch Road

Bearcamp River Trail

Mead Base Conservation Center

START

P

Diamond Ledge Road

6
PERCIVAL-MORGAN LOOP

This fine loop hike takes you over two summits with extensive views over Squam Lake. Some scrambling on rocks and by caves near the summits adds to the climbing experience.

DIRECTIONS

The two small mountains reached by this loop hike have their own trailheads, separated by about 0.4 mile on NH 113 in the town of Holderness on the north side of Squam Lake. The hike up Mount Percival is somewhat steeper with more extensive scrambling over rocks compared to Mount Morgan, so I suggest ascending via Mount Percival. From Exit 24 on I-93, follow US 3/NH 25 through Ashland to Holderness. Make a left onto NH 113, and take a note of your mileage. You soon pass the Squam Lake Natural Science Center and follow the northwest shoreline of Squam Lake. After about 5.0 miles you pass the road that goes right to the Deephaven and Rockywold camps. At 5.6 miles from the junction in Holderness, the parking areas for Mount Morgan and for West Rattlesnake will be on the left and right side of the road, respectively. Continue for another 0.4 mile to the parking area for Mount Percival on the left. There is space for about twenty cars. *GPS coordinates* (Mount Percival Trailhead): 43° 47.53′ N, 71° 32.68′ W.

TRAIL DESCRIPTION

Mount Percival Trail, marked with yellow blazes, starts on a wide carriage road through a forest dominated by white pines. From late spring through summer two wildflowers may immediately catch your eye. Orange hawkweed, also called devil's paintbrush, resembles an orange dandelion. The bright-yellow flowers of common cinquefoil may remind you of a buttercup. Note the five leaflets that give this plant its name. Other wildflowers that are notable for their

LOCATION
Holderness, NH, at trailhead; Campton, NH, at summits

RATING
Moderate

DISTANCE
5.2 miles round-trip

ELEVATION CHANGE
1,550 feet

ESTIMATED TIME:
4.5 hours

MAPS
AMC *White Mountain National Forest Map & Guide*, L6

AMC *White Mountain Guide*, 29th ed. Map 4 Moosilauke-Kinsman, L6

USGS Topo: Squam Mountains, NH

leaf patterns are Solomon's plume (false Solomon's seal) and Indian cucumber root. The former has a single arching stem from which broad, lily-like leaves attach. The latter has a double whorl of leaflets.

There is a small patch of poison ivy along the side of the trail just in from the trailhead, so keep to the middle of the trail here. Poison ivy's three glossy leaflets with wavy edges are the key to its identification. Another plant here that also has three leaflets is hog peanut, so this is a good spot to test your ability to discern poison ivy from similar looking plants. Of course, it is best not to touch.

This lower-elevation forest is host to a symphony of bird songs in late spring through early summer. Species that are likely to serenade you as you begin your ascent include red-eyed vireo, veery, hermit thrush, black-throated green warbler, black-throated blue warbler, and American redstart. Listen for the dry, two-syllable *che-beck* of the least flycatcher, sounding more like an insect than a bird.

At 0.2 mile, Morse Trail comes in from the left. You will use that later to complete the loop but for now continue straight. As you ascend, note some very large white pines. After about 20 minutes (0.9 mile), the trail crosses a small brook called Smith Brook. On a hot day it is a pleasure to douse your face, neck, and

Squam Lake from Mount Percival. The Abenaki called the lake "Keeseenunknipee," which means "goose lake in the highlands."

arms with its cooling water. If you are hiking with your dog, it will appreciate the chance to drink. Soon after, you pass through an old stone wall. The pines, white birch, and stone wall suggest that this area was cleared at some point in the past 100 years.

The white pines slowly drop out and you enter a northern hardwood forest (sugar maple, American beech, yellow birch). At about 1.5 miles, the trail turns sharply to the right and you traverse a boulder field. After the boulder field, the trail turns left and heads steeply uphill. You'll reach a fork after about 1 hour, 20 minutes (1.9 miles). The main trail (marked "Cliff") goes right, scrambling up a steep pitch over ledges. The left fork (marked "Cave") is more strenuous, going through a boulder cave. It would be the more hazardous choice in wet weather and definitely a bad choice if you are hiking with a dog. Both lead in about 0.1 mile to the overlook, with an amazing view of Squam Lake framed by red spruces. To the west is Mount Morgan, your next destination, and Mounts Whiteface and Passaconaway are to the northeast. There are some lowbush blueberries and mountain holly on this ledge.

After enjoying the vista, follow the yellow blazes to the open summit of Mount Percival just beyond. Mount Percival Trail ends in Crawford-Ridgepole Trail (2.0 miles). The view is similar to that from the previous ledge.

Continue on Crawford-Ridgepole Trail west (left) toward Mount Morgan. This section of the loop is a lovely boreal forest walk on the fairly level ridge between the two summits. Red spruce and balsam fir are the dominant trees. On the forest floor, look for the broad leaves of bluebead lily (clintonia) and the four or six whorls of leaflets and red berries of bunchberry dogwood. Wet swales are covered with a lush, green growth of fringed sedge. The birds serenading you are likely to be dark-eyed juncos, several species of warbler, and golden-crowned kinglets.

At 2.8 miles (0.8 mile from Mount Percival), the trail reaches a junction with Mount Morgan Trail. Follow Mount Morgan Trail to the right to reach another great vista of Squam Lake about 0.1 mile ahead. Before reaching the cliff, a spur trail leads to the right to the actual summit of Mount Morgan and a view north to the Sandwich Range. A geographic marker from Boston's Museum of Science marks the actual summit. Note the quartz and feldspar dikes embedded within the metamorphic rocks of the ledge.

If you are on these summits on a warm, sunny day without too much wind,

 you will likely be accompanied by butterflies and dragonflies, which seek out the warmth of sunny openings in a forest. Three large, common butterflies to look for are white admiral, mourning cloak, and eastern tiger swallowtail (illustrated here). Dragonflies include common baskettails early in summer and green and variable darners later on.

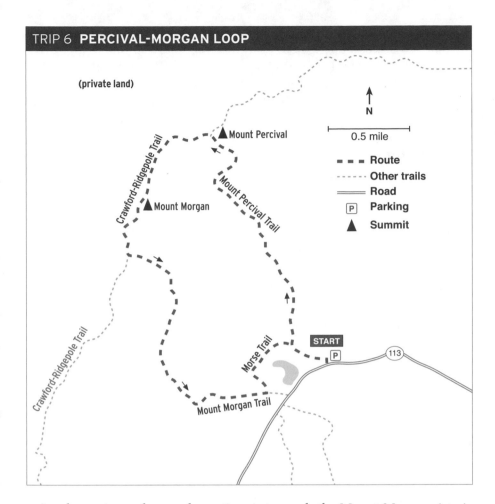

(private land)

N

0.5 mile

Mount Percival

Crawford-Ridgepole Trail

Mount Percival Trail

Mount Morgan

- - - Route
- - - - Other trails
= Road
P Parking
▲ Summit

Crawford-Ridgepole Trail

Crawford-Ridgepole Trail

Morse Trail

START

P

113

Mount Morgan Trail

An alternative and more dramatic way to reach the Mount Morgan vista is to continue on Crawford-Ridgepole Trail, which at this point coincides with Mount Morgan Trail, at the trail junction. The trail descends some steps and shortly reaches a junction with a spur trail that ascends to the right, marked with a sign as a ladder trail. This spur trail is not for anyone uncomfortable with heights. It climbs three ladders, the third of which is offset to the right, so you have to be very careful where you place your feet. The trail then squeezes through a narrow cave where you may need to remove your pack to fit before coming out at the vista. Descending this way is even more challenging.

For the descent, return to the junction with Crawford-Ridgepole Trail and turn right. Mount Morgan Trail runs together with Crawford-Ridgepole Trail for about 0.2 mile. Where they split, turn left for the 1.6-mile, 1.0-hour descent down Mount Morgan Trail. This is a steady downhill through northern hardwoods, becoming gradually less steep as you descend. The trail crosses a few stone walls, once again indicating the human history of the region.

Morse Trail (formerly Morgan-Percival Connector) comes in from the left near the bottom of Mount Morgan Trail. This will connect to your original trailhead at Mount Percival Trail. Turn left on Morse Trail for a pleasant 15-minute walk through northern hardwoods. You cross two streams, one on a wooden bridge. When you reach the junction with the Mount Percival Trail, turn right and walk 0.1 mile to your car.

DID YOU KNOW?

On Golden Pond, the popular 1981 film starring Katharine Hepburn, Henry Fonda, and the local loons, was filmed on Squam Lake.

OTHER ACTIVITIES

The hike up West Rattlesnake Mountain on the south side of NH 113 opposite the Mount Morgan trailhead is one of the most popular family hikes in the Squam Lake region. It is a great first mountain hike for young children.

Five-Finger Point Trail is a wonderful loop hike on a promontory on the northern shore of Squam Lake. It is reached via Pinehurst Road off NH 113 about 0.75 mile west of the Mount Percival trailhead. The trail provides changing vistas of the lake and several opportunities for swimming from small beaches and from one dramatic shoreline rock.

The Squam Lake Natural Science Center in Holderness has interpretive nature trails, a garden, and excellent displays on local ecology and wildlife.

MORE INFORMATION

Much of the land in this loop trail is owned by the Burleigh Land Limited Partnership. Public access comes from a conservation easement held by the Lakes Region Conservation Trust. The Squam Lakes Association provides trail maintenance. There is no fee for parking.

Holderness and Ashland, the nearest towns, have restaurants, gas stations, and motels.

7

WELCH-DICKEY LOOP

This was the most suggested family hike in the White Mountains by all the people I talked to. The summits of Welch and Dickey command excellent views for relatively modest effort. The hike is substantial enough to give you a feeling of accomplishment, yet is manageable for most everyone above age 6 or so.

DIRECTIONS

Welch and Dickey Loop Trail is located off NH 49 at the entrance to Waterville Valley. Take I-93 to the Campton/Waterville Valley exit (Exit 28) and follow NH 49 through Campton toward Waterville Valley. Four and a half miles beyond NH 175 in Campton, turn left (northwest) on Upper Mad River Road (second intersection with this loop road) and cross the river. Follow this road for 0.7 mile, then turn right onto Orris Road. A large parking area with space for about 100 vehicles (in response to the popularity of this trail) is 0.6 mile up this road. Restrooms are at the parking area. *GPS coordinates: 43° 54.24′ N, 71° 35.31′ W.*

TRAIL DESCRIPTION

Welch and Dickey Loop Trail is a good trail choice early in the season, as its lower elevation and relatively southern location ensure that snow disappears earlier here than farther north. For those with less time or energy, a hike up to the first great viewpoint on Welch Mountain requires only about an hour one-way. The large areas of rocky ledges near the summits should present no problems for hikers who are comfortable with scrambling on rocks; however, they could be hazardous if the weather is wet or icy. And remember, these summits, despite their low elevations, are still quite exposed, so do not forget windbreakers and raingear and stay off the open summits if a thunderstorm threatens.

LOCATION
Thornton, NH

RATING
Moderate to strenuous

DISTANCE
4.4-mile loop

ELEVATION CHANGE
1,800 feet

ESTIMATED TIME
3.5-5.0 hours

MAPS
AMC White Mountain National Forest Map & Guide, J5

AMC *White Mountain Guide*, 29th ed. Map 4 Moosilauke–Kinsman, J/K 5, 6

USGS Topo: Waterville Valley

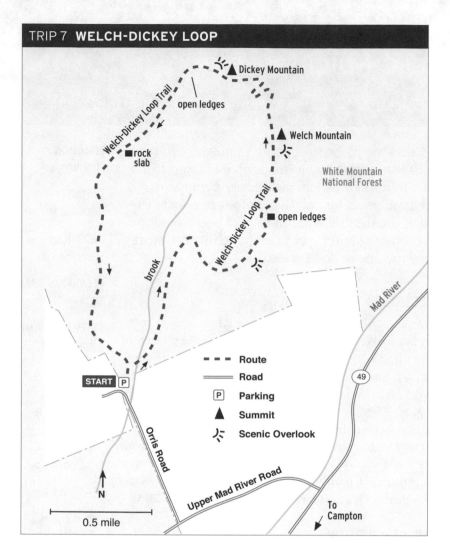

Dickey Mountain

Welch-Dickey Loop Trail

open ledges

■ rock
   slab

■ Welch Mountain

White Mountain
National Forest

Welch-Dickey Loop Trail

■ open ledges

brook

START P

49

Mad River

- - - **Route**
——— **Road**
P **Parking**
▲ **Summit**
)ᵌ **Scenic Overlook**

Orris Road

N

0.5 mile

Upper Mad River Road

To
Campton

I describe going up Welch first because you'll reach a viewpoint sooner. You can turn around there if you want a shorter walk. To begin, take the right fork just beyond the display board and lost-and-found box at the trailhead. The trail is marked with yellow blazes. Although its popularity has led to erosion in some places, the walking is smooth for much of its length.

The trail soon crosses a stream and then follows it through a northern hardwood forest for the first 0.5 mile. There are a number of stream crossings on wooden boards. Notice the glacial erratics scattered throughout the woods. These are often covered with mosses and rock tripe, the latter a type of lichen that, although edible, looks and tastes like a piece of shoe leather.

After about 45 minutes, there is a switchback with steps, the forest changes to red spruce and balsam fir, and the trail then ascends more steeply to the south ledges, the first vista (0.9 mile). Proceed upward, past other ledges, some of which are steep, and through low forests of red spruce, balsam fir, white pine, and oaks. Dogs may need help on these ledges. You'll then reach the summit of Welch (1.5 to 2.0 hours).

From the ledges and summit of Welch, the prominent peaks are Dickey Mountain, the Sandwich Range (southeast), Mount Tecumseh (north—the major ski area for Waterville Valley), and Mount Tripyramid (northeast). You also have an excellent view of the Mad River Valley and a breathtaking view down into the saddle between Welch and Dickey.

Jack pine is abundant on the ledges near the summit of Welch Mountain. This small tree grows in a handful of other locations in the White Mountains, including Carter Ledge and Webster Cliff. You can identify jack pine by its short, stiff needles occurring in bunches of two. It depends upon fires for regeneration because fires open up its cones for seed dispersal and perhaps inhibit other competing vegetation. Why it occurs on Welch but not in similar habitats on Dickey is a mystery.

Recovery areas for small plants on the ledges are delineated by neat lines of small stones. Signs urge hikers to protect the plants from trampling by remaining on the trail or on exposed rocks. Two tiny alpine species protected by this effort are mountain cranberry and mountain sandwort. The thin soil, exposure to the winds, and absence of trees mimic the alpine conditions normally found above about 4,500 feet in the White Mountains, allowing these plants to thrive on Welch and Dickey. You can see them at this lower elevation, where the weather conditions are not as extreme, as the true alpine habitat. Three-toothed cinquefoil, whose small, white flowers bloom in June, is probably the

Hikers arriving at the summit of Mount Dickey. Photo by Ryan Smith.

most abundant plant in the recovery areas. Each of the three leaflets of this low plant has three teeth on its outer edge.

Shrubs are a major component of the vegetation on the open ledges. Blueberries are a popular midsummer attraction, but please make sure your picking does not destroy them or any other vegetation in this fragile habitat. Rhodora, a type of rhododendron, will be in glorious bloom around Memorial Day. It has large, pinkish-purple flowers and bluish-green leaves. Labrador tea, chokeberries, shadbush, and bush honeysuckle are other shrubs on the ledges.

The trail then descends steeply to a saddle before ascending to the Dickey summit. The saddle contains a particularly attractive display of boreal forest plants. Where the shading from the red spruce is not dense, bunchberries and reindeer lichen grow in patterns that look like they were designed by a rock gardener. Mountain holly, wild raisin, the white form of pink lady's slipper, clintonia, and haircap moss grow under the spruce canopy as well.

It takes 20 to 30 minutes (0.5 mile) to hike from Welch to Dickey. The view from Dickey includes much of what you see from Welch and also the Franconia Ridge. You may wonder what has caused rectangular open areas visible in the forest below. These are places where loggers have clear-cut the forest. They are in various states of revegetation, depending on how long it has been since the area was logged. A dense tangle of shrubs, such as raspberries, blueberries, and huckleberries, will grow up within a few years, followed by early successional trees, including paper birch, aspen, and pin cherry.

The open ledges are also excellent places to look for ravens. These large, completely black members of the crow family are considered among the most intelligent of birds. They are frequently observed soaring around ledges in the mountains and sometimes cavort with one another and even fly upside down. Their voice is a hoarse call that sounds like a cross between a crow and a hog. A much smaller bird you are likely to see at higher elevations is the dark-eyed junco, a slate-gray, sparrow-sized bird with a white belly and white outer-tail feathers.

From Dickey, the trail, marked with cairns (piles of stones) in a number of places, descends through more ledges with great views, particularly of Cone Mountain. Here you can find pink corydalis, a wildflower with ferny leaves and small, pink flowers that resemble the heads of birds.

A half hour or so below the Dickey summit, the trail crosses a particularly impressive granite slab. This is laced with stripes that are sills of dark-gray basalt formed from molten lava that penetrated cracks within the granite.

Shortly thereafter, you'll enter a forest of beech, maple, and red oak. This is a rich area for spring wildflowers and ferns. Look for Canada mayflower, wild oats, clintonia, Indian cucumber root, false Solomon's seal, true Solomon's seal, painted trillium, starflower, and goldthread. Around Memorial Day, when the leaves are just emerging, wild sarsaparilla appears, a plant with glossy reddish leaves in groups of three or five. You might think that you have come into contact with poison ivy. Rest assured. Poison ivy does not occur at these elevations.

Partridgeberry is a small, low plant with paired, dark-green leaves that hug the ground and are occasionally punctuated with bright-red berries. The distinctive, arrowhead-shaped leaves of the rattlesnake root are present throughout the year, but its flowers do not appear until late summer.

It's about another mile to the parking lot. Near the end, make sure to stay on the trail as it passes an abandoned road and turns right onto a logging road (to the left is a mountain-bike trail).

DID YOU KNOW?

The town of Thornton, NH, where Welch and Dickey mountains are located, is named for Matthew Thornton, one of the original settlers of the area and a signer of the Declaration of Independence.

OTHER ACTIVITIES

The resort community of Waterville Valley has restaurants, a grocery store, golf, and fishing, among other amenities. Skiing is, of course, a major activity in winter. The village of Campton has a few restaurants and a store where you can pick up groceries, all near the intersection of NH 149 and NH 175.

MORE INFORMATION

Welch and Dickey Loop Trail is within the White Mountain National Forest. A user fee ($3) is required; www.fs.usda.gov/whitemountain; 603-536-6100.

8

MOUNT OSCEOLA

The hike up Mount Osceola from Tripoli Road may be the mellowest route up a 4,000-footer in the White Mountains. A spectacular mountain vista greets you at its summit.

DIRECTIONS

The trailhead for Mount Osceola Trail is off Tripoli Road, 7.0 miles from its junction with I-93 and 4.8 miles beyond the turnoff to Russell Pond Campground. This is close to the highest point reached by Tripoli Road in its passage through Thornton Gap. If you are coming from Waterville Valley, the trailhead is about 4.5 miles west of the junction of Tripoli Road and NH 49. Stay to the right when the road to the ski area splits off to the left.

The trailhead is on the north side of the road. Space is available for about ten vehicles in the parking area. You can also park along the side of Tripoli Road. *GPS coordinates:* 43° 59.01′ N, 71° 33.52′ W.

Tripoli Road is not plowed in winter, and the gates at its I-93 and Waterville Valley ends are closed in snow and mud season. Thus, a winter ascent requires a much longer walk.

TRAIL DESCRIPTION

Mount Osceola Trail is a well-graded path for its entire length, nowhere particularly steep because of well-placed switchbacks. The first section is a bit rocky, passing through a number of boulder fields caused by landslides. There are some broad, flat, slanted ledges at several places that are no problem when dry but could be slippery when wet. Once you reach the ridge, the trail becomes a pleasant, gentle ascent through the boreal forest until you reach the summit ledges.

Leaving the parking area, the trail starts through a mixture of northern hardwoods and boreal forest. It quickly turns to almost complete boreal forest dominated by red

LOCATION
Livermore, NH

RATING
Strenuous

DISTANCE
6.4 miles round-trip

ELEVATION GAIN
2,050 feet

ESTIMATED TIME
5.0–6.0 hours

MAPS
AMC White Mountain National Forest Map & Guide, J6

AMC *White Mountain Guide,* 29th ed. Map 4 Moosilauke-Kinsman, J6

USGS Topo: Waterville Valley at trailhead, then Mount Osceola

spruce, balsam fir, and paper birch. Birds you are likely to hear include red-eyed vireos, hermit thrushes, and black-throated green and black-throated blue warblers. In about 15 minutes, you cross the first of several streams that tumble down the mountain over and around boulders. On a hot day, you will find it refreshing to splash cool water on your brow, and if you have a canine companion, it will appreciate a drink.

At 1.3 miles (about 45 minutes), the trail starts a series of switchbacks and becomes less rocky. At about 2.5 miles, you attain Breadtray Ridge and the grade lessens. You can see the summit of Osceola ahead of you.

After passing another stream, an open area on the right affords a partial view across Waterville Valley to Mount Tecumseh and to the broad ridge of Sandwich Dome. This opening is created by a fir wave, a fascinating phenomenon characteristic of these high-elevation forests. For many years, fir waves were a puzzle to both forest ecologists and hikers. Scientists now have concluded that fir waves represent a common pattern of regeneration in these high-elevation forests (roughly 3,000 to 4,500 feet). All the older balsam fir trees at a certain elevation die in a band parallel to the contour of the mountain. The older trees reach the end of their lifespan (about 80 years), die, get knocked down by winds (often bringing down their neighbors too), and are replaced by regenerating saplings. Look for the many young firs growing up in the midst of the dead and dying older trees. This band of dying older trees and regenerating seedlings gradually moves up the side of the mountain, thus the name "fir wave."

The view northeast from Mount Osceola includes East Osceola and Mount Carrigain.

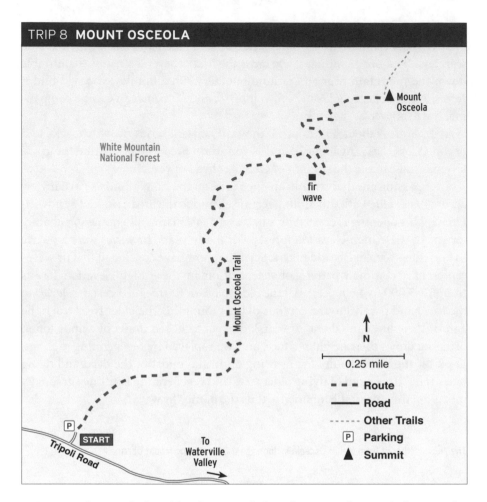

At 3.2 miles, reach the older fire tower's foundation, with open ledges nearby and the foundation of a more modern tower a few yards beyond. Mount Osceola is the tallest mountain south of the Kancamagus Highway, so the view from these ledges is extensive. The village of Waterville Valley, the ski slopes on Mount Tecumseh, and Sandwich Dome are to the south. Moving east, you see the three summits of Mount Tripyramid, with the slide on North Tripyramid particularly prominent. Farther in the distance to the east and northeast are Mounts Passaconaway, Chocorua, and Carrigain; the Moats; and the Presidential Range.

For the best view north, return to the old fire tower foundation and take a spur trail to the north. A large rock enables you to get above the balsam fir for superb views of the Franconia Range, Mount Moosilauke, South Twin, and Mount Bond.

In addition to the balsam fir, the vegetation at the summit ledges includes mountain cranberry, purple crowberry, and poverty grass. Birds you might encounter around the summit include white-throated sparrows, dark-eyed juncos, and yellow-rumped warblers. On a sunny day, large dragonflies (darners) are likely to be patrolling the summit for their insect prey.

Retrace your steps to return to the parking area. Plan for about the same amount of time for the descent, due to the rockiness of the trail in its lower section.

DID YOU KNOW?

Osceola was a Seminole chief who never got within 1,000 miles of the White Mountains. The name may have been applied by a Waterville Valley summer resident in the late 1800s, but there was no obvious reason why this mountain was named for him.

OTHER ACTIVITIES

Mount Osceola Trail continues beyond the summit ledges to East Osceola and eventually descends to a terminus at Greely Ponds Trail (Trip 22). This part of the trail is rougher than the trip we describe here. In particular, the section from East Osceola to Greely Ponds is considered one of the most difficult trails in the White Mountains.

The Waterville Valley Athletic and Improvement Association (WVAIA) maintains a variety of pleasant trails to waterfalls and other destinations in the valley (such as Trip 1).

MORE INFORMATION

There is a $3 daily user fee for parking at the Mount Osceola trailhead.

The village of Waterville Valley has a grocery store, an ice cream shop, restaurants, other shops, public restrooms, and two campgrounds.

9

MOUNT MOOSILAUKE

Mount Moosilauke is a broad, 4,802-foot summit that reaches up into the alpine zone on the western edge of the White Mountains and has wonderful views in all directions. This attractive loop hike follows rushing mountain streams for much of its length.

CAUTION This outing takes you above treeline where the weather can be quite harsh. It will almost always be colder and windier than at lower elevations, and the open area of the alpine tundra leaves you exposed to snow (possible even in summer), rain, harsh winds, and lightning. Be prepared with extra warm clothes and rain gear, and be ready to turn back if the weather changes.

DIRECTIONS

The trailhead is at the Dartmouth Outing Club's Moosilauke Ravine Lodge. From Exit 32 off I-93 (Lincoln/North Woodstock), take NH 112 west for about 3.0 miles. Make a left onto NH 118 and follow that for 7.2 miles. Make a right onto Ravine Lodge Road, an unpaved road, and follow that to its end (1.6 miles). Use the turnaround, and then find parking along the side of the road. Signs make it very clear that you should not park in the turnaround itself. Parking is shared with guests of the Ravine Lodge, so you may need to park a short distance from the actual trailhead and walk back along the road. The trailhead for Gorge Brook Trail is also the trailhead for Al Merrill Loop.

During winter, the road to Ravine Lodge is not plowed. Cars can be parked at the closed gate, and you must be prepared to hike or snowshoe the extra 1.6 miles. *GPS coordinates:* 43° 59.62' N, 71° 48.90' W.

LOCATION
Woodstock, NH, at the trailhead, then Benton, NH

RATING
Strenuous

DISTANCE
7.9 miles for the loop

ELEVATION GAIN
2,700 feet

ESTIMATED TIME
6.0 hours

MAPS
AMC *White Mountain National Forest Map & Guide,* J/I-3

AMC *White Mountain Guide,* 29th ed. Map 4 Moosilauke-Kinsman, J/I-3

USGS Topo: Mount Moosilauke

TRAIL DESCRIPTION

This loop hike ascends to the summit of Mount Moosilauke on Gorge Brook Trail, and then uses Moosilauke Carriage Road, Snapper, and Gorge Brook trails for the descent. The trails are well maintained and marked by the Dartmouth Outing Club, so you should have no trouble following them. On the ascent, a former section of Gorge Brook Trail was washed out by Hurricane Irene in 2011, requiring the trail to be relocated for about 0.6 mile.

From the turnaround at the terminus of Ravine Lodge Road, follow the trail beyond the barrier and descend left to a bridge across the Baker River. As the big trailhead sign indicates, turn left for Gorge Brook Trail, and walk a short distance across an old logging road. Turn right where Hurricane Trail continues straight ahead. This first part of Gorge Brook Trail is a gradual ascent along Gorge Brook, with many attractive small cascades and moss-covered boulders. Red spruce, balsam fir, and paper birch are the dominant trees and hobblebush is the main understory shrub. After your first crossing of Gorge Brook on a

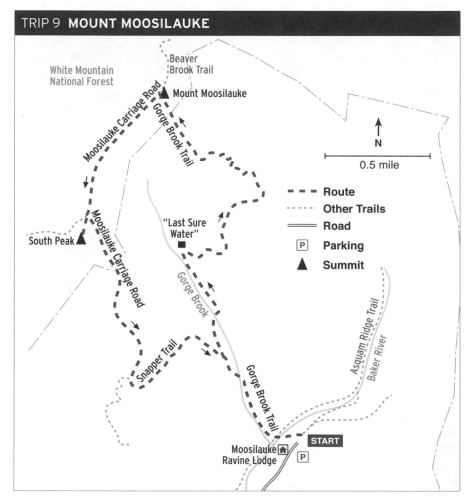

TRIP 9 **MOUNT MOOSILAUKE**

White Mountain
National Forest

Beaver
Brook Trail

Moosilauke Carriage Road

Gorge Brook Trail

▲ Mount Moosilauke

↑
N

0.5 mile

Moosilauke Carriage Road

South Peak ▲

"Last Sure
Water"
■

– – – Route

· · · · · Other Trails

═══ Road

P Parking

▲ Summit

Gorge Brook

Snapper Trail

Gorge Brook Trail

Asquam Ridge Trail

Baker River

Moosilauke
Ravine Lodge 🏠

P

START

bridge (0.6 mile, 25 minutes), the trail continues straight ahead and coincides with Snapper Trail. An old section of Gorge Brook Trail that led to the right at this point has been closed due to hurricane damage. At 0.8 mile, a new section of Gorge Brook Trail diverges right from Snapper Trail and continues uphill high above the brook. It rejoins the original section of Gorge Brook Trail at 1.2 miles and, shortly after, crosses back over the brook on another bridge.

At 1.6 miles (1.0 hour), at 3,300 feet altitude, the trail passes a sign reading "Last Sure Water." You will see a plaque there honoring Ross McKenny, the builder of Ravine Lodge. In winter, only experienced snowshoers should venture beyond this point. The trail turns right, away from the brook, and begins a series of switchbacks that lead you up the east ridge of the mountain.

Bird songs will provide a constant symphony during your ascent through the boreal forest. Two of the most distinctive are those of the winter wren and Swainson's thrush. The winter wren is a tiny, brown bird that you almost never see, but it has a remarkable extended, sweet, twittering song of at least four subsections. You'll wonder how such a small creature does not run out of breath. Swainson's thrushes sing an ethereal, flutelike song of gradually ascending notes, appropriate for a hike to higher altitudes.

At 2.1 miles, you reach a small clearing and continue ascending at a steeper pitch. The spruce and fir trees gradually decline in stature as you ascend, and the paper birches are replaced by heart-leaved birches. If you are hiking in late June through early July, you will be treated to a nice display of bunchberries (a tiny dogwood with four creamy white floral bracts that serve as petals). The berries, produced in mid- to late summer, although not poisonous, are at best emergency food so leave them for the birds. Views to the south gradually open up, Mount Carr being the most prominent peak in that direction.

The next landmark (3.4 miles) is a sign that informs you that you have reached the alpine zone and therefore should stay on the trails to avoid trampling the sensitive tundra vegetation. Between here and the summit at 3.7 miles (2 hours, 45 minutes), you will find plants that thrive in alpine habitats. Two species restricted to alpine and arctic habitats that are common around the Moosilauke summit are Bigelow's sedge and highland rush. These do not have showy flowers so may not attract your attention, except perhaps when the rush turns a rich golden brown in late summer. Some bright flowers include three-toothed cinquefoil (white flowers and three leaflets each tipped with three teeth) and mountain sandwort (small, white flowers and thin, opposite leaves growing in tufts). Mountain cranberry has small, glossy, green leaves and red berries. Alpine (bog) bilberry is a type of blueberry with attractive bluish-green, roundish leaves. (See page 260 for more on alpine habitats.)

Two birds that inhabit this harsh alpine environment are white-throated sparrow (with its sweet-whistled *See old Sam Peabody, Peabody, Peabody* song) and dark-eyed junco (a gray, sparrowlike bird that flashes white outer-tail feathers when it flies).

The grassy alpine summit of Mount Moosilauke. Photo by Jerry Monkman.

On a clear day, Mount Moosilauke's location on the western edge of the White Mountains provides you with fantastic vistas. To the west, you can see the Green Mountains of Vermont and the Adirondacks of New York. The Franconia Range, Twin Range, and Mount Washington are visible to the northeast. If you happen to climb on a cloudy day, enjoy the plants, birds, and isolation of this alpine environment. Students from Dartmouth College serve as alpine stewards, providing trail and other information for hikers who have reached the summit.

For the descent, pick up the signs for Moosilauke Carriage Road, part of the Appalachian Trail. The first 0.5 mile of this trail is on an exposed ridge, so if the weather is threatening, the best idea is to return via Gorge Brook Trail. In good weather, this section of Moosilauke Carriage Road trail is a pleasant, gradual descent through scrub spruce-fir vegetation with excellent vistas. At 4.6 miles (0.9 mile from the summit), you'll reach a three-way junction with Glencliff Trail (the next leg of the Appalachian Trail) and a spur path that ascends South Peak (0.2 mile each way). South Peak provides excellent views south and back to the summit of Moosilauke to the north, so is well worth the detour.

After enjoying the views from South Peak, continue descending down Moosilauke Carriage Road. The trail is relatively wide and is nowhere particularly steep. Observe how the trees gradually increase in stature as you descend.

At about 1.4 miles below the summit, note the stone barrier that was probably erected to keep snowmobiles and ATVs from reaching the summit. Snapper

Trail comes in from the left, 1.9 miles below the summit (6.0 miles total). Turn left onto Snapper Trail and continue your descent. Snapper Trail is another pleasant, gradual downhill. Note the abundant hay-scented ferns in an area of the former route of the trail. This fern favors open, sunny locations, such as this abandoned trail. The trail crosses several bridges over a tributary of Gorge Brook.

At 7.1 miles, Snapper Trail joins the relocated section of Gorge Brook Trail that you took on your ascent. Cross over the brook (7.3 miles) and continue down the Gorge Brook Trail. Turn left (upstream) when you reach a junction with a path to the Class of 1997 Swimming Hole. Cross the stream on a bridge, following signs to the parking area.

DID YOU KNOW?

"Moosilauke" is an Abenaki word thought to mean "bald place." That seems fitting given the smooth appearance of the domed summit. A minority opinion is that it means "good moose place."

OTHER ACTIVITIES

Ravine Lodge is open to the public. You can stay overnight in the main lodge or one of the rustic bunkhouses and enjoy breakfasts and dinners. The lodge is run by students from Dartmouth College.

Although the trails described in this book are not appropriate for cross-country skiing, there are a host of skiing trails around Ravine Lodge, including along the unplowed access road.

MORE INFORMATION

Dartmouth College owns Mount Moosilauke; dartmouth.edu/~doc/moosilauke. There is no fee for parking.

Find services (restaurants, motels, grocery, gas) along NH 112 or US 3 in North Woodstock or along NH 112 in Lincoln.

FRANCONIA NOTCH

The Franconia Notch region is the westernmost part of the White Mountains. It includes the Kinsman Range, Franconia Notch, and the Franconia Range. The latter, with its beautiful cone-shaped peaks, rises above 5,000 feet, making it the second-highest range in the White Mountains. The hiking opportunities described here are easily accessible from I-93. You'll find numerous waterfalls, unique geological formations, and terrific scenery. The Franconia region is a popular tourist destination and includes such well-known sites as the Flume, Echo Lake, and Cannon Mountain.

For fishing enthusiasts with a valid New Hampshire license, Profile Lake is stocked with trout. Nonmotorized boats are permitted. The Pemigewasset River is also a popular fishing spot.

Franconia Notch Bike Path parallels the highway through the notch and provides access to some of the hikes described in this book. It is a paved path, 20 miles round-trip, suitable for families and accessible from parking areas in the notch.

SUPPLIES AND LOGISTICS

The village of Franconia is at the north end of Franconia Notch, off I-93; Lincoln and North Woodstock are a few miles to the south. These have grocery stores, pharmacies, gas stations, restaurants, motels, and country inns. Those traveling to the notch from the north on US 3 may find it more convenient to stop for supplies in Twin Mountain, about 12 miles away.

The visitor center at Flume Gorge is open from May through the end of October. It has tourist information, snack bars, restrooms, a gift shop, and a restaurant (nhstateparks.org/visit/state-parks/flume-gorge.aspx; 603-745-8391). At Profile Lake, there are restrooms, a small interpretive nature center, and a snack bar that serves ice cream and other treats. Echo Lake has a small snack bar and restrooms, and there are restrooms at the Basin.

PUBLIC TRANSPORTATION

Concord Coach Lines goes from Boston's Logan Airport and South Station to Lincoln. From there, you can reserve a shuttle (the Shuttle Connection) to Franconia Notch. Check the web for details. The AMC Hiker Shuttle stops at Lafayette Place (trailhead for Lonesome Lake) and the Old Bridle Path/Falling Waters Trail trailhead; outdoors.org/lodging/lodging-shuttle.cfm; 603-466-2727.

NEARBY CAMPING

Lafayette Campground in Franconia Notch State Park has 97 tentsites as well as picnic tables for day use, restrooms, water, a small camp store with limited groceries, information on trails, and ranger naturalist programs. No dogs are permitted in the campground; nhstateparks.org/visit/state-parks/franconia-notch-state-park .aspx; 603-823-9513.

A number of national forest campgrounds are within a 30-minute drive. Zealand and Sugarloaf campgrounds (the latter providing limited facilities for people with disabilities) are near Twin Mountain. The Big Rock and Hancock campgrounds are at the western end of the Kancamagus Highway. Wildwood Campground is on NH 112, west of Lincoln. Visit www.fs.usda.gov/activity/ whitemountain/recreation/camping-cabins. Private campgrounds are in the North Woodstock/Lincoln area.

10

THE BASIN AND BASIN-CASCADE TRAIL

This trail begins at the Basin, one of the largest, most impressive glacially carved potholes you will ever see. It then follows Cascade Brook, ascending past Kinsman Falls and a series of smaller waterfalls, rapids, and potholes. Large, flat rocks along the brook are perfect for family picnics.

DIRECTIONS

The parking area for the Basin is at a well-marked exit off Franconia Notch Highway. If you approach from the south, the exit is about 5.5 miles north of the Lincoln/North Woodstock exit and 1.5 miles north of the Flume. After parking your vehicle on the east side of the highway, follow the signs to the Basin via a walkway under the highway. If you are coming south through the notch from the Franconia or Twin Mountain areas, the exit for the Basin is about 1.5 miles south of Lafayette Campground, and the parking area is on the west side of the highway.

Those who want to return south from the Basin after their hike need to drive north for 3.0 miles on Franconia Notch Highway to the Cannon Mountain Tramway exit to a turnaround, because there is no place to reverse direction at the Basin itself. Those returning north can reverse direction at the Flume exit. *GPS coordinates:* 44° 07.38′ N, 71° 40.96′ W.

TRAIL DESCRIPTION

The first section of this hike, which takes you a little beyond the Basin, is very easy and suitable for even the youngest child. The second section is moderate but should present no serious problems for children above age 4. It has been heavily eroded by hiking boots, exposing tree roots and rocks in many places, so it takes longer than mileage alone would indicate.

LOCATION
Lincoln, NH

RATING
Easy

DISTANCE
1.6 miles round-trip

ELEVATION GAIN
400 feet

ESTIMATED TIME
45 minutes-1.5 hours

MAPS
AMC *White Mountain National Forest Map & Guide*, H4

AMC *White Mountain Guide*, 29th ed. Map 2 Franconia–Pemigewasset, H4

USGS Topo: Lincoln to Franconia

From the parking area, it is a short, well-marked walk to the Basin, located in a curve of the Pemigewasset River. This glacial pothole is about 30 feet in diameter and 15 feet deep. It was scoured out and polished into a smooth, round surface by sand and small stones thrashing about in water rushing from snowmelt around the time the last continental glacier departed the region (about 12,000 years ago). Take a moment to read the sign describing how it was formed.

After enjoying the Basin, follow the Pemigewasset River downstream, cross over a bridge, turn right on Pemi Trail, and then, after about 200 feet, make a left on Basin-Cascade Trail at the sign. You'll find lots of paths in the area, but you should have no trouble locating this one from the Basin.

Almost immediately the trail passes a large, flat slab of rock in the streambed of Cascade Brook. Unless water levels are unusually high, this is an excellent place for a picnic or snacks. Families with very young children may want to use this spot as their turnaround point. If you go on, you will find numerous other places along the trail where short side paths lead to the stream and to flat rocks, perfect for sunning, picnicking, or wading. You'll have excellent views of the lower part of Franconia Ridge.

The forest along the trail changes from northern hardwoods to red spruce as you ascend. Hemlocks thrive along the brook, creating a cool, shady environment in many locations. There are some huge white pines too. The cooler atmosphere along the brook creates a "refrigerator effect," causing spring wildflowers,

Walk in Thoreau's footsteps at the Basin, a superb example of a glacially carved pothole.
Photo by Jerry Monkman.

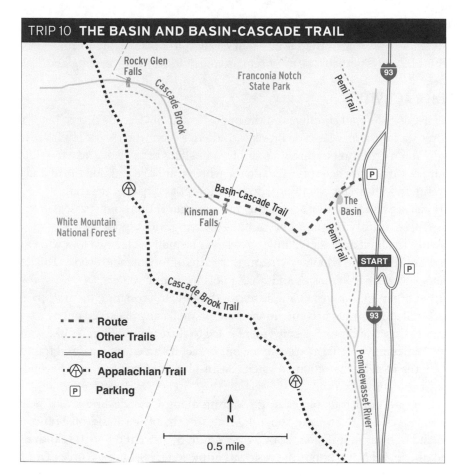

such as clintonia and Canada mayflower, to bloom several weeks later than in surrounding uplands.

At 0.7 mile (about 15 minutes past the Basin), a rough, unmarked side path leads down a slope to the base of Kinsman Falls at a point where the trail is relatively high above the brook. Shortly thereafter (0.8 mile), you reach the crossing of Cascade Brook. This is a good place to turn around because the crossing is challenging. A former bridge at this point was washed out and there are no immediate plans to rebuild it.

Chipmunks are particularly common along Basin-Cascade Trail. Listen for the harsh, birdlike chirp of this children's favorite. You'll probably see a few as well, with their distinctive striped faces and backs and their habit of carrying their tail straight up when they dash about.

Retrace your steps to return to the trailhead.

DID YOU KNOW?

After his 1858 visit to the Basin, Henry David Thoreau wrote in his journal, "This pothole is perhaps the most remarkable of its kind in New England."

OTHER ACTIVITIES

Basin-Cascade Trail continues on the opposite side of Cascade Brook, but it requires wading across Cascade Brook, a challenge even when water levels are not high. You might want to throw a pair of water shoes or sandals and a towel into your pack if you are determined to do the whole trail. Use your judgment and be careful. In high-water conditions, do not attempt that part of the trail.

If you are able to make it across, the trail, rougher at this point, passes through a small, beautiful canyon just beyond the crossing with a pool deep enough for a swim. In about another 0.2 mile, cross over a small bridge two logs wide and then cross a gentle tributary stream that runs into Cascade Brook. This is a pretty spot with lush mosses and small pools for young waders.

In another 15 minutes (0.5 mile above the stream crossing), the trail passes Rocky Glen Falls then becomes more level. A small canyon carved out by a tributary to Cascade Brook is a convenient place to turn around. It looks like someone deliberately created a box canyon, but in fact it's an entirely natural fracturing of the rock by the action of water. (Basin-Cascade Trail ends just beyond at the Cascade Brook Trail.)

There are numerous places to go wading along Cascade Brook. For a real swim, check out Echo Lake about 4.0 miles north of the Basin off Franconia Notch Highway (admission fee of $4 per adult, $2 per child 6 to 11; children 5 and under and New Hampshire residents admitted free). Flume Gorge (Trip 11) is a few miles south of the Basin.

MORE INFORMATION

There is no parking fee at the Basin parking area. Basin-Cascade Trail starts in Franconia Notch State Park (nhstateparks.org/visit/state-parks/franconia-notch -state-park.aspx; 603-745-8391) and ends in the White Mountain National Forest (www.fs.usda.gov/whitemountain; 603-536-6100).

The trail provides access to those using wheelchairs up to the Basin. Restrooms are available but there are no other facilities. A cafeteria with restrooms is at the Flume Gorge Visitor Center just south of the Basin.

11

FLUME GORGE

Stroll along rushing water on a boardwalk through one of the White Mountains' most renowned geological wonders: an extremely narrow gorge bounded by straight, vertical cliffs. This half-day outing also takes you past waterfalls, a giant pothole, huge boulders, and two covered bridges.

DIRECTIONS

The parking area for the Flume is off Exit 34A of Franconia Notch Highway, the extension of I-93 through Franconia Notch. The exit is very well marked and is about 4.0 miles north of the exit on I-93 for North Woodstock, Lincoln, NH 112, and the Kancamagus Highway. Purchase admission tickets and pick up a trail map at the Flume Gorge Visitor Center. *GPS coordinates: 44° 05.81′ N, 71° 40.88′ W.*

TRAIL DESCRIPTION

Flume Gorge is a popular destination at the south end of Franconia Notch State Park and is a perfect half-day outing for families. You can start your hike right from the visitor center or, if you have very young children, you can cover the first 0.7 mile on a school bus that drops you off right where the trail enters the gorge. You'll find a number of overlooks with steep dropoffs throughout this walk, so parents should keep an eye on younger children, especially those who like climbing on split-rail fences.

Starting from the visitor center, pass a huge glacial erratic in about 200 yards. Follow the path through the Flume Covered Bridge and the Boulder Cabin for 0.7 mile to the entrance of Flume Gorge (the school bus stop). Proceed into the Flume on boardwalks, stairs, and bridges for about 0.2 mile. The section through the gorge ends at Avalanche Falls.

LOCATION
Lincoln, NH

RATING
Easy

DISTANCE
2.0-mile loop

ELEVATION GAIN
270 feet

ESTIMATED TIME
2.0 hours

MAPS
AMC White Mountain National Forest Map & Guide, H4

AMC *White Mountain Guide,* 29th ed. Map 2 Franconia–Pemigewasset, H4

USGS Topo: Lincoln, NH

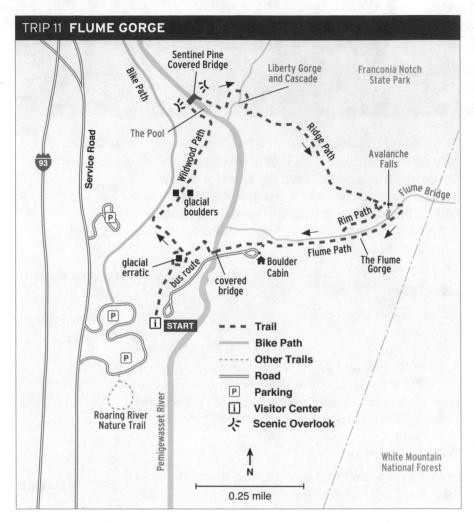

Why are the walls of the Flume so straight? The Flume was formed by erosion of a basalt dike within the granite. Two hundred million years ago, the granite, which tends to crack in straight lines, fractured vertically at the Flume. Lava from deep within the earth then flowed into the fractures, forcing the granite apart and solidifying to form a seam of basalt 12 to 20 feet wide.

Eventually, water began to flow over the granite and basalt, eroding the softer basalt and leaving the steep granite sides of the Flume. The narrowness of the gorge (at times it's as little as 12 feet wide) reflects the width of the original basalt dike. The straightness of the walls shows the fracture planes of the granite. In some places, you can still see remnants of the black basaltic rock.

At Avalanche Falls, you can take a shorter loop back toward the visitor center on Rim Path or continue to the Pool on Ridge Path. The Pool is as spectacular as the Flume Gorge, so I highly recommend you keep going on Ridge Path.

Follow Ridge Path for about 0.7 mile (mostly downhill) to the Pool and the Sentinel Pine Covered Bridge over the Pemigewasset River. From overlooks 130 feet above the Pool, you look down on a giant pothole 150 feet wide and 30 to 40 feet deep within the Pemigewasset River. The Pool was formed by the scouring action of sand and small stones blasted against the rock over a millennia of winter snowmelts and floods.

The Sentinel Pine Covered Bridge crosses the river right at the Pool. Make sure to note the fallen 175-foot white pine that forms the base of the bridge. The best view of the tree is from a short spur trail to the left after you pass through the covered bridge.

From the covered bridge, it is 0.6 mile back to the visitor center on Wildwood Path through a forest laced with boulders.

The vertical granite walls of the Flume Gorge show where the softer basalt dike was eroded away. Photo by Jerry Monkman.

DID YOU KNOW?

The Conway granite that forms the walls of the Flume Gorge was created from magma (molten rock) that welled up from deep within the earth and solidified 3 to 5 miles below the surface during the mid- to late Jurassic Period, about 180 million years ago.

OTHER ACTIVITIES

Roaring River Nature Trail, accessible from the Flume Gorge parking area, is a quiet experience compared with the Flume. Here you can learn about the forces of destruction and renewal that shape the northern hardwood forest. Pick up a self-guided interpretive pamphlet at the visitor center. A gazebo provides a place to listen quietly to the sounds of the forest while looking out at a view of Mount Flume and Mount Liberty, two 4,000-foot peaks of the Franconia Range.

Flume Gorge is convenient to other activities in Franconia Notch State Park, such as Basin-Cascade Trail (Trip 10), which leaves from the same parking area; swimming at Echo Lake Beach (admission fee $4 per adult, $2 per child 6 to 12; free for children 5 and under and for New Hampshire residents); and the Cannon Mountain Aerial Tramway. A paved bike trail starts at the Flume Gorge parking area and runs the length of Franconia Notch.

MORE INFORMATION

The Flume Gorge Visitor Center is open from early May through late October from 9 A.M. to 5 P.M. Admission at the time of this writing was $16 for adults and $13 for youth ages 6 to 12. Children ages 5 and under with a paying adult and New Hampshire residents ages 65 and over may enter for free; nhstateparks.org/visit/state-parks/flume-gorge.aspx; 603-745-8391.

The visitor center has a cafeteria, a gift shop, restrooms, and interpretative exhibits. You can watch a short movie about Franconia Notch State Park.

In winter, the visitor center is closed and some of the boardwalks are removed, but you can still walk in and enjoy a number of the trails. There is no admission fee then.

Dogs are not permitted along the trails in Flume Gorge.

12

BALD MOUNTAIN AND ARTIST'S BLUFF

Bald Mountain and Artist's Bluff command great views of Franconia Notch for relatively little effort. This ideal family outing is short, has a well-defined goal, and begins and ends near Echo Lake, a picturesque swimming beach.

DIRECTIONS

From the south, take Franconia Notch Highway, the extension of I-93 through Franconia Notch. As you approach the north end of the notch, the cliff of Artist's Bluff looms ahead. Take Exit 34C (NH 18/Echo Lake/Peabody Slope), drive about a half-mile west, and park in the lot (indicated by a sign) on the right (north) side of NH 18 by the Peabody Memorial Slope area of Cannon Mountain. The trail enters the woods along the north side of the parking area. From the Twin Mountain area, follow US 3 south toward Franconia Notch and pick up NH 18 at the entrance to the notch, where NH 3 and I-93 come together, and then follow the above directions. *GPS coordinates:* 44° 10.73′ N, 71° 42.10′ W.

TRAIL DESCRIPTION

Bald Mountain, the highest elevation on this trail, is only 2,340 feet; however, it is still a good idea to throw windbreakers in your pack, particularly if you plan to have a picnic on the summit.

 This loop hike has been renamed Veterans Trail in honor of New Hampshire veterans, although as of this writing, much of the signage used an old name, Loop Trail, at least in its lower sections. Loop Trail traditionally has referred to the lower section of the loop so you could avoid hiking back along the road. In any case, the trail, marked with red blazes, is easy to follow and I anticipate that the signage will be updated soon. Veterans Trail starts out fairly steep initially, following an old forest road. After about 10

LOCATION
Franconia, NH

RATING
Moderate

DISTANCE
1.5 miles on the trail

ELEVATION GAIN
550 feet

ESTIMATED TIME
1.0-2.0 hours

MAPS
AMC White Mountain National Forest Map & Guide, G4

AMC *White Mountain Guide*, 29th ed. Map 2 Franconia–Pemigewasset, G4

USGS Topo: Franconia

minutes (0.25 mile) of climbing through northern hardwoods, Bald Mountain Spur, which ascends the summit of Bald Mountain, enters from the left. Follow this to the left and continue ascending, now through a forest of red spruce and balsam fir. A short distance farther, the vegetation becomes scrubby, and a little bit of scrambling on rocks is required before you reach the summit of Bald Mountain, 0.4 mile from the trailhead.

From Bald Mountain, the Peabody Slopes of the Cannon Mountain Ski Area are immediately to the south. Farther to the east (your left) is the glacially carved valley that is Franconia Notch. Try to imagine this area completely covered by ice thousands of feet thick as recently as 12,000 years ago. The glacier acted like a giant piece of sandpaper, grinding and smoothing the walls of the valley as it moved slowly through the region. North–south valleys in the White Mountains such as Franconia Notch were particularly well scoured by the north–south movements of the continental ice sheet and so have characteristically broad bottoms and steep sides.

Mount Lafayette, at 5,260 feet the highest mountain of the Franconia Range, forms the eastern wall of Franconia Notch. You will immediately be struck by how "pointy" the summits of Mount Lafayette and other peaks of the Franconia Range are, compared with the broad, smooth summits of the Presidential Range. This is because the tops of the Presidentials were flattened out by the massive continental glacier; in contrast, the Franconia Ridge was scoured from the sides by mountain glaciers. The freezing and thawing of the ice plucked out chunks of rock from both sides of Franconia Ridge, leaving behind a narrow ridge.

Another noteworthy feature of Mount Lafayette is the steep ravine carved in the side of the mountain by the rushing water of Lafayette Brook. This was formed in postglacial times. Eagle Cliff is the dramatically rugged shoulder of Mount Lafayette. Legend has it that golden eagles used to nest there, and in recent years peregrine falcons have taken up residence (they're very hard to see even with binoculars).

The summit ledges on Bald Mountain are covered with stunted spruce and firs and shrubs such as mountain holly, blueberries, and meadowsweet. Three-toothed cinquefoils grow in cracks in the rocks where some soil collects. These and bunchberries form a nice display of white flowers in mid-June. Notice the so-called flag trees, with branches on only one side of the trunk. The prevailing winter winds, in combination with ice, kill buds on the opposite side of the trunk, so that branches form only on the lee side (i.e., the side away from the direction of the prevailing wind). On Bald Mountain, most of the flag trees point east, indicating that the wind is usually from the west. Exceptions do occur, perhaps where the winds whip around the side of the mountain.

If you are lucky, you may see one of the White Mountains' largest and most charismatic animals from a distance so safe that you'll need binoculars. Black bears, often mother bears with their cubs, occasionally forage for berries in the

Cannon Mountain looms large from Bald Mountain. Photo by Jerry Monkman.

open ski trails high up on Cannon Mountain during daylight. Looking across to those ski slopes from Bald Mountain is about as good a chance as you'll have to see bears in the White Mountains, because they are usually secretive. The bears' presence along the ski trails shows that these trails are not without value to some wildlife.

After enjoying the Bald Mountain summit, retrace your steps on the spur trail to the trail junction. If you have had enough for the day, take the right fork and descend to the parking area. For Artist's Bluff, 0.4 mile away, follow the left fork. The understory vegetation is particularly lush between Bald Mountain and Artist's Bluff, with abundant ferns, mosses, clintonia, club mosses, false Solomon's seal, mountain wood sorrel (particularly near the junction with the Bald Mountain spur), red and painted trillium, and pink lady's slippers (both pink- and white-flowered varieties). Striped and red maples are common understory shrubs. Other plants to look for are bristly and wild sarsaparilla, goldenrods, rattlesnake root, wild oats, and Canada mayflower.

The trail descends to a gravelly gully, passes a huge boulder, ascends over a wooded hump, and then descends steeply for about 5 minutes to the junction with the short spur trail that leads left to Artist's Bluff. Follow the spur trail to the open ledges of Artist's Bluff.

From this vista, Echo Lake is immediately below, and you look directly down the notch. The notch is the north–south divide between two completely different drainage patterns. Below you, Echo Lake has an outlet to the northwest that

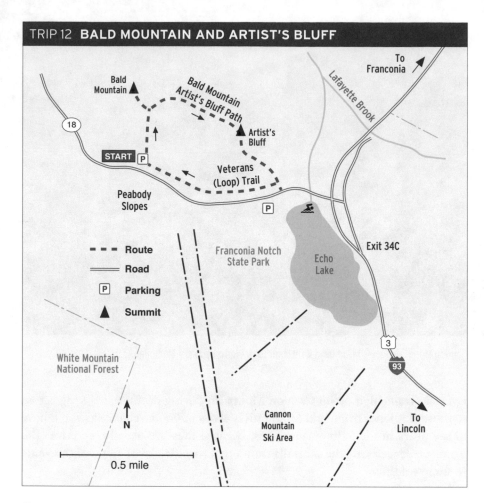

Bald Mountain

Bald Mountain Artist's Bluff Path

18

START

Artist's Bluff

Veterans (Loop) Trail

Peabody Slopes

- - - **Route**

——— **Road**

P **Parking**

▲ **Summit**

White Mountain National Forest

N

0.5 mile

To Franconia

Lafayette Brook

Exit 34C

Franconia Notch State Park

Echo Lake

3

93

Cannon Mountain Ski Area

To Lincoln

flows into the Gale River, which joins the Connecticut River and flows into Long Island Sound. Profile Lake is just a little south of Echo Lake, on the other side of an almost imperceptible rise in the land. A drop of water falling in Profile Lake flows south through the Pemigewasset River to the Merrimack River and eventually reaches the Atlantic Ocean at Newburyport, MA.

From Artist's Bluff the trail descends steeply in a gully, initially on some conveniently placed rocky stairs. In about 10 minutes it intersects with Loop Trail to the right. Veterans Trail comes out along NH 18 just below this junction but it is much more pleasant to take Loop Trail, 0.3 mile back to your car, closely paralleling NH 18. Reward yourself with a swim in Echo Lake.

DID YOU KNOW?

Before the age of Vibram soles and Gore-Tex parkas, hikers in long, frilly dresses, starched collars, and neckties walked up Bald Mountain and Artist's Bluff from the Profile House in Franconia Notch and other grand hotels. These summer hotel guests would purchase paintings from artists who were in residence at the hotels and undoubtedly painted from Artist's Bluff.

OTHER ACTIVITIES

Bald Mountain and Artist's Bluff are very close to the scenic attractions in Franconia Notch State Park: Echo and Profile lakes, Cannon Mountain, the Old Man of the Mountain site, the Basin, and Eagle Cliff. Despite the crowds, these natural wonders are worth a stop before or after your hike.

Echo Lake has a picturesque swimming beach with lifeguards and a bathhouse. The entrance fee is $4 per adult, $2 per child 6 to 11; children 5 and under and New Hampshire residents are admitted free. The area has a snack bar, restrooms, information service, and a picnic area.

MORE INFORMATION

The trail is within Franconia Notch State Park. There is no parking fee; nhstateparks.org/visit/state-parks/franconia-notch-state-park.aspx; 603-745-8391.

13

MOUNT PEMIGEWASSET TRAIL

Mount Pemigewasset Trail climbs to the summit of Mount Pemigewasset, a 2,500-foot peak at the southern end of Franconia Notch and the location of the famed Indian Head profile. The climb is a good one for children because it's never very steep. The views from the top are excellent, and the combination of stream crossings and rocks in the forest makes for an interesting walk.

LOCATION
Lincoln, NH

RATING
Moderate

DISTANCE
3.6 miles round-trip

ELEVATION GAIN
1,300 feet

ESTIMATED TIME
4.0 hours

DIRECTIONS

The trailhead is reached from the parking lot for Flume Gorge in Franconia Notch State Park. This is at Exit 34A of Franconia Notch Highway, the extension of I-93 through Franconia Notch. The exit is about 4.0 miles north of Exit 32 on I-93, the exit for Lincoln, North Woodstock, NH 112, and the Kancamagus Highway. For this trail, it is most convenient to park at the northwest side of the parking lot near the beginning of the bike path that heads north through the notch. The actual trailhead is off the bike path. *GPS coordinates: 44° 05.87′ N, 71° 40.90′ W.*

MAPS
AMC White Mountain National Forest Map & Guide, H4

AMC *White Mountain Guide,* 29th ed.
Map 2 Franconia–Pemigewasset, H4

USGS Topo: Lincoln

TRAIL DESCRIPTION

Mount Pemigewasset Trail is marked with blue blazes, but it would be hard to get lost on this well-trod path even if you didn't see the blazes. Start walking north on the bike path for about 150 yards, and then follow the trail to the left. The trail goes through three tunnels, the first under old Route 3, which is now a service road for the highway, and the second and third for the northbound and southbound sides of I-93.

The trail traverses some open areas that harbor attractive flowers in midsummer, including purple-stemmed asters, pearly everlastings, orange hawkweed, and a variety of goldenrods. The moister sections have jewelweed,

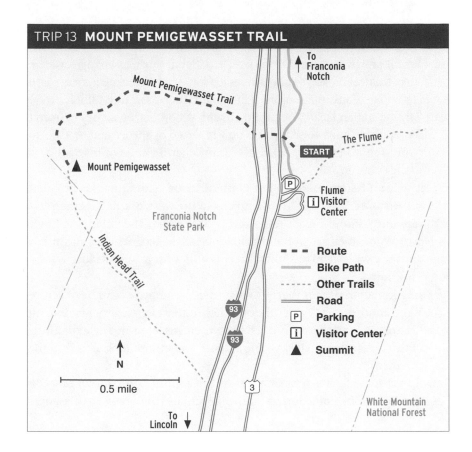

Mount Pemigewasset Trail

To Franconia Notch

The Flume

START

Mount Pemigewasset

P

Flume Visitor Center

Franconia Notch State Park

Indian Head Trail

Route
Bike Path
Other Trails
Road
P Parking
i Visitor Center
▲ Summit

93

93

N

0.5 mile

3

To Lincoln

White Mountain National Forest

hay-scented fern, and fringed sedge. Between the first and second tunnels, you pass through a pleasant balsam fir woodland.

After about 0.5 mile and several stream crossings on bog bridges, the trail heads uphill at a somewhat steeper pitch. At this point, you are walking through a northern hardwood forest, where the dominant trees are yellow birch, American beech, and sugar maple. Hobblebush, with some striped maple, forms the understory. Woodland wildflowers to look for include wild sarsaparilla, partridgeberry, mountain wood sorrel, false Solomon's seal, and white wood-asters. Clintonia (bluebead lily) becomes more frequent as you ascend. Shield ferns, shiny club moss, and a variety of true mosses are also quite common. Mushrooms abound from midsummer through early fall.

The birds you are likely to hear in the forest include black-throated green warblers, black-throated blue warblers, red-eyed vireos, golden-crowned kinglets, and hermit thrushes. Red squirrels and chipmunks scamper about.

Approximately 1.3 miles from the trailhead, the trail makes a bend to the left and passes a huge boulder, a glacial erratic. This is a nice place to stop for a snack or lunch. Just beyond this rock look for some jelly fungus (a bright orange-yellow blob) on a cut log. At a clearing about 50 yards past the boulder, note the shallow root structure of an overturned tree in a small clearing. Plants of the forest understory, such as wild oats, northern fly honeysuckle, and hobble-bush, are still growing where the tree once stood, but this may change over time. The death of this tree creates opportunities for some sun-loving plants such as hay-scented fern to take advantage of the light penetrating to the forest floor.

At 1.7 miles, Indian Head Trail, marked with yellow blazes, comes in from the right. The northern hardwood forest is now replaced by spruce and fir. Continue straight on Mount Pemigewasset Trail for another 0.1 mile to reach the open ledges of the summit.

Great views of surrounding mountains can be had from the broad, flat rocks of the summit. Mount Moosilauke is to the west, South Kinsman to the northwest, and Mounts Flume and Liberty to the east. The villages of Lincoln and North Woodstock are to the south. Some of the ledges at the summit end rather abruptly with steep dropoffs. Parents will want to keep a close watch on young children.

The small, scattered trees that grow around the summit have been sculpted by the wind to form "flag" trees. Look for chimney swifts, very fast and agile birds that zoom about the summit chasing their insect prey. The left and right wings of this streamlined, dusky-colored bird sometimes look as if they move independently.

You'll find some lowbush blueberries at the summit, but you will have lots of competition from both human and nonhuman frugivores at this popular

Snowshoeing to the summit of Mount Pemigewasset. Photo courtesy of Leti Taft-Pearman.

destination. The nonhuman variety include flocks of cedar waxwings—beige, crested birds with yellow bellies, red tips on some of their wing feathers, and black masks through their eyes. They have any inaccessible blueberry-covered ledge all to themselves.

On your return, avoid following the yellow blazes you might see at the summit ledges. These lead down the mountain by a very steep, unmaintained trail. On the return downhill, a small white arrow with a handwritten sign on a balsam fir that reads "To the Flume Parking Lot" is at the junction with Indian Head Trail. Follow this arrow to the right for Mount Pemigewasset Trail. It is possible to return via Indian Head Trail, which ends up on a short gravel road just south of the Indian Head Resort off Route 3. But be warned that Indian Head Trail is not well marked and would require a 0.75-mile walk along the highway to reach your vehicle, unless you park at its trailhead beforehand.

DID YOU KNOW?

The formation of the Indian Head is the result of water seeping into cracks in the granite rock and then freezing and expanding, thereby causing pieces of the granite to break off. What remains behind happens to resemble a human profile. The Indian Head is only a temporary feature of the landscape and will eventually erode into something less than a face, which happened to the Old Man of the Mountain several miles to the north.

OTHER ACTIVITIES

The Indian Head is not obvious from anywhere on the trail on this hike. After the hike, make sure you get a good look at it from the valley in the vicinity of the Indian Head Resort.

Flume Gorge (Trip 11) is accessible from the same parking area (admission is $16 for adults, $13 for children ages 6 to 12; it is free for children ages 5 and under and for New Hampshire residents ages 65 and over).

MORE INFORMATION

There is no fee for parking to use the Mount Pemigewasset Trail; nhstateparks.org/visit/state-parks/franconia-notch-state-park.aspx; 603-745-8391. The closest concentration of restaurants and other tourist facilities is off US 3 and NH 112 in Lincoln and North Woodstock.

14

COPPERMINE TRAIL TO BRIDAL VEIL FALLS

Coppermine Trail takes you on a gentle uphill grade along Coppermine Brook to Bridal Veil Falls, one of the most beautiful waterfalls in the White Mountains. It is a pleasant walk on the western side of Cannon Mountain.

DIRECTIONS

Coppermine Trail is off NH 116, about 3.4 miles south of the village of Franconia. If you are traveling north through Franconia Notch, take the Franconia exit on I-93 (Exit 38) and then go south on NH 116 for 3.4 miles. Alternatively, from the North Woodstock and Lincoln exit on I-93 (Exit 32), travel west on NH 112 for about 8.0 miles and then north on NH 116 for 7.7 miles. Look for Coppermine Road on the east side of NH 116. Park your vehicle where there is ample space on Coppermine Road just after turning off NH 116. *GPS coordinates:* 44° 10.86′ N, 71° 45.34′ W.

TRAIL DESCRIPTION

The hike starts along Coppermine Road, a dirt road, so all distances are from NH 116. Be careful to avoid turning off on one new road (Beechwood Lane) coming off Coppermine Road, and on any new developments.

At 0.4 mile, the trail, marked with yellow blazes, departs from the left side of the road (look for the hiker sign). The trail becomes a pleasant woodland path through a northern hardwood forest. Yellow birch is especially abundant, and American beech and sugar maple are also well represented. Conifers, particularly Canadian hemlock but also red spruce and balsam fir, occur along the north side of the brook where the microclimate is shadier, damper, and cooler. The most abundant understory shrub is hobblebush.

Look for circular clumps of interrupted fern soon after turning off Coppermine Road. The leafy green pinnae (leaflets) of this large fern are "interrupted" along the stalk

LOCATION
Franconia, NH

RATING
Moderate

DISTANCE
5.0 miles round-trip

ELEVATION GAIN
1,100 feet

ESTIMATED TIME
3.0-4.0 hours

MAPS
AMC *White Mountain National Forest Map & Guide,* G4

AMC *White Mountain Guide,* 29th ed. Map 2 Franconia–Pemigewasset, G4

USGS Topo: Sugar Hill to Franconia

The base of Coppermine Falls. Photo by Jerry Monkman.

by brownish reproductive pinnae. You may also notice the raspberries growing in disturbed areas near the road. These make a delicious treat if birds haven't gotten there first.

Most wildflowers growing along the trail bloom in May and June. These include trout lily, foamflower, rosy twisted stalk, Canada mayflower, clintonia, false Solomon's seal, Indian cucumber-root, jack-in-the-pulpit, starflower, wild sarsaparilla, and shinleaf.

Coppermine Brook comes in from the right at about 1.0 mile and is within sight or earshot of the trail for the remainder of its length. If you decide to cut the walk short, several places where the trail runs along the brook make for a pleasant short (or long) stop before you turn around. Soon after, you can look for the mysterious plaque in the river (see page 68).

After about an hour to an hour and a half (2.3 miles), the trail crosses over to the south side of the brook on a wooden bridge and passes the Coppermine Shelter, a lean-to. Mountain maples, with their characteristic arching stems and lobed maple leaves, are at the bridge and around the shelter. You will also notice little caves created by fern- and moss-covered boulders and overhanging tree roots. These look like great dens for animals or for weary elves. The small evergreen ferns that grow right on top of the boulders are appropriately named rock ferns, or Virginia polypody.

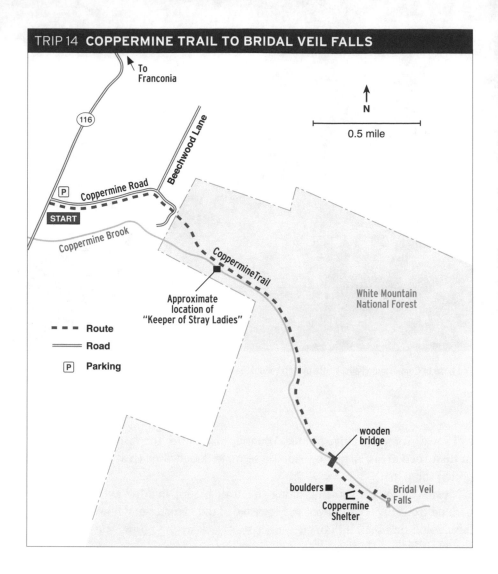

To
Franconia

116

N

0.5 mile

Beechwood Lane

P Coppermine Road

START

Coppermine Brook

Coppermine Trail

Approximate
location of
"Keeper of Stray Ladies"

White Mountain
National Forest

- - - Route
=== Road
P Parking

wooden
bridge

boulders ■

Coppermine
Shelter

Bridal Veil
Falls

The trail crosses back over the stream on well-placed rocks, climbs moderately, and then ends at Bridal Veil Falls, 0.2 mile after the bridge. The more adventurous can scramble up the right side of the waterfall to the top of the falls for a view of a second, very attractive pool that is not visible from the bottom. Bridal Veil Falls is really several connected cascades, some forming "shoots" along sloping rock faces and others tumbling over rocks into pools, like the large one at the bottom. Like most waterfalls in the White Mountains, the best time for viewing them is when water levels are relatively high, either early in the season or just after a rainstorm.

Retrace your steps to return to your vehicle.

OTHER ACTIVITIES

The swimming area at Echo Lake in Franconia Notch State Park is about 10 miles away (admission is $4 per adult, $2 per child 6 to 11; free for children 5 and under and for New Hampshire residents). If you are up for more hiking, the nearest hike described in this book is Bald Peak (Trip 15). Its trailhead is about 1.2 miles farther south on NH 116.

Lost River Reservation (south on NH 116 and east on NH 112) is a gorge with lots of caves with names like Judgment Hall of Pluto. It is run by the Society for the Protection of New Hampshire Forests (admission is $18 per adult, $12 per child 4 to 12) and is a terrific place to take kids.

MORE INFORMATION

There is no fee for parking at Coppermine Trail; however, the first 0.5 mile of this trail goes through private land, so please be respectful of property owners. The remainder of the trail is in the White Mountain National Forest; www.fs.usda.gov/whitemountain; 603-536-6100.

The village of Franconia is the closest place for food and supplies. Stores and restaurants are clustered around the junction of NH 18 and NH 116.

COPPERMINE TRAIL AND THE KEEPER OF STRAY LADIES

After hiking about 1.2 miles on Coppermine Trail (approximately 0.2 mile after the trail joins the brook), look for a plaque on a large boulder in the streambed with an enigmatic inscription:

In Memoriam to Arthur Farnsworth
"The Keeper of Stray Ladies"
Pecketts 1939
Presented by a Grateful One

To find it, look for a steep slope through conifers down to a flat area where people might have pitched tents along the stream. You need to scramble to reach the streambed and then use caution because the rocks are slippery. The boulder juts out into the stream roughly halfway along the flat area. The plaque faces downstream on the same side of the brook as the trail.

For the rest of your hike, you can ponder who Arthur Farnsworth was, why the tribute was placed in this particular location, and who was the "grateful one" that chose to eulogize Mr. Farnsworth in this manner.

The answer, according to an article by Lyn McIntosh in the autumn 1987 issue of *Magnetic North,* is that Arthur Farnsworth was a handsome young Vermonter who was employed at Pecketts, a fashionable, year-round resort in the 1930s on Sugar Hill, just west of Franconia Notch. Guests of Pecketts rode on horseback to land owned by the resort on Coppermine Brook for hiking, fishing, snowshoeing, or simply enjoying the beautiful rushing stream. Farnsworth's job was to make guests feel at home at the lodge. In 1939, the actress Bette Davis came to Pecketts for a period of rest after a particularly exhausting time of moviemaking. In brief, Davis fell in love with Pecketts, the whole region, and Farnsworth. The simple life of the North Country and the strong, honest gentleman who did not find her fame particularly intimidating were just the antidotes Davis needed from her life as a movie star.

Legend has it that Davis strayed from a hiking party at Coppermine Brook, knowing that Farnsworth would be sent to find her. They were married in 1940 and lived happily in California, occasionally escaping to the White Mountains.

Unfortunately, in 1943, tragedy struck. Farnsworth died after he fell down some stairs at their home on Sugar Hill. Davis continued to come back to the White Mountains for a while but eventually sold her home on Sugar Hill in 1961. The plaque mysteriously appeared on Coppermine Brook sometime around then.

The Keeper of Stray Ladies.

15
BALD PEAK VIA MOUNT KINSMAN TRAIL

This hike fits the description of "great views for relatively modest effort." You follow an old logging road past some attractive cascades up to a bare knob on a spur of the Kinsman Range, from which there is a wonderful 360-degree vista.

DIRECTIONS

From the North Woodstock and Lincoln exit on I-93 (Exit 32), travel west on NH 112 for about 8.0 miles to its intersection with NH 116 (Bungay Corner). Turn north (right) on NH 116. The trailhead is on the right, 6.8 miles from the intersection with NH 112 and 1.8 miles north of the Easton town hall. The trailhead for Mount Kinsman Trail has recently been relocated about 0.2 mile south of its former location. As of this writing, the parking area had space for about seven vehicles, but it may be expanded in the future.

If you are traveling through Franconia Notch, take the Franconia exit on I-93 (Exit 38) and then go south on NH 116 for 4.6 miles to the parking area on the left. *GPS coordinates:* 44° 09.91' N, 71° 45.95' W.

TRAIL DESCRIPTION

This is an excellent family hike, with a relatively moderate grade throughout. Mount Kinsman Trail begins on a newly blazed path marked with blue blazes. Very soon you pass through an open area that was probably logged fairly recently. Look for scattered blueberries and steeplebushes, the latter with maroon flower clusters that resemble a steeple.

The path continues gradually uphill along the side of a valley above a stream. The forest is primarily hemlocks and paper birch. At 0.5 mile, the path ends in an old logging road that comes up from the former trailhead on NH 116. Mount Kinsman Trail turns right onto the road. You

LOCATION
Easton, NH

RATING
Moderate

DISTANCE
4.6 miles round-trip

ELEVATION GAIN
1,450 feet

ESTIMATED TIME
4.0 hours

MAPS
AMC White Mountain National Forest Map & Guide, G3-H4

AMC *White Mountain Guide,* 29th ed. Map 2 Franconia–Pemigewasset, G3-H4

USGS Topo: Sugar Hill

won't find a trail sign here, but you will see blue blazes. A sugar house will be on the left just a few steps ahead.

Continuing uphill, Mount Kinsman Trail leaves the old logging road on a path and then joins another logging road. Be careful at every intersection with old roads and paths to follow the blue blazes. At 1.1 mile (about 30 minutes), the trail enters the White Mountain National Forest. The forest floor here is covered with a variety of wildflowers and ferns. Wild sarsaparilla, sharp-leaved asters, and New York fern are particularly abundant. Hay-scented fern grows in more-sunny locations.

You will cross over some small rivulets and then reach the first of three attractive brooks at 1.5 miles. Water bubbling around boulders and cobbles invites you to take a break. Walk uphill from the left side of the brook to see the site of the former Kinsman Cabin. Some of the stonework is still there.

The second brook is reached at 1.8 miles, along with increasing numbers of yellow birches. Here a waterfall streams down a moss-covered rock wall. At 2.1

miles, you cross the third brook, Flume Brook (called Kendall Brook on the USGS topo), and the forest becomes decidedly boreal (spruce-fir).

On the opposite side of Flume Brook, you will see a sign that directs you right "To Flume." Follow this side trail for about 150 yards downhill past Indian pipes and piggy-backed mosses to a view of the Kinsman Flume. Like its better known namesake in Franconia Notch, this flume was formed by the erosion of a basalt dike within the channel of Flume Brook. The viewpoint has a very steep dropoff with no railing, so parents will want to keep an eye on their children. You cannot even see the bottom of the gorge.

Return to the main trail and turn right. In about 70 yards, the spur trail to Bald Peak departs to the right at a point where Mount Kinsman Trail makes a sharp left. Take the spur trail. It heads slightly downhill and passes a fir wave (described in Trip 8). Note the young balsam fir coming up under the dead firs, which indicates that the forest is regenerating despite the loss of the older trees. After a modest ascent, you reach the bare open ledge of Bald Peak (2.3 miles).

A sweeping view greets you in all directions. The closest mountains are those of the Kinsman Ridge to the east, to which Bald Peak is connected. You can see North Kinsman and the back of Cannon Mountain, a completely different perspective on these peaks than the one you get from Franconia Notch. Looking south, the large mountain is Mount Moosilauke. The peaks of the Benton Range are west of Moosilauke. The view due west is of 2,000-foot hills across the nearby valley and of Vermont in the distance. The village of Franconia is to the north.

The low trees at the open ledges include balsam fir, red spruce, and heartleaf birch. A visit in blueberry season could be fruitful. The common grass is called poverty grass because its flower head contains only a few flowers. Reindeer lichen is also common.

When I visited Bald Peak on a warm, sunny day in early August, the peak was swarming with large

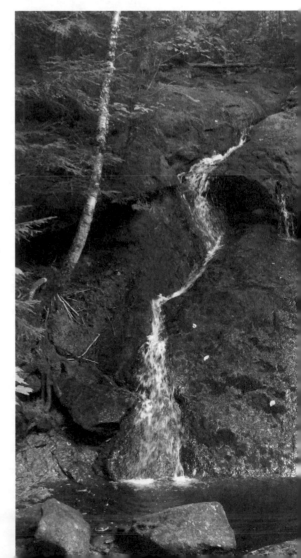

One of the attractive small streams that you encounter on the way to Bald Peak.

dragonflies called variable darners. These are strong fliers, which is essential if they are going to reach these windy hilltop locations. They live in ponds as nymphs (juveniles).

On a larger scale, listen for the hoarse croaking of common ravens, which also are attracted to these remote mountaintop locations. Other birds you might encounter include dark-eyed juncos, white-throated sparrows, and yellow-rumped warblers.

Retrace your steps to return to your vehicle. Remember to turn left off the logging road just after you pass the sugar house.

DID YOU KNOW?

Asa Kinsman, for whom the ridge is named, settled in Easton in the 1780s.

OTHER ACTIVITIES

This trailhead is just over a mile from the trailhead to Coppermine Trail (Trip 14). That offers a scenic hike along a brook.

Swimming is available at Echo Lake Beach in Franconia Notch State Park (follow directions in reverse from Franconia Notch above). An entrance fee is charged ($4 per adult, $2 per child 6 to 11; children 5 and under and New Hampshire residents are admitted free).

MORE INFORMATION

The first part of this trail is on private land, so please respect the rights of the landowners and stay on the trail. The second half is in the White Mountain National Forest; www.fs.usda.gov/whitemountain; 603-536-6100. Parking at the trailhead is free.

16
LONESOME LAKE AND HUT

Lonesome Lake is a beautiful lake reached by a short but somewhat steep climb. You can swim in the lake while enjoying the spectacular view across Franconia Notch to Mount Lafayette. AMC's Lonesome Lake Hut provides overnight accommodations.

DIRECTIONS

Lonesome Lake Trail starts at the Lafayette Campground in Franconia Notch State Park. From the north, take Franconia Notch Highway through the notch to the exit for the campground, about 1.5 miles south of the Old Man of the Mountain site. If you are coming from the south through Lincoln and North Woodstock, exit at the trailhead parking area, about 1.5 miles north of the Basin, then cross over to the west side through a foot tunnel. *GPS coordinates:* 44° 08.52′ N, 71° 41.03′ W.

TRAIL DESCRIPTION

The trail begins at the picnic area at the campground's south parking lot on the west side of the highway. A large sign for the trail and yellow blazes will help you make your way past the picnic area, across the Pemigewasset River, and through the campground without getting off track. After leaving the campground, Lonesome Lake Trail follows an old bridle path once used to reach a private camp on the lake.

After 10 minutes (0.3 mile) of hiking through a dense northern hardwood forest, the trail makes a sharp left turn and crosses a wooden plank bridge over a stream that tumbles down the mountainside. At 0.4 mile, Hi Cannon Trail departs right toward the summit of Cannon Mountain. Lonesome Lake Trail then ascends moderately steeply via three switchbacks. While ascending, listen for the flutelike songs of hermit thrushes and the incredible long bubbly

LOCATION
Lincoln, NH

RATING
Moderate

DISTANCE
3.2 miles round-trip

ELEVATION GAIN
1,000 feet

ESTIMATED TIME
4.0 hours

MAPS
AMC White Mountain National Forest Map & Guide, H4

AMC *White Mountain Guide,* 29th ed. Map 2 Franconia–Pemigewasset, H4

USGS Topo: Franconia

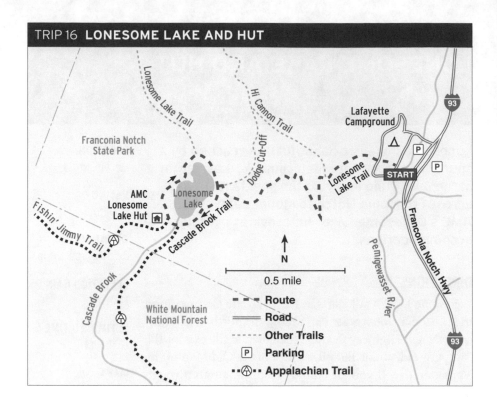

Lonesome Lake Trail

Hi Cannon Trail

Lafayette
Campground

93

P

Franconia Notch
State Park

Dodge Cut-Off

Lonesome
Lake Trail

START

P

AMC
Lonesome
Lake Hut

Lonesome
Lake

Fishin' Jimmy Trail

Cascade Brook Trail

Pemigewasset River

Franconia Notch Hwy

Cascade Brook

White Mountain
National Forest

N

0.5 mile

Route
Road
Other Trails
P Parking
Appalachian Trail

93

warble of the winter wren, two of the White Mountains' finest songsters. The trail then levels off through a pretty boreal forest with red spruce and balsam fir and a lush understory of mosses, goldthread, mountain wood sorrel, and clintonia. The terrain here is very hummocky—it looks like the kind of place where elves might pop out from behind the trees. Lonesome Lake Trail reaches the lake at 1.2 miles at a junction with Cascade Brook Trail.

From here you loop around Lonesome Lake on Around Lonesome Lake Trail, a trail that incorporates sections of Cascade Brook, Fishin' Jimmy, and Lonesome Lake trails. Parts of it may be soggy, particularly in spring. Because it's a loop, you can take it in either direction, but I describe it going clockwise.

Turn left onto Cascade Brook Trail and follow the southeast shoreline of the lake toward Lonesome Lake Hut. From vantage points along the shore you can see North and South Kinsman mountains and the Cannonballs. At 1.4 miles, turn right onto Fishin' Jimmy Trail. In another 0.1 mile you pass the outlet of the lake and then the dock area of Lonesome Lake Hut (1.6 miles), where the best swimming is.

On a hot summer day, after sweating mightily on your ascent, there will be nothing better than a swim, but keep an eye on kids because there are no lifeguards. The lake is about 20 acres in area and averages 3 to 6 feet in depth with a maximum depth of 12 feet. Technically it's a tarn—a mountain pond scoured out of the mountainside by a glacier. This may be the best place in New England to get a beautiful view while practicing your backstroke. Across the notch are Mount Lafayette and other peaks of the Franconia Range. Walker Ravine in Mount Lafayette appears as a deep V in the mountainside.

While sitting around the lake, you will likely see dragonflies hovering and darting above the water. Dragonflies are strong flyers and active predators of other insects around the lake. Dragonfly behavior is fun to watch. Although you might see them chasing prey, much of their activity is related to mating. Territorial males alight on their favorite perches and chase intruding males away. Males and females mate on the wing, and you may even see two dragonflies in such a "tandem flight." The female then deposits her eggs in the water by hovering and touching it periodically with the tip of her abdomen. Some species have specialized appendages to inject their eggs into emergent vegetation.

Look for dragonfly exuviae along the shoreline. These are the discarded exoskeletons of dragonfly nymphs (larvae). The nymphs live in water as voracious predators. When it is time to molt into adulthood, a nymph crawls out onto vegetation, splits its exoskeleton ("skin"), and emerges as an adult, much like a butterfly emerging from a cocoon. The remaining exuviae is left behind on the vegetation and provides a nice record of successful breeding. The newly emerged adult, called a teneral, is soft and vulnerable for at least a few hours until its wings and new exoskeleton harden.

Shrubs growing by the dock include sheep laurel, wild raisin (withe rod), sweet gale, and mountain ash. You may also observe the difference between red spruce (square needles) and balsam fir (flat needles).

After enjoying the lake, visit the hut by following Fishin' Jimmy Trail to the left. Day-hikers can use the restrooms and buy trail snacks, hot and cold drinks, trail maps, T-shirts, and other supplies. Soup is sometimes available midday. Ask at the hut for information about the self-guided nature walk, which uses the next portion of Around Lonesome Lake Trail, or longer trails that take you around the lake to Cannon Mountain or other destinations.

Very tame snowshoe hares hang out around the dock and the hut. These hares change color to match the season, turning brown in summer and white in winter. This camouflages them, although their tameness around the hut leaves the impression that they are not too worried about predators. The grassy areas provide them with forage during summer. In winter they feed on twigs and bark.

If you visit the hut in June, you will hear a symphony of bird songs. Performers include Swainson's thrushes, winter wrens, white-throated sparrows, yellow-rumped warblers, black-capped chickadees, and dark-eyed juncos.

Leaving the hut, Around Lonesome Lake Trail continues clockwise along the western shore of the lake. The trail goes through an open boggy area on split-rail bridges and planks. The planks protect your shoes from the dampness, while at the same time protecting the plants from your shoes. The most abundant shrubs are sheep laurel, sweet gale, and leatherleaf. The pink flowers of sheep laurel, produced in early July, look like smaller versions of those of mountain laurel, a close relative. The crushed leaves of sweet gale smell as sweet as those of its close relative, the bayberry.

Examine the undersides of leaves of several of the shrubs, with a hand lens if possible. Sweet gale leaves have tiny yellow resin dots. The undersides of the thick leaves of leatherleaf are covered by rusty scales. The best leaf "underside" is that of Labrador tea, a shrub with thick, leathery leaves, the undersides of which are covered with dense, reddish-brown, woolly hairs.

Look for sundews in the wetland. These are tiny bog plants that capture small insects by using sticky hairs on the tips of spoon-shaped leaves. The insects are digested and provide nutrients to the plant. The low-nutrient conditions of bogs make them a haven for carnivorous plants, but it takes a sharp eye to find sundews.

Look for larches between the plank trail and the lake. This relative of pines, spruces, and firs is partial to bogs. Unlike pines, which have needles in bunches of two to five, larches have needles in bunches of twenty or so, which give its branches a delicate, lacy appearance.

Beavers have played a large part in creating the wetland landscape around Lonesome Lake. As of this writing they no longer inhabit the lake itself, but their

Snowshoeing across Lonesome Lake. Photo by Dennis Welsh.

legacy remains in the extensive boggy wetlands created by their dams, particularly on the western and northwestern shores. You can still see the old dams too. Beavers are now active downstream from the outlet and upstream of the northwestern shore.

At about 0.3 mile from the hut, the trail reaches the junction with Lonesome Lake Trail. Note the many upturned trees whose intricate root systems are exposed to view. It reveals graphically how shallow the root systems are, due to the thinness of the soil. Here you will also find the large, cabbage-like leaves of Indian poke and an extensive cover of sphagnum moss.

Turn right onto Lonesome Lake Trail to complete the loop in another 0.2 mile. From here you can either descend to your vehicle at Lafayette Place on Lonesome Lake Trail or walk back to the hut.

DID YOU KNOW?

Lonesome Lake Hut is the only one of the eight AMC huts in the White Mountains not located in the White Mountain National Forest. It is within Franconia Notch State Park.

OTHER ACTIVITIES

Lonesome Lake Hut is a great place for families to have their first experience staying overnight at a backcountry hut. The hut requires a relatively short walk and is laid out so that families staying overnight often can have a room to themselves. Hearty breakfasts and dinners are served. Throughout the full-service season, an AMC naturalist is on-site to present an evening program, lead a family-oriented nature walk, or answer your questions about the mountains. Reservations are required for an overnight stay; outdoors.org/whitemountains; 603-466-2727.

MORE INFORMATION

The entire trail, including the parking area, is in Franconia Notch State Park; nhstateparks.org/visit/state-parks/franconia-notch-state-park.aspx; 603-745-8391. There is no parking fee. Fishing is permitted at Lonesome Lake. Contact the New Hampshire Fish and Game Department for a license.

AMC'S HIGH HUTS IN THE WHITE MOUNTAINS

In 1888, the Appalachian Mountain Club built a small, one-room stone hut to provide overnight accommodations at Madison Spring in the col between Mounts Madison and Adams. AMC wanted to provide a protected place that hikers could use as a base to explore the Northern Presidential Range. A number of club members had climbed in Switzerland, and the high-mountain huts there undoubtedly inspired them. Unlike today, with an attentive crew providing meals and managing the hut, early visitors brought their own food and were expected to take care of the hut.

Carter Notch Hut was opened in 1914, using a design similar to that of Madison Spring Hut. A third hut, Lakes of the Clouds, was opened in 1915, partially as a response to the tragic death of two climbers caught in a storm on the Crawford Path in 1900.

The person most responsible for creating the hut system of today was Joe Dodge, who served as manager of the AMC hut system from 1928 through 1959. A legendary personality, he oversaw the creation of the four "western huts," including the acquisition of Lonesome Lake Hut and the construction of Zealand Falls, Galehead, and Greenleaf Huts, expanded the existing huts, promoted the hut system throughout New England, and trained hut crews on managing the huts. Mizpah Spring Hut is the only addition to the hut system since Dodge retired. There are now eight backcountry huts in the White Mountains.

These huts are in wonderful locations and are spaced a day's hike from each other. They provide lodging, meals, and "mountain hospitality." Guests can participate in a naturalist walk and learn about local ecology and human history from displays, books, and members of the "croo." Kids can earn a junior naturalist badge. Snacks, hot drinks, and trail information are available during the day; overnight guests are served breakfast and dinner during the full-service season (see outdoors.org/lodging/huts for information on when certain huts are closed or self-service only). Reservations are required for an overnight stay. For more information or to make a reservation, call 603-466-2727 or visit outdoors. org/lodging/whitemountains.

Four huts make fine destinations for day hikes as well as overnight trips. Those are Lonesome Lake (Trip 16), Zealand Falls (Trip 37), Mizpah Spring (Trip 40), and Carter Notch (Trip 49). For cold-weather hiking, snowshoeing, and skiing enthusiasts, three of those four (Carter, Zealand, and Lonesome Lake) are open in winter on a self-service basis. All other huts close in September or October.

17

CLOUDLAND FALLS AND FRANCONIA RIDGE VIA FALLING WATERS, GREENLEAF, AND OLD BRIDLE PATH TRAILS

The hike across Franconia Ridge from Little Haystack Mountain to Mount Lafayette is one of the White Mountains' most spectacular long day hikes, providing some of the very best scenery in the Northeast. If you want a shorter hike, the portion from Falling Waters Trail to Cloudland Falls will satisfy everyone who loves the intoxicating sound of falling water within a cool, dense forest.

CAUTION The ridge has a 1.6-mile section above treeline fully exposed to the elements, so that part of this hike should be attempted only in good weather by hikers who are in good shape and have the proper gear.

DIRECTIONS

Falling Waters Trail departs from the Lafayette Place parking area in Franconia Notch State Park off the Franconia Notch Parkway (I-93). This is about 1.5 miles north of the Basin and 1.5 miles south of the Old Man of the Mountain site parking area. The parking area for this trail is on both sides of the highway, and which side you end up on depends on whether you are coming from the north or the south. The trail leaves from the east side of the parkway, which is where you park if you have been traveling north through Lincoln and Woodstock. If you are traveling south on the parkway, use the same exit as for the Lafayette Campground and park on the west side of the highway. You reach the trailhead through a tunnel underneath the highway. *GPS coordinates:* 44° 08.53' N, 71° 40.86' W.

LOCATION
Lincoln, NH, to Franconia, NH

RATING
Strenuous for the complete loop; Moderate with a few steep sections to Cloudland Falls

DISTANCE
9.0 miles for the complete loop; 2.6 miles round-trip to Cloudland Falls

ELEVATION GAIN
Mount Lafayette, 3,850 feet; Cloudland Falls, 800 feet

ESTIMATED TIME
7.0 hours for the complete loop; 2.0 hours round-trip to Cloudland Falls only

MAPS
AMC *White Mountain National Forest Map & Guide,* H4-5

AMC *White Mountain Guide,* 29th ed. Map 2 Franconia–Pemigewasset, H4-5

USGS Topo: Franconia

TRAIL DESCRIPTION

Falling Waters Trail as far as Cloudland Falls makes an excellent family hike and should be manageable by young children. It does have several stream crossings that could be challenging in high water. If you are considering hiking beyond the waterfalls up to and across the ridge to Greenleaf Trail, you should check with the hiker information booth at the trailhead for weather conditions above treeline (see caution statement above).

Leaving the parking area, the trail passes the hiker information kiosk and then runs together with Old Bridle Path for the first 0.2 mile. Falling Waters Trail then makes a sharp right turn and crosses Walker Brook on a bridge. The forest at this point is northern hardwoods, with lots of yellow birch, but it very quickly changes to red spruce, balsam fir, and Canadian hemlock as you continue to ascend. Spruce and fir go together in the forests of the White Mountains above 2,000 feet, and hemlocks are frequent denizens of cooler river valleys. The most common understory shrub is hobblebush. Clintonia, bunchberries, and mountain wood sorrel compose much of the herb layer.

Throughout the trail, jumbles of boulders that tumbled down the mountain in landslides form interesting caves that will appeal particularly to younger hikers. Ferns can be difficult to tell apart, but the mountain wood fern, found along this section of this trail, has some distinctive features for those willing to take a close look. A fern frond is equivalent to a leaf, and the mountain wood fern's frond is divided first into pinnae, and then each pinna into pinnules. The second pinnules on the lowest pinna are very uneven in size, such that the lower one hangs down quite a bit. Another feature of this and its close relatives is that its stipe (stem) is covered with rusty scales.

At 0.7 miles, the trail crosses Dry Brook on rocks (use care during high water, when Dry Brook is anything but dry), and then ascends the south bank to Stairs Falls. This is an ideal place to sit on a rocky ledge and enjoy the sounds of falling waters and the smells of the forest.

Continuing above Stairs Falls, the trail passes by some overhanging rocks (Sawtooth Ledges), and then crosses back to the north side of the brook (another potential challenge in high water) just below Swiftwater Falls, a beautiful 60-foot cascade. The trail then crosses a smooth rock slab and ascends past some boulders along the waterfall.

Beyond Swiftwater Falls, the trail continues on some switchbacks and along an old, gravelly logging road to the bottom of Cloudland Falls. Take a moment to enjoy the view looking up from the bottom of this 80-foot cascade, and then ascend a steep and rough segment of the trail to the top of the falls. Here there are views across Franconia Notch to Mount Moosilauke. From this vantage point, also note the two small waterfalls at almost right angles to each other. These are brooks from two different subwatersheds. The brook to the north drains the upper sections of Mount Lincoln, whereas the other drains Little Haystack. Their flows join together to form Dry Brook, which then tumbles down

Cloudland Falls and flows into the Pemigewasset River in Franconia Notch and eventually the Merrimack River.

This is the turnaround spot for the shorter hike. The trail continues more steeply through the boreal forest, crossing back and forth over the brook from Mount Lincoln. After the last crossing, about 0.3 mile beyond Cloudland Falls, the trail follows an old logging road, which takes it away from the stream. Leaving the logging road after about 0.3 mile, the trail ascends a series of switchbacks. At 2.8 miles, a spur trail leads to the right to Shining Rock. This huge, steeply sloped granite slab is usually covered with a thin layer of water, so walking out on it is not recommended because it can be very slippery and dangerous. You can stand at its edge and look across Franconia Notch to the Kinsman Range. This provides a nice break from the enclosed forest in which you have been walking so far.

Back on the main trail, the hike continues steeply through spruce and fir trees that are gradually becoming shorter, hinting that treeline is not far ahead. Falling Waters Trail reaches treeline and shortly thereafter ends in Franconia Ridge

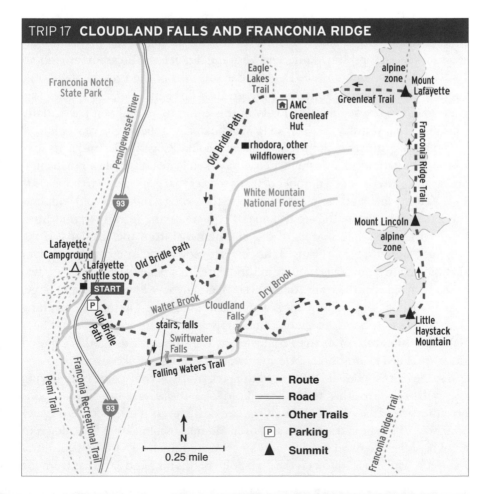

TRIP 17 **CLOUDLAND FALLS AND FRANCONIA RIDGE**

Franconia Notch State Park

Pemigewasset River

93

Eagle Lakes Trail

alpine zone

Mount Lafayette

Greenleaf Trail

AMC Greenleaf Hut

Old Bridle Path

rhodora, other wildflowers

White Mountain National Forest

Franconia Ridge Trail

Mount Lincoln

alpine zone

Lafayette Campground

Lafayette shuttle stop

Old Bridle Path

START

P

Old Bridle Path

Walter Brook

Cloudland Falls

Dry Brook

Little Haystack Mountain

Pemi Trail

Franconia Recreational Trail

93

stairs, falls

Swiftwater Falls

Falling Waters Trail

Franconia Ridge Trail

- - - Route
——— Road
······· Other Trails
P Parking
▲ Summit

N

0.25 mile

Trail at the summit of Little Haystack Mountain (3.4 miles, 4,760 feet). This is another possible turnaround spot.

The views from Little Haystack are wonderful, particularly on a clear day. Mount Lafayette, the highest point in the Franconia Range and the eventual destination for those continuing on, dominates the vista to the north. Looking east there is the Twin Range, Mount Bond, and the vast Pemigewasset Wilderness. Note the large number of bare areas on the mountain slopes, evidence of past landslides. To the south, Franconia Ridge Trail, outlined by cairns, follows the knife-edge ridge toward the sharp peaks of Mounts Liberty and Flume. The cliffs of Cannon Mountain are particularly prominent to the west across the glacially scoured valley that is Franconia Notch.

To continue the hike, turn left (north) on Franconia Ridge Trail, part of the Appalachian Trail. The next 1.6 miles of the hike is above treeline, with this spectacular view as your constant backdrop. It is also completely exposed to the elements, so if the weather is deteriorating, you should return via Falling Waters Trail and not attempt the ridge. In summer, thunderstorms can be particularly dangerous and have resulted in some fatalities.

The alpine zone of Franconia Ridge is one of New England's rarest communities, consisting of isolated "islands" of treeless habitat in the higher mountains of New Hampshire, Maine, and Vermont. Franconia Ridge contains about 1 square mile of alpine zone. The broader summits of the Presidential Range support about 7 square miles and the greatest diversity of alpine species (see page 260 for more details). The rarity of this community makes it particularly important that you stay on the trail to avoid damaging the fragile vegetation.

The most distinctive alpine plant on Franconia Ridge is diapensia. Its low, rounded growth form and small, densely packed leaves resemble a pincushion and are characteristic of a number of plant species that grow above treeline. This growth form enables these plants to survive the strong winds and cold temperatures that characterize the alpine zone. If you are hiking in early to mid-June, small, attractive white flowers of diapensia emerge from the cushions, if the wind or a late frost haven't caused the petals to blow away. Another showy plant that blooms in summer is mountain sandwort. This plant often forms borders along both sides of the trail. Alpine avens has showy yellow flowers and large, kidney-shaped leaves. This plant is endemic to the White Mountains, meaning that it grows only here (except for a small population on an island off Nova Scotia). Knee-high balsam fir trees contorted by the strong winds on this exposed ridge are called krummholz, a German word meaning "crooked wood."

Use the cairns (piles of stones used to mark trails) as your guide in following the trail. In clear weather, the trail is easy to follow because of the steep dropoffs on either side of the ridge, but the cairns can be lifesavers if thick clouds obscure your way. The trail takes you up and over Mount Lincoln (5,089 feet), down to a col between Mounts Lincoln and Lafayette, and finally up to the summit of Lafayette, which at 5,260 feet is the high point of this hike and 5.0 miles from the

The stunning vista along the Franconia Ridge Trail includes Mounts Lincoln, Liberty, and Flume. Photo by Jerry Monkman.

trailhead. Franconia Ridge Trail ends at the summit of Mount Lafayette, near the foundation of the old hotel that used to stand here.

The view from Mount Lafayette is one of the best in the White Mountains. Mount Garfield and its prominent cliff is the large peak to the east and slightly north of Mount Lafayette. Farther east, on a clear day, you can see Mount Washington and the other peaks of the Presidential Range. Lonesome Lake (Trip 16) is a prominent feature on a shoulder of the Kinsman Range to the west. Looking south, you see the whole length of Franconia Ridge, including the summits you just traversed.

From Mount Lafayette, descend to the west via Greenleaf Trail. This descends at a moderately steep grade with spectacular views of Eagle Lakes and AMC's Greenleaf Hut immediately below you and Cannon Mountain across Franconia Notch. In about 0.5 mile from the summit, you leave the alpine zone and enter an area of short spruce and fir trees. If it has been windy, this will provide a nice break.

Just before you reach Greenleaf Hut, you pass the two Eagle Lakes. These are tarns, a term used by geologists to describe glacially scoured lakes on the side of a mountain. It appears that these lakes are rapidly turning into bogs. If you look hard in the boggy areas alongside the trail, you can find cranberries. These are not the same species as the cranberries of commerce, but a species called small (or wren's egg) cranberries. Like their larger, lowland cousins, they grow as low, trailing vines in bogs and produce berries, but their leaves are tiny in comparison. Another interesting plant is three-leafed false Solomon's seal, similar to the false Solomon's seal (or Solomon's plume) of lowland forests except that it has three leaflets per stem.

AMC's Greenleaf Hut is perched on an open ridge at 4,200 feet at 6.1 miles (roughly 1.1 miles from the summit of Mount Lafayette). This is an ideal place to take a break, enjoy the views, get some refreshments, and perhaps use the restrooms. You can also read the educational displays about the ecology of the area.

From Greenleaf Hut, continue your descent on Old Bridle Path. The first mile of this trail follows open ridges from which there are great vistas of Walker Ravine on the side of Mount Lafayette and across Franconia Notch. Some parts are steep and require care with your footing. If you are hiking in late May through early June, the lovely pink flowers of rhodora, a type of rhododendron, will be in bloom along this upper section of Old Bridle Path. Unlike the rhododendron popular in landscaping, the leaves of this shrub are not evergreen, so the flowers actually come out before the leaves do. Another spring wildflower common along this section of Old Bridle Path is trailing arbutus (mayflower). This plant grows low to the ground and has clusters of small, very fragrant white flowers.

The flowers along this trail can be attractive to butterflies. During one hike, we were accompanied by large numbers of eastern swallowtail butterflies feasting on nectar from clintonia (bluebead lily) flowers.

At 7.4 miles (1.3 miles from Greenleaf Hut), the trail descends some stone steps, and you are back in the forest for the remainder of the hike. The grade is moderate for the rest of the way. At about 8.1 miles, you approach the edge of the ravine of Walker Brook. The trail continues to descend and reaches the junction with Falling Waters Trail along Walker Brook at 8.8 miles. Continue straight to your vehicle 2.9 miles from Greenleaf Hut to complete your 9.0-mile loop.

DID YOU KNOW?

If you guessed that Mount Lafayette was named for the Marquis de Lafayette, the French general who played a key role in the American Revolution, you would be right.

OTHER ACTIVITIES

Echo Lake in Franconia Notch State Park is a nice place to cool off and relax after your hike. The swimming area is a short drive north of the parking area.

Lafayette Place Campground (no dogs), across the highway from the trailhead, is a convenient place to camp.

Reservations are essential to stay overnight at Greenleaf Hut; outdoors.org/lodging/whitemountains; 603-466-2727.

MORE INFORMATION

The parking area (no fee) is in Franconia Notch State Park; nhstateparks.org/visit/state-parks/franconia-notch-state-park.aspx; 603-745-8391. Most of the trail is in the White Mountain National Forest (www.fs.usda.gov/whitemountain); 603-536-6100.

AMC's Hiker Shuttle stops at the trailhead; www.outdoors.org/lodging/lodging-shuttle.cfm; 603-466-2727.

Look for information on trail conditions and the weather at the hikers' kiosk at the base of this trail. An information volunteer is often at the kiosk.

The nearest stores and restaurants are on NH 112 in Lincoln to the south and on NH 18 in Franconia to the north.

AMC'S MOUNTAIN WATCH PROGRAM

AMC's Mountain Watch Program is a great way for hikers to collect scientific information on the ecological health of the White Mountains while enjoying their time in the mountains. Mountain Watch has two types of volunteers: plant monitors and visibility reporters. Hikers can volunteer as either or both. The program is relatively informal and does not require attendance at training sessions. Hikers are encouraged to participate by making observations during their regular outdoor experiences. Get more details, sign up for the program, take the online training, and download data forms to take with you on your hike at AMC's website (outdoors.org/mountainwatch).

Plant Monitors

As an outpost of arctic habitat in a relatively southern latitude, the alpine zone of the White Mountains is particularly vulnerable to climate change. By paying attention to whether certain flowers are in bloom during your hike along Franconia Ridge or in the Presidential Range, you can provide valuable information to scientists on how the anticipated climate change may be affecting this rare mountain community and the adjacent high-elevation spruce-fir forest. Phenology, the study of the timing of annual seasonal events in nature, is being used all over the world to examine how the natural world is responding to climate change. Citizen scientists have been recording the arrival times of birds in spring, when frogs start calling in spring, the timing of tree leaf-out, and now, through the efforts of AMC's scientific staff, the blooming times of high-elevation plants. A tendency toward flowering earlier in the year, if measured over decades, would indicate an effect of a warming climate.

Visibility Monitors

One of the obvious highlights of hiking in the White Mountains is to experience the spectacular vista from one of the many summits. Unfortunately, many observers report that the number of days with haze and limited visibility has increased in recent years. The haze is caused by fine particulates originating from coal-fired power plants (possibly from as far away as the Midwest) and automobile emissions. The haze not only detracts from the recreational experience of hikers but may also be harmful to health. Volunteers take photos when they arrive at their vista, and then describe their impressions of the view and whether haze affected their experience. Several of the AMC huts offer a view guide, on which volunteers can report.

OFF THE KANCAMAGUS HIGHWAY

The Kancamagus Highway (NH 112) is a scenic highway running east–west for about 35 miles between the
towns of Conway and Lincoln. It provides access to
many trails. The area is heavily wooded and particularly beautiful—and crowded—during fall color season. The highway follows the Swift River in its eastern
section and the East Branch of the Pemigewasset River
closer to Lincoln, so it is never far from rushing water.
Here you can enjoy waterfalls, mountain ponds, several small mountains that have excellent views for relatively little effort, and a number of 4,000-footers that
provide longer hikes. The White Mountain National
Forest maintains a number of picnic areas, campgrounds, and recreation areas along the highway.

The highway is named for an American Indian
who became chief of the Penacooks in 1685. Kancamagus (pronounced *kank-
a-maw-gus*) was the grandson of Passaconaway and the nephew of Won-
alancet, two other Penacook chiefs who had mountains named after them.
Angered by the continued intrusion of white settlers, Kancamagus led the last
uprising of the Penacooks. Eventually, he and the remainder of his tribe emi-
grated north to Canada.

SUPPLIES AND LOGISTICS

The Saco Ranger Station of the White Mountain National Forest is on the Kancamagus Highway at its eastern terminus at NH 16. The Lincoln Woods Ranger
Station is on the highway about 4 miles east of Lincoln. Stop in for trail information and to pick up the descriptive pamphlets for the guided nature hikes along
the highway. The ranger stations also have water, restrooms, and displays of the
local natural history. Trail information and restrooms can also be found at the
Passaconaway Historical Site, about 3 miles east of Sabbaday Falls. Restrooms
are located at the Rocky Gorge and Lower Falls scenic areas.

You won't find stores or gas stations along the Kancamagus Highway, so make sure you are well supplied with lunch, snacks, and gas before heading out. If you are coming from the east, Conway and North Conway have stores, gas stations, restaurants, motels, and other amenities. Along NH 16, south of Conway, there is a small general store in Chocorua and a few others between Chocorua and the Kancamagus Highway. If you approach from the west, there is a shopping center with a supermarket on NH 112 in Lincoln. Those coming from Crawford Notch will want to stop in Bartlett before traveling south on Bear Notch Road to the highway.

NEARBY CAMPING

The U.S. Forest Service maintains six campgrounds (more than 250 sites) and six picnic facilities spread conveniently along the Kancamagus Highway. White Ledge Campground (28 sites), also run by the national forest, is off NH 16 a few miles south of the highway. The campgrounds fill up on many summer weekends, so check at the information board on NH 112 just off I-93 in Lincoln (west end) or at the Saco Ranger Station (east end) for information on availability before you start your drive on the highway. You can reserve sites beforehand by calling 1-877-444-6777 (International 518-885-3639 or TDD 877-833-6777) or on the web at recreation.gov.

18

SABBADAY FALLS

The short (0.6-mile round-trip) walk to Sabbaday Falls off the Kancamagus Highway has been one of the most popular in the White Mountains ever since tourists started to frequent the region. The wide, flat trail with minimal elevation change is an ideal walk for families with very young children.

DIRECTIONS

The trailhead for Sabbaday Falls is on the south side of the Kancamagus Highway (NH 112), roughly 15 miles west of NH 16 near Conway and about 19 miles east of I-93 in Lincoln. For those coming through Crawford Notch or Bartlett, the trail is 3 miles west of the junction of Bear Notch Road with the Kancamagus Highway. The parking area, near the site of a former hotel, has space for about 30 vehicles. *GPS coordinates: 43° 59.84′ N, 71° 23.57′ W.*

TRAIL DESCRIPTION

Walk along Sabbaday Brook Trail from the parking area. The brook is bordered by hemlocks, but uphill from the brook the forest is northern hardwoods: American beech, sugar maple, and yellow birch. Hobblebush is the most abundant understory shrub.

Turn left at the sign for the falls at 0.3 mile. This is a short loop past the falls that rejoins the main trail. Very soon the loop passes a pool and an interesting small pothole. This pothole is perched above the current level of the brook, suggesting that it was created when water levels were higher than today. If it is filled with rainwater, look for mosquito larvae and other aquatic insects.

Ascend the stone stairs into the gorge created by the falls. It's easy to spend a long time watching the patterns of water rushing over granite ledges, through a narrow flume, and into deep, clear pools. The geological features that created this environment are described on interpretive signs.

LOCATION
Waterville Valley, NH

RATING
Easy

DISTANCE
0.6-mile loop

ELEVATION GAIN
100 feet

ESTIMATED TIME
0.5–1.0 hour

MAPS
AMC *White Mountain National Forest Map & Guide*, J8

AMC *White Mountain Guide*, 29th ed. Map 3 Crawford Notch–Sandwich Range, J8

USGS Topo: Mount Tripyramid, NH

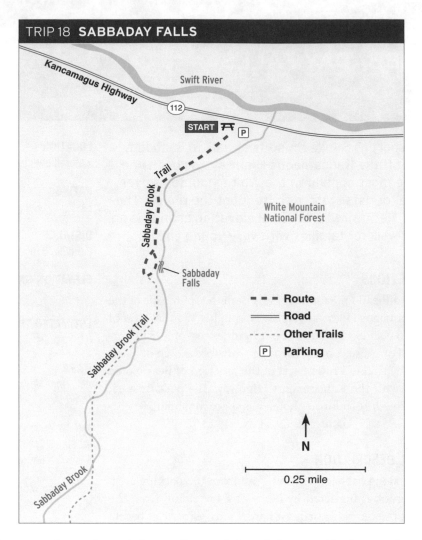

TRIP 18 SABBADAY FALLS

Kancamagus Highway

Swift River

112

START

P

Sabbaday Brook Trail

White Mountain
National Forest

Sabbaday
Falls

Sabbaday Brook Trail

- - - Route
═══ Road
· · · · Other Trails
P Parking

↑
N

0.25 mile

Sabbaday Brook

The gorge, the pools, and the small, rounded potholes in Sabbaday Brook were carved out by sand and small rocks carried by meltwater from the last continental glacier about 12,000 years ago. The floods that accompanied the melting of the glacier must have been tremendous, far surpassing anything we see today. Not only did the glacier unload vast volumes of water onto the landscape, but it also unloaded sand and gravel that, in combination with the fast currents, acted like sandpaper to grind down rocks, creating waterfalls, new stream channels, and pools.

The narrow, straight gorge, or flume, at Sabbaday Falls was formed by the same processes that created the Flume Gorge of Franconia Notch (Trip 11). A layer of basalt that had intruded into a crack in the granite wore away during the last Ice Age, leaving steep-sided granite walls 50 feet or so above the water. You can still see remnants of the gray-black basalt within the flume at its lower end where it enters the lower pool.

The loop crosses a bridge and goes past the upper pool. Both the lower and upper pools were formed by the scouring action of water melting from the glacial ice and during spring floods. Initially, the falls tumbled into the lower pool, but they eventually carved their way back through the basalt dike to form the

Sabbaday Falls, another example of a flume. Some of the basalt layer can be seen on the right. Photo by Jerry Monkman.

flume. The river now makes a sharp, 90-degree turn right below the upper falls where it followed a more easily eroded geological fault in the rocks that was at a right angle to the basalt dike.

At the deep upper pool you can get a feeling for the powerful erosive action of the grit-laden water by observing how the rock underwater has been carved away in a neat curve, creating an overhanging ledge. Keep in mind that the geological processes that created these marvels are still going on today, albeit at a slower rate than in the past because there is no glacial meltwater.

Just after the upper pool, the loop ends at the main trail. Turn right for the short walk back to the parking area.

DID YOU KNOW?

"Sabbaday" is an old New England way of referring to the Sunday Sabbath Day. The falls were named by settlers who were building a road through the area. It was a difficult task, and as winter approached they rested and left their tools near the falls on a Sunday before heading home.

OTHER ACTIVITIES

Enjoy a picnic before or after your walk at the Sabbaday Falls Picnic Area at the trailhead. You can combine this walk with one of the longer hikes off the Kancamagus Highway (Trips 23, 24, or 25) to make a full-day outing.

Sabbaday Brook Trail continues for several miles beyond the falls, ascending Mount Tripyramid. See AMC's *White Mountain Guide* for a description of the hike beyond the falls.

MORE INFORMATION

The trailhead and the falls are in the White Mountain National Forest. A user fee ($3 per day) is required; www.fs.usda.gov/whitemountain; 603-536-6100. The parking area has picnic tables and restrooms.

The nearest restaurants and other amenities are on NH 16 in Conway.

19

FOREST DISCOVERY TRAIL

Interpretive signs along Forest Discovery Trail describe different techniques used by the White Mountain National Forest to manage the forest for multiple uses. You can walk the easy 1.4-mile loop in an hour, or linger longer if you want to sit and enjoy the view of the forest and nearby mountains from one of the many benches placed along the trail.

DIRECTIONS

Forest Discovery Trail is off the Kancamagus Highway, 7.4 miles east of Exit 32 (Lincoln, NH 112) off I-93 and 2.3 miles east of the White Mountain National Forest's Visitor Center at the Lincoln Woods Trail. It is 0.1 mile east of Big Rock Campground on the north side of the highway. *GPS coordinates:* 44° 02.72′ N, 71° 33.34′ W.

TRAIL DESCRIPTION

Forest Discovery Trail is a wide, graded loop with a spur trail that is also a loop. Eleven stations with interpretive signs cover such topics as natural forest succession; selective cutting; maintaining openings for wildlife; and the values of riparian (riverside) forest, old growth, and managing for multiple-age stands. You can see examples of different management techniques along the trail.

The trail leaves the parking area and soon reaches the loop junction. Turn left, and walk along the trail as it gradually ascends. At 0.6 mile, you reach a clearing with a particularly nice view of Scar Ridge and Mount Osceola. This area was clear-cut (all trees were removed 15 to 25 years ago). Look for pin cherries (brick-red bark speckled with linear pores called lenticels), trembling aspen (smooth grayish-green bark), and young American beech (smooth pure-gray bark) growing in this clear-cut. Pin cherries and aspens are characteristic early successional trees that

LOCATION
Lincoln, NH

RATING
Easy

DISTANCE
1.4-mile loop

ELEVATION GAIN
150 feet

ESTIMATED TIME
1.0–2.0 hours

MAPS
AMC White Mountain National Forest Map & Guide, 16

AMC *White Mountain Guide,* 29th ed. Map 2 Franconia-Pemigewasset, 16

USGS Topo: Mount Osceola, NH

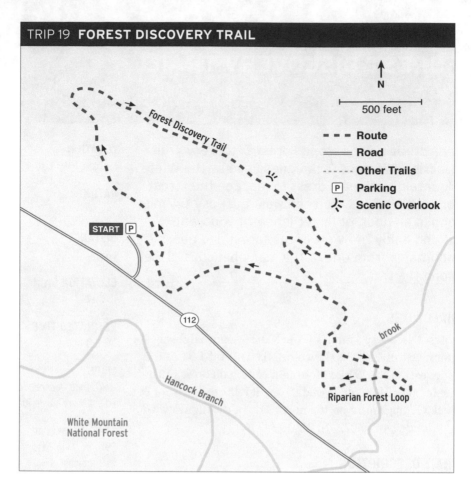

colonize recently disturbed areas, such as clear-cuts or burned areas. Eventually these two species give way to later successional species, such as American beech. Beech does have the ability to reproduce vegetatively from root suckers when cut, which is likely why there are so many young beeches at this spot.

At 0.8 mile, you reach a junction with a spur trail, a 0.3-mile loop. Turn left on this spur for a nice walk through a riparian forest. After crossing a bridge, take the left fork of the spur loop and follow it through small ups and downs. Canadian hemlock is the most common riparian tree in the White Mountains. The hobblebush leaves in the understory of this riparian forest are especially large.

Back at the spur loop junction, retrace your steps to the main trail. Turn left and follow it 0.2 mile back to the parking area.

DID YOU KNOW?

The effects of clear-cuts on wildlife depend on the species. Certain wildlife species, such as moose, deer, and bears, thrive in a mixture of different-aged forests and open land, rather than a continuous dense forest canopy. On the other hand, some mammals and many bird species of the White Mountains require uninterrupted forests.

OTHER ACTIVITIES

Forest Discovery Trail can be combined with one of the other walks off the Kancamagus Highway, such as Lincoln Woods Trail (Trip 21) and Greeley Ponds (Trip 22) for a longer outing.

MORE INFORMATION

This walk is within the White Mountain National Forest: www.fs.usda.gov/whitemountain; 603-536-6100. There is no fee for parking at this trailhead. The national forest visitor center at the Lincoln Woods Trail parking area, 2.3 miles west of here, has trail information and restrooms.

Learn about the history of forest management at the Forest Discovery Trail.

20

ROCKY GORGE AND LOVEQUIST LOOP AROUND FALLS POND

This short, easy hike takes you over a small gorge with swiftly moving water, and then around a quiet, scenic pond surrounded by conifers.

DIRECTIONS

Rocky Gorge Scenic Area is about 9.5 miles west of the intersection of the Kancamagus Highway (NH 112) and NH 16 just south of Conway village. The well-marked turnoff is about 2.0 miles west of the turnoff for Lower Falls, another scenic area. If you are coming from the Crawford Notch area, take US 302 to Bartlett, turn right onto Bear Notch Road, and then turn left (east) when you reach the Kancamagus Highway. The parking area for Rocky Gorge Scenic Area is on the left in about 3.5 miles. Space is available for about 40 vehicles. *GPS coordinates:* 44° 00.16' N, 71° 16.67' W.

TRAIL DESCRIPTION

From the parking area, walk northeast on the paved path along the river. Walk out on the rocks before the bridge for a nice view of the gorge in both directions. The walls of the canyon are mostly rectangular because granite fractures along definite joints. Notice too that the granite rocks are crisscrossed dikes of white pegmatite, an igneous "intrusion" that flowed into the cracks in the granite.

You can still find a few hearty plants hanging on to life despite the challenges of living where there is no obvious soil. Long beech ferns are especially impressive growing from cracks in the rocks on the vertical walls of the gorge. In depressions on the rocks that are filled with water, look for sweet gale (a shrub with sweet-smelling leaves covered by tiny yellow dots), red maple, woolgrass (a sedge with dropping clusters of brown, scaly flowers), and mosses. In cracks where a little soil has accumulated, you'll find

LOCATION
Albany, NH

RATING
Easy

DISTANCE
1.0-mile loop

ELEVATION GAIN
150 feet

ESTIMATED TIME
0.5-1.0 hour

MAPS
AMC *White Mountain National Forest Map & Guide,* 19

AMC *White Mountain Guide,* 29th ed. Map 3 Crawford Notch–Sandwich Range, 19

USGS Topo: Bartlett, NH

flat-topped asters, goldenrods, blueberries, and small white pines. Signs warn you not to swim at Rocky Gorge, as the strong currents in the gorge make it dangerous.

You reach the footbridge over Rocky Gorge in 0.1 mile. Cross the river, and then stroll up the graded path (with benches and interpretive signage) through hemlocks to get to the junction with Lovequist Loop Trail. Before beginning the loop, walk down to the edge of the pond for a nice view. Then head clockwise around the pond on Lovequist Loop Trail, a wide path mostly free of rocks and marked with yellow blazes. The ski trails that intersect this loop are marked with blue diamonds.

As you go up a small hill, note the bracken ferns along the path. These are robust ferns whose main stalks divide into three equal stalks. Unlike most other ferns, the bracken does not seem to mind drier habitats and thrives in sunny areas where the canopy of trees is thin. Also look for Indian cucumber-root, a lily with two tiers of whorled leaves. The top whorl supports creamy flowers in spring and black (inedible) berries later in the season.

Turn right at the next junction (straight ahead is Nanamocomuck Ski Trail), and head up a small hill onto an esker high above Falls Pond. The forest is dominated by tall red spruce with little understory vegetation. Red spruce is easily identified by looking at its needles—they are individually attached on twigs and feel decidedly prickly when you grab them. White pine, another common tree along this walk, has needles in bunches of five and the needles are flexible instead of stiff. Spruce needles are square in cross section; you can twirl them

Rocky Gorge, a great place to relax and be serenaded by flowing waters.

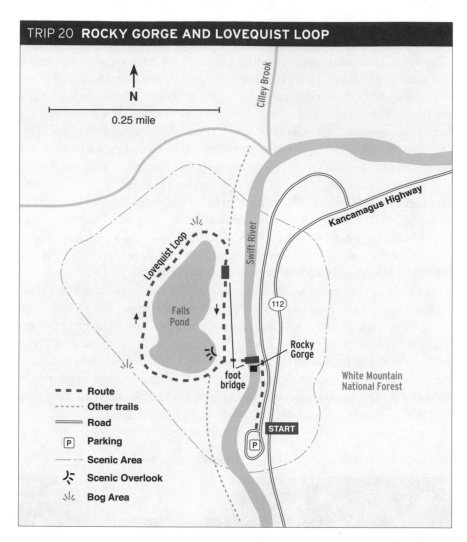

between your fingers, unlike the flat, untwirlable needles of hemlock and balsam fir. One way to remember all this is that to "spruce up" is to look sharp, just like spruce needles.

Red spruce is currently most abundant at midelevations (roughly 2,000 to 4,000 feet) in the White Mountains. The elevation of Falls Pond is only 1,100 feet, so you might wonder why it is so common here. Before there was widespread logging in the White Mountains, red spruce was a dominant part of the forest, even at lower elevations. Unfortunately for the spruce, they were preferred by many loggers, and the forests that replaced them often grew up in northern hardwoods rather than spruce. Take a moment to appreciate this great stand of spruce and the fact that it is apparently sustaining itself well.

The trail goes through a small section of hardwoods roughly halfway around the loop, and then the spruces return. Woodland wildflowers include goldthread, partridgeberry, flowering wintergreen, clintonia (bluebead lily), and pink lady's slipper (blooms in mid-June).

Two short spur trails give you access to the pond shore. Take either or both for a view of the pond and for exploring its shore life. Dragonflies patrol the shoreline, flying back and forth looking for insect prey, for mating opportunities, and to defend their territories. The most striking of the dragonflies are the large darners, voracious predators with very large eyes and patterns of bluish green stripes and blue speckles on their bodies. The shrubs growing in damp, boggy habitats along the pond shore include sweet gale, Labrador tea (rusty-brown fuzz on the undersides of leaves), leatherleaf (rusty scales on the undersides of leaves), sheep laurel, and huckleberry. Red maples, famous for their brilliant, red fall foliage, thrive in the wet areas as well. In the shallow water of the pond are pipeworts, plants that look like hatpins.

At the south end of the pond, the trail crosses over a stream surrounded by a wetland with lots of sphagnum moss (illustrated here). Sphagnum thrives here because the topography does not allow water to drain. Sphagnum moss soaks up water like a sponge and creates acidic conditions in the bog by secreting hydrogen ions. It is the peat moss that we use to condition the soil in our gardens.

Soon after, follow an arrow directing you back to Rocky Gorge. A solid wooden bridge crosses the outlet from the pond (look for white turtlehead flowers in late summer). At the end of the loop, turn left to return to Rocky Gorge and your vehicle.

OTHER ACTIVITIES

Lovequist Loop Trail provides access to Lower Nanamocomuck Ski Trail, a novice-level trail that runs from the Covered Bridge Campground to Bear Notch Road. It connects with more-advanced ski trails.

You can go swimming in the Swift River 2 miles east at the Lower Falls area. Fishing in the pond and along the river requires a New Hampshire fishing license.

MORE INFORMATION

This hike is within the White Mountain National Forest. A user fee ($3 per day) is required; www.fs.usda.gov/whitemountain; 603-536-6100. You'll find restrooms at the parking area.

21

LINCOLN WOODS TRAIL TO BLACK POND AND/OR FRANCONIA FALLS

Lincoln Woods Trail provides easy access to the Pemigewasset Wilderness, a vast protected area in the heart of the White Mountains. It follows the west bank of the East Branch of the Pemigewasset River. Explore Black Pond, a quiet and peaceful pond framed by mountains, and Franconia Falls, an exciting rush of water over rocks.

DIRECTIONS

Lincoln Woods Trail is off the Kancamagus Highway (NH 112), 5.0 miles east of Exit 32 (NH 112, Lincoln) on I-93, just beyond the Hancock Campground. The U.S. Forest Service operates a visitor center at the trailhead, so you can stop in to talk with the rangers about trail conditions and pick up brochures on this and other trails. *GPS coordinates:* 44° 3.84′ N, 71° 35.32′ W.

TRAIL DESCRIPTION

Lincoln Woods Trail is a great trail for anyone who does not like hiking uphill or on rocks but still wants to go for a long walk in the forest. It is straight and wide, and you can often see what seems like at least a half-mile ahead. The elevation gain is imperceptible. The railroad bed along which this trail was built once brought loggers and devastation to the region—sparks from a train engine ignited a devastating forest fire here (see page 187). The seemingly pristine forests and mountains you now experience along this hike are a tribute to the regenerative powers of nature. The trail is heavily used, both by day-hikers and backpackers.

From the national forest visitor center at the trailhead, take the stairs down to the river, cross the East Branch of the Pemigewasset River on a suspension bridge, and then turn right. Lincoln Woods Trail never strays far from the

LOCATION
Lincoln, NH

RATING
Moderate (easy trail but relatively long)

DISTANCE
6.8 miles round-trip to Black Pond, 6.6 miles to Franconia Falls, 8.0 miles to both

ELEVATION GAIN
Black Pond, 500 feet

ESTIMATED TIME
3.0–5.0 hours, depending on route

MAPS
AMC White Mountain National Forest Map & Guide, I5

AMC *White Mountain Guide,* 29th ed. Map 2 Franconia–Pemigewasset Range, I5

USGS Topo: Mount Osceola, NH

river, which will be your constant companion on your right. For the next 2.6 miles, you'll walk on a wide, straight, flat, old logging railroad bed still studded with well-preserved railroad ties made from local hemlock. Sometimes iron rails and spikes are present, and there are places where you can see old stone bridge abutments. (Note: It is illegal to disturb any artifacts.)

Note the influence of Hurricane Irene in 2011—such as a washout of the riverbank, uprooted trees, and a bypass—at about 0.75 mile. At 1.4 miles, Osseo Trail diverges to the left for Mount Flume and Franconia Ridge at a point where a stream also comes in from the left. Just beyond this junction, a small field on the west side of the trail provides a little diversion. This was the site of an old logging camp. It is a good place to look for butterflies fluttering around goldenrod on a sunny summer day. At 1.7 miles, Lincoln Woods Trail closely approaches the riverbank. Stop here to admire the river and the view of Bondcliff. Shortly after that, the trail crosses Birch Island Brook, a tributary of the East Branch. Black Pond Trail departs to the left at 2.6 miles (see below for that destination). Lincoln Woods Trail then passes through the former Franconia Brook tentsite, which has been relocated to Pemi East Side Trail on the other side of the river.

Franconia Falls makes a fine destination from the Lincoln Woods Trail.

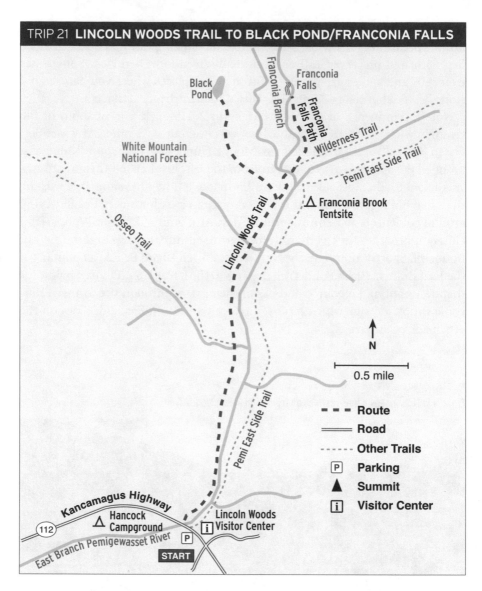

Black
Pond

Franconia
Falls

Franconia Branch

Franconia
Falls Path

Wilderness Trail

Pemi East Side Trail

White Mountain
National Forest

△ Franconia Brook
Tentsite

Lincoln Woods Trail

Osseo Trail

N

0.5 mile

- - - **Route**

═══ **Road**

········ **Other Trails**

P **Parking**

▲ **Summit**

i **Visitor Center**

Pemi East Side Trail

Kancamagus Highway

△ Hancock
Campground

Lincoln Woods
i Visitor Center

112

East Branch Pemigewasset River

P

START

Lincoln Woods Trail officially ends at a stone wall at 2.9 miles. The spur trail to Franconia Falls departs to the left. (Straight ahead, the main trail crosses Franconia Brook on a suspension bridge and continues through the Pemigewasset Wilderness, providing access to a host of backcountry trails and camping opportunities.)

For Black Pond

The first part of the trail to Black Pond is an old spur from the railroad that passes the ice pond used by the logging camps. This pond is rapidly becoming a marsh, and you need to be careful to follow the yellow blazes where flooding has forced the trail to be relocated. The trail follows the northeast bank above Birch Island Brook for about 0.2 mile. It then crosses several small streams and passes the outlet to Black Pond, where there is a nice view of Owl's Head. It reaches Black Pond 0.7 mile from Lincoln Woods Trail at a terrific sitting rock.

Black Pond is framed by a dense spruce-fir forest and by views of Bondcliff and West Bond. With a little bushwhacking, you can explore more of the shoreline and see other mountains, such as Owl's Head. It is a wonderfully peaceful place, where dragonflies patrol over the water and trout swim. You might even see a moose. Their tracks can be obvious in a grassy marsh northwest of the "sitting rock." The shoreline vegetation includes red and green sphagnum mosses, meadowsweet, leatherleaf, and Labrador tea. These plants, along with steeplebush and sedges, also occur around the marsh at the fringes of the ice pond.

For Franconia Falls

Follow Franconia Falls Trail, which leads to the left at the stone wall marking the end of Lincoln Woods Trail. Just when you start this spur trail to the falls, look for a patch of helleborine orchids on the right. These 2-foot-tall plants have broad, lilylike leaves ascending their stems and a spike of small, greenish orchid flowers at the top. Many orchids are vulnerable to collectors, who seek them out for their beauty or rarity. Helleborine orchids are different.

Though native to Europe, they are established and fairly common in the United States. Just beyond the orchids, a yellow birch with a long limb over the brook provides an irresistible photo opportunity.

Continuing on, it is a short, mostly level walk to Franconia Falls (0.4 mile). You'll find plenty of flat sitting rocks spread out over about 50 yards along the brook, so you can enjoy a number of perspectives of the falls. The smooth granite ledges and chutes of water make this a popular spot for swimming and sunning in summer, so you are likely to have lots of company. Along the edge of the brook at the falls, look for speckled alder (rounded, toothed leaves; branchlets with speckles; and cone-like fruits), northern wild raisin (a viburnum with opposite leaves), hobblebush, white pine, and red spruce. One of the largest trembling aspens you will ever see grows along the spur trail opposite the largest cascade. Normally this tree is about 30 to 40 feet tall and has smooth, grayish-green bark. The specimen growing near Franconia Falls is more than 50 feet tall, and its bark is gray but deeply furrowed. When trees are allowed to grow old, they often take on characteristics different from those of younger specimens. Hopefully, this process will be a common occurrence in the Pemigewasset Wilderness for years to come.

Retrace your steps to return to the trailhead.

OTHER ACTIVITIES

Pemi East Side Trail, also called the East Branch Truck Road, departs from the same trailhead and follows along the east bank of the river. You can make a pleasant loop of about 3.0 miles by combining it with Pine Island Trail, a short trail that departs to the left from Pemi East Side Trail at 0.6 mile and rejoins it at 1.4 miles.

You might be tempted to do a longer loop hike and connect up with Lincoln Woods Trail at its terminus in the wilderness area, but keep in mind that there is no bridge for crossing back to Lincoln Woods Trail at that point. Fording the river is at best a nuisance and at worst dangerous if water levels are high.

Because it is flat, wide, and has no hills, Lincoln Woods Trail is excellent for novice cross-country skiers. Intermediate skiers will prefer Pemi East Side Trail (described above) on the other side of the river. This trail has some hills that provide more of a challenge than Lincoln Woods Trail. Both trails are groomed by the Forest Service. Dogs are allowed.

Fishing in the East Branch is allowed with a New Hampshire fishing license. You can swim and wade in pools below Franconia Falls.

MORE INFORMATION

Lincoln Woods Trail is in the White Mountain National Forest; www.fs.usda .gov/whitemountain; 603-536-6100. A user fee ($3 per day) is required for parking at the trailhead.

LOGGING IN THE PEMIGEWASSET WILDERNESS

Logging has had a major impact on the forest around Lincoln Woods Trail and many other sections of the White Mountains. The area that is now called the Pemigewasset Wilderness was still an undisturbed wilderness known only to hunters, trappers, and a few hikers when logging baron J.E. Henry purchased the logging rights in 1892. Henry's company had been busily laying waste to the Zealand Valley since 1880 (see Trip 37), and this purchase was an expansion of his empire. He built the East Branch and Lincoln Railroads, which started in Lincoln, followed the present course of the Kancamagus Highway, and then turned north to follow the East Branch of the Pemigewasset River. One logging camp was built near the present site of the White Mountain National Forest's Visitor Center on the Kancamagus Highway and another near the junction of Lincoln Woods Trail and the spur trail to Black Pond.

At the present site where Lincoln Woods Trail ends, the railroad split into two branches, one continuing north along Franconia Brook and the other heading east along the East Branch of the Pemigewasset River. The former is now Franconia Brook Trail and the latter Bondcliff Trail. These two rail lines were further divided like branches of a tree as J.E. Henry's company expanded deeper into the wilderness. Along with the rail lines came more logging camps.

On weekends, the railroads carried tourists into the mountains to sightsee, visit the logging camps, and pick blueberries. Hikers, hunters, and fishers also used the railroad to gain access to the backcountry.

The logging operations laid waste to the area, and it came to be known as the "so-called Pemigewasset Wilderness." In 1917, J.E. Henry's son sold the land to Parker-Young, another logging company. Parker-Young sold the land to the U.S. government in the 1930s, but retained logging rights through 1946. The railroad ceased operating in 1948. The Pemigewasset Wilderness, encompassing 45,000 acres, began to recover from the logging and was officially designated a wilderness area by an act of Congress in 1984.

The large numbers of white birch, which thrive in recently logged areas, are evidence that this is second-growth forest. Along Lincoln Woods Trail, the typical vegetation is a canopy of northern hardwoods, but in many places the understory is dominated by conifers, particularly red spruce. Eventually the spruce will reclaim their dominant place in the region.

22
GREELEY PONDS

Set dramatically near the height of Mad River Notch between Mounts Osceola and Kancamagus, the Greeley Ponds are classic mountain ponds bordered by rugged slopes that descend abruptly to the shoreline. They are reached by a relatively easy trail that crosses numerous split-log bridges.

DIRECTIONS

The parking area for Greeley Ponds Trail is on the south side of the Kancamagus Highway (NH 112) at a hairpin turn in the road about 9.0 miles east of I-93 in Lincoln. The lot is small and, given the popularity of this trail, it may be full. Parking is also available about 0.25 mile to the west where the cross-country ski trail begins. This trail is also marked with a sign for Greeley Ponds. If you park at the ski trail lot, walk along the road to get to the hiking trailhead. (The ski trail can be covered in knee-deep mud during hiking season.)

If you are heading west on the Kancamagus Highway, the trailhead is about 0.25 mile west of the Hancock Scenic Overlook. The distance from NH 16 in Conway is about 25.0 miles. *GPS coordinates:* 44° 01.89′ N, 71° 31.01′ W.

TRAIL DESCRIPTION

The Greeley Ponds can easily provide a full day of swimming, picnicking, and fishing. The ponds are a popular destination, so do not expect solitude in summer. The trail is heavily eroded due to years of tramping by hiking boots. You'll find lots of exposed tree roots and mud, particularly in the first section. The wettest sections are bridged.

Greeley Ponds Trail is marked with yellow blazes, which helps you stay on course wherever the cross-country ski trail intersects the hiking trail. (The ski trail is marked with blue diamonds.) The trail starts out in a dense forest

LOCATION
Lincoln, NH, at trailhead; Livermore, NH, at destination

RATING
Moderate

DISTANCE
3.2 miles round-trip to the upper pond, or 4.6 miles to both ponds

ELEVATION GAIN
450 feet

ESTIMATED TIME
2.0–4.0 hours

MAPS
AMC *White Mountain National Forest Map & Guide,* 16

AMC *White Mountain Guide,* 29th ed. Map 3 Crawford Notch–Sandwich Range, 16

USGS Topo: Mount Osceola, NH

of balsam fir and soon crosses over two streams and a number of small wet-lands on a series of wooden bog bridges. The trail continues gradually uphill and enters the Greeley Ponds Scenic Area at the height-of-land in Mad River Notch 1.3 miles from the trailhead, where Mount Osceola Trail comes in from the right. (Mount Osceola Trail climbs very steeply to East Osceola peak and is one of the more challenging hikes in the White Mountains.)

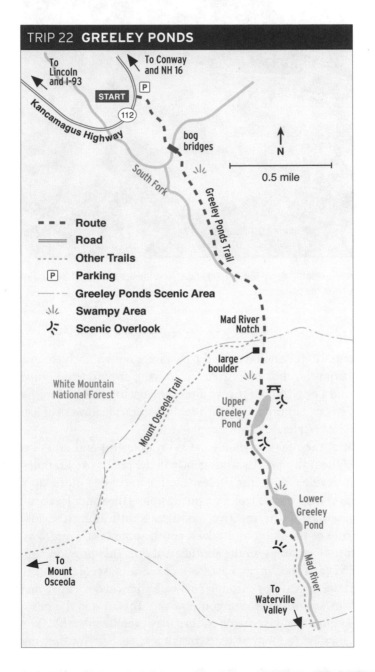

Ebony jewelwing, a colorful damselfly you can find around the Greeley Ponds, particularly where small streams enter the ponds.

Just beyond this junction, you will pass a huge boulder, which probably tumbled down from the cliffs of East Peak. Growing around this boulder are a big balsam fir and a birch whose trunks almost merge together as they twist around each other. In late summer, look for the showy, purple flowers of New England asters near the boulder.

Stay right at the next fork (with the ski trail again) and cross over another bog bridge. The trail then descends gently to the ponds. At 1.6 miles (1.0 to 1.5 hours), a short side path to the left leads to the north end of the upper pond. A flat, sandy area here is excellent for a picnic unless the water levels are too high.

After enjoying this perspective, continue south along the main trail to the south side of the pond and take a short, somewhat overgrown side trail leading left to open areas on the southeast shore. This provides a particularly impressive vista of the craggy East Peak of Mount Osceola. You get a sense of how the glacier that swept through this valley plucked rocks from the side of the mountain, creating the cliff you now see. This also is the best place for a swim. By August, the water temperature may even be tolerable. Watch out for snags in the water. You may also discover a few leeches—or they may discover you—but don't let them deter you. They are generally small and won't likely bother you if you keep moving.

The snags that stick out of the water are terrific perching spots for ebony jewelwings and several different species of dragonflies. Ebony jewelwings, also called black-winged damselflies, are boldly marked with unmistakable electric-green bodies and black wings, striking colors that would be right at home in a tropical jungle rather than this relatively cold region. Damselflies hold their wings vertically when at rest, unlike dragonflies, which hold their wings horizontally.

It takes 10 to 20 minutes along Greeley Ponds Trail to hike from the south end of the upper pond to the lower pond, depending upon how much time you spend enjoying the rich assortment of wildflowers in this section of the trail. You'll see lots of clintonia, goldthread, painted trillium, hobblebush, rosy and clasping-leaved twisted stalks, sharp-leaved asters, and rattlesnake roots (the last having big leaves in three parts and drooping, greenish flowers in late summer). Snowberries, whose tiny rounded leaves smell like wintergreen when crushed, are particularly abundant at the side trail of the south end of the upper pond. In wet swales there are white turtleheads, sedges, sphagnum moss, and hobblebush. Look for blue-colored algae growing on damp, moldy wood, the bright blue looking more like paint than a living thing.

The lower Greeley Pond is about 100 feet lower in elevation than the upper pond. The vistas from its two vantage points (the best is from a small cove near a stand of paper birch at its southwest corner) are not as dramatic as those of the upper pond. Lower Greeley Pond is too shallow for swimming, but it is equally interesting from a natural history perspective. Look for evidence of beaver activity, particularly lots of standing dead trees in the water indicating recent flooding.

At the north end of the lower pond there is a boggy area with lots of sphagnum moss. Leatherleaf, Labrador tea, tall meadow rue, and sweet gale are the most obvious shrubs, and cotton grass, white turtleheads, marsh Saint-John's-Wort, bog club moss, and twig rush are the most common nonwoody plants. Cotton grass, actually a type of sedge, has dense balls of white, cottony hairs that surround its inconspicuous flowers. Its other name is hare's tail.

Inspect the sphagnum mats for sundews, tiny plants whose rounded leaves are bordered with sticky hairs that trap insects. Bogs are low in nutrients, so the sundew feeds itself in a very unplantlike way: by catching and digesting insects. Be careful to avoid trampling the sphagnum when you hunt for sundews.

Retrace your steps for the return trip, but be careful at the various intersections with the ski trail. Just beyond the big rock, make sure you stay right at a fork or the ski trail might take you to Osceola Trail. If you find yourself ascending very steeply, turn around and walk back to the junction of Greeley Ponds Trail.

DID YOU KNOW?

The Greeley Ponds were named for Nathaniel Greeley, who ran an inn in Waterville Valley in the nineteenth century, when the valley was still a quiet, secluded place. He was one of the pioneer trail builders in this part of the White Mountains.

OTHER ACTIVITIES

A moderately difficult cross-country ski trail parallels the hiking trail and crosses it in several places. Dogs are not permitted on the ski trail.

Greeley Ponds Trail can also be approached from Waterville Valley. With two vehicles, you could walk or ski the whole trail from the Kancamagus Highway to Waterville Valley (or vice versa). At the time of this writing, the section of the trail between Waterville Valley and the ponds was subject to midweek closures due to trail maintenance work, so check on trail conditions before planning to do this.

Swimming and fishing (New Hampshire fishing license required) are possible at Greeley Ponds.

MORE INFORMATION

The trail is in the White Mountain National Forest; www.fs.usda/whitemountain; 603-536-6100. A user fee ($3 per day) is required for parking at the trailhead. Dogs are allowed, with the exception of the ski trail.

The nearest restaurants and other services are on NH 112 in Lincoln, about 8 miles west of the trailhead.

23

BOULDER LOOP TRAIL

Boulder Loop Trail passes jumbles of boulders during its 1,000-foot ascent to rocky ledges on a shoulder of the Moat Range. Here there are fine views across the Swift River Valley to a number of 4,000-foot peaks south of the Kancamagus Highway.

DIRECTIONS

Boulder Loop Trail is 6.0 miles west of the intersection of the Kancamagus Highway (NH 112) and NH 16 in Conway. Turn right at the sign to the Covered Bridge Campground on Passaconaway (formerly Dugway) Road and drive through the Albany Covered Bridge (constructed in 1858, renovated in 1970). Park in the first parking area beyond the bridge and find the trailhead at the north side of the road. In winter the bridge is closed to vehicles, so you'll need to park before the bridge.

If you are coming from the Crawford Notch area, take US 302 to Bartlett. Turn right onto Bear Notch Road, and then turn left (east) when you reach the Kancamagus Highway. Passaconaway (Dugway) Road is about 6.0 miles east.

Space is available for about twenty vehicles in the parking area. *GPS coordinates:* 44° 00.30′ N, 71° 14.35′ W.

TRAIL DESCRIPTION

This loop trail is appropriate for younger hikers who have some experience on trails or for those who can be easily carried in a backpack. Boulder Loop Trail is marked by yellow blazes. The loop, which I describe in the clockwise direction, begins 0.2 mile from the parking area.

Turn left, and you soon pass the first large group of boulders. These and the others you see along this trail were formed by landslides. You'll find two especially huge

LOCATION
Albany, NH

RATING
Moderate

DISTANCE
3.1-mile loop

ELEVATION GAIN
950 feet

ESTIMATED TIME
2.0–4.0 hours

MAPS
AMC *White Mountain National Forest Map & Guide*, 110

AMC *White Mountain Guide*, 28th ed. Map 3 Crawford Notch–Sandwich Range, 110

USGS Topo: North Conway West

boulders, one with a crack in it that forms a cave and another covered with rock-tripe lichens, which look a bit like flakes of shoe leather.

The trail starts to ascend through a forest of northern hardwoods (sugar maples, American beech, and yellow birch) with an understory dominated by hobblebush and striped maple. Common woodland wildflowers include Canada mayflower, clintonia, pink lady's slipper, false Solomon's seal, spikenard, wild sarsaparilla, silverrod, various goldenrods, shinleaf, and whorled wood-aster. See if you can find white ash, a broad-leafed tree whose leaves are composed of many leaflets and arranged in pairs along the twigs. Its wood is used for baseball bats. One of the white ashes and some of the pines are riddled with large holes hammered out by pileated woodpeckers, the largest woodpecker in the United States.

As you continue to ascend, you will notice increasing numbers of red spruce, indicating a transition to the boreal forest. After about 0.7 mile, the trail passes an opening that provides the first vista out over the valley and across to ledges. At this and other clearings, the spruce are largely replaced by red oak and white pine, two species that survive better than spruce in drier, sunnier, warmer areas such as these low-elevation open ledges. At 1.3 miles (another 20 minutes), you reach a sign reading "To the View, 0.2 mile." Follow the short spur trail up the stone steps that take you to the ledges. The spur trail extends in the open for about 0.3 mile. The views are all superb, but don't get too close to the edge, particularly if it's rainy, because the dropoff is steep.

At 1,965 feet, these ledges are the highest elevation on the trail. On a clear day you can see Mounts Chocorua, Passaconaway, and Middle Sister, and the Tripyramids. Immediately below is the valley of the Swift River. This river is a tributary of the Saco River, which flows into the Atlantic Ocean in southern Maine. The ecology at the ledges differs from the lower forest, partly because the thin soil supports only a few trees. Like the clearings described earlier, this area receives more sunlight and is drier, so red oaks and white pines are mixed in with some red spruce. Note how the white pines have relatively short needles, possibly an adaptation to reduce water loss in this wind-exposed location. Mountain ash, a small tree of the boreal forest with distinct

A bracket fungus caught the attention of this young hiker.

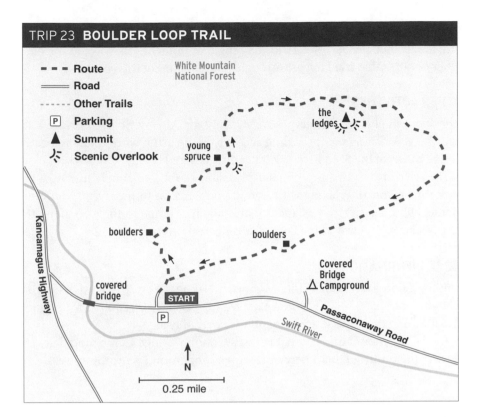

Route
Road
Other Trails
P **Parking**
▲ **Summit**
〳 **Scenic Overlook**

White Mountain
National Forest

the
ledges ▲ 〳 ■

young
spruce ■ 〳

boulders ■

boulders ■

Covered
Bridge
△ Campground

covered
bridge

START

P

Kancamagus Highway

Swift River

Passaconaway Road

↑
N

0.25 mile

compound leaves, is common on the ledges. Mountain ash is really not an ash at all, but a relative of apples and pears. In June it displays showy white flowers; in late summer, its red berries, borne in flat-topped clusters, are relished by birds. Its twigs are a favorite food of moose. Low shrubs at the ledges include lowbush blueberries, shadbush, and dwarf juniper. Wildflowers include goldenrods and cow-wheat. Reindeer lichen—a pale-green, bushy lichen—forms an ornate border around trees and shrubs, giving the feel of a rock garden.

A large yellow spot marks the point where you turn around. Look for bristly sarsaparilla, a thorny relative of the more common wild sarsaparilla, near this yellow spot. After backtracking to the main trail, turn right for the 1.0-hour descent. Just below the ledges, you pass a huge rock that is at least as large as ten blue whales. The descent is particularly rich in hobblebush (colorful berries in late summer) and spinulose wood fern. The trail continues downhill, crosses a small stream, and enters another area of huge boulders strewn by a landslide 2.3 miles from the trailhead. An overhanging rock is a good place to get out of the rain and still be able to sit on a flat rock. Beyond this, the trail flattens out and traverses a few small streams. At the loop junction, go straight to return to the parking area.

DID YOU KNOW?

The name "hobblebush" refers to the tangle of branches that would hobble a hiker or horse that tried to pass through a dense stand of this shrub.

OTHER ACTIVITIES

Check out the historical interpretive signs by the Albany Covered Bridge after your hike. A fishing pier providing access to those using wheelchairs is located on the banks of the Saco River right near the covered bridge.

The river in this area is a popular place for wading, or simply finding a flat rock for a picnic or relaxing with a good book. Access to the river, swimming, picnic tables, and restrooms are available about 1.0 mile to the west along the Kancamagus Highway at the Lower Falls Recreation Area.

MORE INFORMATION

Boulder Loop Trail is in White Mountain National Forest (www.fs.usda.gov/whitemountain; 603-536-6100). A user fee ($3 per day) is required for parking and for using the day-use area around the covered bridge.

The White Mountain National Forest's Covered Bridge Campground is very close to the trailhead. Blackberry Crossing Campground is nearby as well.

24

UNH TRAIL TO HEDGEHOG MOUNTAIN

This loop trail takes you to the summit of 2,532-foot Hedgehog Mountain. Three outlooks provide terrific vistas of 4,000-foot peaks and also have some interesting wildflowers.

DIRECTIONS

The trailhead for UNH Trail is on the south side of the Kancamagus Highway, about 15.0 miles west of its intersection with NH 16, just south of Conway. It is also the trailhead for the Downes Brook and Mount Potash trails. Turn left (south) on a gravel road opposite the Passaconaway Campground to find the trailhead. For those coming from Crawford Notch or Lincoln, the trailhead is about 1.0 mile west of the intersection of the Kancamagus Highway and Bear Notch Road. *GPS coordinates: 43° 59.66' N, 71° 22.17' W.*

TRAIL DESCRIPTION

UNH Trail should be hiked only when the weather is good, for two reasons: First, the ledges around the summit could be hazardous in wet or icy weather; and second, you don't want to miss the views, which on a clear day extend as far as the Presidential Range. The elevation gain is mostly gradual, with a few short, steep sections. Some sections of the trail have recently been rerouted due to extensive damage caused by Hurricane Irene in 2011.

Leaving the parking area, the trail passes a small pond, runs with the Downes Brook and Mount Potash trails for about 60 yards, then turns left and enters the forest. Look for an attractive, dark-green, dense growth of common haircap moss growing near rocks at the point where the trail enters the forest. Named for the hairs that cover the cap on its spore case, this widespread species is one of the most distinctive mosses in New England, looking like tiny spruce trees.

LOCATION
Albany, NH

RATING
Moderate, with some steep sections

DISTANCE
4.8-mile loop

ELEVATION GAIN
1,450 feet

ESTIMATED TIME
3.5–5.0 hours

MAPS
AMC *White Mountain National Forest Map & Guide,* J8

AMC *White Mountain Guide,* 28th ed. Map 3 Crawford Notch–Sandwich Range, J8

USGS Topo: Mount Chocorua, NH

The East Ledges of Hedgehog Mountain affords a fine view of Mount Passaconaway and other nearby peaks.

The trail is well marked with yellow blazes and signs. After 0.2 mile on an old railroad bed, the hiking trail turns right (a ski trail continues straight). Continuing along an old logging road in a spruce forest, UNH Trail crosses another ski trail at 0.3 mile, heads moderately uphill, and reaches the loop junction at 0.8 mile (20 minutes). There is a large (approximately 7-acre) clear-cut to the east that will provide nice views of mountains to the north and some good blackberry picking in season until it grows back. Signs placed by the Forest Service describe the rationale for the clear-cut: removing timber heavily damaged by Hurricane Irene and providing habitat for birds and mammals that thrive in early successional habitats such as shrublands. Blackberries, raspberries, and pin cherry are characteristic of clear-cut areas.

I recommend hiking the loop clockwise by taking the left fork. This provides a more gradual ascent to the East Ledges, which provide the most extensive views. However, if you are short on time and still want to get to one of the vistas, take the right fork of the loop and go as far as Allen's Ledge, 0.3 mile from the junction.

For the complete loop, turn left and follow this new section of the trail. After about 10 minutes of almost-level hiking through northern hardwoods (mostly yellow birch and American beech), the trail turns right onto the original section of the trail and starts ascending. Look for understory plants such as hobblebush, heart-leafed aster, Indian cucumber-root, Solomon's seal, Indian pipes, and shiny club moss.

At 1.6 miles, the trail descends into a small ravine, crosses a brook (could be dry in late summer), and then begins to ascend more steeply. Note the rather abrupt change from the northern hardwood forest to a red spruce forest. The trail comes out on the East Ledges (2.1 miles, about 1 hour, 40 minutes). The East

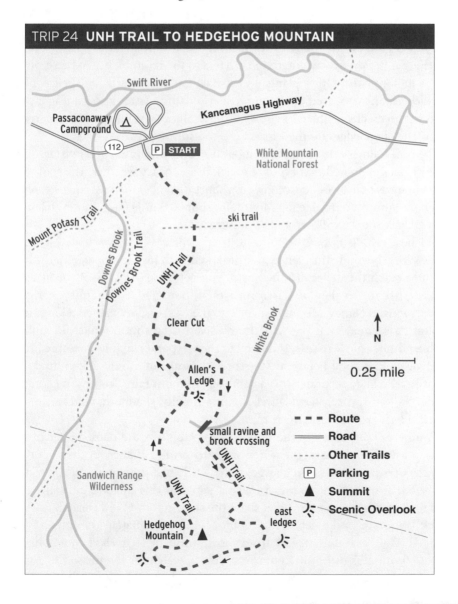

TRIP 24 **UNH TRAIL TO HEDGEHOG MOUNTAIN**

Swift River

Passaconaway Campground

Kancamagus Highway

112

P START

White Mountain National Forest

Mount Potash Trail

Downes Brook

Downes Brook Trail

UNH Trail

ski trail

White Brook

Clear Cut

N

0.25 mile

Allen's Ledge

small ravine and brook crossing

UNH Trail

Sandwich Range Wilderness

UNH Trail

Hedgehog Mountain

east ledges

- - - Route
=== Road
---- Other Trails
P Parking
▲ Summit
Scenic Overlook

Ledges look down over a secluded valley bounded by Mounts Passaconaway and Paugus. Mount Chocorua is in the background, and the Moat Range is prominent to the northeast. Former clear-cuts, now covered with new growth, testify to logging in years past.

Signs at the East Ledges indicate that you are in a habitat for a rare plant and should therefore be careful not to trample on the vegetation. The special plant is White Mountain whitlow-wort, also called silverling, a relative of chickweeds. This species occurs in mountains from Georgia through West Virginia; however, a distinct variety occurs only on rocky ledges in the mountains of New Hampshire and western Maine, and, oddly, also on one small island in the Merrimack River at Newburyport, MA. It is a low, compact plant growing in cracks in the rock where small bits of soil and moisture accumulate. Its inconspicuous flowers are mostly hidden within silvery scales. In fact, the scientific name for this plant, *Paronychia argyrocoma*, refers to the resemblance of these silvery scales to hangnails. Other plants on the East Ledges include red spruce, black huckleberry, heart-leaved birch, and goldenrods (the latter also finding a roothold in the cracks in the rocks). Large dragonflies (several species of darners) patrol the open ledges for their insect prey on sunny days.

The trail follows open ledges for about 0.2 mile, providing great vistas. Some of the ledges are narrow and could be slick in wet or icy weather. The trail reenters the spruce-fir forest, descends for a short distance, then ascends steeply to reach the summit of Hedgehog Mountain, about 0.9 mile (40 minutes) from the East Ledges and 2.9 miles from the trailhead.

The best vista is not at the summit itself, which is heavily wooded, but at a ledge a little beyond. Turn left at an unmarked path just after reaching the high point to reach this ledge. To the north, you get a partial view of the glacially carved U-shaped valley of Carrigain Notch, bordered by Mounts Carrigain, Anderson, and Nancy. Mount Hancock, to the west of Carrigain, is a long ridge. Mount Passaconaway is particularly massive to the south. Potash Mountain, with a number of clear-cuts, is nearby to the west and roughly the same height as Hedgehog. Behind Potash are the three summits of Mount Tripyramid. The Swift River Valley separates this assemblage of mountains from Carrigain and Hancock. Red spruce, sheep laurel, mountain holly, shadbush, wild raisin, and bracken fern grow around the summit.

Two mountains south of the Kancamagus Highway are named after hedgehogs, presumably because the spires of spruce and fir that cover their rounded summits reminded those in charge of the quills of a porcupine. While resting up before your descent, you can make a game of this by looking at the map and finding other mountains that share the same name. Owl's Head, Sugarloaf, Black Mountain, and Blueberry Mountain come immediately to mind.

UNH Trail descends steeply from the summit of Hedgehog Mountain. In about 40 minutes (0.9 mile from the summit), watch for the turnoff to Allen's Ledge to the right, marked by a sign. Take this spur trail back uphill and follow the base of a massive rock to the left and up to the vista. From here Mount Washington is visible on a clear day. In front of Mount Carrigain, Green's Cliff is prominent. You also see Bear Mountain, Mount Chocorua, and Mount Paugus.

Returning to the main trail, it is 1.1 miles (about 30 minutes) to the parking area. The trail descends steeply, crosses a ravine, and descends along a hogback ridge covered with hemlocks. The trail levels out on an old railroad grade, and the cross-country ski trail enters from the left. At the T junction, turn left for the short walk back to your vehicle.

DID YOU KNOW?

UNH Trail is named for a camp that was used by the University of New Hampshire's Forestry Program from the 1940s through the 1960s. The buildings, which were located near the beginning of the loop, are no longer there.

OTHER ACTIVITIES

You can combine this hike with a visit to the Russell-Colbath House, a restored 1830s house that shows how some of the first settlers in the area lived. It is about 1.0 mile east of the trailhead along the Kancamagus Highway. Swimming is available at Lower Falls Recreation Area, about 9.0 miles east of the trailhead on the Kancamagus Highway.

MORE INFORMATION

UNH Trail is in White Mountain National Forest. A user fee ($3 per day) is required for parking; www.fs.usda.gov/whitemountain; 603-536-6100.

BIRD GUILDS IN THE WHITE MOUNTAINS

You may have noticed on your hikes through the White Mountains that you often go a long time without seeing or hearing any birds, and then all of a sudden, you are surrounded by trees full of chickadees, nuthatches, golden-crowned kinglets, warblers, woodpeckers, and other species. They will busily make their way across your trail and eventually move on. Then the quiet of the woods returns. These associations of birds of different species are called guilds, a term that comes from the old Dutch craftsmen's associations. Guilds are multispecies "teams" of birds that forage together, moving from tree to tree in the forest.

With binoculars you can observe that the different species have different ways of feeding. Chickadees and kinglets are acrobats, often hanging upside down as they inspect small twigs for insects or other edible morsels. Nuthatches probe the bark of the main trunk and large branches, while woodpeckers poke holes in branches and trunks to catch the insects deeper within the tree. Warblers and flycatchers sally for flying insects, while juncos and thrushes forage among the leaf litter on the ground. By using different feeding methods, these birds reduce competing with each other, although there is undoubtedly some overlap in their menus. The advantage to feeding in guilds is that large numbers of birds are more efficient at finding and then flushing insects than an individual would be. Also, there are more eyes to watch out for predators like Cooper's hawks and more voices to sound a warning or mob a predator.

If a bird guild should appear while you are walking through the boreal (spruce and fir) forest, keep your eyes open for boreal chickadees. These birds resemble black-capped chickadees, those familiar epicures of sunflower seeds at backyard bird feeders. Boreals are slightly smaller and have a brown, rather than black, bib. Boreal chickadees inhabit the spruce-fir forests in the White Mountains. At the elevation of Hedgehog Mountain, 2,500 feet, you might very well see both species of chickadees, perhaps even together. You might also see red-breasted nuthatches along with the more familiar white-breasted nuthatches. The red-breasted nuthatch is more partial to coniferous forests, whereas its white-breasted cousin prefers broad-leafed trees.

The dark-eyed junco, a small sparrowlike bird, is common in the boreal forest. It often forages with flocks of other species.

25

MOUNT CHOCORUA VIA CHAMPNEY FALLS

Mount Chocorua is one of the White Mountains' most iconic peaks. Its sharp-pointed summit stands alone in the southeastern section of the Whites and is visible for many miles. Trails approach Mount Chocorua from all directions. Champney Falls Trail is perhaps the easiest way to ascend the mountain and has the bonus of passing by waterfalls that are particularly impressive after a rainstorm. For many people, especially those with young children, the falls are a destination by themselves.

DIRECTIONS

The parking area for Champney Falls Trail is on the south side of the Kancamagus Highway (NH 112), about 11.0 miles west of its junction with NH 16, south of Conway and about 1.5 miles east of Bear Notch Road. Space is available for about 30 vehicles. This is a very popular trail, so vehicles may spill over onto the side of the road on summer weekends. *GPS coordinates: 43° 59.40′ N, 71° 17.97′ W.*

TRAIL DESCRIPTION

Mount Chocorua is "only" 3,500 feet in elevation, so you might be lulled into thinking that this is a relatively short and easy hike, at least compared with a 4,000-footer. Don't be fooled. The mountain is a long way from any roads, so it will take you some time before you even start gaining serious elevation. Also, the bare summit cone is steep and may be uncomfortable for people who do not do well with heights.

Snowshoeing is fine to Champney Falls. Beyond that it should be left to the experts.

Champney Falls Trail is marked with yellow blazes. It is heavily used and has a large number of exposed tree roots. It begins by crossing Twin Brook. The bridge that

LOCATION
Albany, NH

RATING
Moderate

DISTANCE
3.5 miles round-trip to the falls only, 7.8 miles round-trip to the summit of Mount Chocorua

ELEVATION GAIN
600 feet to the falls, 2,250 feet to the summit

ESTIMATED TIME
2.5 hours round-trip to the falls, 6.0 hours round-trip to the summit

MAPS
AMC *White Mountain National Forest Map & Guide*, J9

AMC *White Mountain Guide*, 29th ed. Map 3 Crawford Notch–Sandwich Range, J9

USGS Topo: Mount Chocorua, NH

TRIP 25 MOUNT CHOCORUA VIA CHAMPNEY FALLS

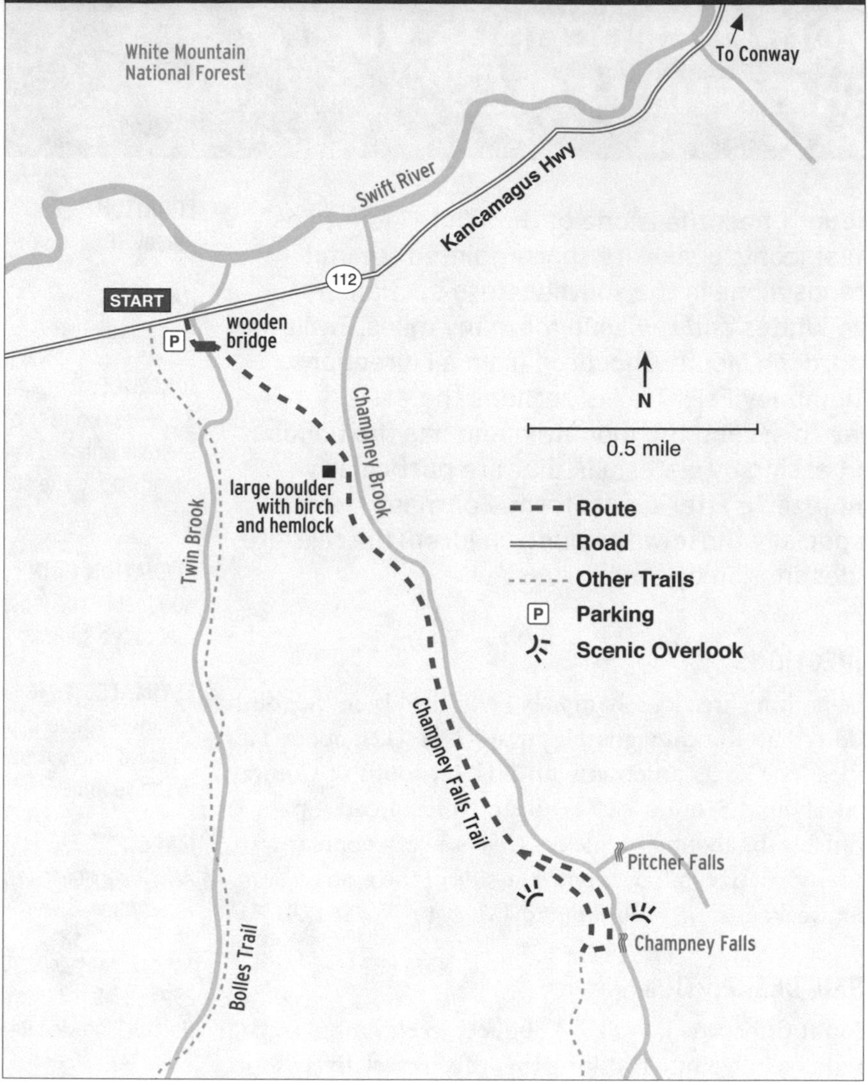
White Mountain National Forest
To Conway
Swift River
Kancamagus Hwy
112
START
wooden bridge
N
0.5 mile
large boulder with birch and hemlock
Champney Brook
Twin Brook
Route
Road
Other Trails
Parking
Scenic Overlook
Champney Falls Trail
Pitcher Falls
Champney Falls
Bolles Trail

formerly traversed the brook got washed out in a storm and it is not clear when and if the Forest Service will replace it. (If the crossing is difficult due to high water, you can avoid it by walking east along the Kancamagus Highway, crossing the brook, and bushwacking along its east side until you reach the trail.) Shortly after the crossing, Bolles Trail goes off to the right.

The forest at this point is northern hardwoods with lots of hemlock, particularly along water. Hobblebush and striped maple form the understory, and Indian cucumber-root, partridgeberry, and shining club moss are common plants of the forest floor. Also, look for painted trillium, shinleaf, rosy twisted stalk, jack-in-the-pulpits, and a few pink lady's slippers.

After 15 to 20 minutes, the trail reaches Champney Brook. Here, look for a marvelous duo of a yellow birch and a hemlock on top of a large boulder. Both trees look like they are growing right out of the rock, and their roots have intertwined as they reach for a foothold in the ground beneath the boulder. The trail parallels the west bank of the brook for the rest of the hike.

At 1.4 miles (1.0 hour, 500-foot elevation gain), take a left at the junction with the loop trail to Champney and Pitcher falls. In about 10 minutes, you pass a small waterfall—more like a shoot—that empties into a pool surrounded by moss-covered rocks. The pool is deep enough for wading, but the shadiness keeps the temperature of the water at a penguin-friendly level for most of the year. Look for water striders in the pools.

Soon after, you reach Champney Falls, where water plunges (or, in dry weather, trickles) over a series of stair-like ledges. A large rectangular boulder is in the streambed at the base of the falls.

After admiring Champney Falls, walk about 100 yards east between two narrow ledges to the base of Pitcher Falls. This beautiful, thin cascade of water looks like it somehow got lost and changed its course. It is in a narrow gorge bounded by two almost-vertical side walls. Instead of being at the far end of the gorge as you might expect, Pitcher Falls plunges over one of the sides. The stream above Pitcher Falls likely changed its course at some point, since erosion by water created the gorge initially.

Continue on the loop trail and ascend the west side of Champney Falls to the top of the falls. You will likely find other people there, perched on rocks admiring the brook and the view of nearby mountains. Even though the view is somewhat obstructed, it is nonetheless refreshing after the long walk through a dense forest. Bunchberries, wintergreen, and hobblebush border the brook right at the ledge above the falls. Be cautious when scrambling around the rocks, because the shade tends to keep them damp and slippery.

Follow the trail away from the falls to the upper junction of the loop trail with Champney Falls Trail (2.0 to 2.25 hours, 700-foot elevation gain). If the falls is your final destination, here is where you turn right and begin the gradual 1.7-mile descent back to your vehicle.

For those continuing on to Mount Chocorua, turn left.[1] The trail continues at a moderate grade until 2.4 miles when it passes a viewpoint to the north and starts ascending more steeply on a series of switchbacks. The forest becomes increasingly boreal (dominated by red spruce and balsam fir trees) in this section of the trail. You will also pass through stands of white (paper) birch, which provide evidence of past forest fires on the mountain slopes. At 3.0 miles, at an elevation of about 3,000 feet, Champney Falls Cutoff (also called Middle Sister

---

[1] I gratefully acknowledge input from Steven D. Smith (co-editor of AMC *White Mountain Guide* and author of *Mount Chocorua, A Guide and History*, Bondcliff Books, 2004) and from Sam Van Etten for the description of the trail and natural history from here to the summit.

Time to take in the view after climbing Mount Chocorua. Photo by Sam Van Etten.

Cutoff) heads left. Shortly after, the trail passes Middle Sister Trail and ends in Piper Trail (3.2 miles).

You will take Piper Trail the remaining 0.7 mile to the summit. Following yellow blazes, the vegetation becomes scrubbier, with more vistas. At 3.4 miles, West Side Trail comes in from the right. Shortly after, the trail breaks out into the open and is exposed for the remainder of the hike. It ascends over ledges, sometimes steeply and requiring occasional scrambling and care to locate the next cairn or yellow blaze. The trail passes over a rocky crag, descends slightly through some scrub vegetation, swings to the west side of the summit cone, then joins Liberty Trail just below the summit. The final ascent to the summit is through a small gully.

Because it stands apart from other mountains, Mount Chocorua provides expansive and spectacular views of much of the White Mountains. To the north on a clear day, you can see Mount Washington and the Presidential Range. To the northeast, Mount Carrigain is prominent. Immediately to the east, Mount Passaconaway looms large and Mount Whiteface is nearby. The sharp, craggy eastern face of the summit of Mount Chocorua that gives the mountain its distinctive appearance is thought to have resulted from erosion from a mountain glacier during the Ice Age.

It is interesting to contemplate why the summit of Mount Chocorua is devoid of trees. At 3,500 feet, Mount Chocorua has a bare summit, not from a true treeline related to temperature and wind, which would generally be about 1,000 feet or more higher in the White Mountains, but as a result of fires that burned off both trees and the underlying soil. According to Smith's *Mount Chocorua, A Guide and History,* there are historical reports of major fires on the mountain in the nineteenth century and early parts of the twentieth century. The absence of tree cover has allowed some plants to flourish on the summit cone that are normally associated with the alpine zone of the White Mountains. These include highland rush, alpine (bog) bilberry, mountain cranberry, and three-toothed cinquefoil. Small shrubs to look for in this barren zone are Labrador tea (fuzzy white flower clusters and leathery leaves with rolled edges and rusty hairs underneath), sheep laurel (pink flowers that resemble those of mountain laurels), purple crowberry (needlelike leaves), and rhodora (a small rhododendron).

Return to the trailhead via the same trails.

DID YOU KNOW?

According to John Mudge (*The White Mountain: Names, Places, and Legends,* The Durand Press, 1995), Chocorua was a Pequawket Indian chief who was either killed or leaped from a cliff to his death in the early 1700s while being pursued by white settlers on the mountain that bears his name. Before dying, Chocorua cursed the white settlers, which settlers blamed for their various tribulations in subsequent years.

Champney Falls was named for Benjamin Champney, a leading White Mountain artist of the nineteenth century. He is considered by many art historians to be the founder of the White Mountain school of artists. They painted in the North Conway area in the second half of that century.

OTHER ACTIVITIES

If you are interested in the human history of the region, a visit to the Russell-Colbath House at the Passaconaway Historic Site should be on your list. It is about 2.0 miles west of the Champney Falls trailhead along the Kancamagus Highway.

MORE INFORMATION

The trail, falls, and mountain are in the White Mountain National Forest. A user fee ($3 per day) is required for parking; www.fs.usda.gov/whitemountain; 603-536-6100.

CONWAY–
NORTH CONWAY REGION

The Conway-North Conway region is in the southeastern part of the White Mountains. The region includes 3,000-foot mountains, bold cliffs popular with rock climbers, the Saco River, and a large number of ponds and streams. Mount Chocorua, a striking cone-shaped peak, is visible from many miles in either direction. One of our suggested hikes (Trip 29) takes you to ledges with wonderful views of this peak, and another (Trip 25 in Section 3, "Off the Kancamangus Highway") to the summit itself. The Green Hills, east of North Conway, provide superb views of the Presidential and Carter ranges for relatively little effort. You'll also find secluded areas that offer excellent wildlife observation opportunities.

SUPPLIES AND LOGISTICS

NH 16 is the main road through this area. Chocorua and other nearby villages, such as Tamworth, are picturesque, small New England communities. These villages are wonderful places to stay, but do not expect to find a wide variety of supplies for your hike. In contrast, Conway Village and North Conway are among the oldest and busiest communities in the White Mountains, with extensive facilities for tourists and lots of traffic. Many outdoor opportunities and amenities for visitors are available, particularly along NH 16.

The Saco Ranger Station is on NH 112 (Kancamagus Highway) just off NH 16 south of Conway Village. It is a terrific place to get the latest information on trail conditions, buy trail and field guides, and peruse displays on White Mountain ecology and geology.

Facing page: The shallow pools of Diana's Baths make
it a popular family destination. The North Conway
region has a number of trails perfect for children.

NEARBY CAMPING

White Ledge Campground, a national forest campground with 28 sites, is off NH 16 about 4.0 miles south of the village of Conway. White Ledge Loop Trail (Trip 29) leaves from this campground. National forest campgrounds along the eastern part of the Kancamagus Highway (NH 112), such as Blackberry Crossing and Covered Bridge campgrounds, are convenient to the region. Campsites can be reserved beforehand on the web at recreation.gov or by calling 1-877-444-6777 (International 518-885-3639 or TDD 877-833-6777).

26

DIANA'S BATHS

Diana's Baths is a popular family destination suitable for the youngest hikers. A short, level, handicapped-accessible walk along the Moat Mountain Trail brings you to a former mill site where you can wade in one of the many pools among numerous cascades or explore the ruins of the old mill.

LOCATION
Conway, NH

RATING
Easy

DISTANCE
1.2 mile round-trip

ELEVATION GAIN
Minimal

ESTIMATED TIME
0.5–1.0 hour

MAPS
AMC *White Mountain National Forest Map & Guide*, I10

AMC *White Mountain Guide*, 29th ed. Map 3 Crawford Notch–Sandwich Range, I10

USGS Topo: North Conway West

DIRECTIONS

From North Conway, turn west onto River Road, which leaves NH 16/US 302 at the traffic light just north of the Eastern Slope Inn. Cross the Saco River and bear right at the next two intersections. You are now headed north on West Side Road. A large, well-marked parking area is on the left about 0.9 mile past the road to Cathedral Ledge (2.4 miles from NH 16 in North Conway).

If you are traveling from the south, pick up West Side Road in Conway Village by turning left from NH 16 onto Passaconaway Road at the intersection where NH 153 goes off to the right. Continue north (straight) as the road turns into West Side Road. About 5.0 miles past Conway, bear left where River Road comes in from the right. Pass the road to Cathedral Ledge and follow the above directions.

From Crawford Notch, travel east on US 302 and turn right onto West Side Road about 4.0 miles east of the turn-off to Bear Notch Road in Bartlett. The large parking area is about 0.3 mile south of the Conway–Bartlett town line. *GPS coordinates:* 44° 04.47′ N, 71° 09.84′ W.

TRAIL DESCRIPTION

Diana's Baths is a pleasant spot to relax and hang out on a summer afternoon. You won't be alone, but the shady forest and the cool water make this an ideal family visit. Diana's Baths is reached by Moat Mountain Trail.

Leaving the parking area, the well-graded, crushed-stone path meanders through the forest, crossing several small rivulets on bridges. Benches along the way invite you to stop and admire the tall white and red pines. In 10 to 15 minutes, you reach Lucy Brook. The mill site is immediately to the left, and Diana's Baths is just a little ahead, also to the left. Moat Mountain Trail continues beyond the baths, but it becomes very steep and is not recommended for families.

Numerous cascades will immediately catch your attention when you arrive at Diana's Baths. Even with the crowds, you will be able to find a flat rock and an interesting stretch of water that you can claim for several hours. Kids will enjoy meandering up the granite terraces to see the wonderful assortment of waterfalls, pools, and rocks upstream. You'll find numerous small, round potholes carved into the flat granite. These were formed by the scouring action of small stones and sand carried around by spring floodwater. Potholes that are perched high above the current level of the water were probably formed during the melting of the last glacier, when water levels were much higher than they are now.

Some gears, pipes, and stone walls from the old mill are still present. This was a gristmill that used the waterpower of Lucy Brook to ground flour.

Diana's Baths is shaded by hemlocks, which keep it pleasantly cool. Three interesting shrubs that grow around the water's edge are rhodora, speckled alder, and mountain holly. If you get here around Memorial Day weekend, rhodora will be in bloom, with showy pinkish flowers that are pretty enough to make you forget the blackflies, at least for a moment. Speckled alders have distinctly spotted twigs and branches, as if they have chicken pox. Mountain hollies are particularly abundant. These shrubs have leaves with smooth edges (i.e., no serrations) and are tipped with a tiny spine

Kids love playing in the many small pools at Diana's Baths. Photo by Leti Taft-Pearman.

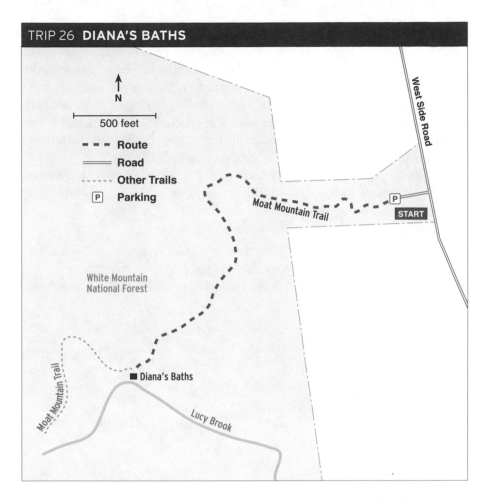

(look carefully, using a hand lens if you have one). The leaves look pale green and delicate in contrast to the dark-gray branches. Look for their small red berries in midsummer. Long beech ferns, with their lower pinnae pointing backward, grow in cracks in the rocky streambed.

Along the trail you will see asters and silverrod in mid- to late summer. Silverrod is actually a type of goldenrod but with silvery, rather than yellow, flowers.

Retrace your steps to return to the parking lot.

DID YOU KNOW?

Diana's Baths is named for the Roman goddess of the hunt, who was often pictured in woodland settings surrounded by animals. Enjoy your swim, and watch out for the water sprites that legend has it used to inhabit the area.

OTHER ACTIVITIES

Echo Lake State Park (not to be confused with Echo Lake in Franconia Notch), just south of the trailhead, has a swimming beach (day-use fee of $4 for adults, $2 for children 6 to 11; children under 6 and New Hampshire residents older than 65 are admitted free). Cathedral Ledge and White Horse Ledge, two popular rock-climbing cliffs, are in the same state park. You need rock-climbing equipment to ascend the cliffs, but there are paths through the forest to the same fine overlooks. You can also drive to the top of Cathedral Ledge.

The North Conway/Intervale/Jackson area has a host of tourist activities, including theme parks popular with children, a scenic railroad, golf, and fishing.

MORE INFORMATION

Diana's Baths is in the White Mountain National Forest; www.fs.usda.gov/whitemountain; 603-536-6100. A user fee ($3 per day) is required for parking at the trailhead. You will find pit toilets at the parking area and picnic benches at the baths.

27
BLACK CAP

Black Cap, a popular family hike in the Green Hills east of North Conway, has one of the finest vistas in the White Mountains for relatively little effort. On a clear day you can see Mount Washington, Kearsarge North, Chocorua, and other peaks of the White Mountains from its 2,370-foot summit.

DIRECTIONS

The trailhead for Black Cap Path is on Hurricane Mountain Road, an experience in itself. This mountain road runs between Intervale and South Chatham. From North Conway, head north on NH 16/US 302 and turn right onto Hurricane Mountain Road just after passing the large visitor information center and scenic overlook. From Crawford Notch or Jackson, head south through Glen on NH 16/US 302 and make a left onto this road just south of Intervale. Wind your way up Hurricane Mountain Road for 3.8 miles (paved, but very steep in spots) to the height-of-land. The parking area has space for about fifteen vehicles.

You can also reach the trailhead from the Evans Notch area by turning right (west) off ME 113 at North Fryeburg onto South Chatham Road. After about 1.5 miles, the road makes a sharp left and heads south as Robbins Ridge Road. Take this for 2.0 miles, and then follow the right fork onto Green Hill Road toward Fryeburg. Take this for 2.0 more miles and turn right onto Hurricane Mountain Road. After 2.5 steep and winding miles on Hurricane Mountain Road, the parking area for the trail will be on your left at the height-of-land. *GPS coordinates: 44° 04.10′ N, 71° 04.31′ W.*

LOCATION
Conway, NH

RATING
Moderate

DISTANCE
2.2 miles round-trip

ELEVATION GAIN
650 feet

ESTIMATED TIME
1.0-2.0 hours

MAPS
AMC *White Mountain National Forest Map & Guide,* I1

AMC *White Mountain Guide,* 29th ed. Map 5, Carter Range-Evans Notch I12

USGS Topo: North Conway East

TRAIL DESCRIPTION

Black Cap Trail, marked with orange blazes and trail signs, is easy to follow and well maintained. Stone barriers channel water off during wet weather. Nonetheless, because this is such a popular trail, it is heavily eroded in places. Please keep to the trail itself to preserve the woodland vegetation. At a reasonable hiking pace, it should take 30 to 45 minutes to get to the summit. Bring along a windbreaker for this exposed summit.

Black Cap Trail begins in a spruce forest. Note the absence of any understory vegetation under the spruce. This is often the case under pure stands of conifer trees, such as spruce, balsam fir, and hemlock. The dense canopy limits light to the forest floor much more completely than in a forest of broad-leafed trees. Even when the broad-leafed trees form a dense canopy, understory herbs and shrubs still get a chance at sunlight in early spring before the trees leaf out. Not so under evergreens. Also, the needles that do fall off the evergreens decompose to an acidic soil rich in tannins, which is not conducive to plant growth.

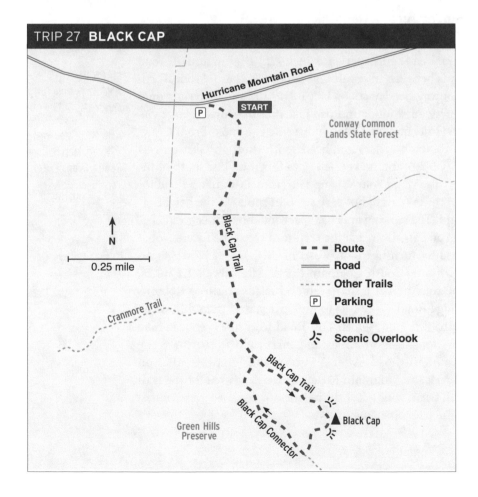

Black Cap provides fine views in all directions after a short hike. This vista looks east toward Maine.

The trail ascends into northern hardwoods. The northern hardwood forest of beech, birch, and sugar maple is much lighter than the spruce forest. Striped maple is the dominant understory shrub. Spring wildflowers include rosy twisted stalk, clintonia, painted and red trillium, and bunchberries. In late summer and fall, look for whorled wood-asters.

At 0.5 mile, The Nature Conservancy has set up a kiosk from which you can obtain a trail map and information. Cranmore Trail departs to the right from Black Cap Path at 0.7 mile. Look for a number of white birches blown over by the wind near this junction. The shallow roots make these trees particularly vulnerable to such mishaps.

At 0.8 mile, Black Cap Connector angles off to the right, heading around the west side of Black Cap. Continue straight following the orange blazes. Soon after, you start reaching open ledges with vistas. The trail ends at 1.1 miles at the Black Cap summit.

You'll need to walk around the summit to get the best vista in each direction. Looking north, the most prominent nearby peak is Mount Kearsarge North, which has a fire tower at its summit. You can also see the Carter and Baldface ranges. To the west are the steep rock faces of Cathedral and Humphrey ledges and the Moat Range, the latter containing one of the few large remnants of truly volcanic rock in the White Mountains. On a clear day, you can see Mount Washington to the northwest, Chocorua and Passaconaway to the southwest, and Mount Carrigain and Carrigain Notch to the west. Conway Lake is due south.

If you are interested in photographing the mountainous scenery to the west and northwest, you should hike Black Cap in the morning, because the mountain views are most striking in the northwest-to-southwest direction. That way you will not be shooting into the sun. A side benefit of an early-morning ascent is that you are more likely to have the scenery to yourself.

At the summit, look for heart-leaved birch, balsam fir, mountain ash, white pine, red pine, red spruce, currant (a small shrub with maple-like leaves), and some blueberries and huckleberries. In spring, the white flowers of shadbushes are in bloom.

A short spur trail, beginning where the label "Maine" is blazed onto the rock, leads to an east outlook that is now fairly overgrown. The landscape of the view in this direction is mostly the low hills and lakes of western Maine. On the way to this east outlook, you pass a wet swale with mosses and a distinct sedge called woolgrass. It has clusters of drooping, brown, scaly flowers from the apex of its 3-foot-high stems.

For the descent, you can make a loop off the summit by hiking a short trail to the right, which descends about 0.2 mile to Black Cap Connector. Turn right on the Connector (watch out for mountain bikes) and follow it for 0.4 mile back to its junction with Black Cap Trail. Turn left for the 0.8-mile descent.

MORE INFORMATION

Black Cap (2,370 feet) is part of The Nature Conservancy's Green Hills Preserve near North Conway; nature.org/wherewework/northamerica/states/newhampshire/preserves/art315.html. The preserve protects some rare plants, including the White Mountain silverling (see Trip 24). The first part of the trail is in Conway State Forest. There is no parking fee.

Hurricane Mountain Road is not maintained for winter travel and is closed from November through mid-May, when snowmobilers use the road.

WHITE MOUNTAIN WEATHER

The summits of Black Cap and other peaks are great places to contemplate White Mountain weather, assuming, of course, that the weather is decent enough to allow you to contemplate anything. Three of the biggest weather-related factors in the mountains are wind, temperature, and clouds.

Wind is evident in the number of uprooted trees you encounter. Wind speeds increase with elevation and topple trees whose roots have difficulty penetrating far into the ground in the thin soil near mountain summits. Evidence of the effect of wind is also apparent in the low, scrubby vegetation that grows on mountain summits, even those that are not technically above treeline. "Flag" or "banner" trees have living branches only on one side—the side that is downwind from the prevailing wind direction. Winter ice that coats the windward side of the trees combines with wind to kill buds.

Temperatures are cooler as you increase in elevation. This is caused by the decline in the density of air with increasing altitude. Less-dense air cannot hold heat as well as air closer to sea level. A typical decline is about 3 degrees Fahrenheit for every 1,000 feet of elevation gain (or 0.5 degrees Celsius for every 100 meters, if you like to think metrically). That sounds great for hikers on a hot summer day, but plants and animals that live at higher elevations must adapt to cooler temperatures and shorter growing seasons.

The cloudiness so prevalent in the White Mountains is related to the cooler temperatures at higher elevations. It is not unusual to see clouds hovering over some of the taller peaks, even when the rest of the region is sunny. On Mount Washington, cloud cover is present an average of 75 percent of the year. As air from the west (where most of our weather systems originate) flows up and over these mountains, it cools and forms clouds. This is because cooler air holds less moisture than warm air, just as the warm, moist air inside your lungs condenses on a cold morning when you breathe out. The Presidential Range has particularly severe weather because it is the highest and therefore coolest range in the region, and is positioned at the convergence of several storm tracks.

Cloud shapes, wind speed and direction, and changes in temperature can help predict the weather. As an example, big, puffy cumulus clouds generally indicate fair weather, but wispy cirrus clouds at very high altitudes indicate that although the current weather is now fair, precipitation may be on its way. A change in wind direction from west to east is often associated with precipitation moving in.

28

MOUNTAIN POND LOOP TRAIL

A clear, quiet body of water, Mountain Pond features beaver lodges, loons, a dense spruce-fir forest, and piles of boulders along the shore.

DIRECTIONS

From North Conway, head north on NH 16/US 302 and turn right onto Town Hall Road in Intervale (left if you are coming south from Jackson or Glen). After 0.1 mile, the road crosses NH 16A. At 2.4 miles, the pavement ends and the road forks. Take the left fork (Slippery Brook Road) and follow it for 4.0 miles. The road passes the trailhead for East Branch Trail, and then Forest Road 38, which goes off to the left. The parking lot and trailhead for Mountain Pond Trail are on the right, about 0.6 mile past the junction with Forest Road 38. Only about the first mile of the unpaved part of the road is plowed in winter. *GPS coordinates:* 44° 10.21′ N, 71° 05.28′ W.

TRAIL DESCRIPTION

Mountain Pond is in a beautiful, secluded part of the White Mountain National Forest, yet it is accessible enough to be a fine family destination. The pond is south of the Baldface Range in the valley of Slippery Brook, east of Jackson and Wildcat mountains. Families with young children (ages 2 to 5) can take a very pleasant short walk even if they decide not to hike the entire loop around the pond. However, this is not a great trail in damp weather. The numerous rocks on the trail become slippery and much of the rest of it gets muddy. Even in dry weather, expect tired feet at the end.

From the parking lot, follow the short, wide path marked with yellow blazes to Mountain Pond Loop Trail. This first section of the trail before you reach the loop is a good place to distinguish four species of maples. Three of them—striped, red, and mountain maple—grow around a small,

LOCATION
Chatham, NH

RATING
Moderate

DISTANCE
2.7 miles

ELEVATION GAIN
Minimal

ESTIMATED TIME
1.5–3.0 hours

MAPS
AMC White Mountain National Forest Map & Guide, G11–12

AMC *White Mountain Guide,* 29th ed. Map 5 Carter Range–Evans Notch, G11–12

USGS Topo: Chatham, NH

wet area; the fourth—sugar maple—is a little farther down the path (see page 142 for more on maples).

The path leads to the loop junction at 0.3 mile. Although you could walk in either direction around the pond, I suggest turning right at the fork. You will come quickly to the outlet of the pond, which could be muddy during spring thaw or right after heavy rains. If passage over this damp area looks doubtful, turn around and take the shorter walk described below. Otherwise, if you start out clockwise, walk almost the entire loop, and then get to the outlet, you may discover that it is too muddy to cross comfortably.

Wetland plants occur around the pond outlet: white turtlehead flowers, meadowsweet (a spirea with fuzzy white flower clusters), sweetgale (a shrub with leaves that smell like bayberry), alders, northern arrowwood, and bur-reed (strap-like leaves right in the stream and pond with burr-like seed heads).

Beyond the outlet, the trail is easy to follow and never far from the shore. The forest is dominated by balsam fir and hemlock, with large boulders strewn about. Trees grow directly on top of the boulders, their roots snaking down to reach the soil below. Dense growth of mosses, mountain wood sorrel, and other plants of the forest floor add to the magical atmosphere.

Two small, common plants—wintergreen and snowberry—are distinctive for their sweet, minty odors. Both have thick, glossy leaves that remain on the

Mountain Pond is a secluded gem. The twin peaks of the Doubleheads appear in the distance. Photo by Ryan Smith.

plant throughout winter. Wintergreen (also called teaberry or checkerberry) is the larger of the two plants, growing as high as 2 inches off the ground. You can crush a leaf to evoke its aroma, reminiscent of chewing gum. (As a conservation lesson, pick a leaf only where the plant is abundant.) The trailing vines of snowberry really hug the ground. The tiny, rounded leaves are stalkless and seem to come off the stems in pairs. The "wintergreen" smell produced by snowberry is not as overpowering as that produced by wintergreen itself.

Mountain Pond is one of the best spots in the White Mountains to find water birds. Look for loons, ducks, and other water birds whenever you pass an opening along the pond shore. If you see loons, take the time to watch these large, handsome birds as they swim silently across the pond, dive for fish, or sound their eerie cries. In summer the loon is unmistakable with its dark head, checkered necklace, speckled back, and large, daggerlike bill.

On one visit, twelve common mergansers were fishing along the shores of the pond. These diving birds are ducks, but instead of having flat bills they have thin ones with serrated edges, which enables the birds to more easily grasp their slippery prey. Mergansers use teamwork to capture fish. A team of mergansers swims in a line to drive the fish toward shore and then dives in tandem to prevent fish from escaping.

Other nesters are black ducks, hooded mergansers, ruffed grouse, hairy woodpeckers, rusty blackbirds, purple finches, and a number of warblers. Beavers are still altering the local hydrology. The last time I hiked here, they had just completed a series of dams on a tributary stream entering the pond, creating tiers of small ponds at different elevations.

When you reach the far end of the pond, stop to appreciate the great view of South Baldface to the north. The bald summit of this 3,500-foot mountain is the result of past wildfires. Back across the pond to the west are the twin peaks of the Doubleheads. A beaver lodge is right by the shore.

The shelter is reached at 1.7 miles. This is the best place in the pond for a swim, but you'll need water shoes to protect you from the rocky bottom. Another potential picnic spot is just before the loop junction (2.3 miles). Look for a short spur trail heading to the left that takes you to the shore of the pond not far from the outlet. The view across the pond is particularly nice here, and it is a good place to see dragonflies, frogs, and some of the same wetland plants described earlier.

The end of the loop is at 2.4 miles. Turn right to return to your vehicle.

For a shorter walk suitable for all ages, go left at the loop junction, walk to the shelter for a picnic, and then retrace your steps to the parking lot (a total distance of about 2.0 miles). Several short spurs lead down to the shore of the pond along this section of the trail.

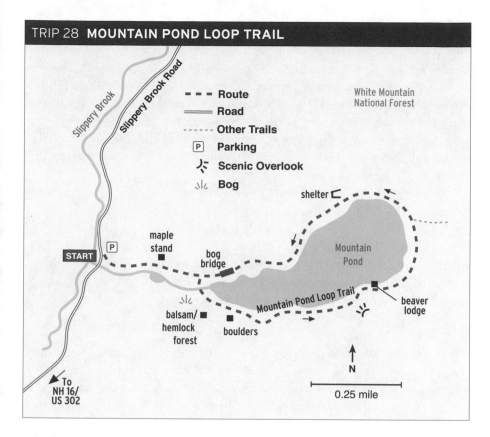

OTHER ACTIVITIES

Fishing is permitted at Mountain Pond with the proper New Hampshire license. You can swim in Mountain Pond but water shoes are recommended.

MORE INFORMATION

This hike is within the White Mountain National Forest (www.fs.usda.gov/ whitemountain; 603-536-6100). There is no user fee for parking. A latrine is located at the shelter.

MAPLES OF THE WHITE MOUNTAINS

Maples are among the most beloved and useful of trees. As a group, they are characterized by three- or five-pointed palmately lobed leaves, brilliant fall colors, helicopter-like winged seeds that spin as they are carried by the wind, and, of course, sweet sap. Another distinguishing feature is that their leaves and twigs are attached to the stems in pairs, what botanists term an "opposite pattern" of branching. They share this characteristic with only a few other types of trees and shrubs: ashes, dogwoods, and viburnums.

Four species of maples are found in the White Mountains, and with a little practice, you can learn to distinguish them. Striped maples are particularly striking and easy to identify. These small trees are named for the distinctive white striping along their bright-green young stems and branches. Their large leaves (up to 10 inches across), with three relatively small pointed lobes, resemble the webbed feet of geese, which is why they are also called goosefoot maples. Beneath these leaves in early summer one can occasionally find drooping flower clusters or winged seeds. The striped maples you see along the trails are usually part of the understory, not more than 10 feet tall. Understory trees such as striped maples that grow in the shade tend to have larger leaves than trees that get more direct sunlight. Even on the same tree, the more-shaded leaves lower on the tree will be larger than those near the top getting more sunlight.

Sugar maples are a large tree of the forest canopy at this elevation. Their leaves are smaller than those of the striped maple and have five pointed lobes, like the shape of a hand. Sugar maple leaves turn brilliant yellow and orange in fall. And, of course, the concentrated sap of this tree is something many people adore, particularly on blueberry pancakes.

Red maples are equally at home in wetlands and on mountain slopes. They can grow as fairly large, straight trees in the forest, or as shrubby, multiple-trunked individuals in wetlands. Their leaves are smaller than those of striped maples and are three-pointed, with sharp angles between the lobes. Red maples turn spectacular shades of red in fall. Their wine-colored flowers bloom before their leaves come out in spring and add a splash of color to wetlands early in the season.

Mountain maples grow only as understory shrubs. Their leaves tend to be three-pointed and rounded, and their twigs are hairy. Long clusters of flowers may be present in spring and early summer, and seeds can be seen in mid- to late summer.

29

WHITE LEDGE LOOP

White Ledge is an extensive open ledge with views of Moat Mountain to the north and Mount Chocorua to the south. White Ledge Trail, an excellent family outing, winds through a hemlock forest, along an esker, past stone walls, through an old pasture, and then up to the viewpoint.

DIRECTIONS

The trailhead is at White Mountain National Forest's White Ledge Campground off the west side of NH 16, about 6.0 miles north of the village of Chocorua and 5.0 miles south of Conway. Park in the day-use picnic area and follow the campground road straight ahead to the trailhead. Space is available for about five vehicles. *GPS coordinates: 43° 57.26′ N, 71° 12.85′ W.*

TRAIL DESCRIPTION

White Ledge Loop Trail, marked with yellow blazes, departs right from the campground road and starts out through a dense hemlock forest. At 0.3 mile, it reaches the loop junction. At this point, it is 2.4 miles to the summit ledge going counterclockwise and 1.4 going clockwise. I describe the loop in the counterclockwise direction.

Shortly after the loop junction, the trail crosses over a stream, which can be difficult to cross when water levels are high. A few minutes later, the trail follows a long, narrow, winding ridge with steep sides composed of loose rocks and sand. This is an esker, an interesting geological feature formed by a river flowing underneath a glacier. The river deposited the sand and rocks, which eventually built up into a hill. The walls of ice on both sides of the river kept the sediment within a narrow path. As you walk along this esker, picture yourself being in a tunnel within the glacier with the river at your feet and ice walls along the banks.

LOCATION
Albany, NH

RATING
Moderate

DISTANCE
4.4 miles round-trip

ELEVATION GAIN
1,450 feet

ESTIMATED TIME
3.0–4.0 hours

MAPS
AMC *White Mountain National Forest Map & Guide,* J10

AMC *White Mountain Guide,* 29th ed. Map 3 Crawford Notch–Sandwich Range, J10

USGS Topo: Silver Lake

White Ledge Loop Trail continues uphill and passes by old stone walls. At about 1.2 miles it levels off, descends for a short distance, and then passes through an overgrown pasture. The stone walls and the overgrown pasture give a hint of what this land was formerly used for: grazing cattle or sheep. New England's landscape is peppered with old stone walls—remnants of its more agrarian past—but there are not many such walls in the White Mountains. The countryside was too rugged to support more than marginal farms.

The old pasture is a laboratory of ecological succession, the process by which cleared land eventually turns back into forest. Look for pin cherry, a tree that is often a pioneer in burned or cutover land (hence its other name, "fire cherry"). It has reddish, flaky bark speckled with narrow pores called lenticels. These help to aerate the tree. Birds relish the cherries, which aids in its dispersal to other open areas. Blackberries and raspberries are also colonizers of cleared land. Young American beech and striped maples are growing in the pasture as well. The beech will eventually become a tree of the canopy, and the striped maple the understory.

After leaving the pasture at about 1.9 miles, the trail turns left and elevates moderately steeply. You'll reach the first set of ledges at about 2.3 miles. The best view of Moat Mountain and other peaks to the north is from the ledges below the actual summit, so take time to enjoy the views on your way up. Moat Mountain is unique in the White Mountains for containing volcanic rock extruded from the earth in the Jurassic Period around 170 million years ago, during the time of

A bracket fungus helps to break down organic matter in the forest. This ensures that valuable nutrients are recycled.

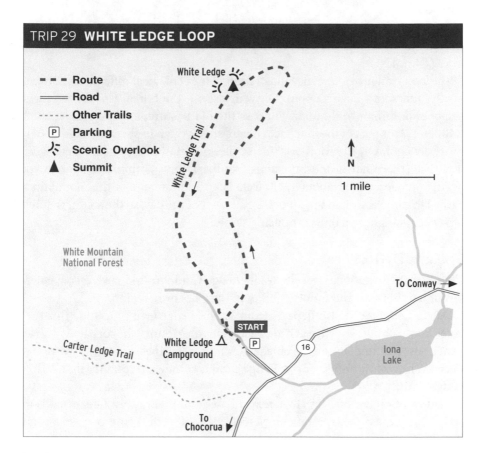

the dinosaurs. Other mountains you can see are Mount Cranmore, Kearsarge North, and Bear Mountain. The summit of Mount Washington is visible just to the east of Moat Mountain.

Follow the blazes and cairns carefully as you continue your ascent up the ledges. The last time I hiked this trail, some of the blazes were faded and hard to see. The ledges have interesting seeps that support growth of sphagnum (peat moss) and other mosses. Common shrubs around the ledges include black huckleberry, lowbush blueberry, and sheep laurel. Three-toothed cinquefoil grows wherever its roots can find enough soil among the rocks.

At 2.7 miles, you reach the summit (2,005 feet), where there is a nice view of lakes and hills to the east. Trees to note include red and white pine, red spruce, and red oak. The trail then begins to descend and very soon passes an excellent vista of Mount Chocorua to the south and then an unmarked side trail, which leads to a view southeast. Continuing your descent, look for some enormous white pines just after the trail makes a sharp left turn (about 3.3 miles). White pines such as these were characteristic of New England forests at the time European settlers first arrived. These huge, straight trees were sought after by the crown for masts of ships, so most were cut.

At about 3.6 miles the trail crosses a stream, and it then follows that stream to the loop junction (4.1 miles). Turn right at the junction to go back to the trailhead (4.4 miles).

The loop trail provides a nice illustration of the ecological differences between north- and south-facing slopes. On your ascent, the boreal (spruce-fir) forest becomes dominant right after you pass the old pasture, an elevation of about 1,400 feet. This part of the loop faces north, so it is often in shadow and therefore relatively cool. On the southern side of the mountain, the boreal forests gives way to northern hardwoods, the more "southern forest," almost as soon as you begin your descent, at about 1,900 feet. The southern side of the mountain is bathed in direct sunlight for a much longer part of the day, so the southern forest type occurs higher up on south-facing slopes.

OTHER ACTIVITIES

Camping at the national forest's White Ledge Campground is very convenient for hiking this trail and for other hikes in the Chocorua region.

Carter Ledge Trail also departs from White Ledge Campground. This trail takes you to another ledge with a nice vista of Mount Chocorua. At Carter Ledge you will find abundant blueberries and jack pines, a relatively rare tree in the White Mountains. Carter Ledge Trail is somewhat rougher than White Ledge Trail.

Madison Boulder off NH 113, a few miles east of the trailhead near Madison, NH, is the largest glacial erratic in New England. It is the centerpiece of a small state natural area.

Swimming at Chocorua Lake, just north of the village of Chocorua, is an excellent way to cool off after your hike.

MORE INFORMATION

White Ledge Loop Trail is within the White Mountain National Forest; www.fs.usda.gov/whitemountain; 603-536-6100. A user fee ($3 per day) is required for parking in the day-use area at White Ledge Campground; Conway to the north and Chocorua to the south are the nearest villages for supplies and restaurants. These can be found in either direction along NH 16.

CRAWFORD NOTCH AND ZEALAND NOTCH

The Crawford Notch/Zealand region lies in the heart of the White Mountains. The area includes two stunning U-shaped valleys and a number of mountains that rise above 4,000 feet. Just getting to this region is a real treat because the drive up US 302 through Crawford Notch and up to the Zealand area is one of the most spectacular in the eastern United States, surpassed only by the drive down US 302. An early explorer, quoted by the Reverend Benjamin G. Willey in his 1856 book, *Incidents in White Mountain History,* described it eloquently: "The sublime and awful grandeur of the Notch baffles all description. Geometry may settle the heights of the mountains, and numerical figures may record the measure; but no words can tell the emotions of the soul as it looks upward and views the almost perpendicular precipices which line the narrow space between them . . . ."

The hiking trails selected here take you to hidden ponds, breathtaking overlooks, good wildlife viewing, and some of the highest waterfalls in the White Mountains. In the secluded Zealand Valley, many trails follow old logging railroads with gentle grades perfect for young hikers.

SUPPLIES AND LOGISTICS

A number of places provide information to hikers as well as an introduction to the rich history of the "Great Notch of the White Mountains." The Macomber Family Information Center at Crawford Depot is located in the historical train station built in 1891, where guests disembarked for the Crawford House Hotel. The depot is just north of the point where US 302 passes through the Gateway of the Notch, the highest and narrowest part of Crawford Notch. The information center is run by AMC and is a short walk from AMC's Highland Center, which offers meals and overnight accommodations (see below). The information center offers displays on the natural and human history of Crawford Notch, restrooms, water for your water bottles, and a store that sells some hiking supplies and souvenirs. The depot also serves as a stop on the Conway Scenic Railroad.

Crawford Notch State Park's Visitor Center is at the Willey House Historic Site off US 302 and has a snack bar, restrooms, and information.

The original hotel at the Gateway of the Notch was built by Abel and Ethan Allen Crawford (father and son) in 1828 and run by Thomas Crawford, brother of Ethan Allen. It evolved into the Crawford House Hotel, which hosted presidents and other dignitaries until it closed in 1975. The building burned down a few years later.

This is an area of small communities and small stores. For picnic and other supplies, stop at one of the stores you pass on US 302 in Glen, Bartlett, Notchland (in the heart of Crawford Notch), Bretton Woods, or Twin Mountain. The

The spectacular view of "The Great Notch of the White Mountains" is one of the scenic highlights of the Whites.

communities of Twin Mountain, Bretton Woods, and Bartlett have a number of restaurants, gas stations, motels, hotels, and tourist cabins.

AMC HIGHLAND CENTER AT CRAWFORD NOTCH

This AMC destination is centrally located for day hikes around Crawford Notch and Zealand. It is a few hundred yards from Crawford Depot and is near the site of the Crawford House Hotel. This green-building facility provides lodging, meals, daily programs on the White Mountains, guided hikes, and a wealth of information for hikers. A store within the center sells hiking supplies, guidebooks, and field guides. Highland Lodge has private rooms with baths for families as well as bunk rooms with shared baths. Breakfast and dinner are included with room packages; trail lunches are available for purchase. The Shapleigh Bunk House, a historical building that was home to artist Frank H. Shapleigh, has two bunk rooms and offers breakfast, showers, and limited facilities for heating your own food. Reservations are needed for both facilities; outdoors.org/highland; 603-466-2727.

PUBLIC TRANSPORTATION

Concord Coach Lines leaves from Boston's Logan Airport and South Station to Lincoln. From there you can reserve a shuttle (the Shuttle Connection) to Crawford Notch. Check the web for details. The AMC Hiker Shuttle (outdoors .org/lodging/lodging-shuttle.cfm) stops at the trailhead for Zealand Trail (Trip 37), AMC's Highland Center (Trips 30, 31, 33, 36, 38, 40, and 41), and the trailhead for Ethan Pond Trail (Trip 38).

NEARBY CAMPING

The Dry River Campground (36 sites) on US 302 is part of Crawford Notch State Park. It is about 1.5 miles south of the turnoff to Ripley Falls and 5.5 miles south of Crawford Depot. The Zealand and Sugarloaf campgrounds of the White Mountain National Forest are in the Zealand area. Zealand Campground, with eleven sites, is right at the junction of US 302 and Zealand Road. The two Sugarloaf campgrounds are 0.5 mile south on Zealand Road. They have a total of 62 sites and have facilities for persons with disabilities. Private campgrounds are located near Bartlett and Twin Mountain.

30

SACO LAKE AND ELEPHANT HEAD

Wooden bridges, the chance to toss stones into the water, and huge rocks make the walk around Saco Lake a great one for small children. Continue up a short climb of Elephant Head for impressive views down Crawford Notch.

DIRECTIONS

From the Jackson–North Conway area, follow US 302 west at Glen where it splits from NH 16. US 302 passes through Bartlett and then heads north through Crawford Notch. At the top of the notch, roughly 20.0 miles from the junction of NH 16 and US 302, the road goes through the narrow pass between two cliffs. If you are not staying at AMC's Highland Center (parking for registered guests only), you should park at the trailhead for Webster-Jackson Trail just past the head of the notch and near the south end of Saco Lake. Plenty of room for vehicles is available on the side of US 302. Saco Lake is on the right as you face north and the Crawford Depot/Macomber Family Information Center is on the left just beyond the pass. You will need to walk about 0.25 mile north on the side of US 302 along the pond to get to Saco Lake trailhead, which is at the north end of the pond just across US 302 from the Highland Center. There is a sign at the trailhead for "Saco Lake, Idlewild."

From Franconia Notch and Twin Mountain, the trailhead is about 8.0 miles south of the junction of US 3 and US 302 in Twin Mountain. Park at the trailhead for Webster-Jackson Trail and walk north along the road to the trailhead, as described above. *GPS coordinates:* 44° 12.94′ N, 71° 24.52′ W.

TRAIL DESCRIPTION

This short walk combines two even shorter walks at the fabled Gateway of the Notch. I describe Saco Lake first followed by Elephant Head, since it is nice to explore the pond

LOCATION
Carroll, NH

RATING
Easy

DISTANCE
1.2 miles round-trip

ELEVATION GAIN
100 feet

ESTIMATED TIME
1.0 hour

MAPS
AMC White Mountain National Forest Map & Guide, G8

AMC *White Mountain Guide*, 29th ed. Map 3 Crawford Notch–Sandwich Range, G8

USGS Topo: Crawford Notch

first and then end with the tremendous vista from Elephant Head. You can, of course, do it the other way, or, if you are short on time, skip one destination or the other. You are rarely out of sight of the road, but you also have constant views of the Willey Range.

From the trailhead, Saco Lake Trail enters the woods and soon crosses a small stream on rocks. In about 5 minutes you reach the shoreline of the pond. This small, unassuming pond off US 302 is the headwater for the Saco River, which flows through Crawford Notch and all the way to the Atlantic Ocean.

A plank bridge aids in traversing a rocky area with 20-foot boulders. This is a good place to study granite. Inspect its coarse texture for crystals of translucent quartz (grayish) mixed in with feldspar (white) and some biotite mica flakes (black or brownish). Also note that the vertical side of one of the huge boulders you pass is very flat, indicating that this rock broke off from an even larger rock along a flat joint. Another rock overhangs the trail. The huge rock formations are covered with rock tripe, a lichen that looks like a piece of boot leather. Trees somehow manage to cling precariously to life on and around the rocks with very little soil. Look for a beaver house tucked in among the rocks, as if designed by a landscape architect.

In summer you are likely to see tree swallows and barn swallows flying over the pond. These small birds are very fast and adept flyers. They fly swiftly, making aerial pirouettes as they catch insects that fly above or emerge from the water.

Saco Lake and Mount Webster after a storm.

See Trip 43 for more on these swallows. Dragonflies will also be patrolling the water for unwary insects. Note the dead trees riddled with woodpecker holes that provide homes for many birds and mammals.

You'll find a variety of wetland plants along the pond shore: speckled alders, meadowsweet, water lobelia, pipeworts, flat-topped asters, goldenrods, and white turtleheads. Across the pond, there is a good view of Mount Tom (4,051 feet), named for Thomas Crawford.

The Idlewild Overlook is reached by a short, steep spur trail. The view there is now partly overgrown. After the overlook, the trail continues along the shore, eventually crossing over the inlet to the pond on another plank bridge. This is a good place to search among the small stones for salamanders. Saco Lake Trail ends at the road near the Webster-Jackson Trail parking area.

To continue the hike to Elephant Head, a round-trip of 30 minutes, continue toward the notch (south) along the highway to the trailhead for Webster-Jackson Trail. Elephant Head is a large, rocky outcropping that overlooks Crawford Notch at the east side of the gateway. It actually looks like the head of an elephant when viewed from the highway near the depot. White lines and spots of white quartz within the grayish granite give the ledge its distinctive profile. You will get a close-up view of the quartz and granite when you reach Elephant Head.

Just past a small field, note the black-eyed Susans, oxeye daisies, and goldenrods. These sun-loving plants would be completely out of place in the forest.

Take Webster-Jackson Trail for less than 0.2 mile to where the Elephant Head Spur diverges right, marked with a sign that reads "Great View of the Notch." You pass through a damp area on wooden planks (look for northern white violets and sedges), and then ascend to an attractive knoll of spruce and fir. In the shade of the forest you will find mountain wood sorrel, spinulose wood fern, goldthread, clintonia (bluebead lily), painted trillium, shiny club moss, and dutchman's breeches.

The trail descends slightly to the open ledge, 0.2 mile from Webster-Jackson Trail. From the top of Elephant Head, there are nice views of mountains, water, and potentially wildlife both up and down the notch. Beavers, ducks, and other animals reside in the wetland across US 302.

This is a good place to observe the drainage patterns of the land. Water in Saco Lake flows south through Crawford Notch and forms the Saco River, ultimately reaching the coast of Maine. Just north of the pond at the Highland Center, water flows north to the Ammonoosuc River and eventually to Long Island Sound via the Connecticut River. After admiring the view and the rocky ledge, retrace your steps to the road.

DID YOU KNOW?

Saco Lake is called a lake, but it is really a pond. A lake is deeper and has distinctive layers of water that differ in temperature. In summer the surface water of a lake is warm but the deep water remains cold, something you can experience

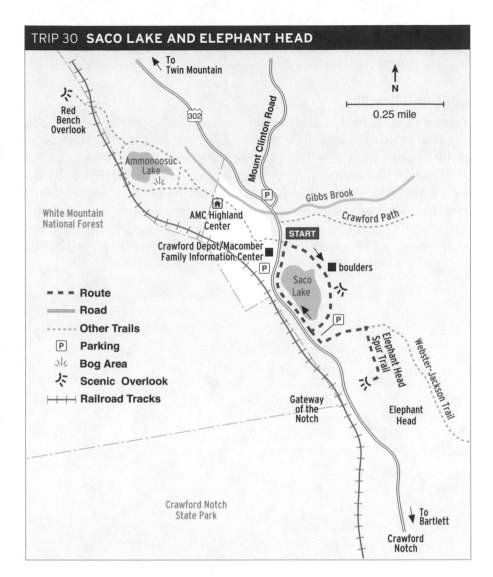

- - - **Route**
===== **Road**
----- **Other Trails**
P **Parking**
⟋⟍ **Bog Area**
⟋⟍ **Scenic Overlook**
+++ **Railroad Tracks**

yourself by diving deep into a lake. There is often a very narrow transition layer between the two layers. Ponds are shallower than lakes and water temperature varies little with depth.

OTHER ACTIVITIES

Saco Lake is stocked with trout. You may fish with the proper New Hampshire license. The Conway Scenic Railway drops you off at Crawford Depot right near the trailhead, so you could arrive there in the style of travelers from 100 years ago.

You can combine this short hike with other hikes in Crawford Notch State Park for a longer outing. The trailheads for the Mount Willard (Trip 33) and Mount Avalon (Trip 36) trails are near the Macomber Family Information Center.

MORE INFORMATION

Saco Lake and Elephant Head are within Crawford Notch State Park (nhstateparks .org/visit/state-parks/crawford-notch-state-park.aspx; 603-374-2272). There is no parking fee if you park near the depot. If you park at the nearby national forest lot on Mount Clinton Road, a $3 per day user fee applies. The AMC Highland Center is a stop on the AMC Hiker Shuttle; outdoors.org/lodging/lodging-shuttle .cfm. Restrooms and trail information are found at the Macomber Family Information Center at Crawford Depot (outdoors.org/lodging/whitemountains/ highland/crawford/crawford-depot.cfm). This is a place to fill up water bottles and purchase last-minute snacks.

31

AMMONOOSUC LAKE VIA AROUND THE LAKE TRAIL

Ammonoosuc Lake feels remote from civilization, yet it is only a 15-minute walk from AMC's Highland Center and US 302. It is a great place to look for moose, beavers, or wood ducks or to take a quick dip in the cool waters. A side trail directs you to the Red Bench, where there is a view of Mount Washington and the Presidential Range.

LOCATION
Carroll, NH

RATING
Easy

DISTANCE
1.0- or 2.0-mile loop

ELEVATION GAIN
150 feet

ESTIMATED TIME
1.0–2.0 hours

MAPS
AMC *White Mountain National Forest Map & Guide*, G7

AMC *White Mountain Guide*, 29th ed. Map 3 Crawford Notch–Sandwich Range, G7

USGS Topo: Crawford Notch

DIRECTIONS

Park at the Macomber Family Information Center at Crawford Depot off US 302. This is on the opposite side of Route 302 from where you park for Saco Lake Trail. See Trip 30 for directions. An alternative is the hikers' parking lot 0.2 mile up Mount Clinton Road (WMNF parking fee applies). Walk north behind AMC's Highland Center and pick up Around the Lake Trail to your left. An alternative way to gain access to the trail is via AMC's Stewardship Trail. This is to the right behind the Highland Center and runs for 0.2 mile with twelve numbered stations before intersecting Around the Lake Trail. You can pick up an audio guide for Stewardship Trail at the Highland Center. *GPS coordinates:* 44° 13.08′ N, 71° 24.66′ W.

TRAIL DESCRIPTION

Around the Lake Trail loops around the shore of Ammonoosuc Lake through a shady forest of evergreens. It should take you no longer than an hour to hike the 1.0-mile loop, but allow extra time for the Red Bench overlook. Make sure you have insect repellent handy, particularly at dawn or dusk. In damp weather or early spring, expect the trail to have muddy spots.

Around the Lake Trail, marked with yellow blazes, heads down toward the lake and in a few minutes reaches the start of the loop. Follow the trail to the left in a clockwise

Winter is a great time to explore Ammonoosuc Lake. Photo by Dennis Welsh.

direction. Cross over Crawford Brook on the bridge, pass a spring, and you will then reach the west shore of the lake.

The forest near the lake is mostly red spruce, balsam fir, and paper birch. In wet areas and at the pond's edge, the understory has red-berried elder, sheep laurel, northern wild raisin, leatherleaf, and Labrador tea. Much of the path around the lake is lined with snowberry, a small plant with tiny, rounded leaves attached to wiry stems that hug the ground. The leaves have a pleasant wintergreen smell when crushed. It is usually hard to find any of the snow-white berries that give this plant its name, but try your luck. Mountain wood sorrel, Canada mayflower, and clintonia grow abundantly around the lake, and you may find trillium and trailing arbutus there too. While admiring these flowers, you will likely be serenaded by the banjo-like plunking of green frogs.

In 15 to 20 minutes, the turnoff to the Red Bench overlook heads left. This side trail to an attractive vista takes 15 minutes (0.3 mile) in each direction. Good patches of goldthread and hobblebush are found right at this trail junction. Follow the Red Bench Trail through the woods away from the lake. It jogs right at the old railroad tracks and crosses over another wooden bridge by a small gorge. The rocky walls of this gorge are covered with ferns. Note that the spruce and firs that lined the lake have given way to deciduous trees—beech, sugar maple, and yellow birch—probably because the soil is drier. Red Bench Trail ends at a clearing in the forest. The clearing is filling in somewhat but still provides views of Mounts Washington (including the cog railway), Clay, Jefferson, and Eisenhower and some relief from the blackflies and mosquitoes that can be a problem on this walk early in the season.

Retrace your steps, return to Around the Lake Trail, and turn left. Take the side path where a sign indicates "Down to the Lake" to the shoreline for a view of Mounts Webster and Willard. Returning to the main trail you cross the outlet of the lake in 10 minutes. The concrete dam with a culvert has been "improved" by beavers, which probably don't trust their human counterparts to make a structure that will last. Guests from the old Crawford House Hotel would swim at this spot. They were apparently not dissuaded by occasional leeches. Many swimmers today brave the leeches as well.

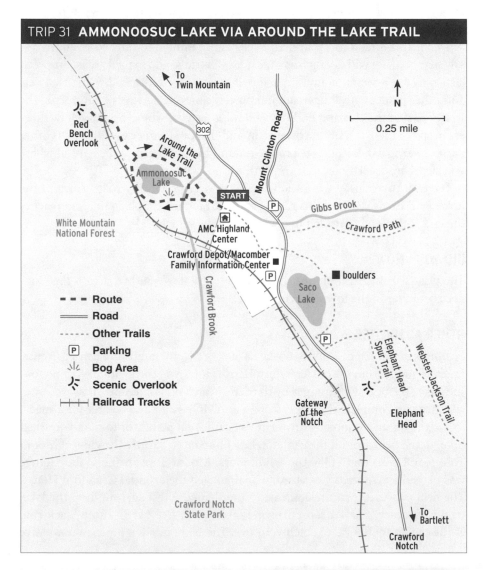

TRIP 31 **AMMONOOSUC LAKE VIA AROUND THE LAKE TRAIL**

If you look carefully at the water flowing out of the lake on the downstream side of the dam, you might notice green fuzz covering some of the rocks. This looks like algae but is actually a freshwater sponge. Most sponges are marine animals, but a number of species live in freshwater. The green color is from symbiotic green algae that live on the surface of the sponge. By turning sunlight into food, the algae provide the sponge with nutrition. Sponges also ingest food particles that are passively filtered out of the flowing water. Freshwater sponges thrive only in unpolluted waters, so the presence of sponge here is a reflection of the cleanliness of Ammonoosuc Lake.

Beyond the dam there is a small clearing on your right, the location of a bathhouse that was used by guests from the Crawford House. Now it has been reclaimed by some attractive wildflowers. One of the most striking is fireweed, a tall (3- to 6-foot) wildflower with a very leafy stem and large, showy, pink flowers with four petals. It is called fireweed because it is one of the first plants to colonize an area after a forest fire. Fireweed is not limited to burned-over areas—any new clearing will do, such as roadsides, ski trails, and logged areas. Fireweed lasts only a few years in any site before it disappears, replaced by shrubs, trees, and other plants with longer staying power (unless the area is kept open). The wetter part of the clearing harbors yellow loosestrife, whose bright-yellow flowers in spires 1 to 3 feet off the ground in mid- to late summer give rise to its other name, swamp candles. If you explore around the wet meadow, be careful where you step, because it's easy to trample this kind of vegetation.

The trail turns away from the lake on an overgrown dirt road. Around the Lake Trail turns right off this road, crosses Crawford Brook again, and reaches the end of the loop. Turn left to get back to your vehicle.

DID YOU KNOW?

The waters from Ammonoosuc Lake eventually flow southwest into the Connecticut River in the town of Woodsville.

OTHER ACTIVITIES

Fishing is permitted in Ammonoosuc Lake with a New Hampshire fishing license. Like the guests from the old Crawford House Hotel, you can swim in Ammonoosuc Lake. The best swimming is by the dam. Watch out for leeches, however.

When you complete this hike, stop in at AMC's Highland Center for a snack, to use the library to look up any critters or unusual plants, or to plan your next hike. In the field around the center, take a moment to admire the view of Mount Tom (4,051 feet) and enjoy the wildflowers. Mount Tom in the Willey Range was named for Thomas Crawford, who managed the original Crawford House. The field provides a sunny contrast to the shaded forest surrounding the lake. In midsummer, small, deep-crimson flowers with five petals and a black ring at the center are bound to catch your eye. These are maiden pinks, a nonnative inhabitant of roadsides and fields. Other nonnative eye-catchers are garden lupines, whose multicolored spikes of pealike flowers put on a gorgeous display along the left side of the dirt road that takes you into the forest. Garden lupines have "escaped" from gardens and now grow along roadsides. Chipping and field sparrows flitter across the field.

MORE INFORMATION

The parking area on Mount Clinton Road is operated by the White Mountain National Forest. A user fee ($3 per day) is required for parking; www.fs.usda .gov/whitemountain; 603-536-6100. Parking along US 302 at Crawford Depot is free.

The AMC Hiker Shuttle stops at the Highland Center; outdoors.org/lodging/lodging-shuttle.cfm.

32

SAWYER POND

Sawyer Pond is a beautiful mountain pond that provides opportunities for swimming, picnicking, camping, fishing, and birding.

DIRECTIONS

The trailhead is off Sawyer River Road, a well-packed dirt road that heads southwest from US 302 about 4.0 miles west of the intersection of US 302 and Bear Notch Road in Bartlett. The parking area is 3.8 miles from US 302, before a gate marking the end of vehicular access. Walk around the gate and look for the trail signs. *GPS coordinates:* 44° 03.20′ N, 71° 24.26′ W.

TRAIL DESCRIPTION

About 100 yards from the gate, Sawyer Pond Trail heads left across a narrow footbridge over the Sawyer River, and then turns left again. The path continues over a second bridge (0.3 mile) and turns left onto an old logging road, which it follows the rest of the way to the pond.

The forest is a transition between northern hardwoods and spruce-fir, so sugar maple, American beech, yellow birch, Canadian hemlock, red spruce, and balsam fir are all to be found. It is a rich forest, something that C. Francis Belcher in *Logging Railroads of the White Mountains* (AMC Books, 1980) attributes to the enlightened lumbering practices of the Saunders family, who owned this region before it became part of the national forest. Unlike most loggers around the turn of the century, the Saunders family did not practice clear-cutting; instead, they did selective logging. They left their legacy in the beautiful, dense forest, as well as the painted trillium, Indian cucumber-root, and other wildflowers, and the verdant patches of shining club moss.

The trail approaches the outlook brook to Sawyer Pond at about 0.5 mile, where there is an attractive cascade. Look

LOCATION
Livermore, NH

RATING
Moderate

DISTANCE
3.0 miles round-trip

ELEVATION GAIN
350 feet

ESTIMATED TIME
1.5–2.0 hours

MAPS
AMC White Mountain National Forest Map & Guide, 18

AMC *White Mountain Guide,* 29th ed. Map 3 Crawford Notch–Sandwich Range, 18;

USGS Topo: Crawford Notch and USGS Topo: Mount Carrigain

for one large glacial erratic, entwined by old roots of trees that used to grow on top, but have since fallen. Nearby, some yellow birch trees appear to be on stilts, much like the mangroves in the tropics. The trees probably sprouted on top of fallen "nurse" logs. As the little trees matured, their roots grew around the logs and down into the ground. Eventually the nurse logs completely decomposed, leaving the bottom of the sapling that had formerly rested on the dead log hanging in the air and connected to the ground by roots. It is an excellent illustration of death and regeneration of the forest.

A sign indicates that you have entered the Sawyer Pond Scenic Area at around 0.8 mile. When you pass a sign indicating the direction to one of the toilets at the campsite, you are almost there. Continue to the pond's outlet and then turn left, leaving Sawyer Pond Trail. Follow the trail that hugs the pond shore, enjoying the vistas and wildlife. This trail passes tent platforms and a shelter, the latter a particularly good place to have a picnic, snack, or swim.

The pond is 47 acres in area, with a maximum depth of 100 feet. This is an impressive depth for a White Mountain pond (technically it's a lake—see Trip 30 for the difference), the result of glacial scouring. Owl's Cliff and the ledges of Mount Tremont form a striking backdrop to the east side of the pond.

Loons may be nesting on the island, so enjoy them from a suitable distance. After the breeding season they may be very friendly and swim right near you if you are quiet. You may hear the rattling calls of belted kingfishers from their perch along the shoreline and as they search for fish. Lake darners, a large dragonfly, patrol the pond's shore. Yellow-rumped warblers, black-capped chickadees, and golden-crowned kinglets inhabit the dense canopy of red spruce and balsam fir surrounding the pond. Make sure the rather tame and saucy

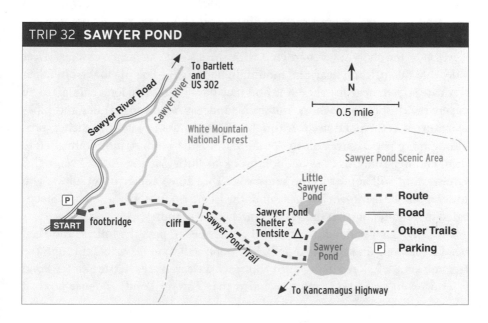

Enjoy Sawyer Pond with your family by hiking in and staying overnight at the shelter.

red squirrels do not make off with your snack. As permanent inhabitants of the place, they clearly believe they are entitled to a share of whatever food you are toting.

Angling for brook trout is a popular activity, and the hiking distance is sufficiently short that it is possible to carry in an inflatable raft. It is a good swimming pond too, with a sandy, gravely shoreline around a number of access points, such as by the shelter.

Much of the shoreline is bordered with shrubs such as meadowsweet, sweet gale, wild raisin, leatherleaf, and mountain holly. Large floating logs from fallen trees are strewn near the shoreline and may have been there long enough to be covered with sphagnum moss and even sundews. Yellow waterlilies and pipeworts grow in the pond itself. A rough trail continues beyond the shelter, providing more perspectives on the pond and its surrounding mountains before dead-ending. You cross the outlook brook to Little Sawyer Pond. Eventually, Green's Cliff will appear to the southwest. The same vantage point allows you to see a unique feature of Sawyer Pond, the island off its northeast shore. Steep-sided mountain ponds in the Whites rarely have islands.

For Little Sawyer Pond, head uphill at the shelter, pass the toilets, and then head right along an unmarked path. The pond will soon be visible through the trees on your left. Keep going until you reach a cleared area. Little Sawyer Pond is 11 acres in area and is more secluded than Sawyer Pond. A dense layer of shrubs limits the view of the pond except at one or two locations, but it is definitely worth seeing.

Retrace your steps to return to the parking area.

DID YOU KNOW?

Sawyer Pond is named for Benjamin Sawyer, one of the early settlers of Crawford Notch. He and Timothy Nash brought a horse through Crawford Notch in 1772, thereby establishing a route south to north through the mountains.

OTHER ACTIVITIES

If you are interested in a longer hike, Sawyer Pond Trail continues beyond the pond and terminates at the Kancamagus Highway, a distance of 6.0 miles. This requires spotting a vehicle at each trailhead.

Sawyer Pond makes a good first overnight backpack destination for beginning hikers. The tent platforms and shelter are first-come, first-served, so you may want to go midweek to avoid crowds and ensure a more mellow experience.

Sawyer Pond Trail is moderately difficult for cross-country skiing. Sawyer River Road is not plowed in winter so you need to ski in from its junction with US 302, an additional 3.8 miles.

You may fish at Sawyer and Little Sawyer ponds with a New Hampshire fishing license.

MORE INFORMATION

This trail is in the White Mountain National Forest; www.fs.usda/whitemountain; 603-536-6100. Parking is free. Two outhouses are located at the camping area but you need to supply your own toilet paper.

AMC's *White Mountain Guide* reflects: "Probably no other spot in the White Mountains affords so grand a view as Mount Willard for so little effort." The hike up this 2,865-foot spur of the Willey Range is pretty steep for some kids, but when you reach the incredible panorama of Crawford Notch, you may declare, as my young nephew did after grumbling the whole way up, "Oh, this was really worth it!"

DIRECTIONS

The trailhead for Mount Willard Trail is located at the Gateway of the Notch behind Crawford Depot and the Macomber Family Information Center off US 302. From the Jackson–North Conway area, follow US 302 west at Glen where it splits from NH 16. US 302 passes through Bartlett and then heads north through Crawford Notch. At the top of the notch, roughly 20.0 miles from the junction of NH 16 and US 302, the road goes through the narrow pass between two cliffs. The parking area for Crawford Depot is a few hundred yards up the road on the left. AMC's Highland Center is about 100 yards north of the trailhead.

From Twin Mountain, take US 302 east. Crawford Depot is on the right just beyond the turnoff for AMC's Highland Center, about 8.0 miles south of the junction of US 3 and US 302. *GPS coordinates:* 44° 13.08′ N, 71° 24.66′ W.

TRAIL DESCRIPTION

Before setting out, throw a windbreaker into your pack. On certain days the wind gets funneled through the notch and really blasts away at the open ledges. The dense cover of conifers provides some shelter near the top, but proper attire will enable you to enjoy the view in more comfort.

Mount Willard Trail starts out with Avalon Trail across the railroad tracks of the old Maine Central line. (It is unsafe

LOCATION
Carroll, NH, to
Hart's Location, NH

RATING
Moderate

DISTANCE
3.2 miles round-trip

ELEVATION GAIN
900 feet

ESTIMATED TIME
3.0–4.0 hours

MAPS
*AMC White Mountain
National Forest Map &
Guide,* G8

AMC *White Mountain
Guide,* 29th ed. Map
3 Crawford Notch–
Sandwich Range, G8

USGS Topo: Crawford
Notch

and illegal to walk along the track because it is used by the Conway Scenic Railroad.) In 0.1 mile at a display board, Mount Willard Trail heads left, while Avalon Trail continues straight ahead.

Mount Willard Trail is marked with blue blazes. It goes uphill at a steady pace, nowhere terribly steep or rocky but nonetheless relentless. Where it follows the old carriage path, Mount Willard Trail is wide enough for parents and children to walk two abreast. The trail crosses several streams soon after leaving Avalon Trail. After 0.5 mile (15 to 20 minutes), Centennial Pool will be to the right. This is a small flume with a pretty "mini waterfall" 10 to 15 feet high. Nice lunch or snack rocks are here if you want a breather.

This lower part of the trail is a forest of northern hardwoods (sugar maple, American beech, and yellow birch) and paper birch, with an understory of wood fern, shining club moss, ground pine, goldthread, hobblebush, shinleaf, and mountain wood sorrel.

At 0.7 mile, the trail turns right and follows the old carriage path. At this point you will notice more and more spruce and fir. The understory includes whorled wood-aster, large-leaved goldenrod, and Canada mayflower. Near the summit you walk through a boreal forest dominated by balsam fir, with an understory composed largely of sphagnum, haircap, and juniper mosses. The summit is reached at 1.6 miles.

Mount Willard provides a spectacular view of Crawford Notch. Photo by Dennis Welsh.

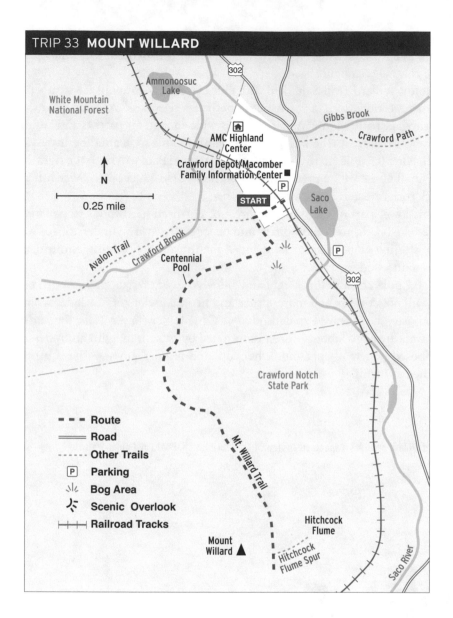

White Mountain
National Forest

Ammonoosuc
Lake

302

Gibbs Brook

Crawford Path

AMC Highland
Center

Crawford Depot/Macomber
Family Information Center

N

0.25 mile

START

Saco
Lake

P

P

302

Avalon Trail

Crawford Brook

Centennial
Pool

Crawford Notch
State Park

- - - Route
=== Road
----- Other Trails
P Parking
⭒ Bog Area
⚹ Scenic Overlook
|+|+| Railroad Tracks

Mt. Willard Trail

Hitchcock
Flume

Mount
Willard ▲

Hitchcock
Flume Spur

Saco River

The view from the ledges of Mount Willard is one of the most famous in the White Mountains. Before you is a breathtaking panorama of a deep, broad notch bounded by steep-sided mountains. Crawford Notch is one of the best examples of a glacially carved U-shaped valley anywhere in the world. Because Crawford Notch runs north and south, it was a perfect channel for the continental ice sheet that covered this area as recently as 12,000 years ago. The glacier advanced along the course of a river, scouring the sides of the mountains and gouging out rocks. What had formerly been a V-shaped valley with a river at the bottom was transformed into a U. In preglacial times, Silver and Flume cascades, which you pass on US 302 just below the Gateway of the Notch, flowed gently into the river at the bottom of Crawford Notch. By steepening the sides of the notch, the glacier left the original valleys of the two streams hanging high above the floor. The two cascades now plunge steeply down the glacially scoured side of the notch, and their courses are aptly termed hanging valleys.

Another prominent feature of the view from Mount Willard is the impressive evidence of rock slides on Mount Webster and Mount Willey. Many landslides and avalanches have occurred in Crawford Notch. The most famous happened in August 1826, when several days of heavy rains caused a huge slide onto the homestead of the Willey family. The entire family was killed. Moving accounts of the tragedy are in Lucy Crawford's *History of the White Mountains* and in the Reverend Benjamin G. Willey's *Incidents in White Mountain History* (both available in some libraries).

The rocky ledges at Mount Willard support an interesting array of plants that can tolerate the exposure and thin soil. Three-toothed cinquefoil and mosses grow very neatly in cracks in the rocks where small amounts of soil accumulate. Whitlow-wort, a rare plant, also grows in these cracks (see Trip 24). You also will find patches of meadowsweet, raspberries, bluejoint grass, sedges, and hay-scented fern.

Attempts have been made in recent years to reintroduce peregrine falcons to the cliffs beneath the Mount Willard summit during nesting season. Peregrines were wiped out in the eastern United States in the 1960s, largely because of DDT. This pesticide was picked up by the falcons in their food and caused the birds to lay eggs with thin, easily broken shells. Since DDT was banned, biologists have successfully reintroduced peregrine falcons into a number of their former eastern haunts. Peregrines nest on inaccessible cliffs, such as those below the summit of Mount Willard, and will even use artificial cliffs (skyscrapers) in cities. If you find that the trail is closed because the peregrines are nesting, you can temper your disappointment with the knowledge that this is a small victory for a spectacular but still-threatened species, and make a point of coming back to Mount Willard some other time.

Retrace your steps to return to the trailhead.

DID YOU KNOW?

Peregrine falcons catch other birds by flying high up in the sky above their target and then diving down through the sky at speeds as fast as 180 to 200 MPH, knocking their unfortunate victims to the ground. Of course their actual speed during one of these "stoops" is almost impossible to measure.

OTHER ACTIVITIES

Mount Willard Trail is an advanced cross-country ski trail, but so many winter hikers go up in snowshoes that it gets pretty well packed. It is best skied right after a fresh snow. Plenty of other great trails are in the area if Mount Willard Trail is closed due to nesting peregrine falcons. The Avalon Trail (Trip 36) is a somewhat longer alternative with a similar view of Crawford Notch.

MORE INFORMATION

Mount Willard is in Crawford Notch State Park (nhstateparks.org/visit/state-parks/crawford-notch-state-park.aspx; 603-374-2272). There is no parking fee.

The Macomber Family Information Center near the trailhead, operated by AMC, has restrooms, water, snacks, and trail information; outdoors.org/lodging/lodges/highland/crawford-notch-depot.cfm. The AMC Hiker Shuttle stops at the Highland Center near the trailhead; outdoors.org/lodging/lodging-shuttle.cfm.

WHY GLACIERS?

Many of the trail descriptions in this book describe U-shaped valleys, glacial erratic boulders, hanging valleys, cirques, tarns, kettle ponds, and eskers. These are all relatively recent features of the landscape created by the vast continental and mountain glaciers that covered much of the northern hemisphere as far south as Long Island, NY, peaking about 20,000 years ago.

This latest Ice Age is but one of many that have occurred in Earth's long history. In fact, the first Ice Age for which there is scientific evidence occurred between 2.4 and 2.1 billion years ago. Since then, there have been times when ice reached almost to the equator and other periods when tropical plants and animals thrived even at the poles. The most recent period of glaciations consisted of several major glacial advances followed by warmer interglacial periods. Some scientists think that the current Ice Age is not over, and that our existing, relatively warm period is actually an interglacial episode, which will be followed by an ice advance in the near future.

The causes of these intermittent periods of glaciation and warming are complex, and they do interact with one another to either enhance or dampen the impacts. One major factor is the shifting of continents (see Geology section in Appendix B). This affects ocean currents, wind patterns, and how much of a landmass there is in the northern hemisphere for snow accumulation and glacial formation. A second factor is the amount of greenhouse gasses, such as carbon dioxide, in the atmosphere, something that varies naturally due to volcanic activity and biological activity (but is now being profoundly altered by humans; see outdoors.org/conservation/issues/climate-change.cfm). A third factor is Milankovitch cycles, named for the Serbian scientist who discovered them. These cycles refer to periodic differences in the distance of Earth from the sun, in the tilt of Earth's axis, and in the wobble of Earth around its axis. These vary in a regular pattern and affect the strength of the sun's energy reaching Earth, therefore affecting temperatures.

During an ice age, glacial activity seems to peak approximately every 100,000 years. This corresponds with the cycle of the eccentricity of Earth's orbit around the sun (the deviation from a circular orbit, which determines how far Earth is from the sun during its annual orbit). Needless to say, the causes of ice ages are still a subject of lively scientific debate.

34
SUGARLOAF TRAIL

You get terrific views from the summits of the Sugarloafs for relatively modest effort, but that's not all this trail has to offer. Huge glacial erratic boulders are located here, and North Sugarloaf has an abandoned quarry where you can find smoky quartz.

DIRECTIONS

The trailhead is on Zealand Road, which branches off south from US 302 at the Zealand Campground, about 2.0 miles east of Twin Mountain and about 6.0 miles northwest of AMC's Highland Center at the head of Crawford Notch. Follow Zealand Road for 1.0 mile from US 302. Park just before the bridge over the Zealand River and look for the trailhead just past the bridge on the right. *GPS coordinates:* 44° 15.29′ N, 71° 30.24′ W.

TRAIL DESCRIPTION

Sugarloaf Trail ascends both North and Middle Sugarloaf (2,310 and 2,539 feet, respectively), and your hike could include one or both of these small mountains. If you have time for only one, the hike to North Sugarloaf takes 1.0 to 1.5 hours, and the hike to Middle Sugarloaf is slightly longer.

Sugarloaf Trail coincides with Trestle Trail for its first 0.2 mile, following the west shore of the Zealand River. It then branches uphill to the left, while Trestle Trail continues straight along the river. Sugarloaf Trail continues moderately steeply through a balsam fir forest, and then through an area dominated by yellow and white birch.

At about 0.5 mile, the trail passes by some huge boulders. These "glacial erratics" were picked up and carried southward for miles by an advancing glacier. When the ice from the glacier melted, the rocks were left behind. They are termed "erratics" because they are originally from somewhere else and were dumped here "erratically" by the

LOCATION
Bethlehem, NH

RATING
Moderate

DISTANCE
3.4 miles round-trip to both peaks

ELEVATION GAIN
North Sugarloaf, 700 feet; Middle Sugarloaf, 900 feet

ESTIMATED TIME
3.0-4.0 hours

MAPS
AMC White Mountain National Forest Map & Guide, F6

AMC *White Mountain Guide*, 29th ed. Map 2 Franconia–Pemigewasset, F6

USGS Topo: Bethlehem, NH

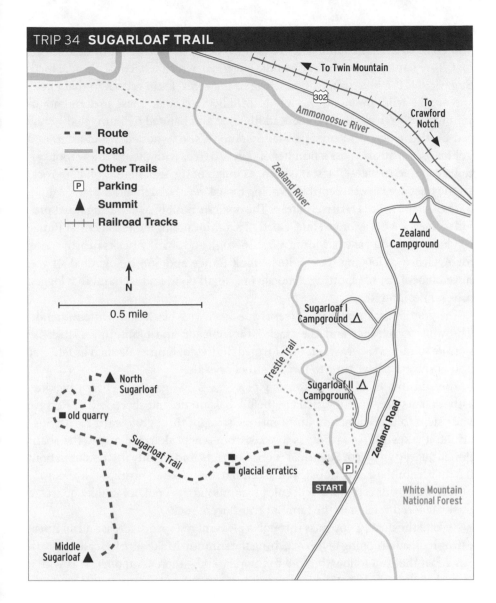

glacier. As you wind your way around these immense boulders, even grown-ups will feel like tiny ants.

Note the lush covering of mosses, rock ferns, and lichens on the boulders. One of the common lichens, rock tripe, forms flat, leathery lobes with dimples. When damp, this lichen turns greenish and even begins to resemble a living organism. It is supposedly edible, but bring along plenty of mayonnaise or mustard. Rock fern (also called Virginia polypody) is a small evergreen fern that thrives on shady cliffs and boulders. If you get a chance, examine the round dots on the underside of its fronds with a hand lens. These are clusters of spore-producing structures.

After the erratics, the trail continues to ascend at a steeper pitch. At 0.9 mile you come to a T junction in the col (saddle) between North and Middle Sugarloaf. Turn left for the summit of Middle Sugarloaf, which is 0.5 mile ahead. North Sugarloaf is 0.3 mile from the junction to the right. I will return to that later.

Note the wildflowers on the way to Middle Sugarloaf. These include mountain wood sorrel, clintonia (bluebead lily), red and painted trillium, goldthread, red-berried elder, wild sarsaparilla, Solomon's seal, whorled wood-aster, and goldenrods. You also pass a number of downed trees with their shallow root systems exposed to view. The soil is thin, as much of the trail here is on bare rock, so the trees are very susceptible to being tossed over by high winds.

The last 0.2 mile is relatively steep. The open summit of Middle Sugarloaf provides fine views of Mount Hale, North Twin Mountain, the Presidential Range (including a good view of Mount Washington), and smaller peaks nearby. Look for evidence of logging on the Rosebrook Range and South Sugarloaf. If you have binoculars, try spotting a moose in a small pond and wetland in a logged area off Zealand Road.

The granite rock under your feet is speckled with black and white minerals. The white is feldspar and the black is hornblende and biotite mica. Because granite solidifies slowly when first formed, individual minerals such as feldspar and hornblende have time to form distinct crystals.

The summit of Middle Sugarloaf provides some good blueberry picking. Other plants are three-toothed cinquefoil, balsam fir, and sheep laurel. Retrace your steps to the T junction and continue straight through toward North Sugarloaf. It takes 30 to 40 minutes to walk from one peak to the other. The abandoned quarry on North Sugarloaf is on your right and slightly up the slope about 0.2 mile from the T junction as you ascend. It looks like an unimpressive jumble of rocks, but kids especially will enjoy scrambling up. Look for smoky quartz, a dusky-colored version of the familiar translucent rock.

Beyond the quarry, you pass through a pleasant red spruce forest and an interesting rock outcropping before reaching the summit. Make sure in scaling North Sugarloaf that you follow the trail to the very end—there is an open area with a vista that you could mistake for the summit just before the actual summit.

The summit of North Sugarloaf is about 200 feet lower than Middle Sugarloaf's. The views are also fine, particularly those of the Zealand Valley, the Presidentials, and Middle Sugarloaf. Reindeer lichen abounds on this summit. This is a pale-green lichen with a delicate branching structure. Lichens thrive on rocky summits with little or no soil because they have the amazing ability to revive even after being almost completely dried out. Birds you might see around the summits of the Sugarloaves are ravens, dark-eyed juncos, and perhaps turkey vultures.

Retrace your steps back to the T junction and turn left there for the walk downhill to the trailhead.

DID YOU KNOW?

Quartz is the most abundant mineral on earth, making up about 12 percent of the planet's crust. Smoky quartz is a variety that is brown or black. It forms as a result of the natural irradiation of quartz over a long time period.

OTHER ACTIVITIES

You can use Trestle Trail, an easy, level trail along the Zealand River, as an extension to this hike. The trail formerly crossed the Zealand River on a trestle that dated to the logging railroad days (it was rebuilt a few times). Unfortunately, the trestle got washed out in 2005 so the crossing is difficult during high water.

Another short walk takes you to Wildlife Pond, 0.2 mile each way on a path heading southeast from the north side of the bridge and across the road from the Sugarloaf trailhead. This provides views of Middle Sugarloaf and its cliffs.

Wading opportunities are available in the Zealand River near the trailhead.

MORE INFORMATION

Sugarloaf Trail is in the White Mountain National Forest (www.fs.usda.gov/whitemountain; 603-536-6100). A day-use fee of $3 is required for parking. The Sugarloaf campgrounds are off Zealand Road right near the trailhead.

Hunting for smoky quartz on North Sugarloaf Mountain.

35

ARETHUSA FALLS AND FRANKENSTEIN CLIFFS

Arethusa Falls is the tallest waterfall in New Hampshire, more than 200 feet high. The falls are an especially stunning sight early in the season. Frankenstein Cliff provides excellent views of Crawford Notch.

DIRECTIONS

From the south, take US 302 north about 8.5 miles from its intersection with Bear Notch Road in Bartlett. The turnoff on a short road to the left is well marked with a sign. From the north, the turnoff for Arethusa Falls is a right turn 6.0 miles south of the Crawford Depot at the head of the notch off US 302. Park in the upper parking lot, which is closer to the trailhead. If that is full, there is ample space at the lower lot just off US 302. *GPS coordinates:* 44° 08.88′ N, 71° 22.20′ W.

TRAIL DESCRIPTION

Arethusa Falls Trail is a pleasant walk along Bemis Brook, and with additional effort, you can also visit several smaller waterfalls. Given its stature as the tallest waterfall in New Hampshire, Arethusa Falls is a popular destination, so expect lots of company, but the view of the falls and the natural history of the area make it more than worth the effort.

You can make a very scenic loop by taking Arethusa-Ripley Falls Trail from the falls to Frankenstein Cliff Trail. You will find some steep ups and downs around Frankenstein Cliffs. In spring and early summer the trail may be closed because of nesting peregrine falcons.

Arethusa Falls Trail is marked with blue blazes and is easy to follow throughout its length. Cross the tracks of the scenic railroad and head into the forest. The trail initially follows an old logging road and almost immediately passes a tree—standing right in the middle of the trail—chiseled out by woodpeckers. In 0.1 mile, Bemis Brook Trail heads

LOCATION
Hart's Location, NH

**ARETHUSA FALLS ONLY:
RATING**
Moderate

DISTANCE
3.0 miles round-trip

ELEVATION GAIN
1,000 feet

ESTIMATED TIME
2.0 hours

**ARETHUSA FALLS TO
FRANKENSTEIN CLIFFS:
RATING**
Moderate, with some steep sections

DISTANCE
4.9 miles round-trip

ELEVATION GAIN
1,500 feet

ESTIMATED TIME
4.0–5.0 hours

MAPS
AMC White Mountain National Forest Map & Guide, H8

AMC *White Mountain Guide,* 29th ed. Map 3 Crawford Notch–Sandwich Range, H8

USGS Topo: Stairs Mountain to Crawford Notch, NH

left to closely follow the shore of Bemis Brook for 0.4 mile before rejoining Arethusa Falls Trail. This side trail takes you past two beautiful small waterfalls, Coliseum Falls and Bemis Brook Falls, but it is rougher and climbs very steeply with lots of exposed roots and rocks before it rejoins the main trail. Take it if you have the time.

Families with young hikers could end their hike at one of these small waterfalls, spend some time lounging on the flat rocks of the streambed, and still have a satisfying outing. The endless patterns that water makes as it cascades over a brink hold an attraction no matter the height of the waterfall.

Most of the trees in the first section of the trail are northern hardwoods (sugar maple, yellow birch, and American beech). Wildflowers and shrubs include pink lady's slipper, painted trillium, clintonia, hobblebush, snowberry, and lowbush blueberry.

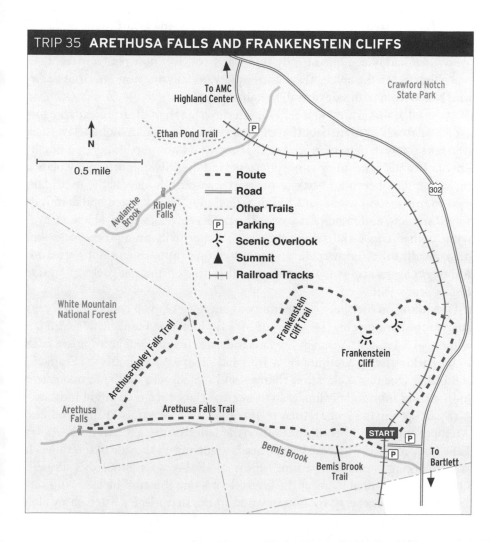

TRIP 35 ARETHUSA FALLS AND FRANKENSTEIN CLIFFS

Arethusa Falls Trail continues on the side of the valley high above Bemis Brook. This section of the trail was relocated—with the help of AmeriCorps volunteers—because of concern about erosion and trampling of vegetation and about the safety of hikers on the slippery rocks near the falls. You will pass a number of fairly recent landslides where paper birch fell over as the earth slipped downward. Other birches were toppled by the ice storm of January 1998.

At 1.3 miles, the trail intersects Arethusa-Ripley Falls Trail, which comes in from the right. For Arethusa Falls, continue to the left for another 0.2 mile until it ends at the viewpoint near the falls.

Arethusa Falls, like nearby Ripley Falls and the waterfalls visible from the roadside in Crawford Notch, is the result of the last continental glacier that covered New England. By flowing in a generally southerly direction, the glaciers deepened the large north–south valleys such as Crawford Notch. Valleys of tributary streams that ran east or west, such as Bemis Brook, were not similarly gouged and so were left high above the valley floor. Geologists call these "hanging valleys" because they are now perched high above the original valley floor. Water that had once flowed gently into the Saco River now plunges steeply to reach the river in the notch. The picturesque waterfalls that now flow into Crawford Notch from both sides are all hanging valleys.

At the falls, which are 750 feet higher in elevation than the trailhead, the forest is a relatively even distribution of trees typically found in higher elevations (the boreal forest: balsam fir and red spruce) and lower elevations (the northern hardwoods). The misty atmosphere around the falls supports many plants, including long beech and oak ferns, northern bush honeysuckle, mountain ash, whorled wood-asters and rough asters, mountain twisted stalk, round-leaved sundew, and mountain avens. The last has broad, kidney-shaped leaves with toothed edges and yellow flowers. It is normally an alpine species but occasionally inhabits lower elevations in the cooler atmosphere along streams. Mountain avens also is found earlier in this hike on the wet rocks alongside Bemis Brook Falls.

Depending on the time of day and your energy level, you could retrace your steps to the parking area (1.5 miles) or hike the loop past Frankenstein Cliff (an additional 3.4 miles). A sign at the falls indicates that it is 1.0 hour or less back to the parking lot by Arethusa Falls Trail and 2.0 to 4.0-plus hours via Frankenstein Cliff. Due to the elevation changes and switchbacks on the Frankenstein loop, it takes substantially longer than a casual glance at a map might indicate.

If you opt for the loop, return to the junction of Arethusa Falls Trail and Arethusa-Ripley Falls Trail and follow the latter to the left. Arethusa-Ripley Falls Trail, marked with blue blazes, heads gradually up the side of the valley. If you are hiking in mid- to late June, this is an ideal spot for pink lady's slippers. Other common inhabitants of the forest floor along this trail include wild sarsaparilla, partridgeberry, mountain wood sorrel, sharp-leafed aster, shiny club moss, and hay-scented fern.

At the base of Arethusa Falls, the tallest waterfall in New Hampshire. Photo by Jerry Monkman.

After a stream crossing, the trail climbs steeply for a short period then levels off along the side of a slope. The trees become shorter, and you get nice views over Crawford Notch through a thinning canopy. This part of Arethusa-Ripley Falls Trail is enjoyable—you're not in a tunnel of trees so typical at this elevation, but instead are visually connected to the surrounding landscape, even within a forest. The large number of blowdowns reveals how shallow the root systems of the trees are. Beech and yellow birch saplings are filling the voids.

Reach the junction with Frankenstein Cliff Trail 1.3 miles from the falls. Look for red spruce, balsam fir, paper birch, yellow birch, blackberries, hobblebush, hay-scented fern, New York fern, and long beech fern at this junction.

Turn right on Frankenstein Cliff Trail. It is marked with yellow blazes and ascends slightly to the height-of-land. The trail then descends through a spruce forest and reaches the outlook ledge on top of the cliffs, 2.1 miles from the falls. The dropoff is dramatic, so you'll want to keep away from the edge, particularly if you are uncomfortable with heights.

Frankenstein Cliff provides a terrific view of the southern part of Crawford Notch. The U-shaped valley was carved out as the last continental glacier moved south through the notch about 20,000 years ago. This is a great spot to get out a compass and a map of the region so you can identify the different peaks. From left to right are Stairs Mountain; Mount Crawford (with a distinct ledge at its summit); Mounts Hope and Chocorua; Bear Mountain; and Mounts Bartlett,

Haystack, Tremont, and Bemis. Arethusa Falls is visible below the long ridge of Mount Bemis. The Saco River threads its way south in the notch, paralleling NH 302 and the railroad. On the ledge where you sit, there are some red pines twisted by the wind and barely hanging on.

Take advantage of the wide vista to look for birds of prey and other wildlife. The cliff has been home to nesting peregrine falcons in recent years. These spectacular birds may linger for a time in the area after they nest. One time I was there, a family of red-tailed hawks was soaring far below in the valley, their screams permeating all the way up to the cliff. Listen for the varied croaking and hoarse cawing of ravens. Sometimes these largest members of the crow family make humanlike noises that make you think you are going to run into a group of hikers on the trail. Chimney swifts are possibilities too. On the ground, friendly chipmunks will probably greet you and expect a handout in return.

From here, it is a steep descent, with steps built into the path in places. Be especially careful of the slippery, gravely footing.

Near the bottom, the trail passes some piles of boulders and then an exposed cliff. The cliff harbors a variety of interesting plants, including joe-pye weed, several species of asters, harebells, spreading dogbane, white snakeroot, flowering raspberries (nice to look at, but the fruits are not edible), and northern-bush honeysuckle. But the extra-special botanical treats at this cliff are round-leafed sundews, growing right in water dripping down the cliff face. These small, carnivorous plants are more typically found in bogs or wet, sandy areas.

The trail levels out, passes under the Frankenstein Trestle of the scenic railroad (the highest railroad trestle in the White Mountains), and then heads south through a nice stand of northern hardwoods. Logs on the forest floor are covered with one of the more picturesque shelf fungi. Its mottled pattern of brown and tan concentric layers gives rise to its common name: turkey tail. Just before you reach the upper parking lot, a short spur heads off left to the lower lot.

DID YOU KNOW?

In Greek mythology, Arethusa was a water nymph (Nereid) who transformed herself into a fountain in order to escape the attentions of a river god. Arethusa is also the name of a very rare New England orchid of bogs and cedar swamps, but its presence in the White Mountains has never been confirmed. Godfrey Frankenstein was an artist who painted in Crawford Notch.

OTHER ACTIVITIES

You could take Arethusa-Ripley Falls Trail from Arethusa Falls to Ripley Falls and then continue out to US 302 on Ethan Pond Trail. This is actually a shorter distance than the loop described above but would require spotting a second vehicle at the Ethan Pond trailhead on US 302. Hiking from this trailhead to Ripley Falls is described in Trip 38.

Visit the Crawford Notch State Park Visitor Center at the Willey House Historic Site before or after your hike for information on the history of Crawford Notch. The site, about 2.5 miles north of the trailhead on US 302, also has restrooms and a snack bar. It is open late spring through midautumn.

MORE INFORMATION

The parking area and trails are in Crawford Notch State Park (nhstateparks.org/visit/state-parks/crawford-notch-state-park.aspx; 603-374-2272). There is no parking fee.

The Dry River Campground, part of Crawford Notch State Park, is about 0.5 mile north of the turnoff to Arethusa Falls on US 302.

36

MOUNT AVALON

The narrow summit of Mount Avalon provides excellent views of Crawford Notch, the Willey Range, and the Southern Presidentials, including Mount Washington. For much of its length, Avalon Trail follows Crawford Brook, with some particularly attractive cascades.

DIRECTIONS

The trailhead for Avalon Trail is across the railroad tracks from Crawford Depot (Macomber Family Information Center) on US 302 at the head of Crawford Notch. It is the same trailhead as for Mount Willard Trail, so see Trip 33 for driving directions. AMC's Highland Center is about 100 yards north of the trailhead. *GPS coordinates:* 44° 13.08′ N, 71° 24.66′ W.

TRAIL DESCRIPTION

Two trails lead from Crawford Depot up the Willey Range to breathtaking, sweeping views of the glacially carved valley of Crawford Notch. Mount Willard Trail is the better traveled and its summit can be reached in 1.5 hours; however, there is little to see along the way. Avalon Trail is longer, with a greater elevation gain, and the trail is more interesting.

Avalon Trail runs together with Mount Willard Trail for the first 0.1 mile. Continue straight where Mount Willard Trail leaves to the left. At about 0.3 mile, the trail crosses Crawford Brook (an easy crossing except if water levels are very high). Beyond the stream crossing, a side trail leads left along the streamside and takes you past Beecher and Pearl cascades.

Beecher Cascade is named for the famous abolitionist Henry Ward Beecher, who spent many summers in the White Mountains in the latter part of the nineteenth century, along with his sister, Harriet Beecher Stowe, author

LOCATION
Carroll, NH, at trailhead; Bethlehem, NH, on Mount Avalon summit

RATING
Moderate, with one steep section

DISTANCE
3.7 miles round-trip

ELEVATION GAIN
1,550 feet

ESTIMATED TIME
3.0-4.0 hours

MAPS
AMC *White Mountain National Forest Map & Guide*, G7

AMC *White Mountain Guide*, 29th ed. Map 3 Crawford Notch–Sandwich Range, G7

USGS Topo: Crawford Notch

of *Uncle Tom's Cabin.* Pearl Cascade is undoubtedly named for its frothy white-water. In summer, both falls are particularly attractive after a rainstorm. At the base of Pearl Cascade, note the small tributary that flows through a mossy gorge with abundant sphagnum moss, Indian cucumber-root, and hobblebush just before it joins Crawford Brook. Sugar maple, American beech, and yellow birch dominate the canopy.

The side trail rejoins the main trail where you will find some good sitting rocks for lunch or a snack. Avalon Trail continues at an easy grade, always within earshot of flowing water. The large number of paper birches suggests that the area was disturbed, perhaps by fire or logging, in the early part of the twentieth century. The trail recrosses the brook at 0.8 mile. At 1.3 miles, A-Z Trail—named after its route, from Avalon to Zealand Trail—comes in from the west. The forest at this point has almost completely transitioned to spruce-fir. Follow Avalon Trail to the left at this junction. The trail then ascends steeply over rocks for the next 0.5 mile, with views through trees over a valley toward Mount Tom. The trail then levels out and a spur path leads left steeply, with some scrambling required, about 100 yards to the summit of Mount Avalon.

Mount Avalon was named so by Moses Sweetser because it reminded him of the Avalon Hills of Newfoundland. Its summit provides a wonderful view of

The glacially carved valley of Crawford Notch from Mount Avalon.

the U-shaped, glacially carved valley of Crawford Notch. This was formed by the north-to-south movement of the last continental glacier that advanced into the area about 100,000 years ago and melted away about 12,000 years ago. The view also includes Mount Webster, with its impressive cliffs, and all the Southern Presidentials through Mount Washington. Looking west, you can see the wooded summits of the Willey Range.

Mount Avalon is at the boundary of two different watersheds. Crawford Brook drains the valley between Mounts Tom and Field, and then flows north to join the Ammonoosuc River streaming down Mount Washington and eventually the Connecticut River. A drop of water flowing over Beecher and Pearl Cascades enters the Atlantic Ocean at Long Island Sound. On the south side of Mount Avalon, the drainage is to the Saco River, which flows into the ocean off southern Maine. Saco Lake, visible from the Mount Avalon summit, is part of the Saco drainage, and AMC's Highland Center, across the road from that lake, sits on the height-of-land that separates the two watersheds.

The small open area at the Mount Avalon summit has scattered short trees, including balsam fir, red spruce, larch, pin cherry, and heart-leaved birch. Bog bilberry, lowbush blueberry, mountain ash, and mountain holly are the main shrubs and flowers, and low "subshrubs" include bunchberry, mountain cranberry, clintonia (bluebead lily), painted trillium, and snowberry. While

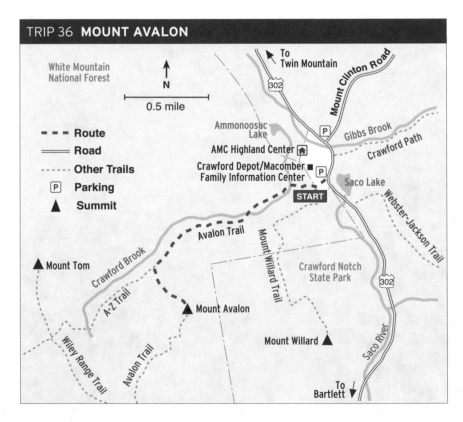

searching for these plants, we were accompanied by golden-crowned kinglets and yellow-rumped warblers, but the birds you might encounter are always hard to predict.

Retrace your steps to return to Avalon Trail. Turn right for the trailhead. If you have time, take a left turn and continue west along the Avalon Trail for several hundred yards beyond the spur trail to an interesting flat ledge with views of Mount Avalon in one direction and the summit of Mounts Tom and Field in the other. Look here for reindeer lichen, a bushy, light-green lichen that thrives in sunny, dry locations with little soil. Mountain cranberry, with leaves that are small, dark green, glossy, and smooth-edged, is interspersed with the lichen. Mountain holly, a shrub noted for its red berries and leaves with a small point on the tip, is also common. Note a narrow band of quartz, which is a dike within the granite along the trail here.

Turn around and follow Avalon Trail back to the trailhead.

DID YOU KNOW?

The Avalon Hills of Newfoundland, for which Mount Avalon was named, were in Paleozoic times part of a small island continent between the predecessors of North America and Europe. Avalonia's rocks are now found both in North America and Great Britain, providing strong evidence for plate tectonics and continental drift., i.e., that our continents are located on plates that have floated on top of the earth's mantle since the beginning of time, constantly changing the arrangement of land masses on earth.

OTHER ACTIVITIES

For a longer hike, make a loop by continuing on Avalon Trail for another mile to the Willey Range Trail just below the summit of 4,340-foot Mount Field. Turn right (northwest) on Willey Range Trail. After 0.9 mile, descend via A-Z Trail and Avalon Trail. The loop is substantially longer than just retracing your steps from Mount Avalon, and is a popular snowshoe route.

MORE INFORMATION

The trailhead is in Crawford Notch State Park (nhstateparks.org/visit/state-parks/crawford-notch-state-park.aspx; 603-374-2272). There is no parking fee. The Macomber Family Information Center near the trailhead, operated by AMC, has restrooms, water, snacks, and trail information; outdoors.org/lodging/lodges/highland/crawford-notch-depot.cfm. The AMC Hiker Shuttle stops at the Highland Center near the trailhead; outdoors.org/lodging/lodging-shuttle.cfm.

37

ZEALAND TRAIL TO ZEALAND FALLS HUT AND ZEALAND POND

This hike takes you to one of the premier locations in the White Mountains for birds and other wildlife, including moose and beavers. From the front porch of AMC's Zealand Hut, you get one of the most spectacular views in the White Mountains, and you can easily spend hours at the falls and river nearby.

LOCATION
Bethlehem, NH

RATING
Moderate

DISTANCE
5.4 miles round-trip

ELEVATION GAIN
650 feet

ESTIMATED TIME
3.0-4.0 hours

MAPS
AMC White Mountain National Forest Map & Guide, G7

AMC White Mountain Guide, 29th ed. Map 2 Franconia–Pemigewasset, G7

USGS Topo: Crawford Notch

DIRECTIONS

The trailhead for Zealand Trail is near Twin Mountain and Bretton Woods. From the Conway–Jackson area, take US 302 west through Crawford Notch. Turn left onto Zealand Road at the Zealand Campground, about 6.0 miles northwest of the Crawford Notch State Park Visitor Center. Follow Zealand Road for about 3.5 miles until its end and park in the lot. The trail is straight ahead, beyond the gate. This is a stop for the AMC Hiker Shuttle. Zealand Road is closed to vehicles from mid-November to mid-May, and hikers and skiers must park across US 302, 0.2 mile from Zealand Road.

From Franconia Notch: Take US 3 north to Twin Mountain. Turn right (east) on US 302 and follow it for 2.0 miles. Turn right at the Zealand Campground and follow Zealand Road until its end as above. From points north: Follow either US 3 or NH 115 south to Twin Mountain. Turn left (east) onto US 302 and follow the directions given above. *GPS coordinates:* 44° 13.49′ N, 71° 28.70′ W.

TRAIL DESCRIPTION

Plan on spending a full day, because there is much for the whole family to see and do along Zealand Trail and around the hut. Zealand Trail is well marked with blue blazes and is relatively easy, except for a steep pitch to the hut in the last 0.1 mile. It follows the bed of an old logging railroad for most of its length. The trail does cross some soggy ter-

The phenomenal view from Zealand Hut is one of the finest in the White Mountains.

rain, and despite wooden bridges and planks, it can still be a bit wet in spring or during wet weather. Be aware that the winter ski trail crosses back and forth over the hiking trail.

Leaving the parking area, ascend on a slight uphill through a dense forest of red spruce with young trees lining the trail. You will soon enter northern hardwoods. After about 20 minutes, the first of many wooden bridges crosses a wet area. At 0.8 mile, approach the Zealand River, where several flat rocks are perfect for having a snack or lunch. At 1.5 miles, the trail crosses the river. You pass through a very attractive balsam fir and white birch woodland with an understory of mountain wood sorrel, clintonia, and hobblebush.

After about 50 minutes (1.8 miles), the trail crosses an open beaver swamp. The Forest Service has to constantly respond to the latest engineering projects of the beavers to keep Zealand Trail above water, and the elevated wooden walkway here is its most recent move. Look for stumps of beaver-chiseled trees, as well as the animals' dams and lodges.

The trail then reenters the forest and skirts open wetlands and wet meadows. At 2.3 miles (about 1.5 hours), A-Z Trail enters from the left, just beyond a beautiful grassy, wet meadow with a view across to Mount Tom. A few years back, this meadow was a beaver pond, but then the beavers disappeared. The pond drained as their dam fell into disrepair, and the pond turned into a meadow.

New beavers moved in, restored the dam, and reflooded the area. In the late nineteenth century, this was neither a pond nor a meadow, but a railroad yard serving the logging industry.

Moose like to feed on tender water plants, so beaver ponds are good places to look for this largest member of the deer family. Moose tracks, resembling large deer tracks, are likely to be in muddy areas around any of the wetlands; their rounded droppings may also be there. The sharpest-eyed member of your group may also find moose teeth marks on bark, where it looks like someone stripped the bark off the tree with a giant comb.

While looking for birds and moose around the beaver ponds, listen for green frogs, which sound like someone plunking the strings of a banjo. Dragonflies patrol for insects over the water. Tall meadow rue, a plant with fuzzy white flowers, is abundant on the shoreline.

Beyond the junction with A-Z Trail, Zealand Trail crosses the inlet to Zealand Pond, following the shore of the pond. AMC trail crews make neat stacks of logs in this area. The wood is used to heat Zealand Hut in winter. Zealand Trail ends at the junction of the Ethan Pond and Twinway trails (2.5 miles).

Turn right onto Twinway Trail to reach Zealand Falls Hut in another 0.2 mile. The last 0.1 mile is rough and steep but stone steps aid your ascent. The bottom of Zealand Falls is to the left, near the base of this steep part.

Situated at 2,700 feet at the head of Zealand Notch, Zealand Falls Hut is one of AMC's eight backcountry huts, which can be reached only by hiking. Day-hikers are welcome to stop in, use the restrooms, fill their water bottles, buy snacks, peruse educational displays, and chat with the "croo" (the friendly staff).

The view from Zealand Falls Hut of Zealand and Carrigain notches is one of the most magnificent in the White Mountains. Zealand Notch, the closer of the two, is a classic U-shaped glacially carved valley. It is bounded on the left (east) by the impressive cliffs of Whitewall Mountain. Rock slides, logging, and fires have left much of Whitewall Mountain barren. The straight horizontal line on the mountainside is a former logging railroad that is now a section of Ethan Pond Trail. Places where logs were dragged down the mountain to the railroad left skid marks, some of which are still visible. The west side of Zealand Notch is bounded by Zealand Ridge, which can be reached by following Twinway Trail very steeply beyond the hut. Carrigain Notch in the distance has an aura of remoteness.

It is hard to imagine when looking out over this verdant scenery that the Zealand Valley was completely ravaged by logging from about 1880 to 1903. During this short period, there was a town with a sawmill, school, post office, and railroad yard just west of the present-day Zealand Campground. Loggers stayed at logging camps near the falls and sent the logs to the sawmill on the railroad. The hut has an interesting display of old photographs on the wall from this period. Sloppy logging activity spawned a number of devastating forest fires, as sparks from the railroad ignited brush left over from the logging operations. The

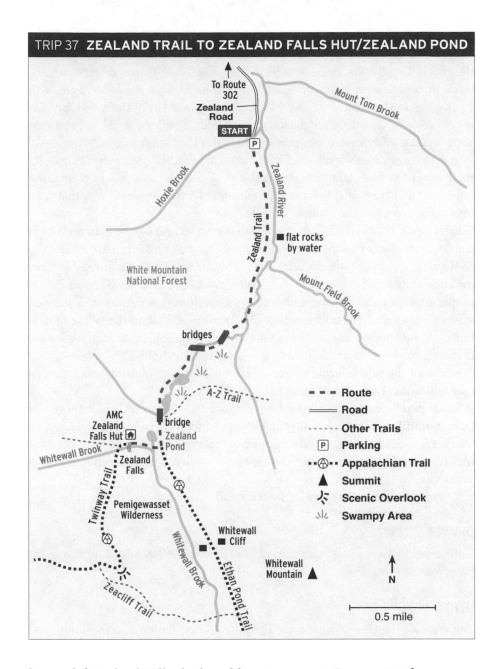

loggers left Zealand Valley looking like a moonscape. See page 105 for more on logging in the White Mountains.

Although the forest has come back, the impact of logging is still evident. The area probably had much more spruce before logging than it currently does, because that was the primary tree sought. Paper birch, which is one of the first species to colonize a disturbed area, still covers large areas that had been clear-cut.

Zealand Falls Hut is popular with birders. In June and July, you can hear the songs of winter wrens, hermit thrushes, and white-throated sparrows right from the porch. These birds, along with purple finches, black-throated blue warblers, black-throated green warblers, redstarts, ovenbirds, and red-eyed vireos, will be singing and calling along the trail, but spotting them in the dense forest is tough. It's easier to see black ducks, wood ducks, blue jays, swallows, and perhaps even a goshawk over the open areas around the beaver ponds.

Just in front of the porch at the hut are a few red-berried elders. This distinctive shrub of wet areas and streamsides has compound leaves in pairs along branches. Red-berried elders produce clusters of small white flowers that turn into small, colorful (but inedible) berries.

Explore the rocky riverbed of Whitewall Brook (except during extremely high water), a few yards beyond the hut. On a hot day, you will immediately feel the cool breeze streaming down the mountain by the brook. This natural refrigerator allows alpine plants to grow at a lower elevation than usual. The showiest is mountain avens, a wildflower with bright-yellow flowers and rounded, scalloped leaves that is found virtually nowhere else in the world but in the White Mountains. Mountain cranberry, a low plant with small, dark-green, evergreen leaves, is also there, wherever there is enough soil for a root to hold. Other plants growing around the brook include three-toothed cinquefoil, meadowsweet, mountain ash, balsam fir, and red spruce.

Many people enjoy sitting on the flat rocks in Whitewall Brook above the falls. A number of pools within the brook are deep enough for swimming or wading, particularly if you walk upstream. Hearty polar bears will jump right in; others will join them if the weather is hot enough. The screeches you hear are decidedly human.

Retrace your steps to return to the trailhead.

DID YOU KNOW?

Rumor has it that the area was named "Zealand" after New Zealand as a testament to its remoteness.

OTHER ACTIVITIES

Zealand Falls Hut is a popular cross-country ski destination, and the hut is open on a self-serve basis in winter. Reservations are required year-round (see below). Because the trail follows an old logging road, it is not difficult except for the last 0.1 mile, where you need to remove your skis. Keep in mind, however, that Zealand Road is closed from mid-November through mid-May, adding 3.5 miles to the journey.

If you have the time and energy for a longer hike (or if you are staying overnight at the hut), you can combine this hike with a hike along Ethan Pond Trail from its junction with Zealand Trail to Thoreau Falls, named for the famous naturalist and philosopher. This takes you along the side of Whitewall Mountain, an area that was once heavily logged. Another option is to hike up the Zeacliff Trail for terrific views of the Pemigewasset Wilderness.

MORE INFORMATION

Zealand Falls Hut offers overnight lodging with breakfast and dinner (reservations essential; outdoors.org/whitemountains; 603-466-2727). Sleeping accommodations are in two large rooms with eighteen bunks each, so the hut is not as comfortable for families with young children as Lonesome Lake Hut. But even a day trip to Zealand Falls Hut is more than worth the effort. If you do stay overnight, the hut is a base for a number of wonderful day hikes.

The Zealand Trail is entirely within the White Mountain National Forest (www.fs.usda.gov/whitemountain; 603-536-6100). A user fee ($3 per day) is required to park at the trailhead.

BEAVERS

Beavers are one of the largest members of the rodent family, which also includes mice, squirrels, and woodchucks. Their webbed feet are perfect for swimming and their scaly flat tails, when slapped on the water, warn other beavers of danger. Beavers use their large front teeth to feed on the nutritious inner bark of trees, favoring aspens, birches, alders, willows, and maples. Grasses and other vegetation are also part of their diets.

Beavers are one of the few animals (along with humans) that modify their entire habitat to suit their needs, building dams and conical houses of sticks and mud. As "ecosystem engineers," beavers have had a major influence on New England and the rest of the country. Their mud-and-stick dams alter the flow of rivers, flooding forests and creating ponds and wetlands that serve not only the beavers but other wildlife as well. Their ponds trap sediments and other pollutants, playing a role in maintaining clear waters downstream.

A beaver family of parents, newborns (kits), and 1-year-olds occupies a lodge. Two-year-olds are driven out of their natal lodge by their parents and may start their own colony nearby. A family will establish a new residence up- or downstream when they have consumed many of their favorite trees. In winter, these rodents stockpile small branches underwater and then remain in their lodges most of the time, venturing out of the underwater entrance only to grab something from their food cache under the ice.

In the first few centuries of European settlement of this country, beavers were trapped in large numbers for their valuable fur. Beaver hats were a fashion rage in Europe, particularly through the early 1800s, so beaver pelts were a major source of revenue for the colonies and the young nation. Under this intense trapping pressure, combined with habitat losses, beavers largely disappeared from New England by the mid-1800s. Their dams fell into disrepair, changing the watery landscape into more uniformly flowing waters. They were reintroduced into New Hampshire around 1930 and have made a remarkable comeback in the state and throughout New England.

Although you can find ample evidence of their presence in beaver-chiseled trees, dams, and lodges, beavers are hard to spot. The best time to look is in the half-light of early dawn or dusk, being as quiet as possible.

Beavers, nature's engineers, can be found in many ponds in the mountains.

38

ETHAN POND AND RIPLEY FALLS

Ethan Allen Crawford described the pond that would be named for him thusly: "For beauty and grandeur it is nowhere surpassed by any spot to me known about these mountains." Ripley Falls is one of the most impressive cascades in the White Mountains.

DIRECTIONS

The trailhead for Ethan Pond Trail and Ripley Falls is at the site of the old Willey House Station off US 302 in Crawford Notch State Park, about 1.0 mile south of the Willey House Historic Site. A sign for Ripley Falls and the Appalachian Trail is located at the turnoff, which leads up a paved road 0.3 mile to a parking area. If that lot is full, you can park off US 302. The turnoff is about 4.0 miles south of Crawford Depot and AMC's Highland Center and 12.0 miles southeast of the junction of US 302 and US 3 in Twin Mountain. If you are coming up through Jackson or North Conway, the turnoff is about 16.0 miles northwest of the intersection of US 302 and NH 16 in Glen. *GPS coordinates:* 44° 10.05' N, 71° 23.16' W.

TRAIL DESCRIPTION

This is a great pond-waterfall combination. Ethan Pond, a remote, 4-acre pond bordered on one side by the steep cliffs of Mount Willey and on the other by a vista across to the Twin Range, was named for Ethan Allen Crawford, who camped there during one of his hunting trips in fall 1829. After hiking to the pond, you can extend your walk by visiting Ripley Falls, only an additional 0.6 mile. Ripley Falls alone is a good hike, even for younger children.

Ethan Pond Trail is part of the Appalachian Trail and is marked with white blazes. It almost immediately crosses the tracks of the Conway Scenic Railroad near a trestle. Avoid the temptation to walk along the railroad tracks and

LOCATION
Hart's Location, NH, to Bethlehem, NH

RATING
Moderate, with one steep section

DISTANCE
6.0 miles round-trip

ELEVATION GAIN
1,600 feet

ESTIMATED TIME
5.0 hours

MAPS
AMC White Mountain National Forest Map & Guide, G7-8

AMC *White Mountain Guide,* 29th ed. Map 3 Crawford Notch–Sandwich Range, G7-8

USGS Topo: Crawford Notch

on the trestle, which is dangerous and illegal. In 0.2 mile, Ripley Falls Trail leads left (you will return to that later) and Ethan Pond Trail continues steeply ahead. In about 0.5 mile, the trail levels off and becomes a very pleasant walk, varying between a gradual ascent and level ground.

The northern hardwood forest here features yellow birch, a few larger sugar maples, many sugar maple saplings, and an understory of striped maple and hobblebush. The shade-tolerant sugar maple saplings await the opportunity afforded by the creation of a gap in the canopy to eventually take their place in the forest canopy. Gaps are created when canopy trees fall over due to wind, disease, or insects. Note a particularly distinctive uprooted paper birch along the trail about 0.5 mile from the trailhead. Its shallow root system, which led to its demise, illustrates how rocky the soil is on these slopes.

As you continue hiking, you will notice the forest becoming increasingly dominated by spruce and fir trees. Kedron Flume Trail enters from the right at 1.3 mile.

(This trail leads past the Kedron Flume to the Willey House Historic Site, but the section between Ethan Pond Trail and the flume is steep and rough.) At 1.6 mile (about 1.0 hour), Willey Range Trail intersects at a point where Ethan Pond Trail turns left. The transition between the lower-elevation deciduous forest and the higher-elevation boreal forest is complete at this point.

Ethan Pond Trail climbs gradually for another 0.3 mile beyond the Willey Range intersection and then passes through a beautiful, level area of boreal forest with lots of small streams, wetlands, and bog bridges. Look

The rocks at the outlet to Ethan Pond provide a view of cliffs on Mount Willey and lead you to the shelter. Photo by Jerry Monkman.

for dense growth of both green and red peat (sphagnum) mosses in this damp area. These two colors actually represent separate species. Peat mosses have an amazing ability to absorb and retain water due to large vacuoles (spaces) in their cells. This is why they are so useful in gardens. Several stands of fringed sedge (long, drooping cylinders of brown flowers) are found in these wetlands too. Other plants include clintonia, goldthread, bunchberries, snowberry, sheep laurel, northern wild raisin, and sharp-leaved and purple-stemmed asters.

The trail crosses the height-of-land (about 2,900 feet) that represents the boundary between the Saco and Pemigewasset/Merrimack River watersheds. You occasionally get views of Mount Willey through the trees. At 2.6 miles, the short spur trail that leads in 0.1 mile to Ethan Pond and the Ethan Pond Campsite comes in from the right. This crosses the inlet at which you get the best view of the pond and the cliff of Mount Willey. The shelter at the campsite is a good place to have lunch, but it does not have a view of the pond.

Take some time to sit on one of the rocks by the inlet and contemplate the surroundings. You can see why this pond was so favored by the legendary woodsman, guide, and innkeeper Ethan Allen Crawford. He appreciated its beauty and its abundance of fish and wildlife. Lucy Crawford's *History of the White Mountains* describes one fishing trip in which the party he guided caught about 70 "salmon trout" (native brook trout) in a very short time and broiled them over a fire on the banks of the pond. He saw ample signs of moose that fed on the waterlilies. Another story, cited in John Mudge's *The White Mountains: Names, Places, and Legends,* describes a hunting trip in which Crawford's group shot two moose at the pond and feasted on moose and trout. They eventually went to sleep within the skins of the moose, paying no attention to the howling of wolves nearby.

Wolves are long gone from Ethan Pond and the rest of the White Mountains, but those camping at the campsite have to be careful to stow their food properly because of bears. A moose in this shallow pond (the greatest depth is 4 feet) is always a possibility.

On the opposite shore of the pond, the outlet drains into the East Branch of the Pemigewasset River. This flows through one of the largest wilderness areas in the White Mountains. In the same direction on a clear day, you can see North and South Twin mountains. Behind you, the cliffs of Mount Willey loom above the campsite, and you may hear the hoarse cawing and croaking of ravens, which roost and possibly nest on the cliff. Peregrines periodically take up residence on the cliffs as well.

The area is covered with vegetation typical of the boreal forest. Immediately along the shoreline, look for larch, Labrador tea, mountain holly, shadbush, alders, and sweet gale. Sweet gale leaves give off the pleasant odor of bayberry when crushed. Black spruce grows along the spur trail leading to the pond. This small tree has short, bluish-green needles and is characteristic of northern bogs. The upland forest surrounding the pond is characterized by red spruce

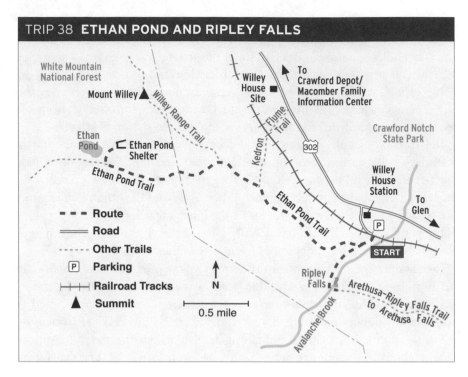

White Mountain
National Forest

Mount Willey ▲

Willey Range Trail

Willey
House
Site

To
Crawford Depot/
Macomber Family
Information Center

Flume Trail

Kedron Trail

302

Crawford Notch
State Park

Ethan
Pond ⊏ Ethan Pond
Shelter

Ethan Pond Trail

Ethan Pond Trail

Willey
House
Station

To
Glen

P

START

Ripley
Falls

Arethusa-Ripley Falls Trail
to Arethusa Falls

Avalanche Brook

- - - **Route**
══ **Road**
····· **Other Trails**
P **Parking**
+++ **Railroad Tracks**
▲ **Summit**

N

0.5 mile

and balsam fir. Birds of this forest include boreal chickadees, red-breasted nuthatches, brown creepers, and several species of warblers.

Retrace your steps to return. When you reach the junction with Arethusa-Ripley Falls Trail (0.2 mile from the trailhead), turn right for Ripley Falls. Arethusa-Ripley Falls Trail was marked with both yellow and blue blazes at the time of this writing. The trail proceeds high above Avalanche Brook, perched on the side of a steep slope for much of the 0.3 mile between Ethan Pond Trail and the falls.

When you approach the falls, note how the cool water and shady gorge make you feel like you just walked into a refrigerator. This feeling is particularly pronounced (and welcome) on a hot day. Be careful of the slippery rocks just underneath the waterfall. Ripley Falls is 100 feet high and flows gracefully down a slab of granite. The falls is named after Henry Wheelock Ripley, who reported its existence in the 1850s. Like many other waterfalls in the area, Ripley Falls is a product of the last glaciations. It is called a hanging valley (see Trip 35 for an explanation).

If you have time, climb up the left side of the waterfall and explore above the falls (but not too close to the brink). This requires you to cross the stream, which could be difficult in high water. The hike up to the top of the falls is steep, but you'll get away from the crowds and also find a few pretty pools in which you can swim. The ledges at the top of the falls can also be slippery, so be extra careful if you explore there.

OTHER ACTIVITIES

Visit the Crawford Notch State Park Visitor Center at the Willey House Historic Site before or after your hike for information on the history of Crawford Notch. The site, about 5.0 miles north of the trailhead on US 302, also has restrooms and a snack bar. It is open from late spring through midautumn.

MORE INFORMATION

This hike begins in Crawford Notch State Park (nhstateparks.org/visit/state-parks/crawford-notch-state-park.aspx 603-374-2272) and ends in the White Mountain National Forest (www.fs.usda.gov/whitemountain; 603-536-6100). There is no fee for parking. The AMC Hiker Shuttle stops at the trailhead; outdoors.org/lodging/lodging-shuttle.cfm.

39

MOUNT CRAWFORD

The 3,119-foot summit of Mount Crawford, surrounded by the Presidential Range and innumerable other peaks in all directions, provides one of the most stunning vistas in the White Mountains. The hike also provides an opportunity to see birds and plants of the boreal forest.

CAUTION Slippery in wet weather with steep dropoffs. Do not attempt in bad weather.

LOCATION
Hart's Location, NH, to Hadley's Purchase, NH

RATING
Strenuous

DISTANCE
5.0 miles round-trip

ELEVATION GAIN
2,100 feet

ESTIMATED TIME
5.0 hours

MAPS
AMC *White Mountain National Forest Map & Guide*, H8

AMC *White Mountain Guide*, 29th ed. Map 3 Crawford Notch–Sandwich Range, H8

USGS Topo: Bartlett to Stairs Mountain, NH

DIRECTIONS

The trailhead for Davis Path is off US 302, 6.3 miles north of where Route 302 crosses Bear Notch Road in Bartlett and 5.6 miles south of the Willey House Historic Site in Crawford Notch. Ample parking is available at a parking lot on the east side of US 302. *GPS coordinates: 44° 07.12′ N, 71° 21.21′ W.*

TRAIL DESCRIPTION

Mount Crawford is reached by Davis Path, one of the oldest hiking trails in the White Mountains. The trail was completed by Nathaniel Davis in 1845 as a bridle path to the summit of Mount Washington. Davis was a son-in-law of Abel Crawford, the "Old Patriarch" of the Crawford family, who brought his family to the area in the 1790s. Abel built the Mount Crawford House near the current trailhead. Davis, who managed the Mount Crawford House, was married to Hannah, the sister of Ethan Allen Crawford. The trail fell into disuse in the 1850s and was brought back as a footpath in 1910 by AMC.

This is a hike to save for a clear day. For much of its distance, it is a relentless ascent within a tunnel of trees, so you want to be sure that you see something at the top. The ledges near the summit can be slippery in wet weather.

Leaving the parking area, the trail follows a dirt road along the west bank of the Saco River for a few hundred yards. It turns right to cross the river on an interesting footbridge, the Bemis Bridge. Samuel Bemis was a dentist from Boston who summered in the White Mountains from 1827 through 1840, eventually retiring here. The home he built, Notchland, is now an inn.

Beyond the bridge, the trail passes through an overgrown field (private property), turns left to follow a power-line right of way for a short distance, and then crosses a streambed that is likely to be dry by late summer. It enters the White Mountain National Forest and follows a small brook, which could be dry. At about 0.5 mile, you pass a sign indicating that you are entering the Presidential Dry River Wilderness (groups limited to ten or fewer; no bikes, no motorized vehicles).

One special wildflower to look for in this lower section of the trail is twinflower (illustrated here), a small plant that trails along the ground. Pairs of

rounded leaves with slightly scalloped edges come off the wiry stem at regular intervals. In July, you can find its two small, pink tubular flowers produced on a single upright stalk, hence its name. Twinflower was a favorite flower of Carolus Linnaeus, the Swedish scientist responsible for developing the system used by all scientists of naming all organisms with a genus and species name in Latin. Linnaeus is often pictured holding a twinflower.

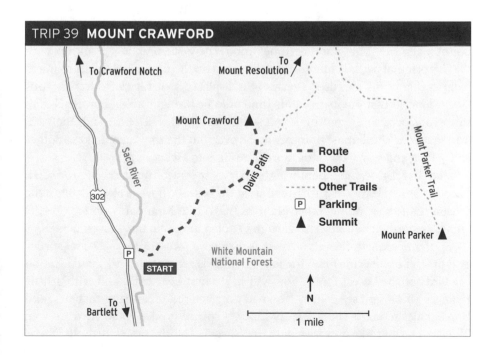

The windswept summit of Mount Crawford has sweeping views and many "flag" trees.
Photo by Jerry Monkman.

Continuing on, you pass a side trail leading right through red pines to a back-country tentsite. The grade becomes moderately steep as you hook up with Davis's original path. While you are chugging up the mountain, take a moment to marvel at how Davis used a series of well-placed switchbacks to traverse this steep slope so that guests from his inn could be brought up on horseback. On numerous occasions, you think you see the top of the ridge through the trees and that your climb must imminently be over, but the trail then makes another sharp turn and somehow finds more mountain to ascend.

Witch hazel grows abundantly in this part of the trail. This shrub has rounded, bluntly toothed leaves that are irregular at the base. Its flowers bloom later in the season than those of any other plant in the White Mountains, so look for its small, greenish-yellow flowers through October and even into November.

At 1.9 miles, the trail levels off, passes through a forest of 10- to 12-foot spruce and fir, and reaches the first vista at a ledge. This general area is a good location for birds of the boreal forest. You will likely first hear calls, and with a little patience you might see golden-crowned kinglets, red-breasted nuthatches, and boreal chickadees. If you are truly lucky, a spruce grouse could surprise you. This is a chicken-like bird with dark, bluish-gray coloring and streaks. It can be surprisingly tame and unafraid of people (or seemingly lacking in intelligence, depending on your perspective).

At 2.2 miles, the spur trail to the summit of Mount Crawford departs to the left at the base of an open ledge. Take care to follow the blazes up the ledge, and go an additional 0.3 mile to the summit. Use caution in wet weather.

The summit of Mount Crawford provides a wonderful 360-degree view. Mount Hope is immediately to the south, and you can see the route of your ascent between this peak and Mount Crawford. Beyond Mount Hope in the same direction are Bear Mountain, Attitash Mountain, Mount Tremont, and the valley of the Sawyer River. The small clear-cuts you see near Bear Mountain are in the Bartlett Experimental Forest and are being studied by the University of New Hampshire. Farther in the distance to the south is Mount Tripyramid. To the east, the most prominent features are Mount Resolution and the steps of Stairs Mountain. To the north, the Southern Presidentials and Mount Washington frame the horizon. Crawford Notch and the Willey Range are to the northeast. Frankenstein Cliff is a prominent feature in that direction. Finally, Mount Carrigain looms large to the west.

The handiwork of the last glacier is evident in this magnificent scenery. It smoothed out the tops of all these peaks, so that many of them are rounded,

The aptly named Giant Stairs on Stairs Mountain can be seen from the summit of Mount Crawford on a clear day.

most notably Mount Eisenhower. Glaciers scooped out deep valleys, such as Crawford Notch below you. The ledges around the summit of Mount Crawford bear parallel scratches etched by small stones squeezed between the moving glacier and the bedrock.

Flag (banner) trees provide evidence of the wind's power on this exposed summit. Many of the spruce and fir on the summit have branches only on one side, the side away from the prevailing wind. Other plants adapted to growing on this exposed summit include a large number of heaths: Labrador tea, bog bilberry, black huckleberry, lowbush blueberry, mountain cranberry, black crowberry, leatherleaf, sheep laurel, and rhodora. Three-toothed cinquefoil, reindeer lichen, and poverty grass also are here.

On your descent from the summit on the spur trail, be careful to follow the blazes back to Davis Path. Retrace your steps to the parking area.

OTHER ACTIVITIES

Visit the Crawford Notch State Park Visitor Center at the Willey House Historic Site before or after your hike for information on the history of Crawford Notch. The site, about 5.0 miles north of the trailhead on US 302, also has restrooms and a snack bar. It is open from late spring through midautumn.

MORE INFORMATION

The first third of a mile of Davis Path is on private land, so please respect the rights of the landowners. The remainder of the trail is in the White Mountain National Forest (www.fs.usda.gov/whitemountain; 603-536-6100). There is no parking fee.

The Dry River Campground, part of Crawford Notch State Park, is about 2.5 miles north of the Davis Path trailhead on US 302; nhstateparks.org/visit/state-parks/crawford-notch-state-park.aspx; 603-374-2272.

THE CRAWFORD FAMILY

Many individuals and organizations have contributed to trail building and maintenance in the White Mountains, and it is impossible in a short essay to do justice to all. One name that has achieved legendary status is Crawford. As described in the Mizpah Spring trip (Trip 40), Crawford Path is considered the oldest continually maintained hiking trail in the Northeast. It was built by Abel and Ethan Allen Crawford in 1819. Abel, the "Old Patriarch" of the Crawford family, came to the Crawford Notch area in 1791 soon after the first road through the notch was opened. First deeded land at what is now Fabyan's Station restaurant (site of the base station of the cog railway), Abel eventually settled in Notchland, near the current trailhead of Davis Path off US 302. Realizing that farming was difficult in this valley, he set up an inn to serve the commercial traffic that used the road to journey between Portland, ME, and points west. Eventually, enough tourists were staying at the inn that Abel and his son, Ethan Allen (at 6 feet, 3 inches called "the Mountain Giant"), were motivated to build a path up the mountains. They completed the 8.25-mile path from the Gateway of the Notch to Mount Washington and used it to guide their guests up the mountains.

The initial Crawford Path was rough and sometimes hard to follow. No doubt the clouds and mist above treeline were similar to what hikers find today, so even the Crawfords would occasionally have to stop to figure out the right direction. Two years after the completion of the original Crawford Path, Ethan built a bridle path from his inn at Fabyan's up Mount Washington. This second route, eventually taken over by the cog railway, became the more popular ascent up Mount Washington through the mid-1800s. In 1840, Thomas Crawford, Ethan's brother, smoothed and expanded the original Crawford Path into a bridle path. According to Laura and Guy Waterman's *Forest and Crag: A History of Hiking, Trail Blazing, and Adventure in the Northeast Mountains* (AMC Books, 1989), Abel, at 74, was the first person to ride up Mount Washington on horseback.

Guests guided up the tallest mountains in New England by the Crawfords included some of the most prominent citizens of New England, such as Daniel Webster, Ralph Waldo Emerson, and Nathaniel Hawthorne. The botanist William Oakes, who wrote one of the first descriptions of the flora of the White Mountains, was a frequent visitor. Many guests would then write about their experiences, enticing people to visit the White Mountains and solidifying the legendary status of the Crawfords.

40

MIZPAH SPRING HUT AND MOUNT PIERCE

Mizpah Spring Hut, located in a clearing in the boreal forest at an elevation of 3,800 feet, is an excellent place to see mountain birds. Continue on to 4,312-foot Mount Pierce for terrific mountain views and a taste of alpine habitat.

CAUTION This section of Crawford Path and the hike over the summit of Mount Eisenhower is mostly above treeline and therefore very exposed to the weather. It should not be attempted in stormy, icy, or very windy conditions.

DIRECTIONS

The trailhead for Crawford Path is near AMC's Highland Center at the head of Crawford Notch. From the Jackson–North Conway area, follow US 302 west at Glen where it splits from NH 16. US 302 passes through Bartlett and then heads north through Crawford Notch. At the top of the notch, roughly 20.0 miles from the junction of NH 16 and US 302, the road goes through the narrow pass between two cliffs. If you are not staying at AMC's Highland Center (parking for registered guests only), park in the hiker lot on Mount Clinton Road. This is a short (about 0.2 mile) distance off US 302, just beyond the Highland Center.

From Franconia Notch and Twin Mountain, the hiker parking lot on Mount Clinton Road is about 8.0 miles south of the junction of US 3 and US 302 in Twin Mountain. *GPS coordinates:* 44° 13.41′ N, 71° 24.69′ W.

TRAIL DESCRIPTION

Much of this hike is on the historical Crawford Path (see page 202). You begin on Crawford Connector, which crosses Mount Clinton Road and links the parking area to Crawford Path. Just before the connector crosses Gibbs Brook, the Crawford Cliff spur trail diverges to the left.

LOCATION
Carroll, NH, to
Hart's Location, NH

RATING
Strenuous

DISTANCE
6.6 miles

ELEVATION GAIN
2,450 feet

ESTIMATED TIME
5.0–6.0 hours

MAPS
AMC White Mountain National Forest Map & Guide, G8

AMC *White Mountain Guide,* 29th ed. Map 1 Presidential Range, G8

USGS Topo: Crawford Notch to Stairs Mountain, NH

This follows the north bank of the brook for a short distance to a pool, and then ascends steeply and roughly to Crawford Cliff, from where there is a fine view of the notch and the Willey Range. The distance to the overlook is 0.4 mile. It is worth a stop if you have the time.

Crawford Connector crosses a bridge over Gibbs Brook and ends at Crawford Path (which comes up directly from US 302 opposite the Highland Center) at 0.4 mile. Turn left and start ascending Crawford Path along the south bank of Gibbs Brook. The trail is nicely graded, varying between slight uphills and more-steep gradients. At 0.6 mile, a short spur path leads left to Gibbs Falls, a popular destination for guests from the old Crawford House Hotel. Men would hike in coat and tie, and women in hoop skirts. After passing the falls, you soon enter the Gibbs Brook Scenic Area. Take note of the old-growth red spruce and some very large yellow birch. Understory plants include hobblebush, clintonia (bluebead lily), mountain wood sorrel, and a variety of mosses.

The trail eventually turns away from the brook at about 1.2 miles. At 1.9 miles, the Mizpah Cutoff comes in from the right. Crawford Path continues straight for the summit of Mount Pierce, but we will save that for the descent. For Mizpah Spring Hut, take Mizpah Cutoff. This steadily ascends about 300 feet, eventually leveling out and passing across boggy sections on logs. The Cutoff joins Webster Cliff Trail 0.1 mile from the hut.

Mizpah Spring Hut is located within the boreal forest zone. It is a great place for mountain birds. Photo by Dennis Welsh.

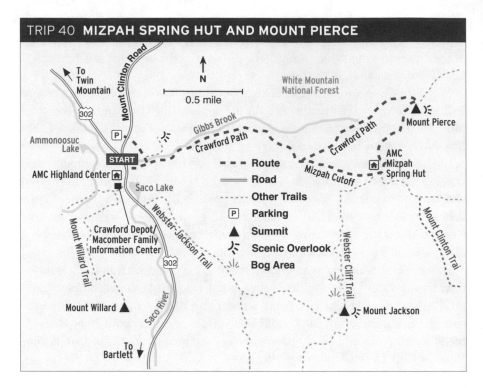

To
Twin
Mountain

↑
N

0.5 mile

White Mountain
National Forest

Mount Clinton Road

Gibbs Brook

Crawford Path

Crawford Path

Mount Pierce

302

Ammonoosuc
Lake

P

START

AMC Highland Center

Saco Lake

AMC
Mizpah
Spring Hut

Mizpah Cutoff

Route

Road

Other Trails

P Parking

▲ Summit

Scenic Overlook

Bog Area

Mount Clinton Trail

Mount Willard Trail

Crawford Depot/
Macomber Family
Information Center

302

Webster-Jackson Trail

Saco River

Webster Cliff Trail

Mount Willard ▲

Mount Jackson

To
Bartlett ↓

Completed in 1964, Mizpah Spring Hut was the last of the backcountry AMC huts to be constructed. It made a much more manageable overnight stop for people hiking between Zealand Falls Hut and Lakes of the Clouds Hut near Mount Washington. Several tent platforms are near the hut. While at the hut, you can use the restrooms, get a snack or a cup of cocoa, eat your lunch, and chat with staff and volunteers. In June the chorus of bird song emanating from the woods around the huts is wonderful. It includes Swainson's thrushes, winter wrens, white-throated sparrows, dark-eyed juncos, and a variety of warblers.

For the summit of Mount Pierce, continue ascending on Webster Cliff Trail. The trail ascends steeply from the hut, assisted at several points by ladders. You pass one open ledge with excellent views south and west, then descend slightly into a col. As the vegetation becomes scrubbier, listen for the song of the Bicknell's thrush, an uncommon species whose existence high up in these mountains is threatened by warming climate. This streaked brown bird sounds a bit like a harpsichord playing a series of notes all at one pitch. There are also a few nice patches of painted trillium (illustrated here) off the trail.

Webster Cliff Trail reaches the open summit of Mount Pierce, 0.8 mile and a 500-foot elevation gain from the hut (total of 3.4 miles from the trailhead). Formerly known as Mount Clinton, after De Witt Clinton, the governor of New York who built the Erie Canal, Mount Pierce was renamed to honor

Franklin Pierce, the only president to have hailed from New Hampshire. Enjoy wonderful, near-360 degree alpine views, including the Southern Presidential Range up to Mount Washington toward the northeast and many peaks in other directions. The summit also provides a sample of the White Mountains' unique alpine (above timberline) habitat. Note the uniquely adapted alpine cushion plants diapensia and alpine azalea, which bloom in early June, and low shrubs such as bog bilberry, Labrador tea, and black crowberry. (See page 260 for more on the alpine zone.)

From the summit of Mount Pierce, continue 0.1 mile on Webster Cliff Trail to its terminus at Crawford Path. Turn left and descend on Crawford Path. This section of the path is a bit eroded and can be wet after heavy rains, but overall the footing is good. Crawford Path reaches Mizpah Cutoff at 4.7 miles (1.2 miles from Webster Cliff Trail). Here you retrace your steps down Crawford Path to Crawford Cutoff (6.2 miles) and the trailhead (6.6 miles).

OTHER ACTIVITIES

If you have two cars, nice weather, and extra time, you could combine this hike with the Mount Eisenhower hike (Trip 41). Leave the second car at Edmands Path trailhead, which is along Mount Clinton Road 2.0 miles east of Crawford Path trailhead. At the summit of Mount Pierce, instead of descending on Crawford Path, you would continue along Crawford Path to the northeast for 1.2 miles until you reach Mount Eisenhower loop. After summiting Mount Eisenhower (0.3 mile), continue on the Loop for another 0.3 mile to Edmands Path, and descend on it for 3.0 miles to Mount Clinton Road.

DID YOU KNOW?

Crawford Path, first built in 1819, is considered the oldest continuously maintained hiking path in the Northeast.

MORE INFORMATION

Crawford Path is in the White Mountain National Forest; www.fs.usda.gov/whitemountain. There is a user fee ($3 per day) for parking in the Mount Clinton Road lot.

THE BIRDS OF MIZPAH SPRING HUT

Mizpah Spring Hut is one of the best locations in the White Mountains to hear and see birds of the boreal forest. Many migratory birds in North America breed in the boreal forest, a vast northern belt of spruce- and fir-dominated forest across the northern latitudes of the continent. The majority of this habitat is in central Canada and Alaska, so most people see these birds only during migration, but the high elevations of the Northeast (as well as the Rocky Mountains) are southern outposts for these birds. You can pick up a bird list at the hut.

If you are at Mizpah during June through mid-July, you will be treated to an enchanting chorus of these birds, particularly early in the morning or late in the afternoon. Swainson's thrush is one of the most accomplished songsters at Mizpah. Its song is flutelike, ethereal, and ascending in pitch, very appropriate for a bird of high elevations. Bicknell's thrush and veery both sound like harpsichords giving a rolling series of notes, the former singing more or less at one pitch and the latter more modulated and typically ending with descending notes. Another amazing songster is the winter wren. This tiny bird is rarely seen, but it gives a loud, boisterous, very extended series of notes that include a number of different phrases. You'll wonder how such a small creature can hold its breath so long.

White-throated sparrows give several clear, sweet whistles that have been described in words as *See old Sam Peabody, Peabody, Peabody*. A musical trill at one pitch given from the top of a spruce or fir is likely to be a dark-eyed junco. This gray, sparrowlike bird flashes white outer-tail feathers when it flies. The purple finch, the state bird of New Hampshire, gives a lively warble. Look and listen also for a number of species of wood warblers that breed around Mizpah Spring. These include yellow-rumped, magnolia, and blackpoll warblers. Warblers are noted for their bold color patterns (often yellows, with black and white streaks) and energetic behavior as they chase their insect prey.

If you are lucky, you could catch a glimpse of a spruce grouse, a chicken-like bird that inhabits the spruce-fir forest.

41

MOUNT EISENHOWER VIA EDMANDS PATH

Ascend above treeline to the alpine tundra on a path created by one of the White Mountains' master trail builders. The summit of Mount Eisenhower provides spectacular views in all directions and a broad area of unique alpine vegetation.

CAUTION This outing takes you above treeline where the weather can be quite harsh. It will almost always be colder and windier than at lower elevations, and the open area of the alpine tundra leaves you exposed to snow (possible even in summer), rain, harsh winds, and lightning. Be prepared with extra warm clothes and rain gear, and be ready to turn back if the weather changes.

DIRECTIONS

The trailhead for Edmands Path is off Mount Clinton Road, which runs from US 302 near AMC's Highland Center to the Base Station Road for the Mount Washington Cog Railway. Mount Clinton Road is closed in winter.

From the Jackson–North Conway area, follow US 302 west at Glen where it splits from NH 16. US 302 passes through Bartlett and then heads north through Crawford Notch. At the top of the notch, roughly 20.0 miles from the junction of NH 16 and US 302, the road goes through the narrow pass between two cliffs. Mount Clinton Road is a short (about 0.2 mile) distance off US 302 just beyond the AMC Highland Center. Take this road for 2.0 miles to the trailhead on the right.

From Franconia Notch and Twin Mountain, Mount Clinton Road is about 8.0 miles south of the junction of US 3 and US 302 in Twin Mountain. Turn left off US 302 and take Mount Clinton Road for 2.0 miles. *GPS coordinates:* 44° 14.94′ N, 71° 23.47′ W.

LOCATION
Crawford's Purchase, NH

RATING
Strenuous

DISTANCE
6.6 miles round-trip

ELEVATION GAIN
2,750 feet

ESTIMATED TIME
6.0 hours

MAPS
AMC White Mountain National Forest Map & Guide, G8

AMC White Mountain Guide, 29th ed. Map 1 Presidential Range, G8

USGS Topo: Crawford Notch, NH, at trailhead, Stairs Mountain at summit

TRAIL DESCRIPTION

J. Rayner Edmands was one of the White Mountains' premier trail builders, active in the early part of the twentieth century. Edmands Path up Mount Eisenhower is arguably his tour de force. His style of trail building, as outlined in Laura and Guy Waterman's *Forest and Crag: A History of Hiking, Trail-Blazing and Adventure in the Northeast Mountains* (AMC Books, 1989), was to make the trail as easy on the hiker as possible, with well-graded pitches, carefully placed stones, and lots of switchbacks. As you might expect, constructing these types of trails is more labor intensive than building trails that take the shortest route to a summit. As such, the Edmands Path, which Edmands reconstructed from an existing route, is one of the most gentle trails to a 4,000-footer in the White Mountains. This is not to say that it is a walk in the park. You need to ascend more than 2,700 feet, and the upper part of the trail is now rocky due to erosion. Edmands could not have anticipated how many hiking boots would eventually use his trail. The part above treeline is exposed to the full brunt of northwest winds, so it can be uncomfortable or dangerous if the weather is bad and coming from that direction.

After several hours of hiking on the well-graded Edmands Path, you break out into the open with sweeping views of Mount Washington and other peaks of the Presidential Range.

The trail begins in a northern hardwood forest at an almost level grade and crosses two small streams on bridges. Some "sinkholes" in the forest suggest that perhaps there were once structures along this part of the trail. Yellow birch is the dominant tree and hobblebush the most abundant understory shrub. The forest floor is carpeted with wildflowers such as goldthread, wild sarsaparilla, bluebead lily (clintonia), and Canada mayflower. The bridge over Abenaki Brook is reached in 0.4 mile. After the bridge, the trail turns right onto an old logging road and starts ascending at a steeper pitch. You will notice an increasing number of balsam fir and red spruce. You can thank Edmands and later trail-maintenance crews for all the stone steps to help your ascent. More recent crews have put in cut-up stumps to help you pass through some wet areas.

After about 1.2 miles (1 hour), pass an open area with sphagnum moss and sedges. At this point, the forest has completely changed to boreal (spruce-fir) and there is little understory vegetation because of the dense growth of conifer trees. The plant with three clover-like leaflets is mountain wood sorrel. Listen for the incredibly lively, long song of the winter wren. Red-breasted nuthatches gives a much simpler nasal *yank, yank, yank* that sounds like a toy horn. Black-throated blue and black-throated green warblers have buzzy, slurred songs.

At 2.0 miles (2 hours), pass a distinctive pile of stones. This is a particularly good area to admire Edmands's handiwork. Note the rock cribbing built into the downslope part of the trail on the left to support it on either side of the stone pile. As you continue upward, the right side of the trail has abundant bunchberries, mountain wood sorrel, and snowberries. These bloom much later in the season here at close to 4,000 feet than they do at lower elevations. To the left, you start getting partial vistas of surrounding mountains through the trees, a hint of the wonderful views you will experience above treeline.

A stream crossing lined by green alder shrubs is reached at 2.5 miles. This crossing could be difficult if conditions are icy. Notice the large, cabbage-like leaves of the false hellebore (Indian poke) here. The trail follows the streambed for a short distance and then continues its gradual ascent. The vistas become more and more frequent and the grade more level as you near treeline (reached at 2.8 miles as you cross a rocky talus slope). One of the first alpine plants to look for as you break out above treeline is bog bilberry, a type of blueberry with round, bluish-green leaves.

Edmands Path ends at Mount Eisenhower Loop at 2.9 miles at the crest of the Southern Presidential Range. Turn right onto the loop for the final 0.4 mile (300 feet) to the summit. You immediately pass a boggy area (once known as Red Pond) full of cotton grass (actually a type of sedge), then follow the trail, well marked with cairns, to the top of the mountain.

If you are fortunate to be there on a clear day, you will have a 360-degree view and see many White Mountain peaks. The most immediate peak to the northeast is Mount Franklin; Mounts Washington and Jefferson loom large beyond Mount Franklin. To the south are the Southern Presidentials: Mounts

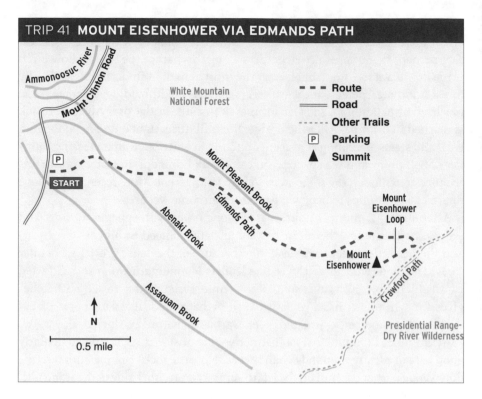

Ammonoosuc River

Mount Clinton Road

White Mountain
National Forest

- - - Route
——— Road
- - - - Other Trails
P Parking
▲ Summit

Mount Pleasant Brook

Edmands Path

Abenaki Brook

Assaguam Brook

START

Mount
Eisenhower
Loop

Mount
Eisenhower ▲

Crawford Path

Presidential Range-
Dry River Wilderness

N

0.5 mile

Pierce and Jackson. The view west includes the Willey and Twin ranges as well as Mount Carrigain.

The broad summit area is a wonderful garden of alpine wildflowers. The display changes as the season progresses. In early to mid-June, white blossoms of diapensia are abundant. This is an alpine cushion plant with small, dark-green leaves in a tight cluster (see Trip 50). In midsummer, the small, white blossoms of mountain sandwort line the trail in profusion, and the bright-yellow flower clusters of alpine goldenrod will surely catch your eye. Another common white flower is three-toothed cinquefoil, identified by its three leaflets, each with three "teeth" along their outer edges. Bearberry willow, a true willow that never grows more than a few inches above the ground, is also common here. (For more information on the alpine zone, see Trip 50 and essay on page 260.)

Retrace your steps to return to the trailhead. You will notice more of the rockiness of the trail on your descent, so you should factor that into your timing.

OTHER ACTIVITIES

For a longer hike, you could combine this hike with a descent via Mount Pierce. It is most conveniently done by having two cars, one at the Edmands Path trailhead and a second at the Crawford Path trailhead (also on Mount Clinton Road). It should be attempted only in good weather because of the extensive amount of hiking above treeline. Going over Mount Pierce adds an additional 1.5 miles to this trip (1 hour). If you do not have two cars, you will need to walk 2.0 additional miles along Mount Clinton Road to get from the Crawford Path trailhead back to the Edmands Path trailhead.

To do the above, after hiking up Mount Eisenhower via Edmands Path and Mount Eisenhower Loop, continue on Mount Eisenhower Loop in the southerly direction for another 0.4 mile (350 foot descent) to Crawford Path. Head southwest toward Mount Pierce for 1.2 miles. Crawford Path goes within 0.1 mile of the summit of Mount Pierce, so you will need to take a short detour onto Webster Cliff Trail to reach the actual summit of Mount Pierce. Then retrace your steps back to Crawford Path and descend for 3.1 miles, being sure to turn right onto Crawford Connector near the bottom to get you to the car at Crawford Path trailhead. The descent of Mount Pierce via Crawford Path is described in Trip 40 under "Other Activities."

MORE INFORMATION

This trail is within the White Mountain National Forest; www.fs.usda.gov/ whitemountain, 603-536-6100. There is no parking fee.

Hotels, restaurants, and gas stations can be found in the towns of Bretton Woods and Twin Mountain, through which you pass on your way to the trailhead if you are coming from the Franconia Notch area. Coming from the south, you will pass the Macomber Family Information Center at Crawford Depot, which has trail information, restrooms, and some basic hiking supplies. The AMC Highland Center (www.outdoors.org/lodging/lodges) at the head of Crawford Notch has lodging and meals for registered guests, a hostel, and public programs.

PINKHAM NOTCH

The Pinkham Notch/Gorham region includes the Presidential Range, the loftiest peaks of the White Mountains. Mount Washington is the highest mountain in the Northeast at 6,288 feet, and five other summits in the range surpass 5,000 feet. In addition to elevation, the Presidential Range is also noted for vast, bowl-shaped ravines. The Carter Range, across Pinkham Notch from the Presidentials, rises above 4,500 feet. The entire region is a magnet for day-hikers and backpackers attracted by the high elevation, rugged scenery, and broad expanse of alpine terrain with extensive vistas and unique ecological characteristics.

A number of trails to ponds, waterfalls, and viewpoints are easy day hikes. These are centered on AMC's Pinkham Notch Visitor Center (PNVC) and the town of Gorham. NH 16 passes right through Pinkham Notch between Jackson and Gorham and provides access to many of the trails described here. Other trails are reached from US 2 west of Gorham.

JOE DODGE LODGE AND PINKHAM NOTCH VISITOR CENTER

AMC's PNVC is the hub of hiking activities and natural history education in the White Mountains. The Trading Post houses an information center, a store, and a dining room. Joe Dodge Lodge offers private rooms, bunkrooms, a library, and meeting rooms. Breakfast and dinner are served to overnight guests and are available to others (advance notification necessary). Lunch is available for purchase. In the evenings, and sometimes during the day, you can hear naturalist lectures and participate in other programs. PNVC is an excellent place to get current information on trails and the weather and to buy U.S. Forest Service parking passes, hiking guides, nature books, T-shirts, trail snacks, and other supplies. The visitor center also has restrooms and showers open to the public.

Facing page: Mid-June in the alpine zone of the White Mountains. Here is a glorious display of diapensia (white flowers) and Lapland rosebay (pink flowers).

While at the visitor center, do not miss the scale model of the Presidential Range, along with displays on mountain geology and ecology. These give a real perspective of the area.

In addition to the hiking trails described in this section, PNVC is the jumping-off point for a network of cross-country ski trails for a variety of skill levels. Check at the visitor center for a map. For reservations for overnight lodging and other information, visit outdoors.org/whitemountains or call 603-466-2721.

SUPPLIES AND LOGISTICS

The Wildcat Mountain Ski Area, about 1 mile north, has all the amenities you might expect in a ski resort: a restaurant, a snack bar, restrooms, coffee machines, and a gift shop. It is open all year; skiwildcat.com; 603-466-3326. If you are coming from the north on NH 16, Gorham has restaurants, inns, motels, stores, and gas stations. From the south, Jackson is the nearest town for supplies.

The Androscoggin Ranger Station of the U.S. Forest Service is located on NH 16 just south of US 2 in Gorham. Stop in for information, trail pamphlets, or to use the restrooms; www.fs.fed.us/r9/forests/white_mountain/contact; 603-466-2713 x0.

PUBLIC TRANSPORTATION

Concord Coach Lines operates daily bus service from Boston's Logan Airport and South Station to Pinkham Notch. Check concordcoachlines.com for schedules. Pinkham Notch is the terminal for the AMC Hiker Shuttle, which also stops at the Appalachia and 19 Mile Brook parking areas; outdoors.org/lodging/lodging-shuttle.cfm; 603-466-2727.

NEARBY CAMPING

The U.S. Forest Service's Dolly Copp Campground is at the junction of NH 16 and Pinkham B Road between Gorham and Pinkham Notch. With 176 campsites, Dolly Copp is the largest public campground in the White Mountains; reservations can be made online at recreation.gov or by calling 877-444-6777. Large groups can camp at Barnes Field Group Area adjacent to Dolly Copp Campground.

42

GLEN ELLIS FALLS

Glen Ellis Falls is a 64-foot waterfall on the Ellis River in Pinkham Notch. It is one of the most impressive falls in the White Mountains and is reached by a very short walk.

DIRECTIONS

The parking area is on the west side of NH 16, 0.7 mile south of the AMC's Pinkham Notch Visitor Center and about 9.0 miles north of the village of Jackson. See Trip 43 for directions to PNVC. *GPS coordinates:* 44° 14.75′ N, 71° 15.20′ W.

TRAIL DESCRIPTION

This is a popular stop, so there are likely to be lots of other people around enjoying the falls. The falls are impressive even in summer, when other nearby waterfalls are likely to be little more than a trickle.

From the parking area, a tunnel underneath NH 16 leads to the well-marked 0.3-mile path to the falls. Walk along the trail, parallel to the river. Several signs along the trail describe the geology of the area. The falls were created when avalanches blocked the flow of the Ellis River, causing it to change its course and tumble over the glacially carved bowl in the side of a mountain.

Stone steps lead you down to the base of the waterfall. Three lookouts—at the top, middle, and bottom of the falls—provide distinct perspectives. At the top you feel potential energy as the water spills through a narrow cut between boulders just before plunging over the lip. Midway, that energy becomes kinetic and you can get dizzy watching the rushing water and spray. From the bottom you get an unobstructed view of the entire falls. Note the deep plunge pool cut by the erosive action of the water.

The shape of the falls pouring over the brink may remind you of water pouring out of a pitcher, and, in fact, Pitcher

LOCATION
Pinkham's Grant, NH

RATING
Easy for all ages

DISTANCE
0.6 mile round-trip

ELEVATION GAIN
Short descent

ESTIMATED TIME
30-40 minutes

MAPS
AMC White Mountain National Forest Map & Guide, G9

AMC *White Mountain Guide*, 29th ed. Map 1 Presidential Range, G9

USGS Topo: Stairs Mountain, NH

Falls was the original name given to Glen Ellis Falls. According to Bruce and Doreen Bolnick's *Waterfalls of the White Mountains* (Backcountry Press, 1999), the name change was suggested in 1852 by Henry Ripley (of Ripley Falls fame) in recognition of its location on the Ellis River.

The pool at the bottom is bounded by lots of flat rocks that invite exploration. When the water levels aren't too high, you will find children and their parents scrambling around these flat rocks. Use caution because mist from the falls keeps everything damp. According to American Indian legend, if you look hard into the mist created by the falls, you can see the shapes of two people hand in hand. These were lovers from different tribes who plunged to their deaths together over the falls when the woman, the daughter of a chief, was promised to someone else.

To return to your vehicle, simply retrace your steps along the river and back through the tunnel under NH 16.

DID YOU KNOW?

The flow over the cliff has been estimated to be a minimum of 600 gallons per minute even in late summer. This is equal to 10 gallons per second.

OTHER ACTIVITIES

This short walk can be combined with a walk to Lost Pond and PNVC for a longer outing. See Trip 43 for details.

MORE INFORMATION

Glen Ellis Falls is in the White Mountain National Forest. The parking area has restrooms, an information board, and a picnic area. There is a $3 day-use fee for parking; www.fs.usda.gov/whitemountain; 603-536-6100.

Glen Ellis Falls is one of the most impressive falls in the White Mountains.

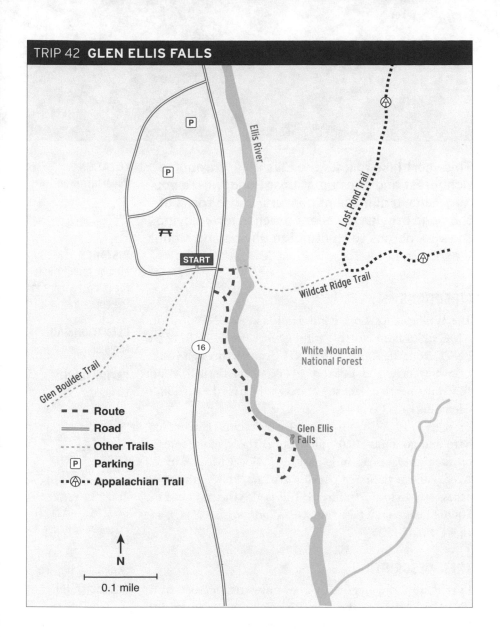

Route
Road
Other Trails
P Parking
Appalachian Trail

Ellis River

Lost Pond Trail

Wildcat Ridge Trail

White Mountain
National Forest

Glen Boulder Trail

16

START

Glen Ellis
Falls

N

0.1 mile

43
LOST POND

This short hike follows the Ellis River through a rich forest and ends up at Lost Pond, where you may catch a glimpse of beavers. Large rocks at the pond provide excellent perches for enjoying the view across to Huntington Ravine and Mount Washington.

DIRECTIONS

The trailhead for Lost Pond Trail is across NH 16 from AMC's Pinkham Notch Visitor Center (PNVC). To get to PNVC from the south, follow NH 16 north through North Conway, Glen, and Jackson. PNVC is on the left, about 10.0 miles north of Jackson and 0.7 mile past the turnoff to Glen Ellis Falls (Trip 42).

To get to PNVC from the north, pick up NH 16 in Gorham and go about 10.0 miles south. The visitor center is on the right, about a mile past the Wildcat Mountain Ski Area. Park at the large parking area for PNVC and walk across NH 16 to the trailhead. This is also the trailhead for Square Ledge Trail (Trip 45). *GPS coordinates (PNVC):* 44° 15.44′ N, 71° 15.17′ W.

TRAIL DESCRIPTION

Lost Pond Trail begins in a swampy area across from PNVC and crosses the Ellis River on a wooden bridge. You may notice two "speckly" shrubs here. Speckled alder is named for its speckled bark, which makes the shrub look like it has chicken pox. The leaves of sweet gale, which grows right next to the wooden bridge, are covered with tiny yellow speckles. Crush a sweet gale leaf in your fingers to get a strong, sweet smell that will remind you of bayberry. White turtlehead flowers bloom in the swamp in August.

From the wooden bridge, a beaver dam is obvious to your left. The dam is composed of tree branches stripped

LOCATION
Pinkham's Grant, NH

RATING
Easy

DISTANCE
1.0 mile round-trip to the pond, 1.8 miles for the entire trail

ELEVATION GAIN
Minimal

ESTIMATED TIME
1.0 hour

MAPS
AMC White Mountain National Forest Map & Guide, F10

AMC *White Mountain Guide,* 29th ed. Map 1 Presidential Range, F10

USGS Topo: Mount Washington, NH

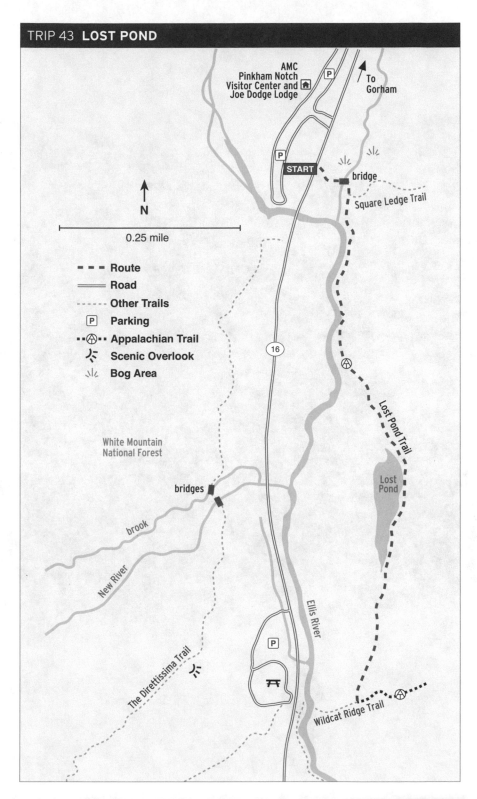

AMC
Pinkham Notch
Visitor Center and
Joe Dodge Lodge

P

To
Gorham

P

START

bridge

Square Ledge Trail

N

0.25 mile

- - - Route
——— Road
----- Other Trails
P Parking
••⊕•• Appalachian Trail
⋏ Scenic Overlook
⋇ Bog Area

Lost Pond Trail

Lost
Pond

White Mountain
National Forest

bridges

16

brook

New River

The Dirittissima Trail

P

Ellis River

Wildcat Ridge Trail

of bark and compacted mud. The beavers eat the inner bark and then use the rest of the branches as lumber for the dam. Beavers build dams to create ponds so they can swim to their supper and have a place for their lodges, safe from predators. By flooding the surrounding woodlands, they can enter their lodges underwater and swim to their major foods, the nutritious inner bark of trees, grasses, and other vegetation. See page 191 for more on beavers.

Swallows are small, graceful birds you are likely to see zooming over the swamp. Barn swallows have distinctive long, forked tails and are bluish black on the back with reddish throats and buff-colored bellies. As their name implies, they sometimes nest in barns and under the eaves of buildings (such as the maintenance building at PNVC). Tree swallows also have blue-black backs but differ from barn swallows in having notched tails and in being completely white underneath. They nest in tree holes and often use nest boxes. These aerial acrobats catch insects while in flight.

The trail turns right after the bridge. Square Ledge Trail immediately departs left and starts to ascend. Lost Pond Trail, which is part of the Appalachian Trail, continues straight ahead along the east side of the Ellis River, initially through a forest of balsam fir and birch and eventually through northern hardwoods with a hobblebush understory. The trail to the pond is wide with little ups and downs and a few rocks, but nothing major.

The Ellis River flow is greatly increased by the addition of the Cutler River flowing down from Tuckerman Ravine. Note how clear the water is in a beautiful, deep pool in the river as you walk by. If you stand quietly by this pool for a minute or two, you may catch a glimpse of brook trout. Water striders may also be present.

In June, look for blooms of Canada mayflower, clintonia, false Solomon's seal, painted trillium, and pink lady's slippers. In damp spots along the trail, wild white violets and inflated sedges abound. Normally, sedges are fairly nondescript, but inflated sedge has amusing, inflated bladders that contain its seeds.

In midsummer, mountain wood sorrel (illustrated here) blooms in profusion here. The three leaves of this small plant will remind you of clover, but it is not related. Other midsummer bloomers are goldenrods (several species) and tall meadow rue.

After about 0.3 mile, the trail angles away from the Ellis River and crosses a tributary over another wooden bridge. You reach the pond in 0.5 mile. The trail becomes rockier, traversing the east shore of the pond. You will pass one particularly large flat rock that is an ideal platform for sitting quietly and enjoying the peaceful scenery, perhaps with a picnic lunch. The view of Mount Washington is impressive—Huntington Ravine stands out, and you can also see Boott Spur, the Lion Head, and the Gulf of Slides from various vantage points. Lost Pond is not far off NH 16 as the crow flies, yet it feels remote and delightfully lost.

At Lost Pond, there are several more beaver lodges. At dusk you stand a chance of seeing the beavers themselves cavorting about. Look for another dam at the outlet of the pond.

Two common plants in the water are waterlilies and wild celery. The leaves of waterlilies float on the surface of the water and provide the underwater parts of the plant with air through a system of gas channels. Wild celery is a favorite duck food with grassy, strap-like leaves.

As you make your way around the pond, you may observe water stains on the rocks and on tree trunks at the shore. These indicate how high the water levels rose during the past spring. Look for bunchberries (illustrated here), a small relative of dogwood that produces creamy, white, dogwood-like flowers in the latter part of June and clusters of red berries during summer. At one point, you may notice a tree that seemingly grows right out of a rock. Its trunk and roots form a little cave. Note also a dead "wildlife" tree laced with woodpecker holes.

The section between the south end of the lake and Wildcat Ridge Trail passes through a riot of boulders. These rocks were deposited by an avalanche off Wildcat Mountain many years ago. Skiers in winter will need a fair accumulation of snow to complete this part of the trail because of the rocks.

The trail ends at Wildcat Ridge Trail (0.9 mile). From here you can retrace your steps, or, if you are feeling adventurous, turn right onto Wildcat Ridge Trail and cross over the Ellis River to reach NH 16. There is no bridge, so you must step carefully from rock to rock, a potentially precarious undertaking at high water. If the river is passable, you can then walk back to your vehicle along NH 16 or walk over to Glen Ellis Falls (Trip 42) and complete the loop described below.

DID YOU KNOW?

The swamp you cross at the beginning of this trail is at the height-of-land of Pinkham Notch. Water drains from this swamp both north to the Peabody River and south to the Ellis.

OTHER ACTIVITIES

Combine the hike with a visit to PNVC or extend the hike to Glen Ellis Falls (Trip 42) and then return via Glen Boulder and Direttissima trails. Lost Pond

Trail can also be combined with Square Ledge Trail (Trip 45) for a more extensive outing. In addition, there is a network of relatively easy day hikes around PNVC. Check the information desk at PNVC for more ideas. Lost Pond Trail is suitable for skiing and links up with other ski trails.

MORE INFORMATION

There is no parking fee for the PNVC parking area; outdoors.org/lodging/whitemountains/pinkham/pnvc-pnvc.cfm; 603-466-2721. PNVC has snacks, trail information, hiking supplies, and restrooms.

The walk is within the White Mountain National Forest; www.fs.usda.gov/whitemountain; 603-536-6100.

Huntington Ravine and Mount Washington loom over this tranquil view of Lost Pond.

44

THOMPSON FALLS TRAIL

A short, easy walk with lots of spring wildflowers leads to a lovely waterfall and cascades near the Wildcat Mountain Ski Area.

DIRECTIONS

The trail is within the Wildcat Mountain Ski Area, roughly halfway between Gorham and Jackson off NH 16. Park in the ski area parking lot on the east side of NH 16, about 1.0 mile north of AMC's Pinkham Notch Visitor Center (PNVC). Walk past the information and ticket booths, cross a bridge, and follow signs pointing left to Way of the Wildcat Nature Trail. The nature trail leads to Thompson Falls Trail. *GPS coordinates: 44° 15.85′ N, 71° 14.34′ W.*

TRAIL DESCRIPTION

You begin along the Way of the Wildcat Nature Trail, an easy, wide, leisurely stroll with sixteen numbered stops. A free pamphlet describing each of these stops is available at the Wildcat Mountain Visitor Center. After about a 10-minute walk, Thompson Falls Trail, marked with yellow blazes, leaves the nature trail at the farthest point in the loop. The trail crosses a small stream on stones, which may be difficult early in the season due to high water, and then crosses a service road.

The next section is still easy, with only a moderate gradient to Thompson Falls. If you are hiking in mid- to late June, you will be treated to a display of pink lady's slippers (see page 227). The distance from the nature trail to the falls is about 0.2 mile.

You will enjoy the graceful stream of water flowing over the falls, but the pool beneath the falls is a little shady for swimming—the smaller potholes and pools above the falls in Thompson Brook are a better bet. Be sure to note riffles and pools, two different habitats within these fast-moving mountain streams. Water striders skim across the pools

LOCATION
Pinkham's Grant, NH

RATING
Easy

DISTANCE
1.4 miles round-trip

ELEVATION GAIN
200 feet

ESTIMATED TIME
1.0-2.0 hours

MAPS
AMC White Mountain National Forest Map & Guide, F10

AMC *White Mountain Guide*, 29th ed. Map 1 Presidential Range, F10

USGS Topo: Carter Dome, NH

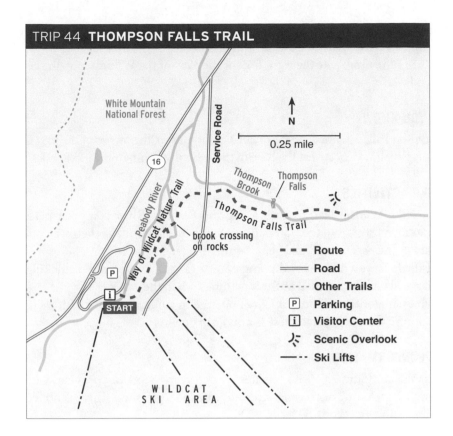

(see Aquatic Insects on page 7 for more information on how they can literally walk on water).

The trail continues more steeply past the falls, so those with very young children may want to stop at this point. You need to do some moderate scrambling up rocks and then cross a stream, which may be difficult in high water. The trail then levels out and provides views of Mount Washington. The scene is particularly attractive in fall, when colorful trees along the brook frame the massive peak. The trail continues along the bank of the brook, passing beautiful cascades and inviting pools until the trail dead-ends about 0.2 mile above Thompson Falls.

Above the falls, you are in a prime example of a boreal forest. The forest floor receives very limited light because of the dense, year-round canopy of conifers. Nonetheless, goldthread (illustrated here), a small plant that thrives in the understory, is abundant along Thompson Falls Trail. This relative of the buttercup has three small leaflets that are roundish with scalloped edges. Delicate white flowers, one per stem with five to seven petals, appear in May at lower elevations. A golden underground stem, technically a rhizome, connects different individuals in the same way that runners connect individual strawberry plants.

Before the advent of modern medicine, goldthread was used to combat a variety of ailments, particularly toothache and other sores of the mouth.

When returning, take the right fork of the Way of the Wildcat loop to see the Peabody River.

DID YOU KNOW?

Thompson Falls is named for Colonel J.M. Thompson, the owner of the first Glen House, which was located at the base of the Mount Washington Auto Road.

OTHER ACTIVITIES

Way of the Wildcat Nature Trail along the Peabody River is a great place to throw fallen leaves into the water and watch them slowly make their way downstream to the ocean (well, maybe not quite that far).

At the falls, you may enjoy dipping your toes in the water and picnicking on the large, flat rocks exposed in the streambed when the water is low.

Cable cars for the Wildcat Ski Area operate in summer to take visitors up to the summit for a fine vista. There is also a zip line.

MORE INFORMATION

The Wildcat Mountain Visitor Center is open year-round and provides various amenities, including restrooms, a restaurant, and a gift shop. There is no fee for parking; skiwildcat.com; 603-466-3326.

Facing page: Pink lady's slipper is common on the Thompson Falls Trail. Photo by Jerry Monkman.

PINK LADY'S SLIPPERS IN THE WHITE MOUNTAINS

The pink lady's slipper is one of the showiest wildflowers in the White Mountains. A typical pink lady's slipper has a pair of large, smooth, almost round, glossy leaves that hug the ground and a single flowering stalk. The flower has a distinctive pink pouch that resembles a shoe (more like a heavy clog than a slipper). The pouch is lined with dark-pink veins. The flower also contains three thin, greenish sepals. Another name for it is "moccasin flower."

As many as one in four of the pink lady's slippers in the White Mountains is not pink at all but white. Why this region should be blessed with so many white ones is a mystery; they do occur elsewhere, but much more rarely.

Pink lady's slippers use deception to get pollinated. Bees are attracted to the fragrance and bright color of the flowers. Once they enter the flower, however, they discover no nectar, but instead become trapped inside the large pouch. In struggling to find the only way out, the bees deposit a pollen mass they had acquired from a previous flower onto the orchid's stigma and then brush up against a sticky mass of pollen that they will deliver to another lady's slipper flower, assuming they have not learned their lesson.

This wildflower occurs below 4,000 feet, particularly in deciduous woodlands, but it is nowhere abundant. It flowers in June; hence, visitors to the White Mountains have a better chance of catching it in bloom than the earlier spring wildflowers such as trilliums and goldthread.

The lady's slipper is a type of orchid, a large family of mostly tropical plants that are much sought after by horticulturists and florists for their beautiful, distinctive flowers. Collectors or others who selfishly want to savor their beauty for themselves or to sell them to unwary gardeners have dug up many orchids, including the pink lady's slipper. This is futile for both the grower and the plant. Pink lady's slippers are very difficult to grow in "captivity," because they have special requirements. Their roots, which are easily damaged upon transplanting, require a special partnership with a fungus in order to take up nutrients from the soil. Tissue culture techniques are now being developed to propagate orchids, so no one needs to destroy wild plants to have them around the house. Enjoy pink lady's slippers in the woods and leave them for the next people who pass by.

45

SQUARE LEDGE

This short trail to an overlook has a terrific view of Pinkham Notch and Mount Washington. This could be a great first experience for young children on a steep trail.

CAUTION The Square Ledge is a steep dropoff; use caution when on the ledge itself. This trail is not a good choice in icy conditions.

DIRECTIONS

The trail begins directly across the road from the Pinkham Notch Visitor Center (PNVC), at the same trailhead as Lost Pond Trail. See Trip 43 for directions. *GPS coordinates* (PNVC): 44° 15.44′ N, 71° 15.17′ W.

TRAIL DESCRIPTION

The trail runs together with Lost Pond Trail for a short distance from NH 16 and crosses a wooden bridge over the Ellis River, where there is an interesting beaver wetland. This is described in Trip 43. The two trails make a sharp right turn, after which Square Ledge Trail makes an immediate left uphill (Lost Pond Trail continues along the river).

The trail is initially wide, with a gradual uphill. Stop at Ladies Lookout (a short spur trail to the left) at 0.1 mile for a view of Pinkham Notch. At the turnoff to Ladies Lookout there is a particularly lush growth of striped maples. In the White Mountains this small tree generally remains in the understory. You will appreciate its bright, green-and-white-striped bark on branches and young trunks and its extremely large, three-lobed leaves (the latter giving rise to the name "goosefoot maple"). Often, trees and shrubs growing in its shade must have very large leaves in order to catch the small amount of light that filters down through the canopy. Striped maple is also called moosewood because it is a favorite food of moose.

LOCATION
Pinkham's Grant, NH

RATING
Moderate

DISTANCE
1.0 mile round-trip

ELEVATION GAIN
500 feet

ESTIMATED TIME
1.0–2.0 hours

MAPS
AMC White Mountain National Forest Map & Guide, F9

AMC *White Mountain Guide*, 29th ed. Map 1 Presidential Range, F9

USGS Topo: Mount Washington, NH

The next landmark is Hangover Rock. It is a large boulder that projects over the trail, making a cozy hangout when it rains. If you are looking for an excuse to take a breather, slow down to enjoy the grove of paper birches.

Shiny club moss is an abundant plant of the forest floor along Square Ledge Trail. These are low, dark-green plants whose upright stems covered with small leaves resemble bottle brushes.

After Hangover Rock, the trail becomes steep and has a short section with loose rocks that may make some children (and even adults) a little uncomfortable. At 0.5 mile, it reaches Square Ledge. Use caution on Square Ledge, as there is a steep dropoff.

The view of the steep headwall of Huntington Ravine is particularly dramatic from Square Ledge. A mountain glacier carved this out during the last Ice Age. J.S. Huntington was a researcher who was one of the first people to spend a winter on the summit of Mount Washington (1870–1871).

Square Ledge itself is composed of schist, the same metamorphic rock that underlies much of the Presidential Range. Look for red spruce, balsam fir, and heart-leaved birch around the ledge.

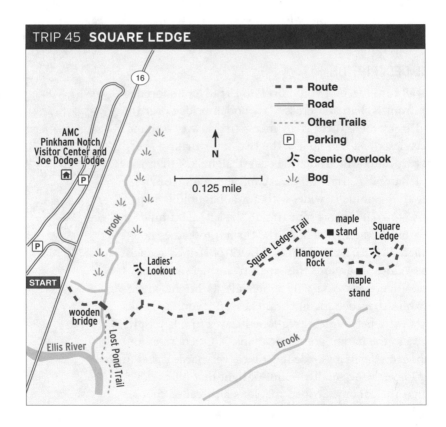

A short, steep walk from Pinkham Notch Visitor Center leads you to the fantastic view of Mount Washington from Square Ledge. Photo by Dennis Welsh.

DID YOU KNOW?

The schist that forms Square Ledge dates back approximately 400 million years and was formed when muds beneath an ancient sea were squeezed together between two colliding continents. Schists appear laminated (in layers) that can sometimes be split apart.

OTHER ACTIVITIES

Square Ledge Trail can be combined with Lost Pond Trail (Trip 43) for a more extensive outing. In addition, there is a network of relatively easy day hikes around PNVC. Check the information desk at PNVC or AMC's *White Mountain Guide* for more ideas.

Pinkham Notch has a number of ski trails, including Square Ledge Loop Ski Trail. This crosses the hiking trail near Ladies Lookout.

MORE INFORMATION

There is no parking fee for the Pinkham Notch Visitor Center parking area. The visitor center has snacks, trail information, hiking supplies, and restrooms; outdoors.org/lodging/whitemountains/pinkham/pnvc-pnvc.cfm; 603-466-2721.

The walk is within the White Mountain National Forest; www.fs.usda.gov/whitemountain; 603-536-6100.

PAPER BIRCH

Paper birch (*Betula papyrifera*), also called white or canoe birch, is the state tree of New Hampshire. These trees are widespread and much appreciated throughout the Granite State.

The ecological role of paper birches in White Mountain forests is more than ceremonial. They range from low elevations up to treeline, thriving in disturbed areas resulting from fire, logging, wind, or other disasters that remove vegetation. As short-lived, temporary residents during the natural succession of a disturbed area from an open field back to mature forest, paper birches are eventually replaced by maples, red spruce, and other more long-lived species. Fortunately for paper birches, and for those who admire their columns of white in a sea of grayish brown and green, natural disturbance to the forest is frequent enough in the White Mountains to ensure a plentiful supply of this species, even in the absence of human activities.

Whoever thought of making a tree with such white bark! The white, peeling bark marked with horizontal dashes makes this an easy tree to identify. The "dashes" are technically called lenticels and are pores through which air passes into the bark. Young saplings and the branches of adult trees are a rich, reddish-brown color that has a more subdued beauty compared with the whiteness of mature trunks. Leaves of paper birch are oval or egg-shaped with serrated (toothed) edges. A high-altitude form, which some botanists consider a separate species, has heart-shaped leaves. The brown flowers of paper birch are in dangling clusters called catkins and are pollinated by the wind. Ruffed grouse, a large, chicken-like bird, and redpolls and other finches that spend winter in northern New England relish their small seeds.

The shagginess of paper birch, along with thoughts of the birch-bark canoes of American Indians, might tempt you to peel off some of the bark. Keep in mind, however, that this will leave a permanent ugly scar on the tree and may kill it, so please resist the temptation.

46

WATERFALL AND VISTA LOOP IN THE NORTHERN PRESIDENTIALS

The first part of this hike features waterfalls and many flat rocks along the brook that invite you to have a picnic, get your feet wet, and relax while listening to the sounds of rushing water. For those looking for a longer outing, the loop hike continues up to stunning views of Mounts Madison and Adams and the northern peaks.

DIRECTIONS

The Fallsway leaves from the Appalachia parking lot off US 2, about 5.4 miles west of the point where NH 16 splits off to the north from US 2 in Gorham and about 0.8 mile west of Pinkham B Road (Dolly Copp Road). If you are coming from the west through the Twin Mountain area, the trailhead is about 7.0 miles east of the junction of US 2 and NH 115. The parking lot is on the south side of US 2.

The parking area is well marked and large, as it is the trailhead for a number of trails into the Northern Presidential Range. The Fallsway leaves from the east side of the parking lot and is well marked. *GPS coordinates:* 44° 22.24′ N, 71° 17.33′ W.

TRAIL DESCRIPTION

You can do a short waterfall loop suitable for children using the Fallsway and Brookbank trails, or extend it with a more rigorous hike to scenic vistas using the Fallsway and sections of the Inlook, Kelton, and Howker Ridge trails, then Sylvan Way and Brookbank. The trail intersections are well marked with signs, so with a little care you should have no trouble following the recommended routes.

The Fallsway starts through a short section of woods before crossing an open area with power lines and an overgrown railroad track. Look for birds (such as common yellowthroats and indigo buntings) and butterflies that thrive in shrubby habitats during your brief walk through

LOCATION
Randolph, NH

RATING
Fallsway-Brookbank trails, easy loop; Inlook-Kelton trails, more strenuous loop

DISTANCE
1.5 miles round-trip, easy loop; 4.0 miles, more strenuous loop

ELEVATION GAIN
400 feet, easy loop; 1,450 feet, more strenuous loop

ESTIMATED TIME
1.0-2.0 hours, easy loop; 3.0-4.0 hours, more strenuous loop

MAPS
AMC White Mountain National Forest Map & Guide, E9

AMC *White Mountain Guide,* 28th ed. Map 1 Presidential Range, E9

USGS Topo: Mount Washington, NH

Gordon Falls is one of the many visual treats along Snyder Brook in the Northern Presidentials.

this right of way. The trail then enters the Snyder Brook Scenic Area of the national forest and meets up with Snyder Brook. The trail follows the west bank of the brook and reaches Gordon Fall, your first stop. The amazing erosive power of rushing water is apparent in the channels and chutes in solid rock. Mosses and ferns thrive along the sides of the waterfalls.

This part of the White Mountains is laced with many short trails and trail junctions, but they are all well marked. Just keep following the signs for the Fallsway. The next waterfalls are Lower and Upper Salroc Falls. An impressive deep plunge pool has been carved out of the streambed by Lower Salroc Falls. This pool will be over the heads of even adults, at least early in the season.

Dikes of basalt and pegmatite are visible in the streambed. The pegmatite appears as whitish stripes of large crystals within the schist rocks of the area; the basalt dikes are black and finely grained. The dikes were formed when molten lava from deep within the earth flowed up into cracks in the schists and then hardened. If it cooled slowly, large crystals had time to form pegmatite. A basalt dike occurs when the lava cools rapidly near the surface of the earth.

A flat rock here is ideal for a picnic if it is not underwater. Hemlocks dominate along the banks of the stream because they favor the cool, shady, damp atmosphere. Away from the water in drier, warmer habitat, northern hardwoods, particularly sugar maples and yellow birches, thrive. From just about any White Mountain viewpoint, dark lines of hemlock reveal the courses of streams.

After passing Lower and Upper Salroc Falls, the Fallsway joins the Valley Way for a short stretch (for a shorter loop, you can return to the parking lot on the Valley Way). At the sign for Fallsway Loop, turn left and walk 0.1 mile to Tama Fall, 0.7 mile from the parking lot. Tama Fall is the largest of the group and arguably the most attractive. A graceful veil of water flows down a natural granite staircase.

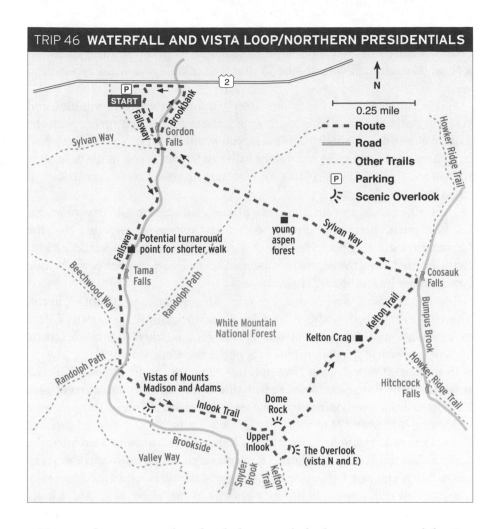

Here is where you need to decide how much farther you want to hike. For those with young children, you can make a loop by using the Brookbank, which descends on the opposite side of Snyder Brook (0.7 mile back to the parking area). Cross over the brook on some flat rocks (no problem except in extremely high water), turn left onto the Brookbank (also marked with yellow blazes), and start your descent. The Brookbank provides good access to the brook at a number of locations and a different perspective of the same waterfalls you saw on the way up. It is an attractive, moss-laden trail with one short, rocky section that may be slick in wet weather or high water. You can also return via the Valley Way, which rejoins the Fallsway at Tama Fall. If the Brookbank is your choice, you can skip the next several paragraphs and pick up the trail description two paragraphs from the end.

For those wanting the more rigorous hike, continue up the Valley Way for another 0.2 mile. Just beyond the point where the Beechwood Way comes in from the right, take the left fork onto Brookside Trail (not to be confused with the Brookbank). This passes a huge glacial erratic in the streambed, and then crosses Snyder Brook in about 0.1 mile (1.0 mile from trailhead) and reaches a three-way junction with Inlook Trail in the middle and Randolph Path to your left.

Follow Inlook Trail. It heads very steeply uphill for about 10 minutes, and you will notice an increasing number of balsam fir and red spruce with the gain in elevation. In about 15 minutes, you reach the first "inlook," an open, ledgy area providing a view across the valley of Snyder Brook to the bare summits of Mounts Madison, Adams, and Quincy Adams. This is a great place to catch your breath.

The trail, marked in cairns in some places, continues uphill at a somewhat less steep pitch, alternating between boreal forest and open viewpoints. Note the Labrador tea growing along the side of the trail. This shrub has leathery leaves that are rolled along the edges. The underside of a new leaf is covered with white fuzz; in older leaves the fuzz is a rusty color.

The trail reaches Dome Rock at 1.6 miles. This is an excellent spot for lunch. The view to the north and east includes Pine Mountain (Trip 47), the village of Randolph, and the Crescent Range. The rock is schist, the characteristic 400-million-year-old metamorphic rock of the Presidential Range.

In another 0.1 mile, Inlook Trail ends in Kelton Trail at the Upper Inlook (1.7 miles from the trailhead). At 2,732 feet, this is the highest point of your hike. The Upper Inlook provides a fine view west and restricted views through trees to Mounts Adams and Madison.

Turn left and start your descent down Kelton Trail. In about 5 minutes, the trail reaches the Overlook, which is largely overgrown but still provides views to the north and east to the Crescent Range, Mahoosucs, and Pine Mountain. The trail descends more steeply now, passing a spring on your left. At 2.3 miles you reach the sign for Kelton Crag, which is just off the main trail. At just a little more than 2,000 feet, you have descended quite a bit from the Upper Inlook, and northern hardwoods are again appearing in the forest. The view from the crag is to the east. Take a moment to crush a leaf of the abundant flowering wintergreen to get its pleasant wintergreen odor. Reindeer lichen is also common on the crag.

Return to the main trail, being sure not to follow a false trail on the opposite side of Kelton Crag. Kelton Trail continues at a less-steep pitch through northern hardwoods and ends at Howker Ridge Trail (2.6 miles). Turn left onto Howker Ridge Trail and follow this for 0.1 mile to the well-marked intersection with Sylvan Way coming in from the left. The sign at the intersection reads "To Gordon Fall, Coldbrook Fall, Appalachia," and you will hear Coosauk Fall through the trees. Go left onto Sylvan Way.

The next mile on Sylvan Way is a fairly level path with nice wildflowers: painted trillium, Solomon's plume, red baneberry, rosy twisted stalk, wild oats, wild sarsaparilla, and foamflower. You will see some huge white ash trees. Check out the pimples on the normally smooth, gray bark of American beech. This is beech bark disease, a serious problem for our beeches that is caused by a one-two punch: a fungus that infests trees that have been attacked by an insect (beech scale).

The trail passes through a logged-over area that has many young aspen saplings and then reenters the forest. Randolph Path crosses at 3.2 miles. After crossing several small streams, you reach Snyder Brook (3.6 miles) just above Gordon Fall, a good place to take a break. Turn right on the Brookbank, which follows the east side of the brook so you do not need to cross it. You won't see a trail sign for the Brookbank, but the yellow blazes are obvious. Follow the Brookbank downstream.

Mosses abound in the cool woods along the Brookbank and on the damp rocks around the waterfalls. One of the most intriguing is named piggyback moss, because new moss "plantlets" grow right out of the "backs" of older shoots. Patches of sphagnum moss also occur.

It takes about 5 minutes (0.3 mile) along the Brookbank from Sylvan Way to reach the power-line right of way. Go through the right of way, turn left, and cross Snyder Brook on an old railroad bridge that has now become part of a bike path. Turn right at the Fallsway to return to the Appalachia parking area (4.0 miles).

Bunchberries carpet the forest floor here and in many other White Mountain trails. Bunchberry is actually a type of dogwood.

OTHER ACTIVITIES

You will find lots of places for wading in the cool water of Snyder Brook. The large network of trails in the Northern Presidentials provides plenty of opportunities for longer excursions to other waterfalls and vistas. Check AMC's *White Mountain Guide* for more ideas if you want to explore further.

MORE INFORMATION

There is no fee for parking in the Appalachia parking area. Except for a small section right at the beginning, the trip is within the White Mountain National Forest; www.fs.usda.gov/whitemountain; 603-536-6100. Much of it is in the Snyder Brook Scenic Area.

Gorham has restaurants, motels, and gas stations. Convenience stores are located along US 2 west of the Appalachia parking area.

47

PINE MOUNTAIN FROM PINKHAM B (DOLLY COPP) ROAD

Pine Mountain is the northernmost peak of the Presidential Range. At 2,405 feet, this geological wonder is lower than its more renowned cousins, but it provides excellent views of the Presidential and Carter ranges for only moderate effort.

LOCATION
Gorham, NH

RATING
Moderate

DISTANCE
3.5 miles round-trip using Pine Mountain Road, Ledge Trail, and Pine Mountain Loop Trail

ELEVATION GAIN
1,450 feet

ESTIMATED TIME
2.0–3.5 hours

MAPS
AMC White Mountain National Forest Map & Guide, E10

AMC *White Mountain Guide*, 29th ed. Map 1 Presidential Range, E10

USGS Topo: Carter Dome, NH

DIRECTIONS

From Jackson or North Conway, head north on NH 16 past Jackson and Pinkham Notch. Make a left onto Pinkham B (Dolly Copp) Road, about 6.5 miles north of AMC's Pinkham Notch Visitor Center (PNVC). The trail to Pine Mountain is 2.4 miles from NH 16 on the right (northeast) side, and opposite the trailhead for Pine Link Trail. Parking is on the left (north) side of the road. There will be signs to the Horton Center (see below), as well as to the trail to Pine Mountain.

If you are coming from the Twin Mountain or Franconia area, take US 3 to NH 115 in Twin Mountain, and then take NH 115 about 12.0 miles to US 2. Make a right onto US 2 and travel about 8.0 miles to Pinkham B (Dolly Copp) Road, which is 0.8 mile past the Appalachia parking area. Make a right onto Pinkham B Road. The trailhead is about 3.0 miles on the left, opposite the trailhead for Pine Link Trail. Pinkham B (Dolly Copp) Road is not maintained for winter travel. *GPS coordinates:* 44° 21.23′ N, 71° 13.89′ W.

TRAIL DESCRIPTION

The trip described here is a loop that starts on Pine Mountain Road; ascends to the summit of Pine Mountain via Ledge Trail; and then returns via Pinkham Ledge Trail, Pine Mountain Loop Trail, and Pine Mountain Road. Pine Mountain Road is a private, unpaved road that leads to the Douglas Horton Center, a retreat run by the United Church of Christ near the summit of Pine Mountain. The center is not open to the public, and recent relocations of the trail are designed to ensure guest privacy at the retreat center.

This hike starts along the unpaved road that leads to the Horton Center. The road is little used but you still need to watch out for the occasional car that passes by. The road formerly passed through a forest dominated by paper birch, but many of the birches were destroyed by an ice storm, so beeches and yellow birch dominate now.

Pine Mountain Road ascends gradually. A common shrub along Pine Mountain Road in wet swales is the red-berried elder. This shrub has compound leaves that branch off in pairs along the stems. The branches themselves are covered with corky spots. Its numerous flowers, produced around early June, are in showy, white, pyramidal clusters. Unfortunately, the dark-red berries found during summer are often inedible, unlike those of its close relative, the elderberry.

Many spring wildflowers and other small plants grow along the trail, an added feature if you are hiking in May or early June. Common ones include painted trillium, Canada mayflower, clintonia, bunchberry, wild sarsaparilla, wild white violet, and starflower. Interrupted ferns and lady ferns (a variety with a red stem) thrive along the edge of the road, and you also should be able to find shining club moss and ground pine. Ground pine, also called princess pine, will remind you of a tiny Christmas tree. Look for pink lady's slippers in June and sharp-leaved and heart-leaved asters in late summer.

The parallel lines on this ridge near the summit of Pine Mountain were scratched into the rock by small stones under a glacier.

At 0.9 mile (about 30 minutes), Ledge Trail leads off to the right. This offers a short (0.6-mile), steep ascent to the summit while providing excellent views from south-facing ledges along the way. It makes a nice, interesting loop over the summit, but as its name implies, it is rocky, requires some scrambling, and is not a good choice in wet or icy weather. Assuming the weather is cooperative, it is easiest to ascend Ledge Trail and descend via Pine Mountain Loop Trail.

The turnoff for Ledge Trail is at a curve where the road becomes a little steeper. The forest becomes boreal (spruce-fir) almost as soon as you leave Pine Mountain Road. When you reach the ledges (in about 15 minutes), note the parallel stripes (called striae) embedded in the flat rocks in a northwest-southeast direction. These are scratches made by the gouging action of stones under the continental glacier as it crept along like a frozen river southwest over Pine Mountain. The rocks, stones, and other debris at the bottom of the glacier, squeezed by the tremendous weight of ice, acted like sandpaper, etching and scouring the earth below. Quartz dikes, which predate the glaciers, are also embedded in the ledges.

The best views of Mounts Washington, Adams, and Madison and of Carter Notch are from ledges just below the summit off Ledge Trail. Carter Notch provides additional clear evidence of glaciation. This beautiful U-shaped notch and the rounded summit of Wildcat Mountain on its southwest side are characteristic features of valleys and mountains smoothed by glaciers.

You reach the summit at 1.5 miles. There is no view from the summit, but you will find a foundation of an old fire tower.

Ravens nest on ledges on Pine Mountain, so your chance of seeing these large, black members of the crow family is good. Depending on the winds, they may effortlessly soar by any of the vistas. They do seem to be enjoying themselves.

The vegetation around the summit ledges is also interesting. Look for reindeer lichen, rhodora, blueberries, Labrador tea, heart-leaved birch, and wild currants. Reindeer lichen is a delicate lichen with thin, bluish-gray, tangled branches. It frequents rocky areas with thin soil in the mountains, often around and under blueberry shrubs. It usually looks so neat and prim that it is hard to believe a landscape gardener didn't deliberately place it there. Rhodora is a small, wild rhododendron with smooth, blue-green leaves. It is common in bogs and on lower summits such as Pine Mountain's. Around Memorial Day, its beautiful large, pink flowers put on a dazzling display, as befits a rhododendron.

The trail, now called Pinkham Ledge Trail, continues beyond the summit at an almost level pace. You should stop to appreciate the views northeast toward the Androscoggin River Valley and the Carter-Moriah Range from several side trails.

Chapel Rock, viewed from the third of the marked overlooks, has a particularly fascinating geologic history. Its rocks are in vertical layers, something more easily seen if you have binoculars. These rocks were once horizontal beds of sandstones and muds that were deposited on the bottom of an ancient sea that predated the modern Atlantic. About 400 million years ago, there was a giant

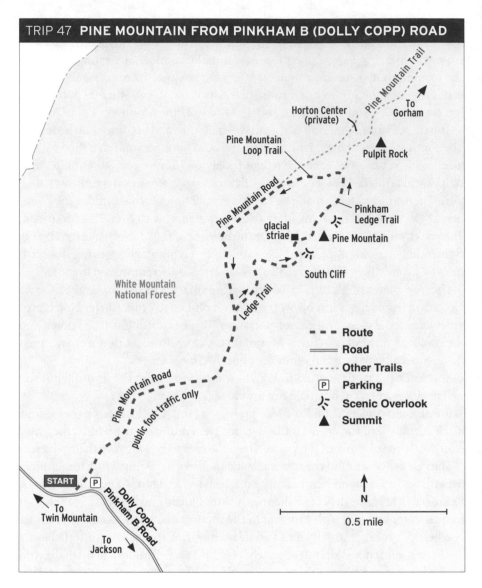

collision between North America and an ancient island continent called Avalonia. The heat and pressure of the crash metamorphosed the deposits into schists and quartzites and folded and thrust them up into their present dramatic, vertical position.

After the Chapel View overlook, the trail descends and reaches a four-way junction at 1.8 miles. Take Pine Mountain Loop Trail to the left. This descends to Pine Mountain Road at 2.1 miles. From here it is 1.3 miles along the road back to the trailhead.

DID YOU KNOW?

Despite its lower stature, Pine Mountain is made up of the same types of rocks (400-million-year-old schists) as the rest of the Presidential mountains.

OTHER ACTIVITIES

If you have extra time, take the short, steep walk along Town Line Brook Trail to Triple Falls. Its trailhead is less than a mile northwest of the Pine Mountain Road trailhead along Pinkham B (Dolly Copp)Road. Look for the sign on the left side of the road.

MORE INFORMATION

The trailhead and the first section of this trail are in the White Mountain National Forest. There is no user fee for parking; www.fs.usda.gov/whitemountain; 603-536-6100. The area around the summit of Pine Mountain and Pine Mountain Road itself is private. Please respect the privacy of guests at the Horton Center so that future hikers will continue to have access to this wonderful small mountain.

Do not confuse Pine Mountain Road with Pine Mountain Trail, which approaches Pine Mountain from the northeast. Its trailhead is in the village of Gorham.

48

LOW'S BALD SPOT VIA OLD JACKSON ROAD

Low's Bald Spot provides a terrific view of the Great Gulf and Mounts Adams and Madison. Along the way you will cross over streams and are likely to see some unusual mushrooms, coral fungi, and interesting wildflowers.

DIRECTIONS

The trail begins at AMC's Pinkham Notch Visitor Center (PNVC) off NH 16 (see Trip 43 for directions). Walk past the outdoor water fountain and scale (for backpackers and kids to weigh their loads). Old Jackson Road Trail branches off from Tuckerman Ravine Trail directly behind the visitor center. *GPS coordinates* (PNVC): 44° 15.44′ N, 71° 15.17′ W.

TRAIL DESCRIPTION

Old Jackson Road was the former carriage route from the town of Jackson to the Mount Washington Auto Road. It has been incorporated into the White Mountain trail system, beginning at AMC's PNVC and meeting the Mount Washington Auto Road at the latter's 2-mile marker. From there a short section of Madison Gulf Trail leads to Low's Bald Spot. The trail ascends gradually, with a few steep sections near the end. Younger children, and those who are not particularly enthusiastic hikers, might find it a bit long.

Old Jackson Road Trail is part of the Appalachian Trail and marked with white-paint blazes. This hike begins not on Old Jackson Road itself, but on a link that brings you shortly to the old road. Be sure to follow carefully the signs to Old Jackson Road, which crosses a maintenance road, a ski trail (indicated by blue diamonds), and other hiking trails.

At 0.4 mile, Old Jackson Road Trail widens and looks like you'd expect an old road to look. Shortly after, the trail crosses a solid wooden bridge right at the point where Crew Cut Trail comes in from the right. Old Jackson Road then

LOCATION
Pinkham's Grant, NH, to Sargent's Purchase, NH

RATING
Moderate

DISTANCE
4.4 miles round-trip

ELEVATION GAIN
950 feet

ESTIMATED TIME
3.0-4.0 hours

MAPS
AMC White Mountain National Forest Map & Guide, F9

AMC *White Mountain Guide,* 29th ed. Map 1 Presidential Range, F9

USGS Topo: Mount Washington, NH

Hikers arriving at Low's Bald Spot, where they can enjoy a sweeping view of the Great Gulf Wilderness and Mount Adams. Photo by Dennis Welsh.

goes uphill moderately steeply and crosses a pleasant, shady gorge with a small waterfall. Take a moment to enjoy the cool, mossy atmosphere and the sound of running water. Soon after, the trail crosses another small gorge (dry in August).

Mushrooms and other fungi abound in the rich, moist soil and on decaying logs along this trail. They come in a rich assortment of colors and odd shapes and become especially abundant in late summer and early fall in the White Mountains. One of the most eye-catching is the coral fungus, which looks like someone stuck a piece of branching coral from a tropical ocean onto a log. Shelf (bracket) fungi growing out of dead trees sometimes reach monstrous sizes. Russulas (robust mushrooms with wide, reddish-brown or yellow caps and thick stalks), mycenas (delicate mushrooms with thin stalks and conical caps), amanitas, and many other types cover the forest floor. Admire them, but consider them all poisonous.

What you actually see of mushrooms or other fungi are their reproductive structures, which are only a small part of their "bodies." The soil below is laced with myriad thin filaments of numerous species of fungi. Some penetrate plant roots and aid the plants in taking up nutrients. Others, such as the coral fungus and the bracket fungus (illustrated here), penetrate into dead wood, breaking it down to basic elements. In this way fungi play a critical role in the ecology of the forest.

Indian pipe (illustrated here), with its distinctive white flower on a white stem, could be mistaken for a fungus because it has no green leaves. It is a flowering plant but gets along without leaves by "feeding" on dead organic matter in the soil rather than producing its own food. Ecologically, it is more like a fungus than a plant.

After about 40 minutes (0.9 mile), the trail reaches a junction with the upper end of George's Gorge Trail and then levels. It crosses a rivulet and passes a swale on the left and then a damp, muddy section traversed by double logs.

Early in summer, look for white bog orchids, 1- to 3-foot-tall plants with slender spikes of small white flowers in the damp open areas alongside the trail. Once we spotted one of these orchids among the dense vegetation at the edge of the largest swale and then watched as a tiger swallowtail butterfly found a number of others, flying from orchid to orchid, ignoring all the other plants. If you have a hand lens, take a close look at one of the flowers. From a distance the flowers don't look like anything special, but close up you will see an exotic shape typical of orchids, with a lower lip and a spur.

In midsummer you can't miss jewelweed and its delicate spurred flowers of orange spotted with black, hanging from juicy-looking leaves. These are followed by fat seed capsules in late summer. When these capsules are touched or squeezed, they explode, releasing the seeds and giving the squeezer a jolt like an electric shock. After trying this a few times it is easy to see why jewelweed is also called "touch-me-not."

In late summer, the white of the bog orchid is replaced by the white of the turtleheads (illustrated here). It may take a little imagination to see the resemblance of this relative of the snapdragon to a turtle, but even if you decide that it looks more like a lizard's head than a turtle's, you will definitely agree that it is a uniquely shaped flower. The flower has two lips, and the top lip overhangs the bottom.

In another 15 minutes, the trail makes a sharp left turn and heads uphill on rock steps at a point where an old section of trail is blocked off. You can hear vehicles from the auto road through the trees, although you still have about 0.5 mile to go before you cross it. Old Jackson Road continues straight past Raymond Path (1.7 miles), crosses a few small rivulets on logs, and then passes Nelson Crag Trail. After this, the trail ascends and opens up a bit, passing through an old gravel pit with a nice view of Nelson Crag (a shoulder of Mount Washington).

Old Jackson Road ends at a parking area on the auto road, 1.9 miles from Pinkham Notch.

To continue on to Low's Bald Spot, walk across the auto road and follow Madison Gulf Trail into the Great Gulf Wilderness. At 0.2 mile beyond the auto road, take the turnoff leading uphill to the right. You won't find a sign

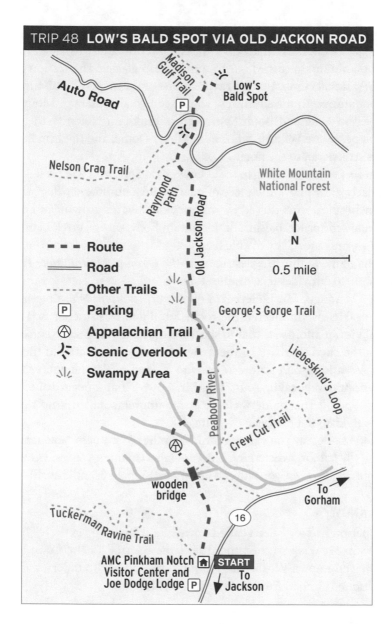

Auto Road

Madison Gulf Trail

Low's Bald Spot

P

Nelson Crag Trail

Raymond Path

White Mountain National Forest

N

0.5 mile

Old Jackson Road

- - - **Route**
═══ **Road**
------ **Other Trails**
P **Parking**
Ⓐ **Appalachian Trail**
☀ **Scenic Overlook**
☀ **Swampy Area**

George's Gorge Trail

Liebeskind's Loop

Peabody River

Crew Cut Trail

Ⓐ

wooden bridge

To Gorham

16

Tuckerman Ravine Trail

AMC Pinkham Notch Visitor Center and Joe Dodge Lodge P

🏠 START

To Jackson

to indicate Low's Bald Spot, but it is easy to find. In another few minutes you reach the viewpoint.

A vast expanse of the Great Gulf Wilderness lies before you from Low's Bald Spot. Mount Adams, the second-highest peak in the White Mountains, is particularly impressive with its symmetrical cone shape. The treeless alpine zone on the upper part of the mountain is very obvious. You can easily see the distinction between the forest dominated by broad-leaved trees at the bottom of the mountain, the boreal forest (spruce and fir) midway up, and the treeless alpine zone.

Between Mount Adams and Mount Madison is Madison Gulf, a tributary ravine of the Great Gulf. Madison Gulf is a cirque—a bowl-shaped ravine on the side of a mountain carved out by a mountain glacier. The section of Madison Gulf Trail that climbs up this ravine is one of the most difficult hikes in the White Mountains. To the southwest you'll see two shoulders of Mount Washington, Nelson Crag and Boott Spur. Across Pinkham Notch to the east, the prominent peaks are Wildcat Mountain, Carter Dome, and the Imp Face. Endless peaks stretch out to the north.

The view isn't the only thing to see at Low's Bald Spot. You will probably notice a particularly gleaming white piece of quartz and a number of "flag" trees with their branching patterns carved by winter winds. Plants growing at Low's Bald Spot include red spruce, balsam fir, mountain holly, sheep laurel, Labrador tea, crowberries, and a few scrawny blueberries.

As to the name of this fine destination, *The Gorham Mountaineer* from September 14, 1910, provides us with the story:

"About a year ago, Mr. J. Herbert Low from Brooklyn, NY, a big man with a thousand friends, discovered the rocky knoll and was so charmed with the delightful view it affords . . . that to share his discovery he marked an easy trail to it from the carriage road. In the first party to be conducted to the outlook was Mrs. Vera Johnson of New York, who evoked peals of laughter from the party by impulsively crying out, 'Oh, Mr. Low! What a beautiful view from your Bald Spot!'" This name was one of the unpremeditated kind that sticks, and Low's Bald Spot it has been ever since.

Return the same way you came. Within 0.4 mile of Pinkham Notch, make sure not to take the left fork where Link Ski Trail (also Connie's Way and Go Back ski trails) comes in. If you do, you will end up on NH 16 about 0.3 mile north of PNVC.

DID YOU KNOW?

The destination had long been called Lowe's Bald Spot. The extra "e" likely was added because it was assumed that the name referred to the Lowe family of Randolph, well-known White Mountain guides and trail-builders, and not the aforementioned Herbert Low from Brooklyn, NY.

OTHER ACTIVITIES

Many loop trails intersect Old Jackson Road if you are interested in a longer outing. Check AMC's *White Mountain Guide* or stop in at PNVC for some ideas. Old Jackson Road is an intermediate-level ski trail.

MORE INFORMATION

There is no fee for parking at PNVC, where you can find hiking supplies, snacks, restrooms, and trail information; outdoors.org/lodging/whitemountains/pinkham/pnvc-pnvc.cfm; 603-466-2721.

49

NINETEEN MILE BROOK TRAIL TO CARTER NOTCH HUT

AMC's Carter Notch Hut is in a remote col between two 4,000-foot mountains. The notch features stunning mountain scenery, two pristine lakes, and a stark pile of boulders called the Ramparts.

DIRECTIONS

The trailhead for Nineteen Mile Brook trail is off NH 16, about 4.0 miles north of AMC's Pinkham Notch Visitor Center (PNVC) and 1.0 mile north of the Mount Washington Auto Road. If you are coming from the north, it is about 6.5 miles south of the intersection of US 2 and NH 16 in Gorham. The large parking area (space for about twenty vehicles) is on the east side of NH 16. *GPS coordinates: 44° 18.13′ N, 71° 13.25′ W.*

TRAIL DESCRIPTION

Nineteen Mile Brook Trail is marked with blue blazes and begins on the route of an old road along the northeast bank of Nineteen Mile Brook. The trail ascends moderately, and the sound of running water is your constant companion for much of this hike. The trail crosses a bridge over a tributary at about 0.4 mile.

About 20 minutes into the hike (about 0.8 mile), you pass a large rock outcropping along the side of the brook. This is schist, a medium-grade metamorphic rock that underlies most of the Presidential Range (see Appendix B, Natural History of the White Mountains). Look for lines of quartz that formed in cracks within the schist. The White Mountains offers visitors fine views of the large, sheet-like rocks that make up the geology of the region. Quartz often occurs in drawn-out grains to such an extent that a particular form called quartz schist is often produced.

LOCATION
Bean's Purchase, NH

RATING
Moderate, with a few steep sections

DISTANCE
7.6 miles round-trip

ELEVATION GAIN
1,900 feet

ESTIMATED TIME
7.0 hours

MAPS
AMC *White Mountain National Forest Map & Guide,* F10

AMC *White Mountain Guide,* 29th ed. Map 5 Carter Range-Evans Notch, F10

USGS Topo: Carter Dome, NH

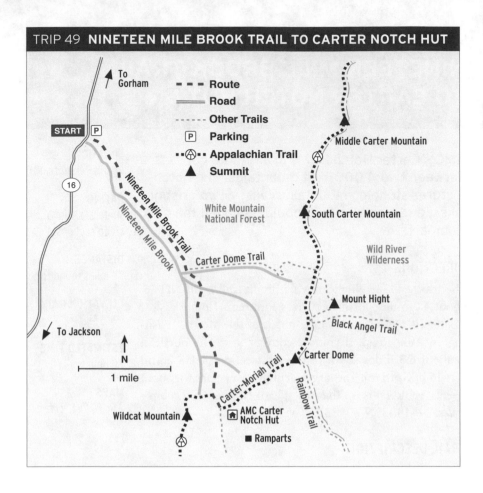

Hemlocks and yellow birch dominate the forest in the first part of the trail. Hemlocks often prevail in the valleys of streams at lower elevations. A number of the yellow birches appear to be growing on stilts. This can take two forms. In one, roots snake down to the ground from a tree growing on top of a large boulder. In the other, the base of the tree trunk is suspended above the ground with the roots forming the struts of a tower. These trees probably grew on top of a log that later rotted away.

At 1.2 miles the trail passes a small dam that creates an inviting swimming hole. After this, the trail becomes rockier, but still ascends moderately. Carter Dome Trail goes off to the left at 1.9 miles (1.0 hour). A few steps beyond, the trail crosses a tributary of Nineteen Mile Brook on a wooden bridge. Another tributary is crossed at 2.2 miles on a log bridge, and the trail then ascends away from the brook. The hemlock and birch gradually give way to a spruce-fir forest with scattered paper birches, the typical forest at elevations of greater than 2,500 feet.

You cross a third tributary at 3.1 miles. The trail ascends at a steeper pitch for a short distance, and then becomes a level, pleasant boreal-forest walk where you catch glimpses through the trees of Wildcat Mountain as it dramatically slopes down to Carter Notch. A final steep section takes you to the height-of-land (elevation 3,400 feet) at the junction with Wildcat Ridge Trail (3.6 miles). Nineteen Mile Brook Trail then descends steeply for 100 feet to the larger of the two Carter lakes. Carter-Moriah Trail departs to the left, and then you pass the smaller Carter Lake and reach the hut at 3.8 miles.

Stop in to see this venerable hut. The original Carter Notch Hut was a log cabin constructed in 1904 as the third backcountry hut built by AMC (after Madison Spring and Lakes of the Clouds). That building no longer stands, but the present stone building was built in 1914 and is the oldest hut still in use in the AMC hut system.

The Carter lakes are an unexpected visual treat when you first see them below you from the height-of-land. The upper Carter Lake supports a number of interesting aquatic plants, including yellow pond lily, bur-reed, and quill-wort. Yellow pond lily has large, attractive yellow flowers and heart-shaped floating leaves. Bur-reed has long, strap-like leaves that flop over on the surface

Carter Notch Hut is surrounded by 4,000-footers in the Carter Range.

of the water. Look for its burr-like fruit. Quillwort is a strange underwater relative of club mosses (nonflowering plants somewhat akin to ferns). Its thin, grasslike leaves are arranged in a circular rosette along the bottom.

Carter Notch is a glacially carved valley. Its walls are the slopes and cliffs of Carter Dome (4,832 feet) and Wildcat Mountain (4,422 feet). The 1,000-foot cliffs on Wildcat that loom over Carter Notch are particularly impressive.

While you are at Carter Notch, you should not miss the Ramparts. Walk about 100 yards south of the bunkhouses on Wildcat River Trail. A trail (signed) leads left to this immense boulder field, formed from boulders crashing down into the notch from the Carter Dome and Wildcat. The going is rough, but for those who are comfortable scrambling on uneven rocks, it is worth exploring. You will be rewarded with a nice view of the hut and the two lakes and an excellent vista to the south. The two Carter lakes owe their existence to the Ramparts, which serves as a natural dam. The outlet of the lower lake flows under the boulders.

Look for caves hidden within the Ramparts, where ice can remain late into summer. Look also for large quartz crystals in the rocks. Mountain cranberry, Labrador tea, and red spruce grow around the boulders.

Another interesting side trip is to hike up Carter-Moriah Trail for 0.3 mile to an excellent viewpoint of the notch near an immense boulder named Pulpit Rock. This is a very steep ascent, but the view is tremendous.

Listen and watch for ravens calling and soaring around the cliffs. They are part of the dramatic scenery of Carter Notch.

Return to your vehicle by retracing your steps on Nineteen Mile Brook Trail.

DID YOU KNOW?

It is not certain who Carter was. By some accounts he was either a lonely hunter in these mountains or a Concord, NH, physician who used to come to the range to study plants.

OTHER ACTIVITIES

Nineteen Mile Brook Trail offers a number of swimming possibilities. The brook has many small pools deep enough for a stop on a hot day even if you do not make it all the way to the notch. Upper Carter Lake is swimmable but has rocks and a mucky bottom. Upper Carter Lake is stocked with trout, so fishing is a possibility with the proper New Hampshire license. Spring peepers also are there.

For those wanting an even longer outing, you can make a nice loop by taking Nineteen Mile Brook Trail to the hut and then hiking up Carter Dome via the steep Carter-Moriah Trail. From there Carter Dome Trail leads back down to Nineteen Mile Brook Trail at its halfway point. That adds 2.6 miles, 1,500 feet, and 2.5 hours to the hike described here.

MORE INFORMATION

This hike is in the White Mountain National Forest. There is a user fee ($3 per day) for parking at the trailhead: www.fs.usda.gov/whitemountain; 603-536-6100. The AMC Hiker Shuttle stops at the Nineteen Mile Brook trailhead: outdoors.org/lodging/lodging-shuttle.cfm.

Carter Notch Hut is open year-round, and there are two bunkhouses along with a dining and kitchen building. During summer and fall, AMC operates it as a full-service hut, providing breakfast and dinner. For the rest of the year, it is open on a self-service basis; you provide your own food, but you have full use of kitchen facilities. Reservations are required at all times; outdoors.org/whitemountains; 603-466-2727.

50

TUCKERMAN RAVINE AND MOUNT WASHINGTON

This rugged hike takes you up to Tuckerman Ravine, one of the most dramatic landscapes in New England, and then on to the summit of the region's tallest mountain.

CAUTION Before beginning, check at AMC's Pinkham Notch Visitor Center (PNVC) for the weather conditions on the summit of Mount Washington, which is likely to be about 20 degrees Fahrenheit colder and much windier than in the valley. You can also check at the Hermit Lake shelters at the base of Tuckerman Ravine for weather updates before ascending any farther, because the hike is well protected from the elements up to that point. Tuckerman Ravine is slightly more benign than the summit, as it is somewhat protected from the westerly winds. But the weather here is notoriously fickle and can change rapidly even with a good forecast. Dense fog and slippery conditions can be hazardous on the headwall because of the steep dropoff, and thunderstorms can pop up rapidly. Don't go beyond Hermit Lake if the weather is questionable, because the route is exposed and rugged. Be prepared to turn back if the weather changes during the hike. A snow arch forms at the base of the headwall in winter and may still be present through early July. Although attractive to look at, it is unstable, so do not climb on or under it. At least one death has resulted from falling ice chunks.

LOCATION
Pinkham's Grant, NH to Sargent's Purchase, NH

RATING
Strenuous

DISTANCE
8.4 miles round-trip

ELEVATION GAIN
4,250 feet

ESTIMATED TIME
8.0 hours

MAPS
AMC White Mountain National Forest Map & Guide, F9

AMC White Mountain Guide, 29th ed. Map 1 Presidential Range, F9

USGS Topo: Mount Washington, NH

DIRECTIONS

The trailhead for Tuckerman Ravine Trail is at AMC's Pinkham Notch Visitor Center (PNVC) on the west side of NH 16. See Trip 43 for directions. Walk past the Trading Post until you see the large sign for this trail. *GPS coordinates* (PNVC): 44° 15.44′ N, 71° 15.17′ W.

TRAIL DESCRIPTION

This is the most popular route up New England's highest mountain and is often crowded with hikers, but it is arguably the most "nature rich" way of ascending Mount Washington. You must have the proper gear, have enough time, and be prepared for rough weather, particularly if your goal is to hike beyond Hermit Lake. Make sure everyone has sturdy shoes and extra clothes. This trail is not appropriate for anyone who is uncomfortable hiking on rocks.

The first part of Tuckerman Ravine Trail is on an old, heavily eroded tractor road along the Cutler River and is moderately steep throughout with virtually no views. Be careful not to get sidetracked by Old Jackson Road, which goes off to the right near the trailhead, or Blanchard Ski Trail, which crosses the trail soon after it starts. At 0.3 mile, the trail makes a sharp left and crosses the river on a solid bridge.

After a short, steep section, you reach the viewing area for the Crystal Cascade. This cascade tumbles over a black volcanic vent of basalt that formed much later in time than the schists that form the surrounding cliffs.

At the junction with Boott Spur Trail (0.4 mile), Tuckerman Ravine Trail turns right and continues climbing relentlessly at a moderately steep rate. Landmarks along this section of the trail are the junction with Huntington Ravine Trail (1.3 mile), a bridge back over to the north side of the Cutler River (1.6 mile), and the junction with Raymond Path (2.1 miles). At 2.3 miles, Lion Head Trail

Tuckerman Ravine is a textbook example of a cirque, a bowl-shaped ravine gouged out of a mountainside by a glacier. Photo by Eric Pedersen.

goes right, and at 2.4 miles you reach the floor of the ravine—and one of the grandest vistas in New England opens up before you. Enjoy the view from conveniently placed benches and check the information hut for the latest weather. There are outhouses, and a well for refilling water bottles.

Tuckerman Ravine is a textbook example of a cirque, a geological term used for a bowl-shaped, glacially carved valley on the side of a mountain. The ravine was carved by a small mountain glacier sometime before the area was completely covered by the last continental ice sheet 50,000 years ago. As the climate cooled, glaciers first formed in the mountains. Water freezing and expanding in cracks in the bedrock plucked rocks from the sides of mountains, leaving the bowl-shaped ravines (cirques) for which the Presidential Range is noted: Tuckerman, Huntington, King, and Great Gulf. Eventually the continental ice sheet covered the whole area, including the summit of Mount Washington.

Follow a trail past one of the shelters to the right to see Hermit Lake. The Cutler River is to the left, crossed by Boott Spur Link.

Hermit Lake, technically a tarn (a glacial lake in the bowl of a cirque), is tiny (less than 0.5 acre) and shallow (less than a foot deep in most places), but its setting is exquisite. The view from Hermit Lake as you face the ravine includes the Lion Head, a particularly impressive rock face on your right that resembles its namesake when seen from NH 16 below, and the long alpine ridge of Boott Spur, with its Hanging Cliffs to the left. The headwall of the ravine is straight ahead.

Tuckerman Ravine Trail continues past the Hermit Lake area, ascending on steps over the Little Headwall, and then at a relatively level pitch to the base of the headwall (3.1 miles, 0.7 mile from the Hermit Lake area). See caution above regarding the snow arch.

The streamside flora is particularly interesting as you approach the headwall. Look for Indian poke (false hellebore), a large, herbaceous plant whose broad, deeply veined leaves look like cabbage. Such a tall herbaceous plant would not survive in exposed areas due to wicked winter winds, but in the floor of the ravine, the thick blanket of winter snow protects it. Green alder is a common streamside shrub. It has rounded, toothed leaves, and its cone-like fruits remain on the plant throughout summer. Meadowsweet is a type of spirea with clusters of white, fuzzy flowers at the tips of branches. This small shrub blooms in early summer at lower elevations, but at the elevation of Tuckerman Ravine, meadowsweet flowers can still be found through late August. They are one of a number of species in the ravine whose bloom times are late because of the heavy winter snow accumulation. In late summer, the sides of streams are lined with the purple flowers of purple-stemmed asters and clusters of the yellow flowers of large-leaved goldenrod.

The vegetation becomes shorter in stature with an increasing number of alpines species the closer you get to the base of the headwall. The elevation at the base of the headwall is 4,500 feet, roughly treeline.

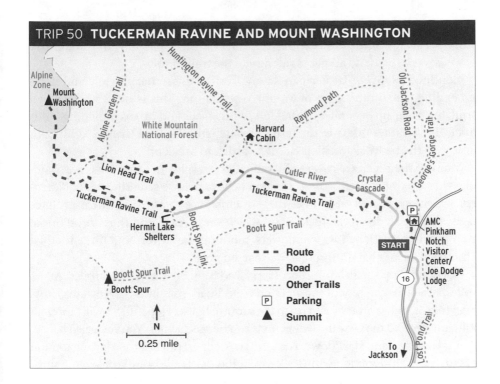

Tuckerman Ravine Trail starts ascending the headwall. Although it looks very intimidating from below, the path is well graded and secure; however, be careful not to dislodge rocks that could potentially injure hikers below. Also, this part of the trail could be hazardous in dense fog or when wet or icy because there are steep dropoffs on either side of you.

The walk up the headwall, although steep and strenuous (elevation gain of 600 feet in 0.3 mile), is very beautiful. Wildflowers, particularly in mid- to late summer, border alpine rivulets that cascade down the mountainside. Among the showiest are pale painted cup, a relative of snapdragons, and arnica, a brilliant-yellow, daisy-like flower. You will also see some lowland species, such as bog orchids, that survive winter here under a protective blanket of deep snow.

At the top of the headwall, you reach a broad alpine plateau. On days with a westerly or northwesterly wind, you will immediately notice the wind picking up at this point. If it is foggy, you will have to be careful to look for the cairns (rock piles) and paint blazes that mark the trail.

Tuckerman Ravine Trail passes Alpine Garden Trail at 3.4 miles (a great trail for alpine wildflowers) and reaches Tuckerman Junction (3.6 mile), a major intersection of a number of trails heading in different directions.

Tuckerman Junction is at the edge of a broad alpine plateau called Bigelow's Lawn, which is another fine area for alpine wildflowers. Some of the botanical superstars in June are diapensia, Lapland rosebay, and mountain avens, the latter particularly partial to alpine streamsides (see page 260). Mountain sand-worts, delicate white flowers with five petals on small plants with thin, grassy leaves, are particularly abundant alongside the trail in July.

Continue following Tuckerman Ravine Trail. It turns sharply right and starts ascending the summit cone of Mount Washington. This is not a well-defined trail, but a way up over piles of boulders, with blazes and cairns providing guidance. The boulder piles are the result of water freezing and then expanding in cracks in the bedrock, causing chunks of rock to break off.

Many of the rocks are covered by yellow-green splotches that look like someone threw paint at them. These are map lichens, whose scientific name, *Rhizocarpon geographicum,* also notes their resemblance to a map. Lichens produce acids that break down the rocks upon which they reside, and thus are an initial step in soil formation. Two wildflowers, mountain sandwort and three-toothed cinquefoil, also inhabit this otherwise barren area.

Continuing up the summit cone, Lion Head Trail comes in at 3.8 miles. At 4.2 miles, you cross the Mount Washington Auto Road, pass by a parking area, cross over the cog railway tracks, and reach the summit house. Hopefully, it will be a crystal-clear day and the view in all directions will be spectacular. You've earned it.

For your descent, start down Tuckerman Ravine Trail but then switch to Lion Head Trail at its junction with Tuckerman Ravine Trail 0.4 mile below the summit. As you will discover on your ascent, Tuckerman Ravine Trail is narrow and particularly crowded on summer weekends, at which time passing a party of hikers going in the opposite direction can be troublesome. Lion Head Trail is steeper, slightly longer and rougher, and more exposed for more of its distance than Tuckerman Ravine Trail, but it has fantastic views of the Carter Range across Pinkham Notch. It follows a ridge along the edge of the Alpine Garden, passes a knob that resembles the head of a lion when seen from below, descends steeply on well-placed steps, enters the boreal forest, and rejoins Tuckerman Ravine Trail 0.1 mile below the Hermit Lake Shelters. From there, return the rest of the way to Pinkham Notch via Tuckerman Ravine Trail. (At less busy times, you can reverse your steps down Tuckerman Ravine Trail.)

DID YOU KNOW?

Dr. Edward Tuckerman was a professor of botany at Amherst College and a well-known lichenologist (a scientist who studies lichens). He initially came to the White Mountains in the 1830s to study the flora and returned many times. Tuckerman was one of the first scientists to describe the effects of elevation on plant communities of the White Mountains.

OTHER ACTIVITIES

Tuckerman Ravine makes a fine day-hike destination in its own right if you have less time or do not want to do the entire hike to the Mount Washington summit.

John Sherburne Ski Trail (for advanced skiers) closely parallels Tuckerman Ravine Trail and leads downhill from Hermit Lake. The ski trail is not open to hikers, so skiers ascend via Tuckerman Ravine Trail before skiing down.

AMC and the White Mountain National Forest run ten shelters (open on one side, they fit eight people each) and three tent platforms at Hermit Lake. If you want to spend more time exploring this exquisite area, consider camping overnight. You must purchase a ticket in person (first come, first served) at PNVC before hiking up.

MORE INFORMATION

Sections of the trail beyond Hermit Lake may be closed to hikers even in June due to heavy snow accumulation. At such times, Lion Head Trail is a logical alternative for ascending Mount Washington from Pinkham Notch. Huntington Ravine Trail is considered the most difficult hiking trail in the White Mountains and is particularly not recommended for descending.

AMC's PNVC at the trailhead has trail and weather information, snacks, restrooms, hiking gear, and field guides; outdoors.org/lodging/whitemountains/pinkham/pnvc-pnvc.cfm; 603-466-2721. You can also get weather information from AMC staff at the Hermit Lake Shelter area; outdoors.org/lodging/campsites/hermit-lake-shelter.cfm; 603-466-8116. This can provide guidance about the wisdom of hiking up to and beyond the bowl of Tuckerman Ravine.

Mount Washington State Park (New Hampshire Division of Parks and Recreation) includes about 60 acres of the summit of the mountain (nhstateparks.org/visit/state-parks/mount-washington-state-park.aspx; 603-466-3347). The Governor Sherman Adams Summit Building at the summit has weather information, restrooms, food service, snacks, souvenirs, telephones, a post office, a museum, and lots of tourists.

THE ALPINE ZONE OF THE WHITE MOUNTAINS

The most unique and exciting landscape in the White Mountains (and arguably all of New England) is the land above treeline. This natural community is an arctic outpost inhabited by rare wildflowers and a few insects, birds, and mammals that are hardy enough to withstand the challenging conditions. The most extensive alpine zone in all of New England is in the Presidential Range, and you can hike to it on the Edmands Path up Mount Eisenhower (Trip 41) or Tuckerman Ravine Trail (Trip 50). Falling Waters Trail (Trip 17) takes you to the alpine zone in the Franconia Range. Mount Moosilauke (Trip 9) also has some alpine tundra.

When ascending to the alpine zone, you pass through three ecological zones: the broad-leafed deciduous forest (or northern hardwoods), the boreal forest, and the alpine tundra. This is a response to the change in climate with elevation. On average, the temperature drops about 1 degree Fahrenheit for every 350 feet you climb, so it will be about 12 degrees cooler at the summit of Mount Washington than at the trailhead in Pinkham Notch, and a lot windier too. By hiking up 4,000 feet in elevation, you have traveled the equivalent of about 1,000 miles north.

The peak time to observe flowers of the alpine tundra in bloom is early to mid-June. This is early in the season for many hikers, so if you miss it, there are still many interesting plants to see all summer.

The first thing to notice about plants in the alpine zone is their small stature. Most never rise more than a few inches above the ground because of the fierce winds. Taller ones are likely to be found only where they are protected from the wind—for example, in the lees of rocks or in ravines or where they are protected by deep snow cover. Balsam fir and black spruce grow as low, gnarled shrubs called krummholz, a German word meaning "crooked wood."

While hiking through the alpine zone in both the Presidential and Franconia ranges, you will notice cushions of dark-green, tightly packed, tiny leaves that

 hug the ground throughout the tundra. These "pin-cushions" are diapensia (illustrated here), a native of North American and Scandinavian arctic realms, as well as the high peaks of New England and the Adirondacks. If you are lucky enough to be in the alpine zone on the Presidential or Franconia ridges in June and the wind and temperature have been cooperative, you will be treated to a profusion of its small, white flowers with five petals. The dark-green leaves act as passive solar collectors, absorbing solar radiation and ensuring that the plant stays warmer than the surroundings.

Alpine azalea also grows as a cushion plant. Its leaves resemble diapensia, but its pink flowers are even smaller—no larger than the head of a matchstick.

They still put on a great show when they all bloom together. Another flower that is bound to catch your eye in June because of its large magenta blossoms is the Lapland rosebay, a very small species of rhododendron.

In keeping with the theme that small is beautiful in the alpine garden, there are tiny willows that never get more than 2 inches high. In June look for pussy willow–type "buds" coming right out of the ground. These are the male and female catkins of the bearberry willow.

The big yellow flower blooming from late June throughout summer is mountain avens. This plant, with relatively large scalloped leaves, grows in only two places in the world: the White Mountains and an island off Nova Scotia. You can sometimes find mountain avens along streams at lower elevations where the microclimate is cool (see Trips 35 and 37).

In July and August, the showiest flower in the alpine zone on Mount Washington is the bluebell (harebell). This flower is common at lower elevations and may not have been native to the alpine garden. There is some speculation that its seeds may have been carried up the mountain in the droppings of donkeys that were used as pack animals in the nineteenth century.

Donkeys are no longer part of the White Mountain landscape, and you will not see large animals in the alpine zone there. You will have to content yourself with the wolf spider, a large, dark spider that scampers over rocks; butterflies; other insects; and an occasional woodchuck or snowshoe hare. Two of the butterflies, the White Mountain butterfly and White Mountain fritillary, are endemic to the Whites. The cold climate of the alpine zone is not generally friendly to amphibians; however, you can hear spring peepers, a small tree frog, into August at Lakes of the Clouds on Mount Washington and Eagle Lake on Mount Lafayette. In the lowlands their shrill chorus of whistles from wetlands is a harbinger of spring and lasts from late March through early May.

The only two species of birds that regularly build nests above the timberline are dark-eyed juncos and white-throated sparrows. The junco is a perky, gray bird with a white belly that flashes white outer-tail feathers when it flies. The white-throated sparrow is famous for its song, a series of clear whistles. The American pipit, a small, streaky, sparrowlike bird with white outer-tail feathers, occasionally nest in the alpine area of the Presidentials. Watch also for ravens cavorting in the air, with their characteristic throaty call that sometimes sounds like the snorting of a hog. Admire their ability to soar over this unique and dramatic habitat.

For an in-depth look at the alpine area, see the AMC *Field Guide to the New England Alpine Summits* (AMC Books, 2014) by Nancy G. Slack and Allison W. Bell.

EVANS NOTCH

Evans Notch is the farthest east of the four major north–south notches that run through the White Mountains. It straddles the New Hampshire–Maine border for much of its length and provides excellent hiking and other recreational opportunities for families and anyone else who prefers their mountains less crowded. Evans Notch is a terrific place to escape the crowds that you might find at the popular notches farther west, and get a sense of what the White Mountains were like in earlier times.

The mountains on its western border include the Baldfaces, the Basin Rim, and the Royces, generally ranging from 3,000 to 3,500 feet in elevation. The mountains on the east side of Evans Notch are lower (1,000 to 2,900 feet) and include Caribou, Speckled, and Blueberry mountains, and Deer Hill. Much of this area is within the Caribou-Speckled Mountain Wilderness.

The lower elevations are ideal for children. Most of the summits have excellent views, flowing water abounds, and there are ample places for picking blueberries. Basin Pond is in a glacially carved bowl between West Royce Mountain and Mount Meader. The pond offers fishing, canoeing, picnicking, and a great chance to spot moose and other wildlife. ME 113 provides access to most of the hiking trails.

Approaching from the south, you pick up ME 113 in Fryeburg. Fryeburg is approximately 8 miles east of Conway and North Conway along NH 113 and US 302, respectively. Keep in mind, particularly when returning to New Hampshire, that NH 113 and ME 113 are two different roads. After leaving Fryeburg, ME 113 passes through Chatham, North Chatham, and Stow. From the north,

Facing page: The Evans Notch region straddles
the border of Maine and New Hampshire. Here,
a storm has just passed by Kezar Lake in Maine.

ME 113 is reached by traveling east on US 2 about 11 miles from Gorham to the former logging town of Gilead.

ME 113 is unplowed through Evans Notch and closed to vehicle traffic during winter. As a result, some of the trails described here are inaccessible then. These include Caribou Mountain and Basin Trail. Roost Trail is located about a mile south of where the gate is closed in winter. If you want to hike or snowshoe to the Roost in winter, you would need to plan on an extra mile to reach the trailhead.

SUPPLIES AND LOGISTICS

The towns closest to Evans Notch—Chatham, North Chatham, Stow, and Gilead—are small, so you may want to pick up the supplies you need for your hike at the larger communities farther away (e.g., Bethel, Fryeburg, Gorham). The Chatham Trails Association (CTA; chathamtrails.org) has produced a detailed trail map of Evans Notch and the Cold River Valley.

The most accessible restrooms in Evans Notch are at Basin Pond, which also has an attractive picnic area. Other public restrooms are at the campgrounds.

The Androscoggin Ranger Station on NH 16 in Gorham (www.fs.usda.gov/whitemountain; 603-466-2713) and the Evans Notch Information Center (207-824-2134) east of Bethel have pamphlets on trails in Evans Notch, as well as information on rock-collecting opportunities.

NEARBY CAMPING

Four national forest campgrounds are in and around Evans Notch: the Cold River, Basin, Hastings, and Wild River campgrounds. The Cold River and Basin campgrounds, with 14 and 21 sites, respectively, are both at the Basin (www.fs.usda.gov/activity/whitemountain/recreation/camping-cabins). Hastings Campground, with 24 sites, is located between the two ends of Roost Trail just off ME 113. It has limited accessibility for people with disabilities (603-466-2713). The Wild River Campground has twelve sites and is reached by a 5.7-mile drive down Wild River Road, an unpaved road off ME 113 (no reservations).

51

LORD HILL

The excursion up Lord Hill combines a relatively short uphill walk to an excellent viewpoint with a visit to an abandoned mine. Amateur rock hobbyists are permitted to collect for their personal use.

DIRECTIONS

From the Conway/North Conway area, take US 302 to Frye-burg, and then head north on ME 113. Turn right (east) onto unpaved Deer Hill Road (Forest Road 9), approximately 4.9 miles north of the little village of Stow. (If you pass AMC's Cold River Camp 0.8 mile beyond that, you have gone too far.) Follow Deer Hill Road past the wildlife-viewing area (2.6 miles from ME 113) to the Horseshoe Pond trailhead on the right, 4.4 miles from ME 113. It is located in a bend in the road where there is room on the right for vehicles to park. Look for the yellow blazes heading off into the forest if a trail sign is not obvious (it seems to keep disappearing!). If you reach an unpaved road heading sharply to the right (Forest Road 50), you have gone about 0.1 mile too far.

From the north or west, take US 2 through Gorham and turn south onto ME 113, which is about 11.0 miles east of the junction of US 2 with NH 16. Travel 13.7 miles on ME 113 through Evans Notch. Turn left onto Deer Hill Road approximately 0.8 mile south of AMC's Cold River Camp and follow the above directions. *GPS coordinates:* 44° 14.14′ N, 70° 56.67′ W.

TRAIL DESCRIPTION

The hike to the summit of Lord Hill (1,257 feet) uses the Horseshoe Pond and Conant trails. Horseshoe Pond Trail, marked with yellow blazes, starts off with a short down-hill section through a beautiful white-pine forest. The trail passes the Styles gravesite, which dates to 1851. After 0.2 mile, turn right onto a forest road, then stay straight

LOCATION
Stoneham, ME

RATING
Easy

DISTANCE
2.8 miles round-trip

ELEVATION GAIN
650 feet

ESTIMATED TIME
2.0–4.0 hours

MAPS
AMC White Mountain National Forest Map & Guide, G13

AMC *White Mountain Guide*, 29th ed. Map 5 Carter Range–Evans Notch, G13

USGS Topo: Center Lovell, ME

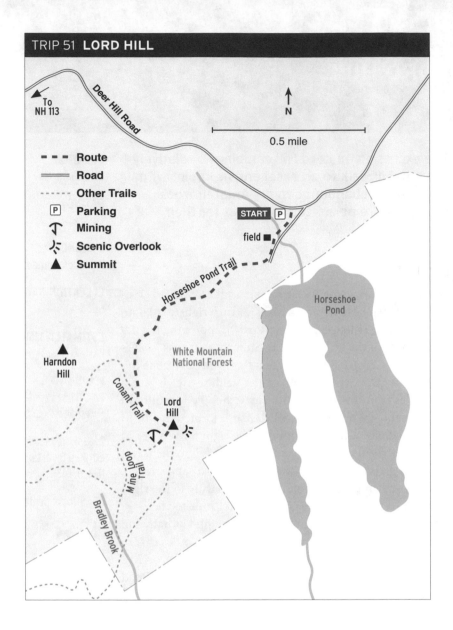

TRIP 51 LORD HILL

To NH 113

Deer Hill Road

N

0.5 mile

- - - Route
━━━ Road
- - - Other Trails
P Parking
⊤ Mining
人 Scenic Overlook
▲ Summit

START P

field ■

Horseshoe Pond Trail

Horseshoe Pond

White Mountain National Forest

▲
Harndon Hill

Conant Trail

Lord Hill ▲ 人

⊤

Mine Loop Trail

Bradley Brook

through a fork. Just before the road widens into what appears to be a parking area, turn right onto a wide, grassy path through a field. Turn left onto the old trail and pick up the yellow blazes.

The trail starts ascending, first through fields and raspberry brambles, then open woodlands, and eventually an evergreen forest. Observe the interesting forest dynamics as you climb up the hill. Stone walls indicate that the area was farmed at one time, and you also may note an old house foundation in the woods. The forest returned after the farms were abandoned. In December 1980, an intense windstorm hit the area. The storm was very patchy in its effects so the forest now alternates between older stands of white pines, hemlocks, and sugar maples, and newer patches of aspens and birches.

Look for piles of hemlock bark that were harvested but never made it to the tannery. Hemlocks, identified by their short, flat, single needles (not in clusters like pines), were extensively logged for tannins before the advent of synthetic substitutes. After trees were cut, the bark was stripped and placed in piles in the woods before being transported to tanneries. Tannins extracted from the bark were used to preserve leather.

Two sweet-smelling plants are common along the trail. Sweet fern, a small, sun-loving shrub with fernlike leaves, grows in the open patches in the forest. Crush a leaf for its bayberry-like scent. The crushed leaves of flowering wintergreen, a low plant with evergreen leaves that grows in shaded parts of the trail, smell like its namesake. Other growing things of note in the understory are goldthread, sharp-toothed nodding asters, and boletus mushrooms. The latter have pores instead of gills on the undersides of their caps.

This trail is a good low-elevation spot for red spruce, a tree that at one time covered much of the lower elevations in the mountains before it was intensively logged. If you feel so inclined, you can make spruce gum out of globs of the resin sticking to the bark. This used to be a popular treat before Mr. Wrigley. You'll need to work it over in your mouth, spitting out the grit. Eventually it will soften up and look like regular chewing gum. For those with less adventurous gustatory inclinations, wait for the blueberries near the summit.

Horseshoe Pond Trail ends at a T intersection with Conant Trail (also called Pine-Lord-Harndon Trail or Pine-Lord Loop). Keep your eyes open for the evidence of pileated woodpeckers that live in the area. If you are lucky, you might catch a glimpse of this crow-sized woodpecker with the flaming red crest. If not, there are a number of trees with softball-sized holes chiseled out and large flakes of wood piled up on the ground below. One of these pileated woodpecker trees is located right at this trail junction.

Turn left and follow Conant Trail for about 0.2 mile. At the summit (1,257 feet), go left to reach the best views from open ledges. The view includes Horseshoe Pond immediately below; long, sinuous Kezar Lake a little farther; and a ridge that includes Speckled Mountain (2,906 feet), Red Rock Cliff, and Blueberry Mountain.

At the summit of Lord Hill there is a nice stand of red pine, a tree with distinctive reddish bark in "plates" and two long needles per bunch. This attractive tree is often planted as an ornamental.

Take Mine Loop Trail to the right for the short (0.1-mile) walk to the abandoned mine. Visiting the old mine on Lord Hill is a dream come true for rock hunters, both young and old. Many early explorers of the White Mountains came seeking riches from minerals locked up in the rocks. Although there is little commercial mining in the White Mountains now, in the past mining probably ranked number two behind lumbering in local commerce. Lord Hill

Large "books" of mica are one of the treasures at the old mine on Lord Hill.

is one of a number of mines in western Maine, some of which are still in commercial operation. The region is still a major source of amethysts and other semiprecious gems.

The White Mountain National Forest allows you to dig for common minerals for your own use without a permit (except for smoky quartz in the Saco Ranger District). Power tools and explosives are forbidden, and a prospecting permit is required if you plan to sell the minerals.

The Lord Hill mine is actually an open depression in the hill, rather than a deep, dark shaft. It can be hot and sunny there on summer days, so bring sun hats and plenty of water. The floor of the hole is littered with small pieces of rock, the remnants of past blasting. Miners at Lord Hill were particularly interested in the large chunks of muscovite, silvery mica that can be divided into paper-thin, flat crystals like the pages of a book. Such thin crystals have been used as capacitors in electronics, although capacitors now usually are made of ceramic. Mica is a common mineral constituent of granite throughout the White Mountains; however, the "books" at Lord Hill are particularly large and impressive. The feldspar at Lord Hill is a white and opaque mineral. At one time it was mined here for use as a porcelainlike material for sinks and bathtubs.

Two gems found at Lord Hill are beryl, a greenish quartz that is high in the element beryllium, and topaz. Beryl crystals 10 to 12 feet long have been found in this part of Maine—one is now at the American Museum of Natural History in New York City. You might initially mistake the clear topaz for quartz because it is also uncolored and translucent, but notice the difference in the arrangement of the angles of the crystals. Topaz has a smoother feel to it. Smoky quartz is also common at Lord Hill, and purple amethysts can be found as well.

These beautiful crystals were formed beneath the earth within the granite that makes up much of the White Mountains. Eons ago, molten rock bubbled up through cracks in the granite, forming pegmatite dikes of feldspar. Within the feldspar, crystals of the minerals formed, becoming large because they cooled very slowly. Later, erosion from water and ice and scouring by glaciers broke up the rock, revealing the minerals to future generations.

Retrace your steps down Mine Loop Trail, Conant Trail, and finally Horseshoe Pond Trail to return to your vehicle.

DID YOU KNOW?

You can find specimens of beryl and amethysts from Lord Hill and other nearby mines at the American Museum of Natural History, Harvard's Mineralogical and Geological Museum, and the Smithsonian Museum of Natural History.

OTHER ACTIVITIES

The Forest Service has set up a wildlife-viewing area on the shores of a wooded pond along Deer Hill Road (Forest Road 9), not far from the Horseshoe Pond trailhead. It makes an excellent stop before or after your hike. Wildlife that frequent the pond and its surrounding shoreline include moose, great blue herons, wood ducks, hooded mergansers, Canada geese, tree swallows, kingbirds, red-winged blackbirds, and warblers. Bring your binoculars.

MORE INFORMATION

This hike is within the White Mountain National Forest. There is no user fee for parking; www.fs.usda.gov/whitemountain; 603-536-6100.

The White Mountain National Forest has produced a guide for rockhounding in the national forest. Go to www.fs.usda.gov/activity/whitemountain/recreation/rocks-minerals for guidelines and rules for collecting rocks and minerals as well as a list of sites, such as Lord Hill, where amateur rock hounds can collect.

This trip is in a relatively remote area, so make sure you pick up any supplies in Fryeburg, Gilead, or one of the other towns you pass through on your way to the trailhead. The nearest restrooms are at Basin Pond, about 2.8 miles north of Deer Hill Road on ME 113.

52

DEER HILL AND DEER HILL SPRING

The hike up the Deer Hills (1,367 feet) is a pleasant half-day outing through forests of maple, beech, birch, and hemlock to a summit with terrific views and blueberries. You can continue on to Deer Hill Spring, a magical place, or visit that as a separate outing.

DIRECTIONS

Deer Hills Trailhead

From the North Conway area, follow ME 113 north from Fryeburg along the Maine–New Hampshire border. The parking area for the trail is on the right about 6.0 miles north of the village of Stow, ME, and 0.2 mile north of AMC's Cold River Camp (facilities for registered guests only). Look for the sign for Baldface Circle Trail, because there is no sign right at the parking area for Deer Hills Trail.

From Gorham or Bethel, take ME 113 south from US 2 in Gilead. The trailhead is about 2.0 miles south of the turnoff to Basin Pond. *GPS coordinates:* 44° 14.25′ N, 71° 00.90′ W.

Deer Hill Spring Trailhead

Deer Hill Spring is a fascinating destination, and can be combined with the hike to the Deer Hills with prior planning. You can hike all the way to Deer Hill Spring from the Deer Hills trailhead on ME 113. To return to your vehicle, you will then have to hike back to the trailhead, unless you have left a second vehicle where Deer Hills Trail comes out on Deer Hill Road, or are willing to walk 2.0 miles back to the original trailhead along roads. An alternative is to return to your vehicle after hiking up the Deer Hills and drive to the Deer Hill Springs trailhead on Deer Hill Road. For this option, drive south on NH 113 from the Baldface Circle/Deer Hill Connector parking lot for about 1.0 mile, turn left onto Deer Hill Road (Forest Road 9) for 1.3 miles, and park where you see the signs for Deer Hills Trail/Deer Hill Spring on the left. *GPS coordinates:* 44° 13.26' N, 70° 59.33' W.

LOCATION
Chatham, NH, to Stow, ME

**LITTLE AND BIG DEER HILLS:
RATING**
Moderate

DISTANCE
4.0 miles round-trip

ELEVATION GAIN
1,000 feet

ESTIMATED TIME
3.0-4.0 hours

**FOR DEER HILL SPRING ONLY:
RATING**
Easy

DISTANCE
1.6 miles round-trip

ELEVATION GAIN
150-foot descent from Deer Hill Road

ESTIMATED TIME
1.0 hour

MAPS
AMC White Mountain National Forest Map & Guide, G13

AMC *White Mountain Guide,* 29th ed. Map 5 Carter Range–Evans Notch, G13

USGS Topo: Chatham, NH, to Center Lovell, ME

TRAIL DESCRIPTION

Little and Big Deer Hills and Deer Hill Spring

You'll see a number of interesting things on the hike up Little and Big Deer hills, so this hike is worthwhile even if you decide not to complete the entire walk. The 1,000-foot rise in elevation up Big Deer Hill is manageable for most families with children but still enough to make you feel like you have gotten exercise. The trail is in relatively good condition and is easy to follow, with some moderately steep, rocky sections and a few sections with roots. A heavy layer of leaves in some steep sections makes the trail slippery when wet.

From the parking area, look for yellow blazes heading east (on the same side of the road) because there is no sign there for Deer Hill Connector. A sign about 0.1 mile from the parking area leads you left down to the Cold River. In about 0.4 mile, the path from AMC's Cold River Camp comes in from the right. Here, pick up Deer Hills Trail and take it across the river on a small dam (a nice place for a swim).

After crossing the river, bear right at the double yellow marker and pass the stone marking the border of New Hampshire and Maine. Few can resist the temptation to have one foot in New Hampshire and the other in Maine. Painted trillium, clintonia, and hobblebush grow abundantly here.

Notice how the river has formed flat, parallel terraces at different heights above its current banks. Each terrace was built up when the river flooded its banks and deposited sand, silt, and mud along its shores. During the melting of the last glacier about 12,000 years ago, Cold River was much deeper and wider than it is today. The terraces it formed at that time are now stranded high above the present water level.

Look for the sign for Little Deer Hill after the old logging road. Yellow blazes mark the trail as it goes uphill at a moderate grade. Several dead wildlife trees stand along the trail between Cold River and Little Deer Hill. Observe the soft-ball-sized holes in these trees and the large wood chips at the base, both the handiwork of pileated woodpeckers.

The trail goes through a northern hardwood forest. Many wildflowers grow alongside the trail, but unfortunately for summer visitors, most bloom in May and June. You can see clintonia, painted trillium, Canada mayflower, Indian cucumber-root, pink lady's slippers, wild anemone, dwarf ginseng, partridge-berry, and wild sarsaparilla. The dominant understory shrub is hobblebush.

About halfway up the trail to Little Deer Hill on the right side, look for a hem-lock with four separate trunks united at the base. More than likely, insects or wind damaged the original trunk, and none of the four branches could dominate and take over. Other trees in the area have double trunks for the same reason.

Where the woods start to thin out as you continue your climb, look for trailing arbutus and flowering wintergreen. The trail then passes over several ledges with views and blueberries, chokeberries, and reindeer moss. It reaches the summit of Little Deer Hill at 1.3 miles. The views and blueberries are great here, so

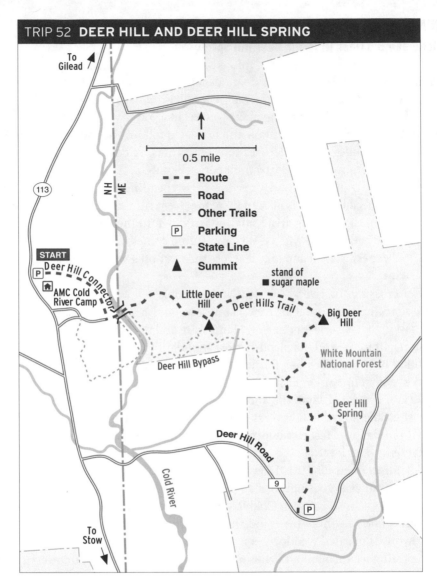

To
Gilead

113

N H
M E

N

0.5 mile

- - - **Route**
────── **Road**
········· **Other Trails**
P **Parking**
—·—·— **State Line**
▲ **Summit**

START
P
AMC Cold
River Camp
Deer Hill Connector

stand of
■ sugar maple

Little Deer
Hill
Deer Hills Trail

Big Deer
Hill ▲

White Mountain
National Forest

Deer Hill Bypass

Deer Hill
Spring

Deer Hill Road

Cold River

9

P

To
Stow

it is a nice place for a picnic and a possible turnaround spot. The bare summits
of the Baldface Range and the impressive cliff face of the Basin are to the west.

The summit of Big Deer Hill is another 0.7 mile beyond (20 to 30 minutes).
The trail descends about 200 feet into the col between Little and Big Deer hills
in a forest dominated by sugar maples, crosses a stream, and then ascends about
400 feet to the summit of Big Deer Hill. The best vista is about 50 yards east of
the true summit. Looking eastward, you'll see hills, lakes, and bogs in Maine.
With binoculars you may get lucky and see a moose in one of the bogs.

Continue on Deer Hills Trail for Deer Hill Spring. You pass Deer Hill Bypass
(2.5 miles, 0.7 mile from Deer Hill) and reach the spur trail to the spring at 2.7

miles. Turning left, you descend about 150 feet and reach the spring in 0.2 mile. After enjoying the spring, return to the main trail.

Your next move is dependent upon whether you left a car at the trailhead for Deer Hill Spring. If so, turn left on Deer Hills Trail, an old logging road at this point. It descends and comes out on Deer Hill Road in 0.6 mile. If instead your car is at the Deer Hill Connector/Baldface Circle trailhead on ME 113, turn right on Deer Hills Trail and retrace your steps. To avoid having to climb back up over the hills, take Deer Hill Bypass, 0.2 mile from the spur to the spring (see map). This joins Deer Hills Trail just before the dam over Cold Brook.

Deer Hill Spring Only

If you have chosen to drive to the Deer Hill Spring trailhead, walk along the old logging road 0.6 mile (still part of Deer Hills Trail), and then turn right onto the 0.2-mile spur trail to the spring. That easy walk should take about 30 minutes.

Deer Hill Spring, also called Bubbling Spring, is in a shady hemlock grove where you are likely to be serenaded by the beautiful flutelike sounds of the hermit thrush or the energetic song of the winter wren. Before you actually see the spring, there is nothing to alert you that something odd is nearby.

Then you notice a porridge of bubbling yellow sand contrasting sharply with the dark surroundings. Water percolates out of the side of the mountain with enough force to keep sand constantly in suspension. Finer particles pass out of the spring with the outflow. You might think you have been magically transported to one of those muddy hot springs at Yellowstone National Park.

Deer Hill Spring bubbles up mysteriously from the side of Deer Hill.

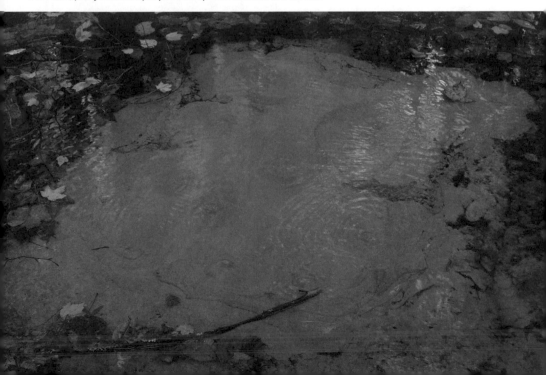

Although the bubbling "quicksand" looks like it might be solid at Deer Hill Spring, you certainly do not want to walk on it. There is a story that a horse was swallowed up by the quicksand years ago, and that its remains still lie somewhere below. That would be a hard rumor to verify. Retrace your steps to return to your vehicle.

OTHER ACTIVITIES

Visit Basin Pond about 2.0 miles north of the Deer Hill/Baldface Circle trailhead after your hike. You can go fishing (New Hampshire license required), paddle around in your canoe, and look for moose and water birds. Two campgrounds in the Basin Pond area are convenient for hiking this and other trails in the Evans Notch region.

The wildlife-viewing area on Deer Hill Road is a nice stop after a visit to Deer Hill Spring. It is 1.3 miles farther east of the Deer Hill Spring trailhead.

MORE INFORMATION

The trail is within the White Mountain National Forest. There is no user fee for parking; www.fs.usda.gov/whitemountain; 603-536-6100.

53

THE ROOST

The Roost is a small hill (1,374 feet) north of Evans Notch that provides terrific views of the Wild River and Evans Brook valleys. It is reached by a short, steep trail off ME 113 near the Hastings Campground at the abandoned village of Hastings.

DIRECTIONS

Roost Trail forms a semicircle with two trailheads on the east side of ME 113. The north trailhead is about 2.7 miles south of US 2, and 0.1 mile north of the bridge over Evans Brook and the junction of ME 113 with Wild River Road. This is 7.0 miles north of the turnoff to Basin Pond. Space is available for only one or two vehicles opposite the trailhead, so you may need to park at the more substantial turnoff on the south side of the bridge. The south trailhead is 0.7 mile south of the north trailhead on ME 113, about 0.1 mile north of its intersection with Forest Road 8. *GPS coordinates:* 44° 21.58′ N, 70° 59.45′ W.

TRAIL DESCRIPTION

The distance to the summit of the Roost is 0.5 mile from the north trailhead and 0.7 mile from the south trailhead. From the north trailhead, the trail immediately climbs some stairs that will definitely get your pulse rate up. You pass through a diverse forest of beech, sugar maple, paper birch, white ash, hop hornbeam (note the vertically scraggly bark), and aspen.

After about 20 minutes of hiking, you reach the summit. Note the red spruce forest. The summit has only a restricted view, so follow the sign that reads "To the Scenic View." This leads you on a rather steep side path downhill to the right for 150 feet and 0.1 mile to open ledges that overlook the Wild River and Evans Brook valleys.

LOCATION
Batchelder's Grant, ME

RATING
Moderate

DISTANCE
2.1 miles round-trip

ELEVATION GAIN
650 feet

ESTIMATED TIME
1.0-1.5 hours

MAPS
AMC White Mountain National Forest Map & Guide, E13

AMC *White Mountain Guide,* 29th ed. Map 5 Carter Range–Evans Notch, E13

USGS Topo: Speckled Mountain, ME

Wild River Valley from the Roost.

The Roost is situated above the confluence of Evans Brook and the Wild River, enabling you to see both valleys. The Wild River Valley, angling off to the southwest, is broader, looking as if glaciers did not carve it quite as deeply as they carved the Evans Brook Valley. The tall peaks on the west slope of the Wild River Valley are the Carter-Moriah Range. The valley is one of the few level areas in this mountainous region, thus the first record of human activity is of farming (see "The Wild River, Logging, and the Town of Hastings" on page 279). Walk down the ledges as far as you safely can for the best view of the Evans Brook Valley toward Evans Notch. You'll be rewarded with a view of a number of small ponds and an oxbow (very sharp curve) in Evans Brook.

From the Roost, look down and see the leaves of trembling aspens shimmering in the breeze. These trees have smooth, light-grayish-green bark, but their most notable feature is their leaves. A very gentle wind that hardly even ruffles the leaves of other trees induces aspen leaves to shake violently and evoke the sound of the wind. This is because the leaf stalk is flattened rather than rounded as in most trees. The flattened stalks enable aspen leaves to bend more readily during a breeze. What function this serves for the aspen is anybody's guess, but what it does for us is to reveal even the slightest breeze.

Aspens, like paper birch, are early colonizers of land where the trees have been cut or blown down. The aspens on the Roost probably moved in after the area was heavily logged from 1891 to 1917. Other trees of note at the ledges are mountain ash, red and white pines, and red spruce. Lowbush blueberries and reindeer lichen are also common.

After climbing back up to the main trail, turn right for the rest of the loop. The trail descends through birch, beech, and sugar maple forest, and then crosses a stream 0.3 mile from the summit. Like most streams in the White Mountains, this one could be trouble early in the season when water levels are high. The trail then turns right on a dirt road; passes some very tall white pine, hemlock, and red spruce; crosses a second stream (fairly flooded last time we were there); and passes through an area of small balsam fir. The main road is just after an old apple grove. The apples are another indication that a town once existed in this area. Turn right onto ME 113 for the walk back to your vehicle.

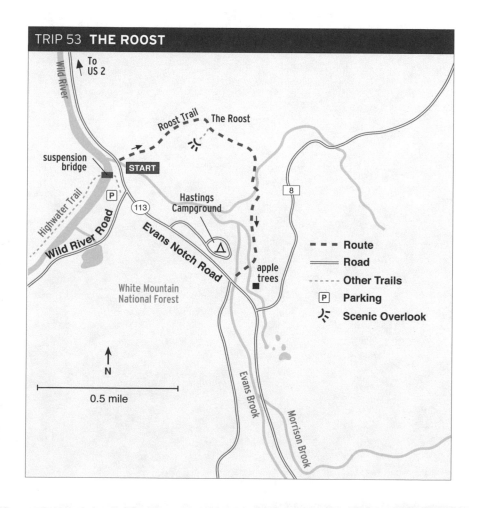

OTHER ACTIVITIES

Take a detour along ME 113 to walk out on the bridge over the Wild River near the parking area for the north trailhead. This bridge recently replaced a suspension bridge that was destroyed by Hurricane Irene in August 2011, showing the Wild River is still capable of living up to its name. A sitting log near the water on the opposite side of the river is a great place to end your hike. Some deeper pools in the river are good for wading and perhaps even a complete dunk.

MORE INFORMATION

This hike is within the White Mountain National Forest. There is no user fee for parking; www.fs.usda.gov/whitemountain; 603-536-6100.

The road through Evans Notch is closed during winter from roughly 1 mile north of the Roost. If you want to snowshoe the trail, you will need to park at the gate and walk that mile along the road.

THE WILD RIVER, LOGGING, AND THE TOWN OF HASTINGS

The following is based on *The Wild River Wilderness* by D.B. Wight (Courier Press, 1971) and *Logging Railroads of the White Mountains* by C.F. Belcher (AMC Books, 1980):

The Wild River looks quiet and peaceful now, but it once was a hub of human activity and industry in the mountains. In the mid-nineteenth century the floodplain around the Hastings Campground, where Evans Brook joins the Wild River, had been farmed by an escaped slave who, as legend has it, had to abandon his farm and flee the area when his former master came looking for him. Then the loggers came.

Before 1890, logging operations in the Wild River Valley were small. Logs were either floated down the river or dragged by teams of horses to a mill at the village of Gilead, currently where ME 113 joins US 2. In 1891, the Wild River Railroad was built to transport wood products down the valley, and logging efforts began in earnest. Hemlock bark was taken for tanneries and red spruce for pulp. The village of Hastings, with a population of more than 300, sprang up almost overnight in the V between the two rivers. The village had sawmills, a school, a post office, houses for workers, and a plant that produced wood alcohol. The Wild River Railroad ran alongside the Wild River about 15 miles south into the valley, following the course of present-day ME 113 south from Gilead, and then Wild River Road and Wild River Trail.

Like Zealand Valley (Trip 37), there were a number of logging camps, trestles, railroad yards, and spur lines along the railroad. Also like Zealand, the logging activity removed many acres of trees and spawned fires and erosion, causing devastation where a few years before a wilderness had existed. Disaster came in 1903 when the Wild River lived up to its name. A tremendous flood from March 11 to March 20 inundated Hastings and destroyed much of the Wild River Railroad. This was followed in 1904 by a very dry year with many forest fires.

When the loggers left, the wilderness returned, and it prevails today. Now, it is hard to imagine a village had been there. The abandoned apple groves near the Hastings Campground are one of the few reminders of that once-thriving community. Even with the landscape returning to a more forested condition, the river continues to alter its surroundings, particularly during major storms. From the bridge over the Wild River, you can see evidence of new landslides from the erosion of riverbanks. And as mentioned in Trip 53, one of the most recent storms, Hurricane Irene (2011), took out the former bridge over the Wild River where the old village of Hastings once stood.

54

BASIN TRAIL TO BASIN RIM

The Basin is an impressive glacial cirque (a bowl-shaped ravine carved out by a glacier) in the Evans Notch region. The best view of it, which includes impressive cliffs and Basin Pond, is from the Basin Rim, a ridge in the Baldface-Royce Range.

DIRECTIONS

The drive to the trailhead includes a 5.7-mile stretch on unpaved Wild River Road (Forest Road 12) that follows the route of the former Wild River Railroad. The road, marked by a sign to the Wild River Campground, heads southwest off Evans Notch Road (ME 113) 2.8 miles south of the town of Gilead (where ME 113 intersects with US 2) and about 7.0 miles north of the Basin and Cold River campgrounds. The parking area for hikers is at the end of the road, just before you enter the campground. *GPS coordinates:* 44°18.38' N, 71° 03.85' W.

TRAIL DESCRIPTION

Basin Trail runs 4.5 miles from the Wild River Valley up and over the Basin Rim and then down to Evans Notch by the Basin Campground and Recreation Area, so you can ascend to the rim from either direction. The approach from the Wild River Valley is more gradual and allows you to hike along Blue Brook for a good distance, and we feature that part of the trail here. With two vehicles you could hike the entire trail.

Basin Trail, marked by yellow blazes, starts out as a gentle path through a rich, deciduous woodland with a number of bog bridges. Expect some muddy spots in spring or after rain. Signs of moose are everywhere. Look for their very large hoof prints in muddy parts of the trail and their droppings in piles scattered here and there.

LOCATION
Bean's Purchase, NH

RATING
Moderate

DISTANCE
4.6 miles round-trip

ELEVATION GAIN
800 feet

ESTIMATED TIME
4.0–6.0 hours

MAPS
AMC White Mountain National Forest Map & Guide, F12

AMC *White Mountain Guide,* 29th ed. Map 5 Carter Range-Evans Notch, F12

USGS Topo: Wild River, NH

Wildflowers abound along the trail. Look for the clover-like three leaflets of the mountain wood sorrel. It produces white flowers lined with pink from late June through early August. Bunchberries, trillium, clintonia, Indian cucumber-root, and pink lady's slippers may be in bloom, depending on the time of year. Cinnamon fern is common in damp areas. These large ferns are named for their cinnamon-colored fertile frond (the part that bears the spores) rising straight up from a circle of green fronds. Its stipe (stalk) is covered with cinnamon-colored chaff.

At 1.3 miles, the trail crosses Blue Brook at a good lunch or snack spot and then begins to ascend on the east bank of the brook. This 0.3-mile part of the trail may delight you as much as the vista from the Basin Rim. The water rushes through some small canyons, forming miniature waterfalls and quieter pools. When water levels are low, there are places where you can walk across the brook by hopping from rock to rock. Small caves and passageways between large boulders invite exploration. Bring a bathing suit if you want a chance for the brook to turn you the color of its name. One particularly good spot to explore is where the brook flows near an impressive cliff face that rises up on the opposite bank. It could be a turnaround point.

The trail then turns away from the brook and ascends more steeply. It reaches the Rim Junction at 2.2 miles, where it intersects with Basin Rim Trail.

The view of Basin Pond from the Basin Rim. The pond is within a cirque, a glacially carved ravine on the side of a mountain.

Continue on Basin Trail for about another 0.1 mile to a small, open ledge facing eastward, slightly off the trail and just before it begins to descend into the Basin. Another great overlook is located about 0.1 mile south of Rim Junction on Basin Rim Trail.

The view from the Basin Rim, which includes the cliffs of West Royce, Basin Pond, Blueberry Mountain, and other peaks in Maine, allows you to contemplate the glacial geology of the Basin. The Basin is the Evans Notch counterpart to Tuckerman Ravine, an eastward-facing bowl created by a mountain glacier during the last Ice Age (1 million to 12,000 years ago). The carving of the steep headwall occurred over a long period of time as a result of the abrasive action of small stones, pebbles, and sand within the ice. Also, rocks were plucked from the side of the mountain when water under the glacier thawed, flowed into cracks in the rocks, and then refroze. The plucked rocks collect in a heap toward the bottom of the bowl. The flat bottoms of glacial cirques are frequently filled with ponds (tarns).

From these viewpoints, Basin Pond and its surrounding wetlands stand out like gems. On a nice summer day, you will probably see people down below in canoes fishing or silently paddling. If you have a pair of binoculars and are lucky, you may even be able to spot moose in the marshy areas of Basin Pond below.

The Basin Rim provides a bird's-eye view of birds too. On a sunny day in June, I watched four turkey vultures soaring majestically with outstretched wings at eye level over the valley. These birds are master gliders, riding warm thermal air currents created as the day heats up. It enables them to save energy that would be required for flapping while they search for their lunch of dead animals. You might also see ravens, swifts, and peregrine falcons, all of which build nests on the cliffs. Warblers such as yellow-rumped magnolias, black-throated green warblers, black-throated blue warblers, and redstarts flitter around the trees on the ridge.

This vista is a good spot to have lunch before retracing your steps. On the way back, follow the sign for Basin Trail (not to be confused with Basin Rim Trail) and Wild River Campground at Rim Junction.

About 0.2 mile from the parking lot, be sure to follow an arrow pointing to the right at a fork with the old trail.

For those who have spotted a second vehicle at Basin Pond and are hiking the entire Basin Trail, it is a 1,300-foot descent and 2.3 miles from Rim Junction to the parking area at Basin Pond. Make sure to stop at Hermit Falls during your descent.

OTHER ACTIVITIES

Basin Pond itself invites exploration, either by driving there after the hike or, if you have spotted a second vehicle at the pond, by hiking down its steep headwall. It has picnic tables, restrooms, a campground, and canoe access. Walk out on the dam, stroll along the shoreline, or look out over the pond for ducks,

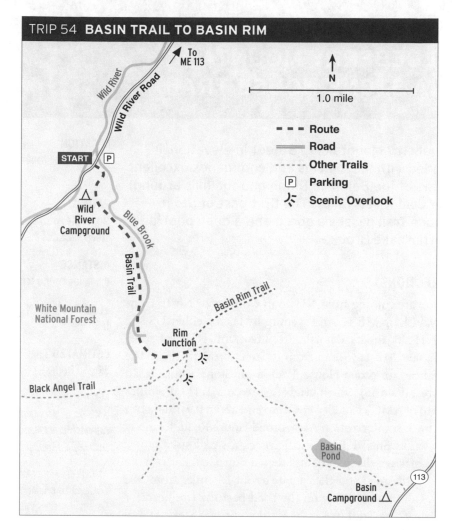

spotted sandpipers, swallows, signs of beavers, or an elusive moose. Bring your canoe if you have one. It makes a fitting end to a great day of hiking.

MORE INFORMATION

This hike is within the White Mountain National Forest. A parking fee ($3 per day) is required at the trailhead; www.fs.usda.gov/whitemountain; 603-536-6100.

Wild River Campground (twelve sites) is adjacent to this trailhead.

Wild River Road and ME 113 are closed to vehicle traffic during winter, so this trail is inaccessible then.

55

BLUEBERRY MOUNTAIN VIA STONE HOUSE TRAIL

Blueberry Mountain, 1,781 feet in elevation, is loaded with blueberries and commands excellent views of the Baldface Ridge and the hills around the Cold River Valley. The first part of Stone House Trail passes a gorge and a deep pool in Rattlesnake Brook.

LOCATION
Stow, ME, to Stoneham, ME

RATING
Moderate, with some steep sections

DISTANCE
4.5 miles round-trip

ELEVATION GAIN
1,150 feet

ESTIMATED TIME
3.0–5.0 hours

MAP
AMC *White Mountain National Forest Map & Guide*, F13

AMC *White Mountain Guide*, 29th ed. Map 5 Carter Range–Evans Notch, F13

USGS Topo: Speckled Mountain, ME

DIRECTIONS

If you are coming from NH 16 in Conway or North Conway, pick up ME 113 in Fryeburg by taking either US 302 or NH 113, and head north. From Gorham, NH, or Bethel, ME, take ME 113 south from its junction with US 2. The trailhead for Stone House Trail is off Stone House Road (Forest Road 16), which heads east from ME 113, 1.3 miles north of AMC's Cold River Camp and about 0.9 mile south of the Basin Recreation Area. Stone House Road, formerly known as Shell Pond Road, crosses a small stream and then makes a sharp right and then a sharp left. Park on the side of the road at a closed gate about 1.1 miles from ME 113. Continue walking on the road past the trailhead for White Cairn Trail (0.3 mile) until you reach Stone House Trail going off to the left, about 0.5 mile from the gate. The road continues on as Shell Pond Trail, past the Stone House and a private airstrip. *GPS coordinates:* 44° 15.12′ N, 70° 59.46′ W.

TRAIL DESCRIPTION

Blueberry Mountain conjures up images of an August afternoon blissfully spent picking sweet blue morsels from low shrubs while looking out over a pretty valley and surrounding mountains. The next morning there's a feast of blueberry pancakes around a campfire. Well, that aptly describes this trail.

Stone House Trail, named for an attractive stone building (private) near the trailhead, provides the easiest ascent

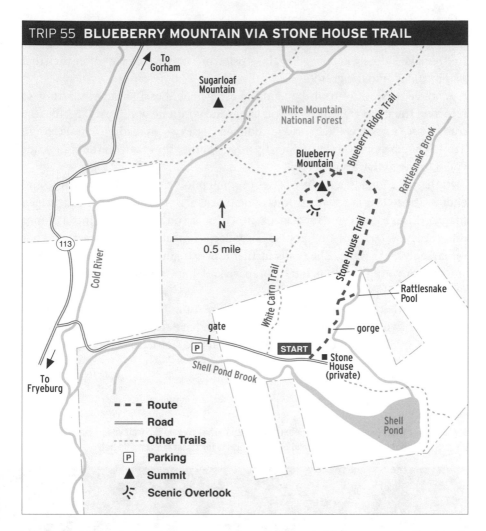

To
Gorham

Sugarloaf
Mountain

White Mountain
National Forest

Blueberry
Mountain

Blueberry Ridge Trail

Rattlesnake Brook

Stone House Trail

N

0.5 mile

113

Cold River

White Cairn Trail

Rattlesnake
Pool

gate

gorge

P

START

To
Fryeburg

Shell Pond Brook

Stone
House
(private)

Shell
Pond

- - - Route
═══ Road
----- Other Trails
P   Parking
▲   Summit
⅄   Scenic Overlook

of Blueberry Mountain and is the most suitable for children. It is initially a gradual ascent, but the upper part is steeper and has a few rocky sections. A 0.7-mile loop around the summit gives you access to several outlooks.

Stone House Trail is well marked with Chatham Trail Association (CTA) signs and some yellow blazes. The trail passes through private land for the first mile, so stay on the main trail marked by the CTA signs and blazes, except for detours to Rattlesnake Flume and Pool.

The first part of the trail is a very gradual uphill on an old logging road. After 0.2 mile, a private path from the Stone House enters right. A few paces beyond, a spur trail to the right marked with an arrow leads you to the gorge over Rattlesnake Flume. It is definitely worth the 30-yard detour to a little wooden bridge over the flume. Here you can watch the waters of Rattlesnake Brook rushing through a narrow gorge with straight walls rising about 25 feet above the water. Rock ferns and rock tripe lichen cover the damp walls of the flume. On the opposite side of the brook, look for the exquisite flowers of trailing arbutus (in May) and twinflower (in July). Like the well-known flume of Franconia Notch, Rattlesnake Flume was created by the erosion of a narrow dike of softer rock that had intruded into the granite.

A whole network of trails beyond the bridge could easily lead you astray, so return to the main trail the way you came and continue uphill. At 0.5 mile, the trail crosses a small wooden bridge and then passes a sign reading "Stone House Trail to Blueberry Mountain." Shortly after, another spur trail on the right leads you 0.1 mile to Rattlesnake Pool.

Rattlesnake Pool is actually a series of small pools connected by cascades and chutes. The setting is a shady woods of hemlock, beech, yellow birch, and striped maple. This is a good spot for a snack, lunch, or, if you are truly daring, a plunge into the icy waters. The first pool is fairly deep (probably about 15 feet) and has remarkably clear water. The pools farther downstream are shallower and more suitable for young children, but be prepared for some scrambling over boulders that may be slippery.

After Rattlesnake Pool, return to the main trail. This is a possible place to turn back if you are hiking with children who have reached their limit. If not, continue uphill on Stone House Trail, being sure to stay left at a fork as indicated by a CTA sign.

A young hiker picks blueberries on Blueberry Mountain. While picking the fruit seems irresistible, keep in mind that wild creatures depend on these bushes for survival and we do not.

At 0.8 mile, the trail enters the Caribou-Speckled Mountain Wilderness Area and becomes steeper, passing through a thick forest of beech. You will find beechdrops, a unique plant that grows only under beech trees. All you ever see of this 6-to-18-inch plant are its small white flowers with reddish-brown splotches scattered along a colorless stalk. It has no green leaves because it gets all of its nutrition by parasitizing the roots of beech trees. Beechdrops do no obvious damage to their host beech trees. Whenever there are beechdrops, you are bound to find beeches.

Listen for bird songs in June and July, and you may hear the flutelike songs of hermit thrushes near the trailhead and Swainson's thrushes higher up. Also, keep your eyes open for guilds of forest birds, including chickadees, nuthatches, downy woodpeckers, blue jays, and some finches.

Near the summit of Blueberry Mountain, red spruce and balsam fir take over. Make sure to follow the yellow blazes carefully at this point. The trail reaches the junction with the Blueberry Ridge Trail 1.5 miles from the start of the trail (2.0 miles from your vehicle). For the best vistas and blueberries, take a left (west) onto Blueberry Ridge Trail and follow it past a few small cairns for about 50 yards to its junction with Overlook Loop. Take Overlook Loop to the left.

Overlook Loop around the summit of Blueberry Mountain has great views from a number of open, rocky ledges. I first visited the summit on a magical day in fall when the scene was at first muted and dull because of fog. Then the fog began to lift, unveiling incredibly vivid fall foliage. The peaks of the Baldface Range slowly came into view and eventually loomed over everything. Special moments like this can make you forget all the damp days of hiking in the mist when you cannot see much past your own nose.

The most abundant plants around Overlook Loop are blueberries, huckleberries, and sheep laurel. Lowbush blueberry shrubs are everywhere on Blueberry Mountain, so bring a container for your hike mid-July through late August. Do not ignore the darker, blue-black huckleberries—they are seedier but also quite tasty. The huckleberries can be distinguished from blueberries by their leaves; huckleberry leaves are covered by small, yellow resin dots on their undersides (easier to see if you have a hand lens). Other plants to note around the ledges are rhodora, which has beautiful large, pink flowers around Memorial Day weekend; three-toothed cinquefoil; red pine; white pine; and red spruce. Possible birds and mammals to spot include ravens, dark-eyed juncos, and snowshoe hares.

Overlook Loop passes a small bog that provides a good illustration of why bogs form where they do. The water that collects in this depression is stagnant, with no flow to replenish nutrients once plants use them up. The sphagnum mosses that grow so abundantly in the bog make life even more difficult for plants, and for the fungi and bacteria that decompose dead leaves and recycle nutrients, because they increase the acidity of the water. As a result, plants that live in bogs have to be able to tolerate acidity and very low levels of nutrients.

One beautiful tree that manages to grow quite well in this and other bogs is larch (illustrated here), a conifer whose gracefully curved branches, 10–30 needles per bunch, and light, airy appearance make it seem lacy  and oriental. You may spot cotton grass, with its unmistakable white cottony balls at the top of leafless, grasslike stems. Bog bilberry, rhodora, and mountain holly also grow here.

Overlook Loop ends in 0.5 mile back at Blueberry Ridge Trail. Turn right for the 0.2-mile walk back to Stone House Trail and your descent.

DID YOU KNOW?

The Stone House near the trailhead was built from granite carted down from the Baldface Ridge by oxen about 200 years ago. Looking across to the ledges on the Baldfaces from the summit of Blueberry Mountain, you cannot help but be impressed by what a task that must have been.

OTHER ACTIVITIES

Stone House Trail can be combined with Blueberry Ridge and White Cairn trails to make a nice loop, but be aware that White Cairn Trail has some steep, rocky sections that could be a problem, particularly in wet weather. In addition, beaver activity may make it necessary to bushwhack around flooded sections near the bottom of the trail. If you choose this option, it is best to ascend via White Cairn Trail and descend via Stone House Trail.

MORE INFORMATION

The trail begins on private land and enters the White Mountain National Forest after about 0.5 mile. There is no parking fee; www.fs.usda.gov/whitemountain; 603-536-6100.

The area around the summit of Blueberry Mountain is part of the Caribou-Speckled Mountain Wilderness Area. Hiking groups must be limited to ten or fewer individuals and geocaching is prohibited; www.fs.usda.gov/detail/whitemountain/specialplaces/?cid=stelprdb5186041.

56

CARIBOU MOUNTAIN

This loop hike takes you through a wilderness area past beautiful cascades to the broad open summit of Caribou Mountain (2,870 feet), one of the highest peaks in the Evans Notch region. The summit has breathtaking views as well as alpine plants.

DIRECTIONS

The same parking area serves both Caribou Trail and Mud Brook Trail, the two trails used for this loop. From Gorham, NH, follow US 2 east to Gilead (about 11.0 miles) and turn right onto NH 113. Travel about 4.7 miles south. The parking area is on the left. Space is available for about fifteen vehicles.

From the North Conway area, follow ME 113 north from Fryeburg, ME. It follows the Maine–New Hampshire border, passing through the Maine villages of North Fryeburg and Stow. The trailhead is on the right about 5.5 miles north of the national forest's Basin Pond picnic and camping area. *GPS coordinates: 44° 20.16′ N, 70° 58.52′ W.*

TRAIL DESCRIPTION

This loop hike ascends via Caribou Trail, and then uses Mud Brook Trail for the final climb to the actual summit and for the descent. Caribou Trail leaves from the left (north) side of the parking area with your back to the road.

The trail begins by descending slightly and crossing over Morrison Brook by rock-hopping. There had formerly been a bridge here but it washed out in a storm. This is the first of at least six stream crossings, none of which should present difficulties except in extreme high water. In about 15 minutes, the trail returns to the side of the brook and begins a long ascent alongside it.

After an hour of ascending (2.0 miles), the trail approaches Kees Falls, a beautiful 60-foot cascade. The trail follows the right side of the falls and then crosses over the stream at the top. The best view of the falls is achieved by scrambling down

LOCATION
Batchelder's Grant, ME

RATING
Strenuous

DISTANCE
6.9-mile loop

ELEVATION GAIN
1,900 feet

ESTIMATED TIME
6.0 hours

MAPS
AMC White Mountain National Forest Map & Guide, E13

AMC *White Mountain Guide,* 29th ed. Map 5 Carter Range–Evans Notch, E13

USGS Topo: Speckled Mountain, ME

carefully after crossing the stream. This is an ideal lunch spot. A pool at the bottom of the falls is deep enough for a swim.

After you have enjoyed the falls, the trail continues by crossing over to the right side of the brook, then back again, with waterfalls on all sides from two streams that join up. Large yellow birches and hemlocks dominate the forest. The trail continues its ascent, finally turns away from the stream, becomes steeper, and levels out before reaching the junction with Mud Brook Trail at 3.0 miles. A small, wet, grassy swale at this junction may even harbor a moose.

Turn right onto Mud Brook Trail to continue your ascent. (Caribou Trail descends from this point to a second trailhead on a dirt road off US 2 a long way from where you parked your vehicle, so you want to be sure to follow Mud Brook Trail here.) The trail continues its ascent, and the northern hardwoods give way to boreal forest (red spruce and balsam fir) characteristic of higher elevations in the White Mountains. See if you can detect the former location of a shelter in a flat area about 0.3 mile from the trail junction. Caribou Spring is there as well, but it is an unreliable water source during the dry days of summer.

An open ledge providing a vista, to the north, is reached about 20 minutes from the trail junction. In 5 more minutes you are at the actual summit (3.6 miles from the trailhead; 2 hours, 40 minutes). The 360-degree view from Caribou Mountain includes many White Mountain peaks. Immediately to your south is Speckled Mountain. Moving west, you can see Evans Notch between Speckled Mountain and East Royce. The Baldfaces are behind them and the Carter Range forms the long ridge farther to your west. Note the remote Wild River Valley between the Carters and East Royce. On a clear day, Mounts Madison, Adams, and Washington are visible beyond the Carter Range. Lakes dominate the view to the southeast. The north view includes the peaks of the Kilkenny and Crescent ridges.

After enjoying the view, take a moment to appreciate the plants that inhabit this open summit. Signs around the summit tell you that this is a special habitat for rare alpine plants, so please avoid trampling the plants. A number of the species on the Caribou summit are common in the higher elevations of the Presidential Range, so it is a treat to see them at this relatively low elevation. One of the most eye-catching is mountain sandwort, a short, delicate plant that forms clumps with small white flowers and fine leaves. Three low, shrubby plants that produce edible berries are lowbush blueberry, bog bilberry, and mountain cranberry. A rare species that occurs only in the White Mountains (except for one clump on an island in Newburyport, MA) is White Mountain silverling (also called White Mountain whitlow-wort; see Trip 24). Reindeer lichen, a light-bluish-green species that looks like a tiny bush, is interspersed with these plants, making the area look like a rock garden. If you are hiking in late June or early July, the bright-pink flowers of the sheep laurel will be in bloom. They resemble a smaller version of their close relative, the mountain laurel. Bird songs that might accompany you as you enjoy the summit include

A well-deserved rest on the way to Caribou Mountain.

the flutelike sounds of Swainson's and hermit thrushes and the clear-whistled notes of the white-throated sparrow.

The trail can be a little difficult to follow from one side of the broad summit to the other. Let the yellow paint blazes (somewhat faded the last time I hiked here) and occasional cairns be your guide. Look for a small boggy area with cotton grass, Labrador tea, and leatherleaf near a second high point on the summit.

Continue following the yellow blazes of Mud Brook Trail when you are ready to descend. After about 15 minutes, the trail passes open ledges with a very steep dropoff that provides a vista east (3.9 miles). The trail then descends steeply through an attractive boreal forest with lots of clintonia, a lily that produces glossy blue berries (inedible) in summer. The boreal forest is more extensive on your descent than ascent. Eventually, you do return to northern hardwoods, which you will recognize by the increasing numbers of sugar and striped maples, yellow birches, and American beech.

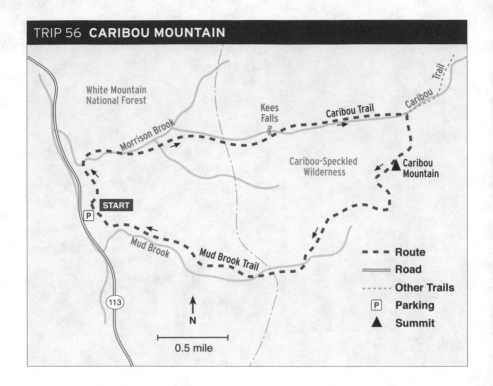

White Mountain
National Forest

Kees
Falls

Caribou Trail

Caribou Trail

Caribou Trail

Morrison Brook

Caribou-Speckled
Wilderness

Caribou
Mountain

START

P

Mud Brook

Mud Brook Trail

113

N

0.5 mile

- - - Route
━━━ Road
----- Other Trails
P Parking
▲ Summit

After about an hour of a fairly steep descent, the trail levels out somewhat and reaches the first of several crossings of Mud Brook (5.0 miles). Soon after, you pass a sign indicating that you are leaving the wilderness area. The trail follows the brook for most of the remainder of the descent, often high above it. After another 30 to 40 minutes, the path widens and the grade becomes even gentler. In 20 more minutes, the trail swings away from the brook, and shortly thereafter arrives at the trailhead (6.9 miles).

DID YOU KNOW?

Caribou do not currently inhabit the White Mountains, although they did in the immediate aftermath of the Ice Age. According to the White Mountain National Forest website (see URL below), Caribou Mountain got its name after two brothers shot what was considered to be the last caribou in the White Mountains in 1854.

OTHER ACTIVITIES

Basin Pond, about 5.5 miles south of the trailhead, is a nice place for picnic. You can canoe and fish there or camp at one of the two campgrounds.

There are a number of places along the Wild River where you can hang out on flat rocks by the edge of the water. Park at Hastings, about 1.5 miles north of the trailhead, and walk across the bridge to find your spot.

MORE INFORMATION

This walk is entirely within the White Mountain National Forest (www.fs.usda
.gov/whitemountain; 603-536-6100), and a good portion of it is a wilderness area
(www.fs.usda.gov/detail/whitemountain/specialplaces/?cid=stelprdb5186041).
Group sizes should be fewer than ten people. An outhouse and a kiosk with trail
information are at this trailhead. There is no parking fee.

NORTH COUNTRY

The North Country is the northernmost section of the White Mountains, above US 2 and Gorham, NH. It tends to be less crowded than the busy notches farther south because it is a longer drive for visitors from the south, its mountains are not as tall as the Presidential or the Franconia ranges, and the area is still a center of logging operations. Much of the area is wild and not well developed for tourists. Nevertheless, the North Country has a certain mystique for backpackers and others who want to escape crowds. It is the White Mountains as they might have been 50 years ago. Several peaks in the Kilkenny Range, which forms the central "spine" of this region, are more than 4,000 feet.

SUPPLIES AND LOGISTICS

Berlin is the largest city in this section of the White Mountains. Pick up supplies there or in other towns you pass through on your way up, such as Gorham, Lancaster, or Twin Mountain. The nearest community to the South Pond Recreation Area (see Trip 57) is Stark, several miles west of the access road to the recreation area. You will find a bathhouse, restrooms, and picnic tables at South Pond.

NEARBY CAMPING

No national forest campgrounds are in this region. The Nay Pond Campground is in West Milan off NH 110. Moose Brook State Park in Gorham has 42 tentsites.

Facing page: The North Country is the most remote and least traveled region of the White Mountains. Photo by Ryan Smith.

The Devil's Hopyard is a narrow, picturesque gorge where ice may linger even in summer and a stream occasionally disappears beneath moss-covered boulders.

CAUTION The Devil's Hopyard is always wet and slippery; take caution not to slip on the rocks.

DIRECTIONS

Take NH 16 north from Gorham 4.5 miles to Berlin. Bear left on NH 110 heading north (to West Milan). It is a little tricky following NH 110 as it winds its way through Berlin because the directional arrows are rather tiny. Take a left onto Madigan Street and then a right onto Wight Street. Stay on NH 110 through West Milan. South Pond Road is on the left 14.7 miles after you turn onto NH 110 in Berlin. A number of mailboxes and a hiking sign are at the intersection, but the sign for the South Pond Recreation Area may not be there in the off-season.

Bear right at a fork in 0.7 mile. During the off-season, there will be a closed gate a short distance after the fork. Park your vehicle outside the gate and walk the remainder of the distance to the pond (about a mile). If the gate is open, continue on to the large parking area.

From Franconia Notch or Twin Mountain, take US 3 north about 25.0 miles past Twin Mountain to its intersection with NH 110 in Groveton. This drive will take you near the town of Guildhall, VT, notable as the ancestral home of the Crawford family before they settled in the notch that now bears their name (see the essay on page 202). Follow NH 110 through Stark, another 8.0 miles or so, and turn right onto South Pond Road about 1.7 miles past a historical marker along the road. Follow the above directions from there. *GPS coordinates:* 44° 35.87′ N, 71° 22.09′ W.

LOCATION
Stark, NH

RATING
Easy

DISTANCE
2.6 miles round-trip (4.6 miles if the gate is closed)

ELEVATION GAIN
250 feet

ESTIMATED TIME
1.0–2.0 hours, longer if the gate is closed

MAPS
AMC *White Mountain National Forest Map & Guide*, Kilkenny inset

AMC *White Mountain Guide*, 29th ed. Map 6 North Country–Mahoosuc Range, B8

USGS Topo: West Milan, NH

TRAIL DESCRIPTION

The beginning section of the trail to the Devil's Hopyard is a wheelchair-accessible path (880 feet), which means it is also ideal for strollers and very young walkers. Within the Devil's Hopyard itself, the trail requires some scrambling on rocks, so this section is not recommended for families with young children (2 to 5 years old). Caution is required at all times for everyone because the rocks in the shady gorge are wet and slippery most of the time. The Devil's Hopyard is an exquisite spot, however, and it is certainly worth the walk, even if you don't get very far into it.

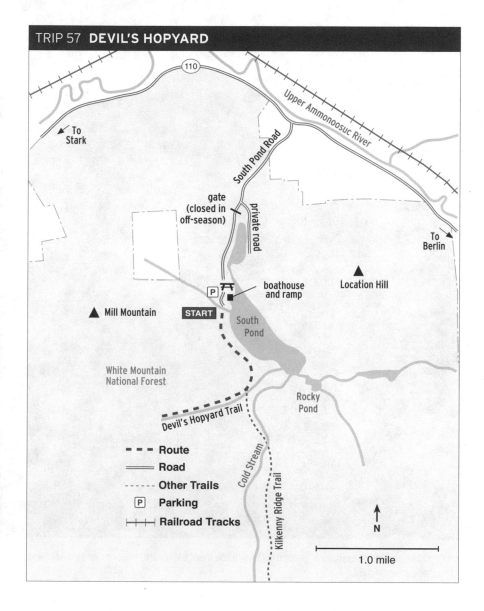

Devil's Hopyard Stream disappears under boulders in the Devil's Hopyard. Mosses and ferns abound in this damp environment.

To start the hike, walk past the bathhouse at the South Pond Recreation Area, following signs to Kilkenny Ridge Trail and the wheelchair-accessible trail. These start out together along South Pond as a level gravel path for several hundred yards. Along the way there are benches at which you can stop and admire the pond, pull out a fishing rod, or throw stones into the water.

The rich deciduous forest here is the type that dominates the lower elevations of the White Mountains. Trees include American beech, sugar maple, yellow birch, and Canadian hemlock. Beech trees have distinct smooth, gray bark that looks like it was meant for someone to carve their initials into (of course, you won't do that!). Sugar maples have the familiar five-lobed leaves. The bark of yellow birch, which peels naturally, is yellowish brown and marked with short horizontal lines.

Two shorter woody plants along this part of the trail are striped maple and hobblebush. Striped maple is a small tree with large, lobed leaves that look like a goose's foot and distinctly green-and-white-striped bark. Hobblebush forms impenetrable thickets that will hobble anyone who dares to lumber through. It has large, rounded leaves that are arranged along its skinny branches in pairs. In May it produces striking, flat-topped clusters of white flowers. Its red berries in summer provide a nice splash of color to the forest understory.

The flowers of the hobblebush show a fascinating division of labor. The outer flowers are all show but no business. They serve to attract insects to the cluster but are themselves sterile. The innocuous-looking flowers in the center of the cluster lack the showy petals but have the stamens and pistils needed to produce fruits and seeds. Insects attracted to the cluster by the showy flowers brush up against the inner ones, pollinating them. Later in the season, clusters of fruits that start out red and eventually turn bluish-black show that this unique arrangement does work.

The trail extends as a path beyond the handicapped trail. Here, it could be muddy in spots. A common woodland wildflower with roundish leaves and a spike of nodding white flowers is round-leaf pyrola.

The trail crosses Devil's Hopyard Stream and, at 0.7 mile, the trail to the Devil's Hopyard forks off to the right where Kilkenny Ridge Trail continues on straight. Shining club moss is abundant on the forest floor at this junction. It resembles an upright moss with erect, 6-inch stems that are covered by tightly whorled "leaves," each from an eighth- to a quarter-inch long. The plants are small and easily overlooked, but millions of years ago their distant relatives were as large as trees. Much of the coal we burn for fuel came from the fossilized ancestors of the little club mosses.

At 0.8 mile, Devil's Hopyard Trail crosses the stream on a bridge. Beyond the bridge the gradient steepens, and the stream alternates between fast-moving riffles and calm pools. Aquatic animals, including insects, show distinct preferences for either riffles or pools. Water striders, for example, will seek out the calmer pools, whereas blackfly larvae prefer the faster-moving riffles.

The trail enters the gorge, and you will instantly notice that it has gotten cooler, as if you've just walked into a refrigerator. The cooler temperature results from the cold water of the rushing stream and the dense shade within the steep walls of the gorge. Even in midsummer, lingering ice can be found in holes between the rocks. At times you might feel as if you are walking on top of the stream, and indeed you are. The stream is often hidden underneath a jumble of large rocks that are part of the trail. Gurgling sounds from holes between the rocks reveal that the stream has gone underground. Imagine the many creatures that find refuge within the abundant caves formed by the boulders.

Mosses and ferns thrive in this cool, damp habitat. One of the most abundant mosses is the common piggyback moss, named so because the new, delicate, ferny branches ride directly on top of the old ones. This moss is also called fern moss because of its delicate, ferny appearance. It covers many of the boulders in a lush coat of green.

The trail becomes increasingly steep before ending at 1.3 miles, having climbed about 250 feet. The shady gorge remains damp long after rainstorms have passed. Use your judgment to determine how much farther everyone should scramble before turning around.

DID YOU KNOW?

Hops are a cultivated vine used in brewing beer, so a hopyard is a field where hops are grown. What that has to do with the White Mountains, where hops are not cultivated, is a mystery.

OTHER ACTIVITIES

The South Pond Recreation Area is ideal for families either before or after a walk to the Devil's Hopyard. It is an easily accessible, developed Forest Service recreational area with picnic tables, a swimming beach, a bathhouse, and boater access. A family can spend a whole day in the area, hanging out at the recreation area for part of the time and hiking for the remainder.

Dogs are not allowed on the beach or in the bathhouse. If you have your dog with you, tell the person at the gate that you are hiking the trails.

MORE INFORMATION

The recreation area is open from 10 A.M. to 8 P.M. during the summer season. An entrance fee is charged ($7 per vehicle at the time of this writing). Before 10 A.M. and during the off-season, a barrier blocks the access road about a mile from the parking area. Hikers can go around the barrier but need to walk about 20 minutes to get to the pond itself and to Hopyard Trail.

This trail is in the White Mountain National Forest; www.fs.usda.gov/whitemountain; 603-536-6100.

58
MOUNT CRAG

Mount Crag is a small mountain that affords superb views of the Androscoggin Valley and surrounding mountains for very little effort. The hike described here is a pleasant, well-graded trail through hemlock and northern hardwoods to the viewpoint.

DIRECTIONS

From the intersection of US 2 and NH 16 in Gorham, head east along US2 toward Bethel, ME. After 3.4 miles, turn left onto North Road. This crosses the Androscoggin River by a dam site. Continue for 3.2 miles along North Road. The trail-head for Austin Brook Trail is just before the road crosses Austin Brook. There are spaces for several cars on either side of the bridge. You pass through a turnstile to start your hike. *GPS coordinates: 44° 24.75′ N, 71° 4.09′ W.*

TRAIL DESCRIPTION

Note the dam and waterfall at the beginning of the trail just after passing through the turnstile. Running along the brook, Austin Brook Trail is along an old forest road. It passes a small pond and some lawns and then enters a forest of hemlocks.

At 0.4 mile you reach the junction with Yellow Trail, which originates at the Philbrook Farm Inn. Turn left for Mount Crag. Yellow Trail, a woodland path, starts out in a dark hemlock forest, but the forest changes to northern hard-woods (primarily American beech and yellow birch) as you begin your ascent. The trail is nicely graded, never too steep, but still enough of an uphill to make you feel like you earned your lunch or snack at the top.

Beech drop, a plant that is parasitic on the roots of beeches, is particularly abundant along the trail. It is a small herb, typically about 6 inches high, with a reddish brown stalk, on top of which is its flower. Because it gets all its nutrition from the beech it parasitizes, beech drop has no green leaves.

LOCATION
Shelburne, NH

RATING
Moderate

DISTANCE
2.4 miles round-trip

ELEVATION GAIN
700 feet

ESTIMATED TIME
2.0 hours

MAPS
AMC *White Mountain Guide*, 29th ed. Map 6 North Country–Mahoosuc, E12 (trailhead), D12 (summit)

USGS Topo: Shelburne, NH

Yellow Trail reaches the summit ledges of Mount Crag at 1.2 miles (45 minutes). This is 0.8 miles from its junction with Austin Brook Trail. Enjoy the great view of the Androscoggin River Valley. Last time we were there, someone had even provided lawn chairs to enhance the experience. The Androscoggin River has its source in Lake Umbagog north of Mount Crag. It flows south past the New Hampshire towns of Berlin and Gorham, then east into Maine, where it turns southeast and joins the Kennebec River in Merrymeeting Bay near Bath, ME.

Mount Moriah, a 4,000-footer, is the prominent peak across the valley to the southwest. By walking out on the ledge and looking west, you can see the peaks of the Northern Presidentials.

The vegetation at and near the summit of Mount Crag differs from that on your ascent. Summit trees include red spruce, red and white pine, hemlock, and red oak. Trailing arbutus, sheep laurel, huckleberries, lowbush blueberries (not super abundant), Canada mayflower, flowering wintergreen, and reindeer lichen form much of the understory.

Retrace your steps to the trailhead. The descent should take about 40 minutes.

The Northern Presidential Range in the clouds, as viewed from Mount Crag.

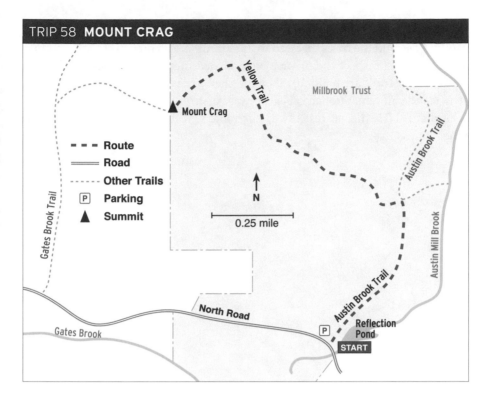

- - - **Route**
===== **Road**
····· **Other Trails**
P **Parking**
▲ **Summit**

Mount Crag

Yellow Trail

Millbrook Trust

Austin Brook Trail

Austin Mill Brook

Gates Brook Trail

N

0.25 mile

North Road

Gates Brook

Austin Brook Trail

P

Reflection Pond

START

OTHER ACTIVITIES

You can also pick up Yellow Trail at the Philbrook Farm Inn, which is about a mile east of the Austin Brook trailhead on North Road. This is a somewhat longer hike (3.6 miles) and requires a crossing of Austin Brook that could be challenging during high water. It is a good idea to stop in at the inn before starting your hike to check on where they want you to park.

The trailhead for Yellow Trail is not obvious from the inn itself. You need to walk along a service road that goes from the west side of the inn. It passes by several cottages, enters the woods, and reaches the joint trailhead for Yellow, Red, and Blue trails. Follow the yellow blazes. Most of Yellow Trail in this section is along a grassy woodland road, but you need to follow the blazes carefully to avoid turning off on other unmarked paths.

Recent logging activity is evident along the path. Yellow Trail reaches Austin Brook in about 0.9 mile, where you can ford by carefully stepping on rocks or have the option of taking a slight detour to a unique, hand-powered cable car to aid your crossing. (A sign indicates that you use that at your own risk.) Once safely across the brook, you enter a hemlock forest and reach the junction with Austin Brook Trail, 1.0 mile from the Philbrook Farm Inn. From this point, you can follow the Trail Description above.

MORE INFORMATION

Mount Crag and the trails that lead to its summit are all on private conservation land, so please respect the privacy of residences near the trailhead and along the trail. The trails are maintained by the Shelburne Trail Club, which also constructed the aforementioned cable car over Austin Brook.

Gorham, NH, the nearest town, has motels, restaurants, gas stations, and other stores.

Lookout Ledge is a rocky outcropping on the side of Mount Randolph that affords a wonderful view of King Ravine and Mounts Adams and Madison, plus some of the peaks of the Carter Range. Ledge Trail provides a relatively direct ascent, steep in a few places but for the most part well graded.

DIRECTIONS

The trailhead for Ledge Trail is at the Ravine House site on Durand Road in Randolph. From Franconia Notch, Crawford Notch, and Twin Mountain, take US 3 north at its junction with US 302 in Twin Mountain. After about 2.0 miles, turn right onto NH 115 and take it for about 10.0 miles to US 2. Turn right onto US 2, take it for about 6.0 miles, and then make a left onto Durand Road, which parallels US 2 closely. The Ravine House site is well marked on the left in about 1.6 miles. The trailhead is on the west side of the Ravine House site, where there is room for several vehicles. (Durand Road eventually rejoins US 2 about 1.0 mile east of the Ravine House.)

From North Conway and Pinkham Notch, take NH 16 into Gorham, where it meets US 2. Travel west on US 2 for about 4.5 miles past its split with NH 16. Make a right at the east intersection of Durand Road with US 2 and take it for 1.1 miles to the Ravine House site on the right. *GPS coordinates: 44° 22.48′ N, 71° 17.48′ W.*

TRAIL DESCRIPTION

Ledge Trail is not heavily used, so it may be overgrown in sections, but it is well marked with orange blazes. The first few paces are on blacktop, then it joins a steep old logging road. At a small stream it turns right, leaves the logging

LOCATION
Randolph, NH

RATING
Moderate

DISTANCE
2.6 miles round-trip

ELEVATION GAIN
1,000 feet

ESTIMATED TIME
2.0–3.0 hours

MAPS
AMC White Mountain National Forest Map & Guide, E8 and Kilkenny inset

AMC *White Mountain Guide*, 29th ed. Map 6 North Country–Mahoosuc Range, E9

USGS Topo: Mount Washington to Pliny Range, NH

road, and parallels the stream uphill. In 0.6 mile, the trail makes a sharp bend to the left where the Notchway comes in.

You could think of this trail as the hay-scented fern walk. The forest is in transition, and there is an extraordinary number of downed trees, the result of the ice storm of January 1998. Sunlight that now penetrates to the forest floor has stimulated the rampant growth of hay-scented fern. These ferns are able to exploit forest gaps because once they take root they spread rapidly. All the hay-scented ferns in one forest opening may actually be connected by underground rhizomes and therefore be one individual plant. Eventually, saplings of sugar maple, yellow birch, and American beech, spawned from nearby trees that survived the storm, will likely fill in the open patches, perhaps preceded by paper birch. For the trees, periodic setbacks from storms, harsh winters, drought, flooding, disease, and insect outbreaks are part of what they must tolerate if they are going to thrive in the White Mountains.

Two other types of ferns grow in an obvious place along the trail. Look for New York fern, with its smallish, lacy frond tapered at both ends, and sensitive fern along the driveway at the beginning of the trail. Sensitive ferns produce clusters of small, round spore cases (sori) on a stem separate from its leafy frond. You might have seen these "fertile fronds" in dried flower arrangements, where they are usually spray-painted silver.

Lookout Ledge provides fine views of the Northern Presidentials. Photo by Jerry Monkman.

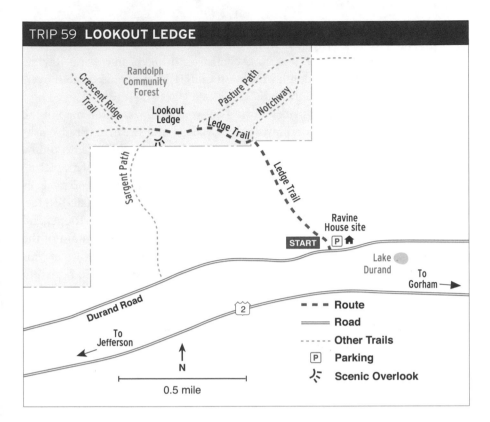

Randolph
Community
Forest

Crescent Ridge Trail

Lookout
Ledge

Pasture Path

Notchway

Ledge Trail

Sargent Path

Ledge Trail

Ravine
House site

START P

Lake
Durand

To
Gorham →

Durand Road

2

To
Jefferson

N

0.5 mile

- - - **Route**

—— **Road**

----- **Other Trails**

P **Parking**

人 **Scenic Overlook**

A wildflower that grows in abundance along Ledge Trail is Solomon's seal. This member of the lily family has unbranched, arching stems with broad, lance-shaped leaves. In spring, pairs of small, greenish-yellow flowers hang underneath the stem. In summer, these turn into blue-black berries. The name Solomon's seal is derived from the pattern of the scar left on the rootstock when the stem is broken off. It presumably resembles the official seal of the ancient king. Other wildflowers to look for include clintonia, doll's-eyes (white bane-berry), wild sarsaparilla, white lettuce, sharp-leaved aster, and lobelia.

In the area of many downed maples, beeches, and birches, look for the strong, straight trunks of white ash trees still standing. The bark of the ash has distinct vertical ridges, and its compound leaves attach to the branches in pairs.

The trail continues climbing steeply, joins another overgrown logging road for a time, and reaches a junction with Pasture Path at 1.1 miles. The forest has largely transitioned into spruce-fir, and you may particularly enjoy looking at the caves made by roots of trees and rock.

Follow Ledge Trail for another 0.2 mile, past a viewpoint to Lookout Ledge, right where the trail meets Crescent Ridge Trail and Sargent Path. The most striking view from Lookout Ledge is of the glacial cirque of King Ravine on the upper slope of Mount Adams. It is a classic U-shaped ravine, as if it were taken straight from the pages of a geology textbook (see Trip 33 for more on U-shaped valleys). With binoculars you can easily see the boulders that fell from the sides of the ravine and now litter its floor. Although the boulders look small from Lookout Ledge, they present a serious challenge to hikers into King Ravine. Look for Crag Camp, a Randolph Mountain Club (RMC)-operated cabin overlooking King Ravine on its right wall.

Lookout Ledge is an ideal place to bring out your compass and a map of the region in order to identify mountains, ridges, valleys, and streams. (Brad Washburn's map, *Mount Washington and the Heart of Presidential Range,* would be perfect for this task.) Mounts Adams and Madison, with their pointed, picturesque summits, loom large in the foreground. The col between the two peaks is the location of AMC's Madison Hut. From west to east are Castellated Ridge, Nowell Ridge, King Ravine, Durand Ridge, Snyder Brook, Gordon Ridge, and Howker Ridge. To the southeast are Pine Mountain and Imp Mountain of the Carter-Moriah Range. The Mahoosuc Range and the Androscoggin River Valley are to the east. Durand Lake is right below. Retrace your steps to return to your vehicle.

DID YOU KNOW?

John Durand, for whom the road was named, was a Londoner who received the original grant to settle in the region. The town of Randolph was originally known as Durand.

OTHER ACTIVITIES

A network of trails in this area could make for a longer hike. Sargent Path could be used for the descent, but you would need to spot a second vehicle at its trailhead or walk the 0.75 mile along Durand Road. It is steeper than Ledge Trail.

MORE INFORMATION

Ledge Trail and Lookout Ledge are on private land. Lookout Ledge can be approached by a number of trails north of US 2 maintained by the RMC (randolphmountainclub.org). There is no fee for parking.

Gorham has restaurants, motels, gas stations, and other stores.

THE RAVINE HOUSE

The Ravine House site at the trailhead for Ledge Trail should be a place of pilgrimage for anyone interested in the history of trail-building in the White Mountains. First opened to guests in 1877, it became a summer hangout for people who built and hiked trails in the Northern Presidentials and the Randolph area. According to Guy and Laura Waterman's *Forest and Crag: A History of Hiking, Trail Blazing, and Adventure in the Northeast Mountains* (AMC Books, 1989), the Ravine House was not an opulent hotel cut from the gilded age, such as the still-extant Mount Washington Hotel in Bretton Woods; rather, it was a comfortable, rambling inn, grand in its own way. Like visitors today to AMC huts, the hikers of those days must have looked forward to returning to the Ravine House each evening for dinner and discussion with the other guests about the trails they had hiked that day and what they were planning next. When they were done with such discussions they might get together to play music.

If the guests at the table included one of the premier trail-builders, such as Laban Watson, there was undoubtedly conversation about new trails needing to be built or a report on a trail in progress. Watson's trails were legendary for being the shortest, steepest, most direct routes up to a summit.

Perhaps someone might have bantered, "You can't be serious about building such a steep trail up Mount Adams!" J. Rayner Edmands, another master trail-builder, preferred smoother, more-graded paths—more labor-intensive to build, but easier on weary hikers' legs.

The Ravine House closed in 1960, but the town of Randolph continues the tradition of trail work and community spirit fostered by the Ravine House and several other now-defunct hotels in the area. Many of the trails in Randolph and the Northern Presidentials across US 2 are maintained by the Randolph Mountain Club, which was formed in the early 1900s to restore and maintain trails that had been obscured by logging activity at the turn of the century.

60

UNKNOWN POND FROM MILL BROOK ROAD

This trip offers a pleasant ascent to a remote, boreal mountain pond bordered by conifers. The hike follows a stream and then ascends through an attractive paper birch forest.

DIRECTIONS

The trailhead is reached from NH 110 on an unpaved road. The road is in good condition but is not maintained for winter travel.

Take NH 16 north from Gorham 4.5 miles to Berlin. Bear left onto NH 110 heading north (to West Milan). It is a little tricky following NH 110 as it winds its way through Berlin because the directional arrows are rather tiny. It makes a left onto Madigan Street and then a right onto Wight Street. Once out of Berlin, stay on NH 110 past the road to the South Pond Recreation Area. Mill Brook Road is on the left about 3.0 miles past South Pond Road, about 18.0 miles from Berlin, and just before the village of Stark Bridge. A hiker sign is at the intersection.

Follow Mill Brook Road (unpaved) south for 4.6 miles. Park just over the second bridge (space for several vehicles) and walk back over the bridge. The trailhead is on the east side of the road (right side if you are facing north) just before the bridge. The hiker sign is a little set back under vegetation, so you might not see it at first glance. *GPS coordinates: 44° 33.23′ N, 71° 24.62′ W.*

TRAIL DESCRIPTION

Part of the charm of Unknown Pond is that it is in a quiet part of the White Mountains. You are likely to run into few, if any, fellow hikers on this trail. The trail begins as a well-graded path along one of the branches of Mill Brook. The spruce-fir forest at the trailhead quickly changes to a rich northern hardwood forest with abundant wildflowers: Indian cucumber-root, painted trillium, bunchberries,

LOCATION
Stark, NH, to Kilkenny, NH

RATING
Moderate

DISTANCE
4.4 miles

ELEVATION GAIN
1,400 feet

ESTIMATED TIME
3.5 hours

MAPS
AMC White Mountain National Forest Map & Guide, Kilkenny inset

AMC *White Mountain Guide,* 29th ed. Map 6 North Country–Mahoosuc Range, C8

USGS Topo: Stark, NH

A foggy morning at Unknown Pond. At 3,200-feet elevation, the pond is in the heart of the boreal (spruce-fir) forest.

and foamflower, to name a few. This first section of the trail could be muddy, particularly right after a rainstorm.

This part of the trail had one of the greatest concentrations of moose droppings and hoof prints that I have ever seen, so keep your eyes open for moose. On the other side of the size-and-grace spectrum, look for the white admiral butterfly, a large brown butterfly with a bold white stripe on its fore- and hindwings. Oddly, the butterflies have an affinity for the moose droppings, and it is not uncommon to see clusters of these creatures wherever there are such deposits.

In about 1.0 mile (a half hour), the trail reaches a small clearing where a tributary comes in, and the more serious ascent begins. This is accompanied by yellow birch and paper (white) birch. Eventually, the yellow birches drop out and the forest becomes almost pure paper birch, a beautiful backdrop to your climb. The presence of this tree is a legacy to logging activities that formerly occurred in this region. Red spruce and balsam fir, the dominant trees above about 2,500 feet, will eventually replace the birches. Where the trees are a little thin, you get occasional views of the nearby ridge of the Pilot Range to the southwest.

At about 2.0 mile (1 hour, 15 minutes), the trail levels out and crosses a small, rushing stream in an open area. This is a nice place to take a short break. The vegetation along the stream includes goldenrods and asters that provide midsummer color, tall meadow rue (fuzzy white flowers), and lady fern. Bunchberries, whose flowers have long since bloomed near the trailhead, may still be in bloom here, a result of the delayed season at higher elevations. Shortly after the stream, you pass a sign providing information about backcountry camping opportunities at Unknown Pond, so you know you are getting close.

Continuing on, Unknown Pond Trail intersects Kilkenny Ridge Trail at 2.2 miles (1.5 hours) at the northeast corner of the pond. For a good view of the pond, turn right (south) on Kilkenny Ridge Trail for about 100 feet and walk a few paces to the left to the edge of the pond. On a clear day, the Horn, an impressively sharp peak that is part of the Kilkenny Ridge, makes a striking backdrop to the pond.

Campers and hikers straying off trails had seriously eroded the shoreline at Unknown Pond. The Forest Service has addressed this by clearly marking camping and revegetation areas. As the signs indicate, avoid entering the revegetation areas and, for those who are camping, stay in the designated areas.

Return to the trail junction and continue to the right. At this point, the Unknown Pond and Kilkenny Ridge trails run together for about 100 yards. For the second excellent viewing area, follow Unknown Pond Trail past where Kilkenny Ridge Trail departs to the north. Look for an open area on the right just beyond where the spur path to the tentsites goes off to the left. This is the best lunch spot.

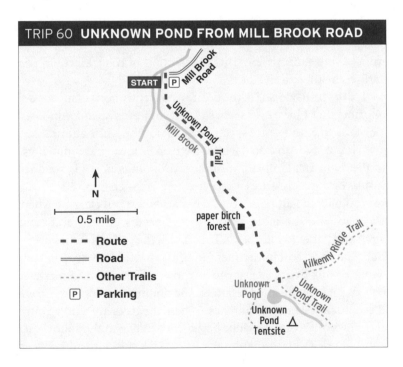

TRIP 60 **UNKNOWN POND FROM MILL BROOK ROAD**

The shoreline is fringed with Labrador tea, a shrub with thick, leathery leaves with rolled edges and white or rusty wooly hairs on their undersides. Yellow waterlilies grow in the shallows.

At 3,170 feet elevation, Unknown Pond is noted for its boreal birdlife. Rusty blackbirds, looking like red-winged blackbirds without the red wings, nest around the backside of the pond. Boreal chickadees, with their brown caps, are a high-elevation spruce-fir counterpart of the familiar black-capped chickadees. Swainson's thrushes, winter wrens, and white-throated sparrows vie for the title of the most accomplished songster at Unknown Pond. Yellow-rumped and blackpoll warblers, cedar waxwings, and dark-eyed juncos can also be found.

Retrace your steps to return to your vehicle.

DID YOU KNOW?

According to Steven D. Smith's *Ponds and Lakes of the White Mountains* (Backcountry Press, 1998), Unknown Pond did not make it into AMC's *White Mountain Guide* until 1940—hence, the appropriateness of its name.

OTHER ACTIVITIES

South Pond Recreation Area offers swimming and boating. It has a bathhouse and restrooms (entry fee charged). The WMNF has designated six tentsites off Unknown Pond Trail for backcountry camping at the south end of the pond. Camping is permitted only in those sites.

For a more extended hike, the Horn is about 2.0 miles south of Unknown Pond via Kilkenny Ridge Trail and a spur trail. It provides a wonderful view of the pond and peaks of the North Country. You'll find some difficult scrambles to reach its summit.

Unknown Pond Trail continues past the pond for another 3.3 miles to a second trailhead on York Pond Road, 2.1 miles past the Berlin Fish Hatchery. Although one could spot a second vehicle at that trailhead, be aware that the gate at the fish hatchery is open only between 8 A.M. and 4:30 P.M. so you would need to be done with your hike before closing time.

MORE INFORMATION

Unknown Pond Trail is in a region of very small villages and limited services, so you may want to pick up supplies in Gorham or Berlin on your way up.

The trail is within the White Mountain National Forest. There is no fee for parking at the trailhead; www.fs.usda.gov/whitemountain; 603-536-6100.

Given the remoteness of this region, the outhouse at the camping area at the pond can come in handy.

APPENDIX A
HIKING WITH CHILDREN

Hiking with children requires flexibility, a sense of humor, and patience. You need to slow down and encourage children to explore the natural world around them—the sights, the sounds, and the smells—even if it means you might not make it to that scenic overlook or waterfall. You have a wonderful opportunity to expose your children to the wonders of the natural world at an early age and you have the opportunity to enjoy nature as your child sees it.

Our recommendations are based on our experiences and those of many AMC staffers and friends, but please keep in mind that it's difficult to generalize about what a child can handle at a given age. Some precocious and energetic 5-year-olds are ready for a 4,000-footer. Some 10-year-olds may not be willing to hike very far at all.

Don't be afraid to start your kids early. Our daughter slept through her first hike in a front carrier at 2 months of age. Hiking with a 1-year-old in a backpack is actually much easier than negotiating with a toddler. Pack diapers, baby food, and other items just as you would on any daylong outing, and be prepared with extra clothes.

WHAT KINDS OF HIKES DO KIDS LIKE?

With the right spirit, every trail can be fun for adults and children alike, but some will engage children more easily than others. In our hikes with children, we've noticed a few especially winning features.

Children love to be around water. The White Mountains have an abundance of waterfalls and lakes that are popular destinations for family hikes. You can swim or wade, look for small critters, throw stones into the water, or have a picnic or a snack on big, flat boulders while dangling your feet in the water. It is also much more fun to hike along a river or a small babbling stream than through unchanging woodland.

Children love to walk on wooden plank bridges that cross streams and wetlands and on split logs that traverse muddy areas. Covered bridges are even better, but there are only a few in the White Mountains.

Kids like to stop and look at little things, such as an odd-looking bug crossing the path, a colorful leaf in autumn, or a brightly colored fungus. It is hard to predict what will strike their fancy. One friend remembered her nephew's fascination with small conifer trees that were his own height. Take the time to enjoy those things with them, rather than hurrying off to the next destination.

Rocks and big boulders so common along many trails in the White Mountains are great opportunities for climbing and exploration. Especially intriguing are those that form caves or overhang the trail. Beginning hikers will proudly show you how they have "conquered" even a small rock in the middle of a trail.

Similarly, kids love scrambling around rocky ledges, particularly after they have been hiking through a dense forest. At a ledgy scenic overlook, the scenery itself is likely to play second fiddle to the scrambling. (Of course, if their parents *ooh* and *aah* over enough views, children may eventually start *oohing* and *aah-ing* too.) Rocky ledges are like a substitute jungle gym. Remember to keep your eyes on children, because there are no railings on most trails.

Most kids love picking and eating blueberries. They may not persevere long enough to collect a stash for tomorrow morning's blueberry pancakes, but they will certainly enjoy this activity for a while. The summits of many of the smaller mountains listed in this book are loaded with ripe blueberries toward the end of July and throughout August. Huckleberries, blackberries, and raspberries are also there for the picking.

Some kids love wildflowers and brightly colored mushrooms, although others may not notice them. Keeping children from picking flowers may be the hardest job you'll have on the trail, but once they get into the habit of just looking, they'll keep it for life.

Kids like to see creatures. In the White Mountains, squirrels, chipmunks, toads, red efts (a salamander), and butterflies are usually popular in a child's bestiary. Look for tadpoles, frogs, fish, and water striders along the edges of ponds. Trees riddled with woodpecker holes, bark stripped by moose, or trees scarred by bear claws are great things to point out.

Birds are hard for many children to enjoy because they are much more often heard than seen in the White Mountains. Encourage children to listen to the beautiful bird songs in the forest, but don't push it. You'll be more successful if you show them either big birds of open spaces and wetlands, such as hawks, herons, and ducks, or sassy, tame birds like gray jays and chickadees that seem as curious about you as you are about them.

Before we had children, many of us sought out quiet, backcountry trails to get a refreshing break from our hectic work lives and our urban or suburban existence. Children are less likely to feel the need for such a wilderness experience than their parents. In fact, they may enjoy the crowds at such places as the Flume or Glen Ellis Falls.

Few people enjoy walking through an endless tunnel of trees with no scenic or watery breaks. Adults can tolerate those kinds of trails in anticipation of a reward at the end in the form of a summit or a waterfall. When you are hiking with children, however, there is no guarantee that you will make it to the end, so pick a hike that won't be disappointing, even if you turn around before completing it.

Navigating can be a fun challenge. Some younger kids will be motivated by the responsibility of spotting the next blaze. Older kids may want to learn how to read trail maps and use a compass and GPS. They may enjoy helping to plan the hike as well.

Bring a friend. Your children may enjoy the hike more if they have a friend along. They can chat and joke with each other along the trail and encourage each other. Of course, you will have to be sure that the friend is someone who takes well to hiking or this could backfire.

FAVORITE DISTRACTIONS

Inevitably, kids will hit a low point while on some hikes. Here's where you need to be creative and prepared.

Some children love singing songs on the trail. Camp songs and songs they have learned in school are great when the trail seems never-ending. Let them pick out the songs, but be ready with your own.

Stories and tales of what you did when you were their age work wonders at distracting children. Ask them a nature question they can answer along the hike—look at the hike descriptions for suggestions. Often there's something close at hand that can be made into a game, such as balsam blisters, spruce gum, or jewelweed.

Make the hike into a scavenger hunt. Have a list of items kids can search for, and be ready to pull it out at a strategic moment. Possible items are mushrooms, spiderwebs, Indian pipes, pinecones, maple leaves, or whatever you can glean from reading the trail descriptions. You can also impart a valuable conservation lesson if you encourage them to leave the items in the forest, rather than collecting them in a bag.

ADDITIONAL THOUGHTS

Be flexible and allow plenty of extra time. Be ready to change your plans midhike and always encourage kids to investigate the natural world. Time spent watching a moose feeding on water plants or a moth caught in a spiderweb will likely be remembered much longer than whether they made it to that last waterfall.

Be goal oriented if getting to that waterfall can stimulate your children to overcome these first pangs of tiredness or lack of motivation, but be ready to bail out if it isn't working or if the children get engrossed in little things they see along the trail and time runs out. The idea is to have fun, not to make this into a forced march. On the other hand, don't necessarily turn back at the first complaint either, particularly if there is something you're sure they'll really enjoy with just a little more effort.

Children have an amazing ability to do a complete 180-degree recovery just after they have insisted that they can't possibly move their legs another inch.

Inspecting a mushroom. This young hiker has mastered the art of "look, but don't touch," which is vital for protecting the natural environment.

We've been saved many times by something like a toad magically appearing on the trail and stimulating a mood change just when it seemed all was lost.

Sometimes picking kids up, clowning around, and carrying them for a short period will get them back on track. And be liberal with praise for how well they are doing.

Just about all the trails described in this book have interesting things for both adults and children to see along the way so that the trip will be worthwhile, even if you do not complete the entire hike. The text suggests logical places at which to turn around before reaching the end, such as a nice view or a swimming hole.

Remember, it is much more important for you to instill an appreciation for the natural world in your kids than to impart facts about nature. Sooner or later a kid will ask something that even the most expert naturalist can't answer. Make it into a game and help them look it up in a field guide. A pad and pencil are useful to record field notes and questions.

Your own enthusiasm for the hike will rub off on them.

APPENDIX B
NATURAL HISTORY OF
THE WHITE MOUNTAINS

The White Mountains are a special place, not only for the scenery and outdoor recreational opportunities, but also for the wonderful diversity of natural history. This brief description of the region's geology, plants, and animals hopefully will enrich your hiking experience. Look for additional information in the individual hike descriptions and in the sidebars. A complete guide to the natural history of the White Mountains would take up several volumes, so seek out additional books if you'd like to know more.

GEOGRAPHY

The White Mountains of north-central New Hampshire and western Maine are the largest expanse of mountains in New England. Forty-three peaks exceed 4,000 feet in elevation and seven exceed 5,000 feet. Most of the region is included in the White Mountain National Forest and several state parks. The area has an extensive network of hiking trails maintained by the national forest and volunteer organizations such as AMC and the Randolph Mountain Club.

Because of their elevation, the White Mountains have a cooler climate and a more "northern" ecology than one would expect at their latitude. Snow remains in some mountain ravines into June, and trees generally do not grow above 4,500 feet. The higher peaks are notorious for damp, misty, and windy weather, so you should particularly cherish a beautiful summer day when there are extensive views. Mount Washington still holds the record for the strongest wind ever recorded in the United States: 231 MPH on April 12, 1934.

A major geographic feature is the north-to-south-running valleys (called notches) that separate the major mountain ranges. From west to east, these are Franconia Notch, Zealand Notch, Crawford Notch, Pinkham Notch, and Evans Notch. Roads traverse all except Zealand.

GEOLOGY

Where did the White Mountains come from? The story is one of enormous collisions and rifts of ancient continents drifting across the earth. Eons ago there was a sea here instead of mountains. About 400 million years ago, the thick layers of sand and mud at the bottom of this sea were squeezed between two colliding continents, North America and an ancient island continent called Avalon. Under this immense pressure, these layers hardened to form the schists, gneisses, and quartzites of the Presidential Range and were then uplifted to the surface of the earth. Pine Mountain and Stinson Mountain are great places to see how these layers of metamorphic rock were actually twisted by these powerful forces.

A second major geologic event occurred 230 to 180 million years ago when the granite that forms the bedrock of much of the rest of the White Mountains solidified from molten rock deep within the earth as ancient continents split apart. Subsequent uplift and erosion of layers of softer, overlying rocks brought the granite to the surface. Volcanic eruptions at that same time created additional rocks.

The rocks along the trails in the White Mountains are almost all granites or schists. Both have a salt-and-pepper appearance because they are composed of different-colored minerals. Granites are composed primarily of crystals of feldspar (whitish or pink) and quartz (translucent white or gray). Usually there are smaller amounts of mica flakes (biotite if brown or black; muscovite if white or silvery) and hornblende (black). The mineral crystals in schist are smaller than those in granite.

Gleaming white quartzes and glossy mica flakes are evident along just about any trail. Rock hounds will especially enjoy a visit to one of the abandoned mines, such as those on Lord Hill or North Sugarloaf. At these mines you can find large crystals of mica, feldspar, and, if you look hard enough, topaz, garnets, beryl, smoky quartz, and even amethysts.

When hiking through White Mountain forests, you will undoubtedly come upon some monstrous boulders. Jumbles of boulders at the base of a mountain, such as on Boulder Loop Trail or Mount Osceola Trail, probably tumbled down during landslides. Isolated boulders may be erratics carried to their destinations by glaciers and left behind when the glacier melted. You'll find large glacial erratics at the Flume, at "the boulder" near the Cascade Path in Waterville Valley, and on Sugarloaf Trail.

Many of the hikes take you past huge outcroppings (visible exposures) of bedrock. Famous profiles such as the Indian Head near Franconia Notch and the Elephant Head at Crawford Notch are outcrops of bedrock visible from highways. On most outcroppings of bedrock you can find narrow bands of white or black rocks, called dikes, crisscrossing the grayer granite. Dikes form when molten rock, heated by forces deep within the earth, flow into cracks in the granite and then cool. Pegmatite dikes are typically white and contain relatively large crystals of feldspars and sometimes other minerals. Basalt dikes are black and do not appear to have any crystalline structure at all, because the magma (molten rock) flowed near the surface of the earth and cooled rapidly, not allowing time for crystal formation. Narrow, steep-sided gorges, called flumes, form where flowing water has eroded the softer dike and left the relatively harder granite walls.

The erosive action of glaciers had a profound effect on the White Mountain landscape. Mountain glaciers high up on the sides of peaks carved the famous bowl-shaped ravines (called cirques) in the Presidential Range. These include Tuckerman, Huntington, and King ravines and the Great Gulf. Mountain glaciers also carved the sharp, narrow ridge of the Franconia Range.

The continental glaciers that covered much of North America during the Ice Age had an even more widespread impact than the mountain glaciers. Four separate advances and retreats of glaciers occurred between 1 million and 12,000 years ago. The last glacier covered even Mount Washington with several thousand feet of ice. Its erosive action smoothed out the summits of the Presidential Range and carved out U-shaped, north–south valleys such as Crawford and Zealand notches. Pine Mountain is a good place to see scratches in the bedrock etched by stones dragged along by the movement of ice.

Recent investigations by the New Hampshire Historic Preservation Office have shown that people inhabited the area around Jefferson, NH, about 11,000 years ago, indicating that the glaciers were no longer covering the White Mountains by then. Archaeological investigations since 1995 have uncovered tools, fluted spear points, and other artifacts.

FORESTS

The White Mountains are densely forested, a fact many easterners may not appreciate unless they have spent time in the Sierra Nevada or other western ranges. Many walks described in this book pass through two different types of forest: the northern hardwood at lower elevations and the boreal forest higher up.

Three broad-leaved trees dominate northern hardwood forests: sugar maple, American beech, and yellow birch. Canadian hemlock, a needle-bearing tree, is abundant along streams in shady gorges. Hobblebush and striped maples are common shrubs in the understory. Northern hardwoods cover a wide band of the northern United States and southern Canada from Maine through Minnesota. This forest glows with beautiful colors in autumn—a great, bug-free time to hike.

Some lower-elevation trails have abundant oaks and white pines mixed in with the northern hardwoods. These species are more characteristic of southern New England forests.

As you ascend above 2,000 feet, you will notice an increasing number of conifers—cone-bearing trees with needle leaves. The two most common species are red spruce and balsam fir. Spruce and fir, along with pines, are often called evergreens because they keep their needles year-round; however, conifer is a better term because some broad-leafed shrubs, such as rhododendrons, are also "evergreen."

Above 2,500 to 3,000 feet, a dark forest of conifers—the boreal forest—completely replaces the northern hardwoods. Boreas, the Greek god of the north wind, was portrayed in mythology as blowing a cold wind across the land, and, indeed, the boreal forest occurs in colder places such as the middle latitudes of Canada and Russia. An ascent of several thousand feet in the White Mountains is ecologically equivalent to driving several hundred miles north of Montreal. The summit of Mount Washington, the highest point in the White Mountains at 6,288 feet, is roughly equivalent to the environment of northern Labrador.

The boreal forest, also called the spruce-fir forest, is a fantasyland of dense "Christmas" trees with a soft, dark, mossy understory. Red spruce (illustrated at left) tends to be more abundant in the lower part of the boreal forest (below 3,500 feet), while balsam fir (illustrated below) dominates higher up. Scattered throughout the forest, particularly in clearings, are a few broad-leafed trees and shrubs such as paper birch and mountain ash. The upper part of the boreal forest grades into dwarf trees and scrub near treeline. The German word krummholz, which means crooked wood, is used to describe the low, twisted trees around treeline.

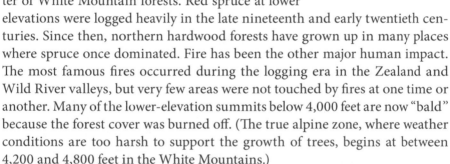

Humans have had a major impact on the character of White Mountain forests. Red spruce at lower elevations were logged heavily in the late nineteenth and early twentieth centuries. Since then, northern hardwood forests have grown up in many places where spruce once dominated. Fire has been the other major human impact. The most famous fires occurred during the logging era in the Zealand and Wild River valleys, but very few areas were not touched by fires at one time or another. Many of the lower-elevation summits below 4,000 feet are now "bald" because the forest cover was burned off. (The true alpine zone, where weather conditions are too harsh to support the growth of trees, begins at between 4,200 and 4,800 feet in the White Mountains.)

On summits, trees are often contorted into odd shapes. This is the result of wind exposure. Flag trees (also called banner trees) have branches on one side only. These occur when the combination of ice and wind kills the branches that attempt to grow into the prevailing winds, which are generally from the west or northwest. The surviving branches point away from the wind, just like a flag rippling in a stiff breeze.

APPENDIX C
A PRIMER ON FLORA AND FAUNA

COMMON TREES

Maples are among the most common trees of the northern hardwood forest. Their leaves have three or five lobes, somewhat like the palm of a hand, and are attached to branches in pairs (opposite-leaved). Read more about maples in the essay "Maples of the White Mountains" on page 142.

American beech has distinct smooth, gray bark. The combination of smooth, gray bark and long, pointed buds makes this an easy tree to identify, even in winter. The bark peels in horizontal layers. Leaves are heart-shaped at the base and serrated along the edges.

Paper birch has unmistakable white bark that peels into horizontal strips. The bark is lined with distinct horizontal pores called lenticels. Paper birch is often the first tree species to colonize an area clear-cut by loggers. Yellow birch also has lenticels but has yellowish-brown or gray bark. Its twigs taste like wintergreen when chewed.

Canadian hemlock is a sprawling evergreen conifer of cool ravines and stream sides at lower elevations. It has short, half-inch needles with two white lines underneath.

Balsam fir is one of the two major trees of the boreal forest. Balsam fir's flat needles are longer (up to 1.5 inches) than hemlock needles and emit a wonderful balsam fragrance when crushed. It is the only conifer with cones that sit upright on branches.

Red spruce is the other major tree of the boreal forest. Its 0.75-to-1.5-inch needles are attached singly to branches, are square in cross-section, and sharp to the touch. If you can roll a needle between your thumb and forefinger, it is a red spruce.

White pine has needles in bunches of five. The 3-to-5-inch needles are soft and flexible, so they won't prickle you.

Larch, also called tamarack, is a tree of open boggy areas. The 1-inch needles grow in clusters of ten to 30. The larch is unique among conifers in that it drops its needles in fall after they turn a beautiful bright yellow.

COMMON SHRUBS

Several species of **blueberries** occur on open, low summits and ledges, where they are often less than a foot high. Delicate white clusters of small, bell-shaped flowers in May and June precede the berries, which ripen in July through about mid-August.

Hobblebush is the most abundant shrub in the forest understory of most hikes. Rounded, paired leaves with toothed edges and heart-shaped bases run along straggling stems. Hobblebush produces flat-topped white clusters of flowers in May and clusters of inedible red berries during summer.

Raspberries and **blackberries** grow as thin, arching "canes" covered with thorns and prickles. White flowers appear in June and the fruits in July and August. Raspberries and blackberries are colonizers of forest clearings, roadsides, and recently logged areas.

Labrador tea is a small (1-to-2-foot) shrub of bogs and boggy shorelines of ponds. Its dark-green, leathery leaves are rolled underneath at the edges and remain on the plant all year. The undersides of the leaves are covered with dense, rust-colored hairs (white on new leaves).

SPRING WILDFLOWERS

Clintonia is a lily with large, shiny, smooth-edged leaves that hug the ground. A single flowering stalk produces several yellowish-green flowers with six "petals" in late May through June. Summer visitors are more likely to see the glossy blue-black berries that give rise to its other name, blue-bead lily. Do not eat the berry.

Painted trillium is one of the grandest of the White Mountain woodland wildflowers. It is unmistakable, containing a whorl of three leaves on a 1-foot stem. The stem is topped with a single white, three-petaled flower with a purple center. In summer, a large red berry replaces the flower.

Canada mayflower is a small plant abundant in many woodlands at both low and high elevations. It has two or three smooth-edged, heart-shaped leaves. Its white, fuzzy spike of small flowers develops first into white-and-red-speckled berries, eventually turning all red.

Pink lady's slipper is a native orchid. The hanging flower is shaped like a shoe or moccasin. See the essay "Pink Lady's Slippers in the White Mountains" on page 228 for a detailed description of this exquisite wildflower.

Goldthread is a small flower of shady, mossy woods with three small, rounded leaflets, each with scalloped edges. In spring, a single white flower with five to seven petals arises from a separate stem. Goldthread has a bright yellow underground stem that connects different individual plants.

Starflower has delicate white flowers that really do resemble stars. Typically, two white "stars" with six to eight petals each are on top of a whorl of five to seven narrow, pointed leaves on a 4-to-8-inch stem.

Alpine wildflowers have always been a key enticement for climbing to higher elevations in the White Mountains. A number of showy species bloom in early to mid-June. See the essay "The Alpine Zone of the White Mountains" on page 260 for more information.

SUMMER WILDFLOWERS

Bunchberries are cheery white wildflowers that usually occur in large colonies on the forest floor. The flower is also called Canada dogwood, since it is related to the flowering dogwood tree. Bunchberries produce a whorl of four or six smooth-edged leaves. They bloom in June at low elevations and in early July at higher elevations.

Mountain wood sorrel, another wildflower of the forest floor, will remind you of a shamrock. Its three leaflets, notched at the apex, are a common sight in cool woods. Mountain wood sorrel has attractive, delicate white flowers with five petals inscribed with thin pink lines and (usually) a pink circle surrounding the center.

Indian pipes occur in isolated small groups in the forest. They are odd looking, easily mistaken for a fungus because of their ghostly white appearance and lack of green leaves. Drooping white flowers are produced on top of 6-to-8-inch stems.

Bluet flowers have four light-blue petals surrounding a yellow center. They are less than half an inch in diameter and three inches tall but grow in dense colonies that can be quite showy. Look for bluets in sunny areas along trails and along roadsides and fields.

Whorled aster is the most common aster in the northern hardwood forest. Its leaves appear to be whorled (attached at or near the same point) around the stem. Its other name, sharp-toothed nodding aster, relates to its coarsely toothed leaves that are tapered at both ends. Blooming from mid-August through September, its flower heads are daisy-like.

Goldenrods are showy late-summer flowers of fields, roadsides, and occasionally sunny spots in forests. Distinguishing the many species is challenging, but it is not hard to enjoy the bright-yellow color they add to the landscape in August and September.

Orange hawkweed looks like a small orange dandelion. It is not native to North America but provides a striking splash of orange color along roadsides and in cultivated areas such as ski trails and around AMC huts.

FERNS AND LYCOPHYTES

Ferns have attractive, feathery leaves called fronds that are divided into leaflets called pinnae. Most pinnae are further subdivided into pinnules. Spores used for reproduction occur in clusters.

Long beech fern is very common in moist forests and on damp ledges around waterfalls. It is roughly triangular in shape, with its two lowest pinnae pointing downward.

Rock fern, also called Virginia polypody, grows on rocks wherever enough soil has accumulated. It is a small (1 foot) evergreen fern whose fronds are divided only once. Look at the underside of a frond to see the round spore clusters.

Interrupted fern is a large (3 to 4 feet) fern. It gets its name from the brown, spore-containing section of fertile fronds that occurs between the green pinnae along the stem. This fern grows in wet areas, often in clearings and along roadsides. A similar species, cinnamon fern, has dense tufts of rusty hairs where the pinnae join the stem.

Hay-scented fern is a lacy, medium-sized fern that grows in dense colonies in small clearings in the woods, such as those created by fallen trees. It gives off the sweet smell of freshly mown grass when the fronds have dried out in late September and October.

Bracken fern is a robust fern with a triangular frond divided into three parts. Unlike most ferns, it grows in sunny, weedy locales, such as along roadsides. A number of wood ferns are common on the forest floor. These large ferns have finely cut fronds and brown scales along the stem.

Club mosses are a group of primitive plants that are not actually mosses but are in their own group, the lycophytes. In prehistoric times they formed trees but the current living species are never more than a few inches tall where they look like miniature cedar, pine, or spruce trees.

MOSSES

Mosses are small, primitive plants that provide a beautiful cover of greenery in damp forests. In the boreal forest they cover rocks, logs, and old stumps, often being the only understory vegetation.

Haircap moss is one of the most common woodland mosses. Its upright branches are covered with small, needlelike leaves. This moss gets its name from the hairy cap that covers its spore-containing capsules. The spores are shot out of the capsule as it dries.

Fern moss, also called piggyback moss, is feathery and fernlike. Smaller plants grow by piggybacking on top of larger ones.

Sphagnum moss, or peat moss, is the most economically important moss. It has a tremendous capacity to hold water, which is why it is so useful to gardeners as a soil conditioner. Sphagnum mosses covers bogs with green or red colors, depending on the particular species.

FUNGI AND LICHENS

Fungi come in an assortment of odd shapes with occasionally vivid colors. They are like icebergs—what you see above ground, their reproductive structures, is only a small part of the whole. Below ground or within a decaying log, myriad fungal filaments break down dead plant matter, helping to create soil. Other types of fungi penetrate plant roots, where they aid plants in the essential process of taking nutrients up from the soil.

Mushrooms, with their classic umbrella-shaped cap, are the best-known fungi. Most types have gills on the underside. These radiate around a central axis, like myriad spokes of an umbrella. Another group of mushrooms, the boletes, have pores rather than gills on their undersides. The best time to find a variety of mushrooms in the White Mountains is in late summer. Mushrooms are eye-catching but can be dangerous. They are a challenge to identify, often changing shape as they develop. One common genus of mushrooms, the Amanitas, are almost all deadly poisonous. Leave picking and eating wild mushrooms to the experts.

Lichens are fungi that have the trapped cells of algae within them. The tiny algal cells produce food for the organism, and the fungus provides the algae with some nutrients and with protection from the environment. Lichens can live in harsh places, such as the bare rocks above treeline, because they provide for their own nutrition and have an amazing ability to resuscitate after being almost completely dried out. These symbiotic organisms grow so slowly and live so long that individual ones can be used to track the slow, frost-induced movement of the rocks upon which they live. Lichens are abundant on rocky ledges, summits, and drier forests of the White Mountains. They come in three general shapes: crusty, leafy, and bushy.

Map lichen creates green and yellow splashes of color with a black background on boulders on open ledges and summits. These brightly colored lichens grow as flat crusts in patches that resemble the patterns of rivers, oceans, and islands on a map.

Rock tripe is a leafy lichen abundant on boulders in the forest. It looks like overlapping pieces of black or dark-brown rubber, each 1 to 2 inches across and irregular in shape. Each piece is attached to rock by a central stalk.

Reindeer lichen is bushy, with many pale-yellow-green entangled branches arising from individual stalks. It grows on open, scrubby ledges, often in large patches that look so neat and well-manicured that you might think a gardener deliberately planted them there.

ANIMALS

Insects, Spiders, and Other Invertebrates

There might be many admirers of insects were it not for two notorious inhabitants of the White Mountains, **blackflies** and **mosquitoes**. Learn more about them and other aquatic insects from the essay "Aquatic Insects in the White Mountains" on page 7.

Butterflies are sometimes called flying flowers, a tribute to their lovely colors and perhaps to their affinity for feeding on nectar. Two of the most common and striking are **eastern tiger swallowtails** and **mourning cloaks**. Eastern tiger swallowtails are yellow with black stripes and two "tails," one projecting from each hind wing. Boldly patterned mourning cloaks, brownish-purple wings edged with bright yellow, dart from flower to flower. Some years, **white**

admirals are very abundant. These are brown butterflies with bold white bands across their fore and hindwings.

Dragonflies and **damselflies**, members of the same insect order, Odonata, are common around the edges of ponds. They are striking insects, often colored with iridescent blues and greens with bold-yellow stripes. Some are red or orange and black. Dragonflies are strong flyers, moving straight ahead rapidly on outspread wings like little airplanes and changing direction abruptly. They have very large eyes that for most species touch each other. Darners, big, strong dragonflies with mottled blue-and-brown abdomens and green or blue stripes on their thoraxes, can often be seen hunting insects over summits and rocky ledges or along the shores of mountain ponds. Damselflies are smaller and more delicate than dragonflies and their smaller eyes are well separated on their heads. Their flight is typically erratic, like a butterfly's. Dragonflies hold their wings horizontally when at rest whereas damselflies bring their wings together over their bodies.

Large black **wolf spiders** are often observed scurrying across rocks on open summits and ledges. These eight-legged relatives of insects are predators of other insects. Unlike most spiders, wolf spiders catch their prey without the use of a web. Of course, you can also find many spiders that spin traditional webs to snare their prey in the White Mountains.

Fallen trees often harbor a variety of invertebrate life that aids in decomposing the tree and recycling nutrients. **Ants** and **termites** create networks of chambers under bark and scatter wildly when you uncover them. **Centipedes**, **millipedes**, **sowbugs (pillbugs)**, **slugs**, and **worms** of various sorts take up residence in decaying logs. (Make sure you return any logs you overturn to their original positions.)

Reptiles and Amphibians

The long, cold winters and damp summers of the White Mountains do not make an ideal climate for reptiles. These scaly vertebrates are more diverse in drier, warmer climates. There are no poisonous snakes in the White Mountains.

If you do find a snake, it is likely to be an **eastern garter snake**. It is brownish with three yellow stripes running along the entire length of its body. Although harmless, this snake won't like being picked up and may try to bite or rub a very stinky fluid on you if you try. Garter snakes feed on insects and small vertebrates.

Painted turtles are occasionally seen basking on rocks and logs in ponds at lower elevations. Their heads are marked with short yellow stripes, and their shells are bordered with red.

Amphibians, which include frogs, toads, and salamanders, are much more tied to water than reptiles. They lay their eggs and develop as tadpoles with gills in water. Many species remain in, or close to, water as adults, even though they breathe air.

The **American toad** is the most wide-ranging amphibian in the region. You'll often find them along trails in the forest far from water, as high up in elevation as treeline. They blend in very well with the dead leaves of the forest floor, and your first clue to them is a rustling sound as they move about. Their leathery, warty skin allows them to wander farther from dampness than most amphibians, although they return to water to lay their eggs.

Frogs of various kinds inhabit ponds and wetlands of the White Mountains. It is much easier to identify them by their sounds than to actually see them. In early spring the birdlike chorus of spring peepers is a familiar sound. Since early spring is a relative term in the White Mountains, choruses of **spring peepers** can be heard in April at low elevations and in July at high-elevation ponds. **Green frogs**, which sound like someone plucking a string of a banjo, are heard in late spring and summer.

Salamanders are creatures of damp woods, mountain streams, and ponds. They generally remain hidden and are difficult to see unless you look under dead logs in the woods or flat stones by water. Despite their secretive habits, the abundance of some species, such as the **red-backed salamander**, makes them very important to the ecology of the soil and leaf litter of White Mountain forests.

The only salamander bold enough to cross a trail out in the open is the **red eft**. This bright-red salamander with greenish spots can afford to be more brazen than other salamanders because it is very toxic. The red eft is actually a juvenile, the land stage of the **red-spotted newt**, an aquatic salamander common in mountain ponds.

BIRDS

Birds are more often heard than seen in the White Mountains. Their calls and songs fill the forests and summits of the Whites. A few songs are particularly characteristic and easy to identify.

White-throated sparrows sing a number of clear, sweet-whistled notes varying in pitch, followed by several wavy notes. Their song sounds like *See old Sam Peabody, Peabody, Peabody* and is very easy to imitate.

Winter wrens have an amazingly extensive, bubbly song that varies in pitch. They make a lot of noise for such a small bird.

If you hear repeated nasal notes that sound like a child's toy horn, that is a **red-breasted nuthatch**.

The song of the **hermit thrush** is flutelike and ethereal. It starts with a long, high note, followed by shorter notes that modulate up and down in scale. Usually hermit thrushes sing from shrubs or the lower branches of trees of the northern hardwoods forest. At higher elevations in the boreal forest, the thrush you are most likely to encounter is the **Swainson's thrush**. Its song is similar to that of the hermit thrush, but ascends up the scale and lacks the characteristic single, long opening note.

Ovenbirds belt out a raucous, booming, two-syllable *t'cher, t'cher, t'cher* that increases gradually in volume. These warblers sing from the ground.

Black-capped chickadees are a favorite of children because they are perky, relatively tame, and are constantly saying their own name. You'll see and hear them on most hikes.

Dark-eyed juncos are small, sparrowlike, gray birds with white bellies and white outer-tail feathers. They spend much of their time on summits and ledges.

Ravens make a hoarse *caw caw* or a series of piglike snorts as they fly overhead. They can sometimes sound like a screaming person.

In addition to songs, the presence of birds is evident in dead trees riddled with holes created by woodpeckers. The little **downy woodpecker** is the one you are most likely to see. It is about the size of a cardinal and is speckled with black and white. Downies produce a lively descending whinny when they land.

Woodpeckers are essential to the ecology of the forest because their holes are used as homes by many kinds of birds and mammals. Because of this, the Forest Service has a policy of protecting "wildlife trees."

MAMMALS

In the White Mountains it is not easy to see many types of mammals, particularly large ones. Nonetheless, they leave ample signs of their presences in tracks, holes in trees, scratch marks on bark, and beaver dams.

Beavers are abundant here. Many of the trails take you by beaver ponds where you can see their wooden lodges, dams of sticks and mud, canals, and chewed trees. The animals themselves can sometimes be seen around dusk or dawn. Lost Pond in Pinkham Notch has been a good place to see beavers in recent years.

Red squirrels are the most frequently encountered mammal in the White Mountains. They scold hikers entering their territories with a rattling chatter usually delivered from a red spruce or balsam fir.

Chipmunks are also popular campground rodents. Chipmunks chirp like birds and scamper on the forest floor over fallen logs and into holes in the ground much more often than squirrels.

Snowshoe hares look somewhat like cottontail rabbits of lowlands but with larger ears and feet that appear a bit too big for their bodies. Their large feet act as snowshoes, helping them to stay on top of deep snow in winter. Snowshoe hares are white in winter and turn brown in summer.

Moose-watching has become a popular pastime in the White Mountains as their population has increased. These largest members of the deer family occasionally can be seen along roadsides around dusk. The wetlands along the Kancamagus Highway near the Passaconaway Historic Site are particularly good places to look for moose. In fall rutting season, males can be ill-tempered, so give them a wide berth. Moose leave characteristic stripe marks on trees with their teeth.

Hikers on the trails rarely encounter **black bears**, but you may see the claw marks they leave on trees to mark their territories. Bears are omnivores, feeding on a variety of mammals, insects, fruits, and nuts.

APPENDIX D
SELECTED RESOURCES

NATURAL HISTORY GUIDES

DeGraaf, Richard M., and Yuriko Yamisaki, *New England Wildlife: Habitat, Natural History, and Distribution,* Lebanon, NH: University Press of New England, 2000.

Eusden, J. Dykstra, *The Geology of New Hampshire's White Mountains,* Etna, NH: The Durand Press, 2013.

GoBotany! New England Wildflower Society, gobotany.newenglandwild.org

Haines, Arthur, *Flora Novae Angliae: A Manual for the Identification of Native and Naturalized Higher Vascular Plants of New England,* New Haven, CT: Yale Press, 2011.

Johnson, Charles W., *Bogs of the Northeast,* Hanover, NH: University Press of New England, 1985.

Marchand, Peter J., *Nature Guide to the Northern Forest,* Boston, MA: Appalachian Mountain Club Books, 2010.

Murray, Tom, *Insects of New England and New York*, Boston, MA: Kollath-Stensaas Publishing, 2012.

Newcomb, Lawrence, and Gordon Morrison, *Newcomb's Wildflower Guide,* Boston, MA: Little, Brown & Co., 1989.

Pope, Ralph, *Lichens above the Treeline,* Lebanon, NH: University Press of New England, 2005.

Raymo, Chet, and Maureen Raymo, *Written in Stone: A Geological History of the Northeastern United States,* Hensonville, NY: Black Dome Press Corp., 2001.

Sibley, David, *The Sibley Field Guide to Birds of Eastern North America,* New York, NY: Alfred A. Knopf, 2003.

Slack, Nancy G., and Allison W. Bell, *Field Guide to the New England Mountain Summits,* 3rd Edition, Boston, MA: Appalachian Mountain Club Books, 2014.

Various authors, *Peterson Field Guide Series,* Boston, MA: Houghton Mifflin Co.

NATURE WITH CHILDREN

Cornell, Joseph, *Sharing Nature with Children,* 2nd Edition, Nevada City, CA: Dawn Publishing Co., 1998.

Hipple, Ethan, and Yemaya St.Clair, *Outdoors with Kids Maine, New Hampshire, Vermont: 75 of the Best Family Hiking, Camping, and Paddling Trips,* Boston, MA: Appalachian Mountain Club Books, 2014.

WHITE MOUNTAINS GUIDES AND HISTORIES

Bolnick, Bruce, and Doreen Bolnick, *Waterfalls of the White Mountains: 30 Trips to 100 Waterfalls,* 2nd Edition, Woodstock, VT: Backcountry Publications, 1999.

Crawford, Lucy, *History of the White Mountains,* Etna, NH: The Durand Press, 1999.

Dickerman, Mike, *White Mountains Hiking History: Trailblazers of the Granite State,* Mount Pleasant, SC: The History Press, 2013.

Mudge, John T.B., *The White Mountains: Names, Places, Legends,* 2nd Edition, Etna, NH: The Durand Press, 1995.

Randall, Peter E., *Mount Washington: A Guide & Short History,* Woodstock, VT: The Countryman Press, 1992.

Smith, Steven D., *Ponds & Lakes of the White Mountains: From Wayside to Wilderness,* 2nd Edition, Woodstock, VT: Backcountry Publications, 1998.

Smith, Steven D., *Mount Chocorua: A Guide and History,* Littleton, NH: Bondcliff Books, 2006.

Smith, Steven D., and Mike Dickerman, *White Mountain Guide: AMC's Comprehensive Guide to Hiking Trails in the White Mountain National Forest,* 29th Edition, Boston, MA: Appalachian Mountain Club Books, 2012.

Wivell, Ty, *Passport to AMC's High Huts in the White Mountains,* Boston, MA: Appalachian Mountain Club Books, 2011.

INDEX

ABOUT THE AUTHOR

Robert N. Buchsbaum has both a professional interest in and a passion for the natural history of New England. He received a bachelor of science degree in natural resources from Cornell University and a PhD in marine ecology from the Boston University Marine Program at Woods Hole. A native New Yorker, he moved to New England in 1978 and has since spent many of his free weekends and vacations exploring the White Mountains. As an AMC volunteer naturalist since 1986, Buchsbaum has presented programs in the huts, lodges, and elsewhere in the Whites on a wide variety of topics, including botany, alpine ecology, birds, and geology.

Buchsbaum resides in Beverly, MA, with his wife, Nancy Schalch. Their two children, Alison and Gabriel, were along for many of these hikes and share an enthusiasm for the outdoors. Buchsbaum works for Mass Audubon as a conservation scientist, carrying out research related to conservation initiatives. He has written numerous magazine articles on natural history and has published extensively in technical journals and books.

ABOUT THE AMC IN NEW HAMPSHIRE

The Appalachian Mountain Club's New Hampshire Chapter has 10,000 members, and offers hundreds of trips each year. Well-trained and dedicated leaders guide hiking, paddling, skiing, and climbing excursions. The chapter is also active in trail work and conservation projects. You can learn more about this chapter by visiting outdoors.org/chapters. To view a list of AMC activities in New Hampshire and other parts of the Northeast, visit trips.outdoors.org.

AMC BOOK UPDATES

AMC Books strives to keep our guidebooks as up-to-date as possible to help you plan safe and enjoyable adventures. If after publishing a book we learn that trails are relocated or route or contact information has changed, we will post the updated information online. Before you hit the trail, check for updates at outdoors. org/publications/books/updates.

While hiking or paddling, if you notice discrepancies with the trail description or map, or if you find any other errors in the book, please let us know by submitting them to amcbookupdates@outdoors.org or in writing to Books Editor, c/o AMC, 5 Joy Street, Boston, MA 02108. We will verify all submissions and post key updates each month.

AMC Books is dedicated to being a recognized leader in outdoor publishing. Thank you for your participation.

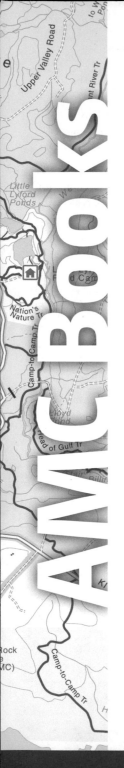

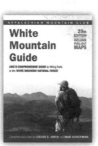